THE CORPORATE CULTURE SOURCEBOOK

Edited by

Richard Bellingham, Ed.D.
Assistant Vice President
Northern Telecom
Mississauga, Ontario

Barry Cohen, Ph.D.
President
Possibilities, Inc.
Concord, Massachusetts

Mark Edwards, Ph.D.
Director, LIDR
College of Engineering, ASU
Tempe, Arizona

Judd Allen, Ph.D.
President
HRI
Burlington, Vermont

Human Resource Development Press
Amherst, Massachusetts

Published by Human Resource Development Press, Inc.
            22 Amherst Road
            Amherst, Massachusetts 01002

© 1990 by Human Resource Development Press, Inc.

Printed in the United States of America

ISBN 0-87425-117-6

Production services provided by The Magazine Group, Inc.
Printing and Binding by Bookcrafters, Inc.

First printing, November 1989

Contents

PREFACE

This book addresses the thorny problems and tremendous potential related to corporate culture change. It describes what culture change is, explains how culture effects several critical dimensions of the organization and provides formulas, suggestions and resources for managing culture change efforts. "The Corporate Culture Sourcebook" presents a unique combination of materials that are useful for human resource development and organizational development professionals. We have included what we believe are the best reference articles on a number of culture change issues. Also included are guidelines for implementing a constructive, corporate culture change process and some resources for practitioners.

Following the format of the "Sourcebook" series, our checklists, questionnaires, models and analyses can be duplicated, converted to overhead transparencies, or modified in any way that makes them useful to you. Of course, materials referenced from other publications are copyrighted by those publishers and appropriate permission should be sought from them.

We would like to acknowledge the organizations and practitioners that have given us the opportunities to be involved in their HRD and OD efforts. From them we have learned what works. We are particularly gratified to the associates at AT&T, M&M Mars, Digital Equipment, Westinghouse, Chase Manhattan Bank, Prime Computer, Southwestern Bell Telephone Company, Samaritan Health Service, Disney, Gulf Oil, Eastman Kodak, NCR, Dupont, Motorola and Northern Telecom with whom we have worked extensively. We are also indebted to the authors and publishers who have given us permission to include their materials.

Realizing the rapid evaluation of corporate culture change technology, we will be updating these materials as more advanced and insightful ones become available. Your suggestions and contributions are always welcome. Feel free to send them to us:

Richard Bellingham
Assistant Vice President
Northern Telecom
3 Robert Speck Parkway
Mississauga, Ontario L4Z 3C8

Barry Cohen
President
Possibilities, Inc.
649 Sudbury Road
Concord, MA 01742

Judd Allen
President
Human Resource Institute
80 Austin Drive #232
Burlington, VT 05401

Mark Edwards
Director
LIDR
College of Engineering, ASU
Tempe, AZ 85287

PURPOSE AND USE OF THE CORPORATE CULTURE SOURCEBOOK

Purpose

Managing corporate culture change has emerged as a top priority for most business leaders. Cultural norms, values and rituals are being increasingly recognized as the key factors which either enhance or retard change initiatives. Indeed, if corporate culture is not compatible with business strategies, hopes for success and growth are dim.

But for many leaders, corporate culture change seems so esoteric and "soft" that deciding to shape it, manage it, or change it seems overwhelming. This book will help to de-mystify the notion of corporate culture change. The purposes of this book are to help leaders and professionals:

1) explore what corporate culture means,

2) understand the effects of culture on the aspects of the organization that are cause for concern and/or celebration, and

3) change those aspects that need changing.

How to Use This Book

To help you manage your corporate culture change efforts, we include in this Sourcebook different types of materials; readings as well as guidelines for implementation and resources. The readings will give you an overview of culture change and a representative sample of current research in each of several areas; the guidelines will provide practical steps for designing and implementing a constructive corporate culture change process; and the resource section will give you a wealth of information from which to draw.

If you are using this book to initiate a culture change effort, we suggest you follow the sequence in which the articles are presented. This approach will help you understand some of the more global issues before you proceed to the specific interventions.

If you are using this book to improve upon an already existing program, we suggest you still review the earlier sections to see how your image compares to several leaders in the field. You may, however, wish to proceed immediately to a section that you consider most important.

PART ONE

EXPLORING CULTURE AND CULTURE CHANGE

SECTION I
INTRODUCTION AND OVERVIEW

Anthropologists and other social scientists have long studied the dynamics of culture in the everyday lives of people. As readers of National Geographic and viewers of international news reels, we have been fascinated, sometimes perplexed, and occasionally horrified by the vast array of customs, traditions, world views, and norms which humans have adopted.

Strangely, the power of culture in our own lives has gone largely unexamined. As if by magic, we accept our own cultural ways as a given. The culture has become our organizational unconscious: "It's just the way we do things around here."

Those working with corporate culture believe that people can and should plan an active role in choosing the cultural environments in which they work. The common thread in the articles found in this volume is an interest in empowering people to understand and shape their work cultures. The book is directed at sharing the many strategies now employed to bring culture under the conscious control of those engaged in work.

The articles in this introductory section explore themes which re-emerge in corporate culture work. In "How an Organization's Rites Reveal its Culture," Janice Beyer and Harrison Trice share insights which can be gained by examining common rites and rituals in organizational cultures. The second article, "Corporate Culture" discusses the merits of closing the gap between existing group norms and desired group norms. The last article in this section, "Are You Corporate Cultured?" reveals structures within organizational environments which reinforce the existing culture.

How an Organization's Rites Reveal Its Culture

By Janice M. Beyer and Harrison M. Trice

The concept of corporate culture has great popular appeal; this appeal is obvious from the recent phenomenal sale of books on the subject. But is "corporate culture" just another buzzword that will pass out of fashion? Can any new, lasting, practical insights be gained by looking at our corporations and other organizations as cultures? We believe the answer to both questions is yes; the purpose of this article is to show why.

Popular treatments of organizational culture usually gravitate toward one of two extreme views: (1) An organization's culture is so obvious it can be immediately sensed by outsiders when they step in the door, or (2) an organization's culture is so elusive it can be revealed—and then only partially—only by outside experts after lengthy study.

The trouble with the first view is that it holds scant promise of telling managers anything new. In this view, culture becomes an all-encompassing concept with few distinguishing characteristics; it merely provides a new vocabulary to repackage familiar ideas and prescriptions about styles of leadership, employee attitudes, interpersonal relations, organizational structure, and strategy, with an admixture of cultural features such as symbols, myths, values, or norms. The trouble with the second view is that it is frustrating. If organizational cultures are so inaccessible, it is unclear what, if anything, managers can do to understand, manage, or change them. While the first view is unsatisfying because it deals with superficialities that can yield only shallow insights, the second view tantalizes with the promise of deep insights waiting to be discovered, then makes their discovery too difficult to be practical.

A way out of this dilemma is to explore natural, observable outcroppings of culture—places where the cultural understanding beneath the surface of organizational life are partially exposed. By analyzing

these outcroppings in their own organizations, managers can gain practical insights.

Rites as Outcroppings of Culture

Organizational culture is usually defined in management literature as a network of shared understandings, norms, and values that are taken for granted and that lie beneath the surface of organizational life. However, culture is more than this. In order to create and maintain a culture, these understandings, norms, and values must somehow be affirmed and communicated to an organization's members in some tangible way. We call this tangible part of culture "cultural forms"; such forms are occasions in which underlying, unstated understandings are brought to the surface. In this sense, cultural forms are outcroppings of culture. Exhibit 1 provides a list of definitions of some cultural forms.

Organizational stories provide familiar examples of cultural forms. Stories about top managers usually express and affirm important organizational norms and values. For example, the story that former IBM president Tom Watson praised an employee who denied him entry into a restricted area of the company because he was not wearing his badge shows that IBM employees should and do uphold company rules.

We do not mean to imply, however, that the occasions that qualify as cultural forms have only expressive consequences. In order to survive, most organizations need to produce something of practical value to society. Most organizational activities are intended to realize practical ends; however, they may also have an expressive, cultural function. The British anthropologist Edmund Leach has pointed out that human actions can serve both to do and to say things; thus people's organizational activities often have a mixture of practical and expressive consequences. Some of these activities—such as telling the story about Tom Watson—are primarily expressive of cultural values. Other examples,

EXHIBIT 1
A List of Definitions of Frequently Studied Cultural Forms*

Rite	A relatively elaborate, dramatic, planned set of activities that combines various forms of cultural expressions and that often has both practical and expressive consequences.
Ritual	A standardized, detailed set of techniques and behaviors that manages anxieties but seldom produces intended, practical consequences of any importance.
Myth	A dramatic narrative of imagined events, usually used to explain origins or transformations of something. Also, an unquestioned belief about the practical benefits of certain techniques and behaviors that is not supported by demonstrated facts.
Saga	An historical narrative describing (usually in heroic terms) the unique accomplishments of a group and its leaders.
Legend	A handed-down narrative of some wonderful event that has a historical basis but has been embellished with fictional details.
Story	A narrative based on true events—often a combination of truth and fiction.
Folktale	A completely fictional narrative.
Symbol	Any object, act, event, quality, or relation that serves as a vehicle for conveying meaning, usually by representing another thing.
Language	A particular manner in which members of a group use vocal sounds and written signs to convey meanings to each other.
Gesture	Movements of parts of the body used to express meanings.
Physical Setting	Those things that physically surround people and provide them with immediate sensory stimuli as they carry out culturally expressive activities.
Artifact	Material objects manufactured by people to facilitate culturally expressive activities.

*Adapted from Janice M. Beyer and Harrison M. Trice, "Studying Organizational Cultures Through Rites and Ceremonials" (*Academy of Management Review*, October 184).

such as management training and committee meetings, have both practical and expressive consequences.

In the following analysis, we will emphasize the expressive, cultural side of organizational events because we think this side is often overlooked. We do not want to deny the practical side, only to balance it with the awareness that most practical activities also generate expressive consequences. To overlook these expressive consequences is to miss much of the significance of what is really happening in organizations. It is also to miss opportunities to convey desired cultural messages and thus help to shape an organization's culture. Only by attending to both sets of consequences can we really understand and effectively manage organizations.

This article deals primarily with organizational rites because, in performing the activities of a rite, people generally use other cultural forms—certain customary language, gestures, ritualized behaviors, artifacts, settings, and other symbols—to heighten the expression of shared understandings appropriate to the occasion. These shared understandings are also frequently conveyed through myths, sagas, legends, or other stories associated with the occasion. Thus rites provide a richer outcropping of cultural understanding than do single cultural forms.

In addition, we focus on rites because they are tangible, accessible, and visible. Identifying the meanings they carry, however, requires interpretive skills not ordinarily taught in business schools or used by practicing managers. We believe, however, that experienced managers are familiar enough with the organizational context to make a working interpretation of organizational rites. We also believe that many managers can learn to interpret their organizations' rites and that the insights they gain in the process will be useful for the enlightened managing and changing of their organizations' cultures.

However, the most important reason for focusing on organizational rites is that many managers conduct or sponsor them without being fully aware of it. Many practical managerial activities also act as cultural rites that are interpreted by employees and others as reflecting what management believes in, values, and finds acceptable. Unless expressive consequences are considered, both the activities chosen and the ways of carrying them out may inadvertently convey cultural messages that are inconsistent with the desired culture.

For example, corporate drug-testing programs that administer reliable tests on an involuntary, random basis might, practically speaking, be very effective in locating drug users, but such "efficient" programs could undermine existing corporate cultures and thus be disastrous in expressive terms. They carry the unmistakable message that all employees are under suspicion; they also cost a lot of money. Thus many managements have decided to employ drug testing only in cases where drug abuse is a suspected cause of poor work performance and to link such testing to employee assistance programs designed to help confirmed abusers rehabilitate themselves. The latter type of program may be relatively "inefficient" in locating drug users in practical terms, but it will probably be effective in expressive terms because it is more consistent with most corporate cultures and with the general values of U.S. workers.

Managers must become sensitive to the possible expressive consequences of their activities; moreover, they must modify those activities to remove culturally inconsistent elements. This is the only way they can ensure that strong cultural messages are being sent about what their organizations stand for. Managers who understand the duality of their actions will be better able to make those actions effective in both practical and cultural terms.

The Social Consequences of Rites

Human actions have both practical and expressive consequences at the same time; moreover, people tend to be more aware of some of these consequences than they are of others. Some of the consequences are evident; others may be hidden. As Exhibit 2 shows, a common rite such as training new managers can have four kinds of consequences. In one program we studied, in addition to the selection and training of promising candidates (thereby marking them as transformed sufficiently to deserve being elevated to managerial roles), cultural messages were conveyed to participants and others who knew of the programs about the relative priorities of different managerial tasks in the company, the managers who provided role models to be emulated, and the true importance of the managerial role. In the terminology of cultural anthropology, this program was a rite of passage—a rite whose main cultural function is to ease the transition of people who are moving from one social status to another.

Our research on organizational life suggested that there are other sets of common activities that

function as cultural rites but that have different expressive consequences. By comparing anthropological accounts of tribal societies with management writers' descriptions of life in modern organizations, we were able to identify five other common rites that had distinctly different expressive consequences; they are presented in Exhibit 3, along with a brief summary of the discussion that follows. We will begin our discussion with a more detailed description of rites of passage.

Rites of Passage

In his book *Rites of Passage* (Emil Mourry, 1909), the Dutch scholar Arnold Van Gennep mentioned similarities in many different tribal societies in customary behaviors that accompany universal and unavoidable events: pregnancy and childbirth, the onset of sexual maturity, betrothal and marriage, and death. Because such events create marked changes in status for the individuals involved, Van Gennep called their attendant customary behaviors "rites of passage." He grouped these behaviors into three distinct consecutive subsets, which he called rites of separation, rites of transition, and rites of incorporation. The apparently intended consequence of these rites was to restore equilibrium in social relations that had been disturbed by an individual's transition from one social status to another.

A good example of rites of passage in modern organizational life is the process of induction and basic training in the United States Army. The rites of separation begin when a recruit reports to an induction center and is then transported to a camp where he receives a uniform and a severe haircut, has to make his own bed in a ritualized fashion, learns to salute and march, is repeatedly humiliated, and is in many other ways stripped of his past identity and status. The next phase, the rites of transition, occurs during basic training, when the raw recruit learns the practical skills associated with his new identity—shooting guns, marching, and obeying promptly and without question. Even his body is rebuilt—through calisthenics; long, arduous marches; and other physically demanding exercises. Toward the end of the transition period, the recruit is repeatedly tested, presumably to determine what new permanent role he is capable of assuming in the organization. The rites of incorporation begin with a relatively permanent assignment to a specific unit, followed by parades, a flag ceremony, speeches, and the issuing of awards to recruits who have performed exceptionally well.

EXHIBIT 2
Examples of Four Types of Social Consequences of Rites for Training New Managers

Practical Consequences

Evident   A thorough evaluation of candidates' potential and improvement in their administrative skills so that only the best qualified candidates are promoted to management positions.

Hidden   The relative priorities placed on various areas of performance in the company are communicated and enforced; members of management who act as trainers sharpen and reinforce their own skills; new and old managers size up one another's strengths and weaknesses.

Expressive consequences

Evident   The transformation of the successful candidate's social identity among people both within and outside of the organization.

Hidden   The enhancement of the prestige of the managerial role within the company; the motivation of nonmanagement personnel to perform according to priorities; the development of social and emotional bonds among managers.

The culmination of the incorporation rite is the issuing of insignia designating the recruit's newly assigned, relatively permanent status. At this point, the recruit is frequently given a leave; he then goes home to discover that he has indeed been transformed and has received a new identity.

Although this example may seem irrelevant to modern corporate life, Thomas Rohlen observed in his book *For Harmony and Strength: Japanese White Collar Organizations in Anthropological Perspective* (University of California Press, 1974) that managerial trainees in the Japanese banking industry go through similarly intensive rites of passage. Rohlen reported that similar in-company training rites are employed by as many as one-third of all medium-to-large Japanese companies, with apparently successful consequences in terms of employee productivity and commitment. The training he observed at the Uedagin Bank illustrates how elaborate the sequence of events can be. In the rite of separation, trainees and their parents were invited to an entrance ceremony, during which the president of the bank gave a speech congratulating the parents on raising such fine children and reassuring the trainees and their families that taking this job would be like joining a large family that takes good care of its members. The presence of current trainees in uniform, the prominent display of the company logo, the singing of the company song—all symbolized the cohesiveness and continuity of the trainees' new "family."

The next step in the training program was the successful completing of several rites of transition, each demanding that the trainees submit to new ordeals. The first rite was a two-day trip to a nearby army camp where the trainees were subjected to some of the rigors of basic training; marching under the direction of a sergeant and sweating their way over obstacle courses, they wore castoff army fatigues that symbolized their shared lowly status. They were told that a large company required order and discipline and that military training was the best way to teach these qualities—and they accepted this explanation. They were also taken periodically to a Zen temple for a two-day session in meditation and other Zen practices. At the temple they were subjected to a strict regimen that included eating tasteless gruel and meticulously observing a whole series of rituals.

Perhaps the most arduous ordeal of all was a 25-mile marathon walk held at the end of the training. Trainees were told to walk the first 9 miles together in a single body, the next 9 in designated groups, and the last 7 alone and in silence. Past trainees monitored their conformity to the rules and tempted them with cold drinks, which they were not allowed to accept. The first phase, walking and talking together, was relatively pleasant. During the second phase, intergroup competition emerged, leading the trainees to escalate their pace even though competition had not been encouraged. The result was that many trainees could not stand the pace and had to drop out. The final phase was very painful and difficult, but the trainees who finished took great personal pride in that accomplishment. Rohlen suggests that the marathon walk taught the values of perseverance, self-denial, and rejection of competition as the route to collective accomplishment.

In addition to these ordeals, the trainees were expected to achieve practical expertise; they studied bank operations and pursued a variety of other scheduled activities. Rohlen reports that every day except Sunday was filled with 14 hours of supervised activity. Unfortunately, he did not describe the final phase of these rites—the rite in which the employees were incorporated into the bank.

EXHIBIT 3
A Typology of Rites by Their Evident, Expressive Social Consequences

Types of Rites	Example	Evident Expressive Consequences	Examples of Possible Hidden Expressive Consequences
Rites of passage	Induction and basic training, U.S. Army	Facilitate transition of persons into social roles and statuses that are new for them.	Minimize changes in ways people carry out social roles. Reestablish equilibrium in ongoing social relations.
Rites of degradation	Firing and replacing top executive	Dissolve social identities and their power.	Publicly acknowledge that problems exist and discuss their details. Defend group boundaries by redefining who belongs and who doesn't. Reaffirm social importance and value of role involved.
Rites of enhancement	Mary Kay seminars	Enhance social identities and their power.	Spread good news about the organization. Provide public recognition of individuals for their accomplishments; motivate others to similar efforts. Enable organizations to take some credit for individual accomplishments. Emphasize social value of performance of social roles.
Rites of renewal	Organizational development activities	Refurbish social structures and improve their functioning.	Reassure members that something is being done about problems. Disguise nature of problems. Defer acknowledgment of problems. Focus attention toward some problems and away from others. Legitimize and reinforce existing systems of power and authority.
Rites of conflict reduction	Collective bargaining	Reduce conflict and aggression.	Deflect attention away from solving problems. Compartmentalize conflict and its disruptive effects. Reestablish equilibrium in disturbed social relations.
Rites of integration	Office Christmas party	Encourage and revive common feelings that bind members together and commit them to a social system.	Permit venting of emotion and temporary loosening of various norms. Reassert and reaffirm, by contrast, moral rightness of usual norms.

All complete rites of passage have the three phases identified by Van Gennep. In a company in upstate New York, the separation phase included several days of testing and screening a large group of self-selected candidates. Those candidates who survived the initial screening were then sent to three days of further evaluation at a live-in assessment center. These two successive screenings helped successful trainees let go of their prior status and assigned them a temporary, limbo-like status. The next phase, transition, usually puts initiates through a series of ordeals designed to introduce them to new experiences. These ordeals also symbolize the difficulties they must overcome and the rigors they must practice in their new roles. Managerial trainees in this company were subjected to one week of fast-paced, difficult instruction and one week of sensitivity training. The last phase, the rite of incorporation, introduces initiates to surrounding social networks as new members of that status. In the company observed, all production was stopped and new managers were introduced to other employees in a brief speech by the production superintendent on the shop floor. The speech was followed by a cocktail party, which top management attended.

Researchers at the University of Michigan recently identified another rite of passage called "parting ceremonies." The rite was given this name because it occurred in organizations that were going out of business—that is, in organizations in which the employees were parting from one another. In these rites, members of the "dying" organizations held social gatherings to ease both their leave-taking and the changing of their social identities. Many of the behaviors observed at parting ceremonies—the telling of stories, the discussion of new jobs, the partying, the picture taking, and the exchange of addresses—also frequently occur when individual members or small groups leave an organization. The most formalized of these occasions is the retirement dinner, but smaller parties are often held for members who leave for other reasons.

We began this section with the examples from the U.S. army and the Japanese bank because these particular rites are both powerful and elaborate. They illustrate what rites of passage could be, not what they are currently like in U.S. corporations. Even the example of management training in the upstate New York company we described earlier—which is the most complete rite of passage we have observed in U.S. industry—lacked the drama and impact of the military and Japanese examples. Typical U.S. corporate training programs seem pale and ineffectual by comparison.

Powerful, extensive rites of passage do, however, exist in U.S. worklife. They ease the entry into risky occupations such as law enforcement, fire fighting, and mining, but they generally occur in educational institutions or through informal socialization by fellow workers on the job rather than in internal management-sponsored programs. Thus managers have little impact on these potent occupational rites in the United States. In the absence of comparable organization-based rites and other cultural forms, U.S. workers often form stronger allegiances to their occupations than they do to their work organizations—an outcome that may be neither desirable nor inevitable.

Rites of Degradation

In his article "Conditions of Successful Degradation Ceremonies" (*American Sociological Review*, March 1956), the sociologist Harold Garfinkel named the next type of rite the degradation ceremony. A vivid example of this rite can be found in a ceremonial practice of the Ashanti, a tribal society in central Ghana in West Africa. The Ashanti chief was placed on an ancestral stool as part of his installment into office; if the tribe decided that it no longer wanted him to be chief, he was "destooled." His sandals were removed so that he had to walk barefoot, and he was placed on the ancestral stool, which was then withdrawn from under him so that his buttocks bumped on the ground. In this way he was reduced to being a commoner.

The procedures used in the rites of degradation that sometimes accompany the removal of high-status officials in modern organizations rarely inflict physical pain, but they can be just as humiliating as the experience of the Ashanti chief. As in rites of passage, the events in rites of degradation seem to fall into stages. First, other organizational members focus attention on the person to be degraded and publicly associate his or her behavior with organizational problems and failures. An important part of this initial stage is the language used by these other organizational members—language that Michael Moch has called "degradation talk" or "chewing ass." Moch observed a production manager being repeatedly degraded by his plant manager's references to difficulties in his private life and by the plant manager's attribution of various problems to the production manager's failures.

Second, the individual is discredited by some supposedly objective report. In the firing of chief executives, consultants are often hired to produce data and analyses documenting that certain detected problems are associated with the CEO. The consultants' status as outsiders and the credentials they possess symbolize their supposed objectivity; their activities are actually rituals designed to produce a necessary artifact—a report that demonstrates to all the erroneous decisions made by those to be deposed.

Third, the person is publicly removed from his or her position. Military organizations again provide a telling example: the dramatic cashiering and "drumming out" of officers from the U.S. Marine Corps and similar ceremonies in the other services. Businesses often skip the ceremony and take abrupt action; in one company, some managers came in Monday morning and found that all their furniture, plants, and pictures had been removed over the weekend. At Apple Computer, on the other hand, the recent removal of cofounder Steven Jobs was painfully drawn out. After months of tension and conflict, President John Sculley, backed by the board of directors, first removed Jobs's remaining operating authority as head of the Macintosh Division, then moved his office across the street, and finally announced to the press that there was no role for Jobs in the future of the firm.

In the final step of rites of degradation, a successor is chosen, often with such ceremonial activities as search committees, an extensive search for and wooing of candidates, and the expenditure of much time and effort—all of which symbolize the importance of the position involved.

A dramatic example of a truncated degradation rite was provided by the events surrounding the impeachment proceedings against Richard M. Nixon and his subsequent resignation from the presidency. Another example may be found in the personal attack that, Lee Iacocca reports, were launched against him in 1975 by Henry Ford II. As in the cases of Jobs, Nixon, and Iacocca, degradation rites stop when the degraded person "voluntarily" withdraws from office or from membership in the system.

Truncated degradation rites are probably not as effective as full-fledged degradation rites because the information power of the degraded person is not totally dissolved. In the cases of Nixon and Iacocca, there are no signs that the deposed men have much remaining influence in the organizations they left, though Iacocca has repeatedly raided Ford's executive ranks. But neither individual has sunk into total obscurity, and Iacocca has, of course, more power and influence now as head of Chrysler than he ever had at Ford. The case of Steven Jobs probably represents an unsuccessful rite of degradation, one that was complicated by the fact that Jobs was cofounder of Apple and held a substantial portion of its stock. Whether for these reasons or because of his personal qualities, Jobs had enough influence with important members of the firm to hire away five of Apple's key people. His case suggests that the ceremonial degradation of persons with ownership rights is harder to achieve than the degradation of appointed or elected officials.

The evident intended consequences of rites of degradation are to dissolve the social status and associated power of those persons who are subjected to the degradation. In corporations and other modern organizations, these rites occur relatively infrequently; they are usually reserved for the removal of relatively high-status or otherwise influential members. However, with the current rash of hostile takeovers and other mergers, such rites are likely to occur more frequently. Some hidden consequences can be detected from our examples: These rites provide a way to publicly acknowledge problems and to discuss their details; group boundaries are defended by redefining which individuals belong to groups and which do not; and the importance and social value of the role involved are reaffirmed. Of course, the most important practical consequence is that the no-longer-desired leader is forced to leave a position of power.

Rites of Enhancement

We have given the name "rites of enhancement" to ceremonial activities that enhance the personal status and social identities of organizational members. The U.S. presidential inauguration ceremony is one well-known example of rites of enhancement. Other examples include the ceremonious conferral of knighthood in England, the awarding of Nobel prizes to scientists and statesmen in Sweden, and the Oscar and Emmy awards given to U.S. motion picture and television performers.

The Mary Kay Cosmetics company may provide the best-known examples of the corporate use of rites of enhancement. The plethora of awards and titles given by this company to its high-performing members is clearly intended to enhance the identities of those who receive them. During elaborate meetings called Mary Kay seminars, gold and diamond pins, fur stoles, and the use of pink Cadillacs are awarded to saleswomen who achieve sales quotas. The awards are presented in a setting reminiscent of Miss America pageants; they are held in a large auditorium, on a stage in front of a large, cheering audience, with all the participants dressed in glamorous evening clothes.

Underlying this dramatic rite is the story of how Mary Kay's determination and optimism enables her to overcome personal hardships and to found her own company. The company's bee-shaped pin is a symbol of Mary Kay's optimistic belief that with help and encouragement everyone can "find their wings and fly." The pink Cadillac is clearly a symbol of exalted status, since Mary Kay herself drives one.

Other corporate examples abound: the awarding of bronze stars at Addison-Wesley Publishing, the "You Want It When?" award at Versatec, special jackets at Diamond International, and so forth. Most companies have some type of award; however, few are bestowed as ceremoniously as the awards at the Mary Kay seminars. All awards are intended to realize the practical consequence of rewarding desired behaviors so that these behaviors will be repeated and emulated by other employees.

These examples also illustrate a hidden expressive consequence of rites of enhancement, a consequence that is diametrically opposed to the consequence of degradation ceremonies: Rites of enhancement spread good news about the organization. Besides providing public recognition of individual accomplishments that all members benefit from, these rites enable the organization to take some share of the credit for these accomplishments. Another hidden consequence of other familiar examples of rites of enhancement, such as the conferral of tenure in academia or the accession of persons to office in associations in general, is the affirmation of the importance of that social role's performance for the organization.

Rites of Renewal

This type of rite includes a variety of elaborate activities intended to strengthen existing social structures and thus improve their functioning. Examples include most organization development (OD) activities; management-by-objectives (MBO) programs, job redesign, team building, quality-of-worklife programs, quality circles, and so forth. These activities tend to fine-tune rather than to fundamentally change organizational systems; they are based on a combination of humanistic and scientific values. For example, team building is justified by the belief that there is a family-life bond within work groups that can be used for the company's benefit. Job design is justified by scientific findings showing that workers' feelings are affected by the nature of their work and by the belief that making constructive changes in that work will result in higher productivity.

Most OD programs use certain standardized sets of techniques; such techniques are rituals in the sense that few have been demonstrated to have intended, practical effects. Team building efforts typically involve a sequence of rituals. The consultant begins by interviewing participants to generate themes for discussion. These interviews are followed by group discussions in which the participants rank and examine problems and then attempt to find and work on solutions and devise steps to realize them. A more extensive intervention called Grid Organization Development has six specific phases, usually lasts for three to five years, and is built around an artifact called the managerial grid, a rather simple two-dimensional scheme for representing the practices of individual managers. Other artifacts commonly used in OD activities include questionnaires and inventories, organizational charts and other diagrams, blackboards and flip charts, and closed-circuit television systems. A large vocabulary of specialized language, including

words like "feedback," "behavior mod," and "confrontation," is used by the initiated to describe these activities.

To label these OD activities as rites of renewal is not to deny that they sometimes have important practical consequences. We are suggesting, however, that they seldom drastically alter existing organizations and that many of their important consequences are symbolic and expressive. Some of the possible hidden consequences of such rites of renewal include reassuring members that something is being done about problems, disguising the nature of real problems, deferring the problems' acknowledgement, and focusing attention toward some problems and away from others. In addition, rites of renewal generally reinforce the existing power systems that form the basis for the renewed social arrangements.

Rites of Conflict Reduction

A variety of features in organizational life—hierarchies of formal authority, social stratification, division of labor, differential power and resources of age groups, and all sorts of other differences between persons—tend to produce pervasive conflict and aggressive behavior. Some of the conflicts produced are so pervasive that they give rise to subcultures and even countercultures. Because this kind of conflict and the accompanying aggression are disruptive and potentially damaging to social life, people develop rites to reduce conflicts.

A.R. Radcliffe-Brown's descriptions of the peacemaking ceremonies of the North Andamen Islanders in his book *The Andamen Islanders* (New York Free Press, 1964) provide a vivid example. In these ceremonies, dancers from two contending factions mingled randomly to form two groups, each new group consisting of about equal numbers from each faction. One group of dancers then gave outlet to their feelings of aggression by violently shaking the members of the other party. In response, members of the other group showed complete passivity, expressing neither fear nor resentment. In this manner collective anger was appeased, wrongs were forgiven, and peace was temporarily restored.

A familiar example of a rite developed to reduce conflict in modern work organizations is collective bargaining. This rite often begins when union and management present each other with a long, widely divergent list of demands and proposals. Each side prepares these artifacts (1) to disguise its real position and to prepare to explore problems causing conflict and (2) to reassure constituents and other observers that specific complaints will be considered. The lists also symbolically evoke the myth that this rite involves bargaining between equals, as does the setting in which the rites take place. Buried somewhere in the profusion of demands are the realistic outcomes expected by both sides. Both sets of bargainers may have a good idea what the final settlement will be, but union members and many segments of management do not have such inside knowledge. To demonstrate resistance to "unfair" demands to constituents, numerous ritualized "false fights" take place; these fights sometimes last late into the night, symbolizing the tough resistance each side is making to the demands of the other. In reality, these fights involve considerable informal cooperation. For example, when the parties are getting close to tacit agreement, a union representative may become openly hostile, threaten to walk out, and start to leave the bargaining table. Members of management will calm that person down, speak of possible compromises, point to troublesome areas where cooperation is emerging, and generally attempt in ritualistic ways to reduce the union representative's ritualistically generated anger.

Another common conflict-reduction rite in modern organizations is the committee. Organizations form joint labor-management committees, affirmative action committees, and so forth. Widely practiced rituals such as agendas, minutes, and motions provide accepted ways for these committees to proceed. Committees do not need to make substantive changes in order to reduce conflict because their very existence and their activities symbolize the organization's willingness to cope with problems and discontent. The mere holding of meetings with local managers helped a new manager of General Motors' Chevrolet Division to reduce the fears and hostilities of local managers. In similar ways, the activities of university ombudsmen, committees on judicial ethics in the American Bar Association, consumer affairs departments in retail stores, and faculty senates help to mollify hostile parties.

Conflict-reduction rites often include other important symbols. As taking action symbolizes authorities' willingness to cope with problems, encouraging participation symbolizes their willingness to pay attention to the complaints and ideas of the participants. The settings and procedures used symbolize how far authorities are willing to go in recognizing the claims of participants. Membership alone puts members on a symbolically equal footing. Many techniques such as brainstorming, nominal groups, and the delphi procedure have been developed to facilitate participation from all committee members. Most of the techniques utilize some method that ensures equal participation, and the meetings take place in settings that are designed to symbolize equality. All these symbols help committees realize their major expressive consequences: to minimize and at least temporarily smooth over differences that cause conflict. At a practical level, committees often realize agreement and cooperation in the process.

However, these rites also have a variety of hidden expressive consequences. One such consequences is to divert attention from solving the problems that generated the conflict. Other consequences include containing the conflict and reestablishing social relations that have been disrupted by it.

Rites of Integration

As organizations and other social systems grow larger, they differentiate internally into subgroups. The major evident expressive consequence of rites of integration is the revival of shared feelings that unite subgroups and commit them to the larger system by increasing their interaction. Such ceremonials are consequently very inclusive and public. The mix of participants is especially important; its integrative effects will depend on how successfully a particular rite incorporates members of diverse subgroups. Most large organizations (and all societies) have many rites of integration.

As their businesses grow, exceptional managers seem to recognize the need for rites of integration. One of the many lessons Tom Watson learned from John H. Patterson, the long-term president of the National Cash Register Company, was the value of bringing far-flung sales staff together for conventions. As Thomas and Maria Belden observed in their book *The Lengthening Shadow: The Life of Thomas J. Watson* (Little, Brown, and Company, 1962), "There were conventions for all of the company salesmen at which bands played, flags flew in the gusty Ohio winds, and men were exhorted to work and to love their work and to know how to work." These conventions not only gave the salesmen valuable information about selling, they "unified the far-flung company, bound it into a family with the factory serving as home and the officers as the center of loyalty. The sales convention was Patterson's . . . way of maintaining unity as the NCR stretched to the far corners of the country, of keeping a small-company spirit along with big-company organization and dividends."

After World War II, when International Business Machines had grown into "gray shapelessness," Watson developed similar but more encompassing rites of integration to unify both field and factory personnel. Huge conventions were held in an elaborate tent city constructed on thirty acres near the IBM factory at Endicott, New York. Paved streets ran between the tents, and terraces planted with flowers surrounded them. Meetings were held in a Barnum and Bailey circus tent. There were many ceremonial events: the group picture, tours of the factory, awards, songs of praise, and visits by distinguished guests. By 1950, however, even with the "tent flaps raised, there was no longer room for the swelling ranks of the company." Thereafter, regional meetings were held and the color and inclusiveness of the Endicott meetings faded. Many companies, of course, have annual conventions of their salespeople; the contents of such rites reflect the cultures of the companies involved.

Christmas parties and annual picnics are other common examples of rites of integration that occur in many organizations. During these rites, managers and nonmanagerial employees interact in settings and activities that lessen the social distance between them. Eating, talking, and drinking together symbolize shared values favoring equality and community. The use of alcohol lowers inhibitions, permitting less guarded interactions than are usual among persons of divergent status. Participants may engage in patting, backslapping, hugging, kissing, and other gestures of affection and approval rarely used in regular work settings. Under such circumstances, they may achieve a temporary sense of closeness. At Christmas parties, some of the rituals and artifacts associated with the Christmas legend are usually included, such as the Christmas tree, traditional food and drink, and the exchange of gifts, often distributed by someone dressed as Santa Claus. Annual picnics often involve ritualized games (like a softball game between different work units or statuses) that act out conflicts from the work setting.

Work-related social gatherings that serve as rites of integration have perhaps the fewest practical consequences of any set of rites; they come closest to being purely cultural or expressive occasions. Even at these events, however, practical matters are often discussed and other business is conducted. Thus while practical consequences are not essential to these rites, they occur nonetheless, making even company parties a mixture of the practical and the expressive.

The annual meetings of corporate boards of directors and of the governing boards of nonprofit organizations provide other examples of rites of integration. These meetings act out and preserve the myth of the effective influence of such constituencies. Reports are given by management, tough and embarrassing questions are asked and ritualistically responded to, and votes are taken according to well-established rites. However, the major consequence is expressive: Members of potentially disparate groups are united to voice concern for the prosperity and continuity for the organizations involved. Helen Schwartzman's analysis of meetings in her article "The Meeting as a Neglected Form in Organizational Studies" in Barry M. Staw and L.L. Cummings, Eds., *Research in Organizational Studies*, Vol. 8 (JAI Press, 1986) concludes that "a meeting is a powerful and ongoing symbol for an organization because it assembles a variety of individuals and groups together and labels the assembly as 'organizational action.' In this way . . . it . . . constitutes and reconstitutes the organization over time." These expressive, symbolic consequences can occur whether or not the meetings result in any important decisions or have other practical results.

Annual meetings of professional associations are another example of integrative rites. Members give and hear papers, do recruiting and job hunting, and participate in many other practical activities. Their expressive, integrative function is evident as participants party and feast in various groupings, usually with considerable alcohol consumption and relatively uninhibited conviviality. In these gatherings, members often make special efforts to interact with strangers and knit them into the group. These powerful rites, however, do not promote integration within professional organizations; rather, they pull professional members away from employing organizations toward integration within a cosmopolitan professional community.

The Practical Implications of Rites

This analysis is intended as a first step in understanding rites and ceremonials as outcroppings of organizational culture. The six types we have identified are important, widespread, and frequent occurrences in corporations and other organizations. Our types are intended to help managers and other analysts think about these familiar events in new ways and call their attention to important occurrences that they might otherwise have overlooked. Like all pure types, our types will not fit the observed instances perfectly, but they provide useful yardsticks against which observed events can be compared and assessed. In particular, some events may be a mixture of more than one type of rite. We do not believe that our list of types is exhaustive; it is merely a reasonable starting point for further refinements and additions.

Managing Cultures

Because they communicate and affirm taken-for-granted shared understandings of an organization's culture, the six types of rites also provide entry points for managing and changing organizational cultures. At the most basic level, managers must learn to assess not only the technical consequences of their own activities and the activities of those they supervise, but also their possible expressive consequences as rites. Managers must know whether the ceremonial, expressive side of their programs reinforces or undermines desired, existing cultural values and beliefs. Because of their intended technical consequences, organizational rites are unfortunately often designed and carried out by technical experts who are unaware of their expressive side. Managers who are less involved with technical details may be better able to detect and assess the cultural messages carried by company programs. Practical, culturally effective alternatives can usually be chosen and implemented.

In addition, research has shown that such familiar activities as training, recruitment and selection, and program evaluation may have expressive consequences that are more important than their technical ones. For example, one study found that the desired technical effects of management training (changes in knowledge and performance) were minimal compared with expressive effects that significantly reduced anxiety about organizational change. In another example, a program evaluation study was responsible not only for goals clarification (an intended technical consequence) but also for generating further negotiation and compromise between subcultures (an expressive conflict-reducing outcome). Managers who are insensitive to the valuable expressive consequences of these rites might discontinue them on technical grounds, thereby unwittingly losing their expressive benefits. Only by becoming sensitive to such expressive consequences of their activities and programs can managers adequately evaluate and manage all aspects of them.

Because rites are important activities in any organization, managers also need to learn and practice ceremonial skills. Some flair for the dramatic and the expressive in speech and action are clear assets for conducting effective rites. For managerial roles with many ceremonial duties, these skills probably should be among the stated qualifications. Karl Weick expressed the point in more general terms in his article "Cognitive Processes in Organizations," in Volume 1 of *Research in Organizations,* edited by Barry M. Staw (JAI Press, 1979): "Managerial work can be viewed as managing myth, symbols, and labels because managers traffic so often in images; the appropriate role for the manager may be the evangelist rather than the accountant."

Managers must also realize that because rites help maintain the continuity of cultural systems, they may impede organizational adaptability. Managers must consequently pay close attention to managing organizational rites so that they do not dampen or divert change efforts. Existing rites can have unintended, even deleterious consequences for planned change, and may thus need to be modified or supplanted as part of change efforts. Managers should therefore learn how to gauge the extent of both the desired and undesired consequences of rites. An effective manager will be able to make and use such assessments to continue, modify, or terminate ceremonial organizational activities.

One caveat is in order, however: Because rites arise so frequently and universally in human societies, managers probably will not be able to suppress popular rites whenever they want. A better strategy may be to try to "domesticate" such rites—to shape their practice and manage their occurrence so that their conservative consequences can be minimized.

Managers who wish to cultivate change must think creatively in order to modify existing rites or to invent new ones to express new ideas and values. In the process, they will need to find ways to build upon the old rites, for no organization is likely to welcome the wholesale alteration of its culture. Managers will encounter less resistance if they understand and appreciate the existing culture before they try to change it, and then use that understanding and appreciation to affirm and reinforce the direction of the desired change. New beliefs and values can be expressed by adding new forms or changing those used in current popular rites; some of the meanings conveyed by existing rites could be changed simply by changing one or two elements, such as the setting and the performers. For example, the cultural meaning of an internal appeals committee might be changed by moving its deliberations away from the general manager's office to a location on the plant floor, or by including fellow employees as well as members of management in those deliberations. In like manner, the cultural meanings of existing rites of passage could be changed by incorporating previously neglected stories about the organization and its early heroes that reflect desired beliefs and values.

As managers begin to evaluate their activities as rites, they will find that some of these rites are ineffective as cultural forms. Desired cultural values will be absent or compromised to the extent that they convey no consistent messages about the desired culture. In such instances, managers will need to decide whether to create new, more vigorous rites or to try to revive tired old ones. New cultural forms can be added to try to invigorate old rites, but managers may find the gradual replacement of such rites more effective. They should avoid immediate substitutions for or drastic overhauls of such rites; even tired ceremonies may have residual sentiments attached to them, and management may awaken resentment if it callously eliminates them. For example, a new bank president who had tried to reinvigorate a formal company dinner as a meaningful rite of integration felt he was unsuccessful. Instead of recommending that he discontinue the dinner, a consultant suggested that he try instituting a picnic or other informal social event, as well as other activities that would help people lose their awareness of differences in status. If the picnic becomes popular and works better as a rite of integration, he can gradually try again to modify the dinner, or perhaps allow it to wither away by gradually withdrawing financial support.

The cultural forms needed to modify existing rites are occasionally already present in organizational subcultures. If such elements can be incorporated, the modified rites may be more acceptable to the organization's members than rites that are entirely new. As we suggested to the bank manager, managers can also invent and establish new rites that express values consonant with the direction of desired change. If the new rites are successful, the old rites that express old values may lose their appeal and wither away. Rites of passage and enhancement are good places to begin; rites of integration and conflict reduction should be useful in dealing with conflicts that emerge during the change. Rites of degradation are problematic because they provoke resentment and make people feel insecure, but they may be necessary in instances that require drastic change.

Existing rites of renewal are dangerous; they should be used only to effect minor cultural change and should be avoided when major change is desired.

Possible New Rites

There are many gaps in our typology waiting to be filled by other observers. For example, a new type of rite is badly needed to se major change processes into motion. Major change requires the invention and establishment of new patterns of behavior—new roles that must be devised, accepted, learned, and enacted. The social interactions required to invent and establish new roles could be called "rites of creation"—rites for establishing new scripts of behavior and embedding them in ongoing social arrangements. Once established, individuals could be resocialized to fill the new roles through special rites of passage, and rewarded when they performed well in those roles through rites of enhancement.

Rites of creation are probably more likely to succeed if they are carried out initially on a small scale. Limiting participation will make it easier to choose participants whose beliefs and values are in line with whatever changes are involved. Furthermore, the desired changes can be treated as a pilot project; if they don't come up to expectations, they can be dismantled with less expense, embarrassment, and disruption.

Other areas in which organizations could benefit from appropriate rites include eliminating a role without degrading its occupants and introducing technology (such as robotics) that takes over some employee tasks. Perhaps such rites have already been invented. Intuitive managers often recognize the need for ceremony; if they don't, workers will often invent a ceremony of their own. People have always managed to develop and celebrate shared understandings; wise managers will help them do so.

Selected Bibliography

Readers interested in additional, in-depth examinations of rites and ceremonials in the workplace can find them described in detail in Harrison M. Trice, "Rites and Ceremonials in Organizational Cultures" in *Research in the Sociology of Organizations,* Vol. 4, edited by Sam Bachrach (JAI Press, 1985); in Harrison M. Trice and Janice M. Beyer, "Studying Organizational Cultures through Rites and Ceremonials" (*Academy of Management Review,* October 1984) and in Harrison M. Trice, James Belasco, and Joseph Alutto, "The Role of

Ceremonials in Organizational Behavior" (*Industrial and Labor Relations Review*, October 1969).

For a discussion of the twins of "do" and "say" in human actions, see Edmund R. Leach's article "Ritual" in *International Encyclopedia of the Social Sciences*, Vol. 13 (Free Press, 1968). For a definitive statement of manifest and latent consequences, see Robert K. Merton, "The Unintended Consequences of Purposive Social Action" (*American Sociological Review*, December 1936). A fascinating account of rites and ceremonials in a Japanese organization may be found in Thomas P. Rohlen's article "Spiritual Education in a Japanese Bank" (*American Anthropologist*, October 1974) and in his book *For Harmony and Strength: A Japanese White Collar Organization in Anthropological Perspective* (University of California Press, 1974). On the American scene, the following pieces are strongly recommended: Stanley G. Harris and Robert I. Sutton, "Functions of Parting Ceremonies in Dying Organizations: (*Academy of Management Journal*, March 1986) and Albert A. Blum, "Collective Bargaining: Ritual or Reality" (*Harvard Business Review*, November–December, 1961). The accounts of events at International Business Machines and the quotations used come from Thomas Graham Belden and Maria Robins Belden, *The Lengthening Shadow: The Life of Thomas J. Watson*, (Little, Brown, and Company, 1962). For a good example of a company picnic as a rite of integration, see R. Richard Ritti and G. Ray Funkhauser, *The Ropes to Skip and the Ropes to Know: Studies in Organizational Behavior* (Grid, 1977); for a dramatic description of a rite of degradation, see N.W. Biggart, "The Creative-Destructive Process of Organizational Change: The Case of the Post Office" (*Administrative Science Quarterly*, September 1977); and for an applied approach to the role of rites in changing cultures, Harrison M. Trice and Janice M. Beyer, "Using Six Organizational Rites to Change Culture" in Ralph H. Kilmann, Mary J. Saxton, and Roy Serpa (Eds.), *Gaining control of the Corporate Culture* (Jossey Bass, 1985). A very real application to routine worklife can be found in Helen Schwartzman's study of the ubiquitous meeting, "The Meeting as a Neglected Form in Organizational Studies" in Barry M. Staw and L. L. Cummings (Eds.), *Research in Organizational Behavior*, Vol. 8 (JAI Press, 1986). Finally, because these cultural forms carry meanings, a reference to the nature of ideologies in organizational behavior is appropriate. Such a reference may be found in Janice M. Beyer, "Ideologies, Values, and Decision Making in Organizations" in Paul C. Nystrom and William H. Starbuck (Eds.), *Handbook of Organizational Design*, Vol. 2 (Oxford University Press, 1981).

Corporate Culture

By Ralph H. Kilmann

Success in business is determined not by an executive's skills alone, nor by the visible features—the strategy, structure and reward system—of the organization. Rather, the organization itself has an invisible quality—a certain style, a character, a way of doing things—that may be more powerful than the dictates of any one person or any formal system. To understand the soul of the organization requires that we travel below the charts, rule books, machines and buildings into the underground world of corporate cultures.

Culture provides meaning, direction and mobilization, a social energy that moves the corporation into either productive action or destruction. I have encountered many organizations in which this social energy has barely been tapped; whether diffused in all directions or even deactivated, it is not mobilized to help the company. Most members seem apathetic or depressed about their jobs. They no longer pressure one another to do well. Pronouncements by top managers that they will improve the situation fall on the deaf ears of employees who have heard these promises before. Nothing seems to matter. The soul of the organization is slowly dying.

Other companies show considerable energy, but it is driving employees in the wrong direction. The organization lives in an immense 'culture gap. The social energy pressures members to persist in types of behavior that may have worked well in the past but are clearly dysfunctional today. The gap between the outdated culture and what is needed for organizational success gradually develops into a culture rut—a habitual, unquestioning way of behaving. There is no adaptation or change, only routine motions, despite the fact that the company is unsuccessful. This rut can go on for years, even though morale and performance suffer. Bad habits die hard. Culture shock occurs when the sleeping organization awakes and finds that it has lost touch with its original mission. The new world has left the insulated company behind—a Rip Van Winkle story on a grand scale.

On the other hand, one has merely to experience the energy that flows from shared commitments among group members to know it—the power that emanates from mutual influence and esprit de corps. Why does one organization have a very adaptive culture while another has a culture mired in the past? Is one a case of good fortune and the other a result of bad luck? On the contrary, it seems that any organization can find itself with an outdated culture if the culture itself is not managed explicitly. I have found that, unattended, a company's culture almost always becomes dysfunctional. Normal human fear, insecurity, oversensitivity, dependency and paranoia seem to take over unless there is a concerted effort to establish an adaptive culture. People cope with uncertainty and perceived threats by protecting themselves, by being cautious, by minimizing their risks, by going along with a culture that builds protective barriers around work units and around the whole organization. An adaptive culture, alternatively, requires risk and trust; employees must actively support one another's efforts to identify problems and adapt to solutions. The latter can be accomplished only by a very conscious, well-planned effort at managing culture.

A company's culture sometimes supports self-defeating individual behavior that persists in spite of its many disruptive effects on morale and performance: doing the minimum to get by; purposely resisting or even sabotaging innovation; and being very negative in general about the organization's capacity to change. Worse, such behavior may even include lying, cheating and stealing as well as intimidating, harassing and hurting others. The most detrimental behavior in the long run, however, is persisting in once-adaptive patterns rather than changing to meet the dynamic complexity of the present. The challenge is to get out of the culture rut.

How Do Cultures Form?

When an organization is born, a tremendous burst of energy is released as members struggle to make it work. A corporate culture seems to form rather

Kilmann, Ralph H. "Corporate Culture." In *Psychology Today*, April 1985, pp. 62–69. Adapted from Killmann, R.H. *Beyond The Quick Fix: Managing Five Tracks To Organizational Success.* San Francisco: Jossey-Bass Inc., 1984. Used with permission.

quickly, based on the organization's mission, setting and requirements for success: high quality, efficiency, product reliability, customer service, innovation, hard work and loyalty. The culture captures everyone's drive and imagination. As the reward systems, policies and work procedures are formally documented, they suggest what kinds of behavior and attitudes are important for success.

Such situational forces, while important in shaping culture, cannot compete with actions of key individuals. For example, the founder's objectives, principles, values and especially behavior provide important clues as to what is really wanted from all employees, both now and in the future. Carrying on in the traditions of the founder, other top executives affect the culture of the company by their example.

Employees also take note of all critical incidents that stem from management action—such as the time that so-and-so was reprimanded for doing a good job when not asked to do it beforehand or the time that another worker was fired for publicly disagreeing with the company's position. Incidents such as these become an enduring part of the company folklore, indicating what the corporation really wants, what really counts in getting ahead or, alternatively, how to stay out of trouble. They are the unwritten rules of the game.

A culture may be very functional at first. But in time it becomes a separate entity, independent of its initial purpose. The culture becomes distinct from the formal strategy, structure and reward systems of the organization. In a similar vein, culture becomes distinct from workers and even top managers. All members of the organization are taught to follow the cultural norms without questioning them. After employees have been around for a few years, they have already learned the ropes. Even new top executives who vow that things will be different find out—often the hard way—how the culture is "bigger" and more powerful than they are. A top manager can get individual commitments to some new policy from his subordinates, but after they walk out the office door and once again become part of the corporate culture, the boss finds the new plan bitterly opposed.

Top management is also caught in the grip of the firm's separate and distinct culture. Employees wonder from below why managers play it so safe, why they refuse to approach things differently, why they keep applying the same old management practices that clearly do not work. They wonder why management is so blind to the world around them. Is management "mean" or just "stupid"?

How Are Cultures Maintained?

The force controlling group behavior at every level in the organization—a force that can brainwash workers into believing that what they are doing is automatically good for the company, their community and their family—must be very powerful. Is it magic or is it the psychology of group membership that explains the potency of corporate culture? Social scientists speak of "norms" as the unwritten rules of behavior. In a company, for example, a norm might be: Don't disagree with your boss in public. If a norm is violated, there is immediate and strong pressure to get the offending party to change behavior. Consider, for example, an individual who persists in presenting reservations about the company's new product at a group meeting—just after the boss has argued strongly for investing heavily in its advertising campaign. The bold employee receives stares and frowns, eyes roll—all nonverbal messages to sit down and shut up. If these efforts do not work, the underling will hear about it later, from coworkers if not from the boss.

The human need to be accepted by a group—whether family, friends, coworkers or neighbors—gives the group leverage to demand compliance to its norms. Were such a need not so widespread, groups would have little hold on people other than formal sanctions. The nonconformists and mavericks who defy pressures to adhere to group norms always do so at a considerable price.

Simple experiments conducted by Solomon Asch in the early 1950s demonstrate just how powerfully the group can influence its deviants. The experiments were described to the research subjects as a study in perception. Three lines—A, B and C, all of different lengths—were shown on a single card. Subjects were asked to indicate which of these three lines was identical in length to a fourth line, D, shown on a second card. In one experiment, seven people sat in a row. One by one they indicated their choices. While line C was in fact identical to line D, each of the first six, all confederates of the experimenter, said that line D was identical to A. The seventh person was the unknowing subject. As each person deliberately gave the wrong answer, the seventh subject became increasingly uneasy, anxious and doubtful of his or her own perceptions. When it came time to respond, the seventh subject agreed with the rest almost one-third of the time. Without such group influence there were hardly any errors.

Imagine just how easily such distorted perceptions of reality can be maintained when backed up by formal sanctions—pay, promotions and other rewards.

The group can reward its members so that they ignore the disruptive behavior of "troublemakers." The members collectively believe that everything is fine, continue to reinforce the myth and reward one another for maintaining it. In essence, everyone agrees that the dysfunctional ways can continue without question. Any deviant who thinks otherwise is severely punished and eventually banished from the tribe.

Asch's classic study demonstrates that the impact of a group on its members is very powerful indeed. And if the group is cohesive, if there is a strong sense of community and loyalty, there will be even stronger pressures on each member to adopt whatever the cultural norms specify. Other studies have shown that if the cultural norms of a cohesive group support the organization's mission, the workers' performance will be high; the culture is said to be adaptive.

Alternatively, if the norms endorsed by a highly cohesive group oppose the corporate goals, then the culture will foster low performance and morale. It is better to have an uncohesive group with mediocre performance than a highly cohesive counterculture. The latter will result in consistently low performance and headaches for everyone.

Given the crucial role of corporate culture in shaping behavior, and the especially powerful effects of group norms, one way to turn around a maladaptive company is to change its culture by managing its norms. Even norms that dictate appropriate behavior, opinions and facial expressions can be brought to the surface, discussed and altered.

In my corporate consulting work, I have found it helpful to have all group members (generally in a workshop setting) list the actual norms that currently guide their behavior and attitudes. This can be done for one or many groups, departments and divisions. Sometimes it takes a little prodding and a few illustrations to get the process started, but once it begins members are quick to suggest many norms. In fact, they seem to delight in being able to articulate what was never written in any document and rarely mentioned even in casual conversation between themselves.

In an organization with a culture deeply rooted in the past, some of the norms people list are: Don't disagree with your boss; don't rock the boat; treat women as second-class citizens; put down your organization; don't enjoy your work; don't share information with other groups; treat subordinates as incompetent and lazy; cheat on your expense account; look busy even when you're not; don't reward employees on the basis of merit; laugh at those who suggest new ways of doing things; don't smile much; openly criticize company policies to outsiders; complain a lot; don't trust anyone who seems sincere. And, ironically, the one common norm that must be violated in this group process is: Don't make norms explicit.

Other frequently listed norms include: Don't be the bearer of bad news; don't say what the boss doesn't want to hear, don't think of things that are not likely to happen; don't spoil the party; don't be associated with an ugly event; see no evil, hear no evil and speak no evil.

As these norms are listed for everyone to see, there is considerable laughter and amazement. The members become aware that they have been seducing one another into abiding by these counterproductive rules. But no individual made a conscious choice to behave this way; rather, as workers entered the organization, they were taught what was expected—often in quite subtle ways. The more cohesive the group, the more forcefully the sanctions are applied and the more rapidly the learning takes place. In the extreme case, a highly cohesive group that has been around for a long time has members who look, act, think and talk like one another.

In the projects in which I had managers and all employees of a company list their norms, it was surprising to discover that most norms cited were negative. In a number of cases, more than 90 percent of the listed norms had at least mildly negative connotations. It may be, of course, that employees felt I was looking for the dysfunctions in their organizations rather than for the adaptive aspects. Then again, maybe many organizations are plagued with a high proportion of negative norms from their bureaucrtic cultures.

The next step is for all group members to discuss where the organization is headed and what type of behavior is necessary to move forward. Even when a corporation has inherited a very dysfunctional culture from the past, individual employees are often aware of what changes are needed in order for the organization to adapt and survive. Similarly, they are aware of what work environment they prefer for their own sanity and satisfaction.

A certain amount of planning and problem solving may have to occur before any new directions can be articulated. In groups that have fallen into a culture rut, members are so absorbed with the negatives that they have not spent much time thinking about or discussing what they would prefer. Sometimes it is helpful to ask them to reflect upon their ideal organization: If they could design their own from scratch, what would it be like? This generally shows what could be changed in the present organization—often things that are accepted merely because they are traditional.

The third step is for all group members to develop a list of new norms for organizational success. What new norms, for example, would encourage a more adaptive stance toward the organization's changing environment? Likewise, what new norms would allow groups to discuss difficult and uncomfortable issues that affect the long-range success of the firm? What cultural norms would bring difficult internal problems out into the open so that they could be resolved?

At this point, employees usually grasp how unwritten rules have affected their behavior. They experience a sense of relief at contemplating a new way of life, realizing that they no longer have to pressure one another to behave in dysfunctional ways. They can create a new social order within their work groups and within their own organization. Part of this sense of relief comes from recognizing that their dissatisfaction and ineffectiveness are not due to their own incompetence: Psychologically, it is much easier to blame the invisible force called culture—as long as they take responsibility for changing it.

In organizations needing to be more adaptive, flexible and responsive to modern times, some of the norms often listed are: Treat everyone with respect and as a potential source of valuable insight and expertise; be willing to take on responsibility; initiate changes to improve performance; congratulate those who suggest new ideas and new ways of doing things; be cost conscious; speak with pride about your organization and work group; budget your time according to the importance of tasks for accomplishing objectives; don't criticize the organization in front of clients or customers; enjoy your work and show your enthusiasm for a job well done; be helpful and supportive of other groups in the organization.

New norms that directly pertain to complex and difficult problems include: Bring uncomfortable issues out into the open; persist in drawing attention to problems even if others seem reluctant to consider the implications of what you are saying; listen to other members' viewpoints even if you disagree with them; encourage zany and bizarre perspectives to insure that nothing important and possible has been overlooked; make people aware when a topic that should generate a heated debate has not.

Spotting Culture Gaps

The contrast between desired norms and actual norms can be immense. My colleague, Mary Jane Saxton, and I refer to this contrast as a "culture gap." We have developed a measurement tool for detecting the gap between what the current culture is and what it should be: Kilmann-Saxton Culture-Gap Survey.

The survey was developed by first collecting more than 400 norms from managers and employees in more than 25 different types of organizations. Many of these norms were also developed through projects in which cultural norms were assessed and changed. The final set of 28 norm pairs that appears on the survey was derived from statistical and clinical analysis of the most consistent norms that were operating in most of the organizations we studied. An example of a norm pair is: A) Share information only when it benefits your own work groups versus B) Share information to help the organization make better decisions. Each employee chooses either A) or B) for each norm pair in two ways: first, according to the pressures the work group puts on its members (actual norms); and second, according to which norms should be operating in order to promote high performance and morale (desired norms).

The differences between the actual norms and the desired norms represent the culture gaps. There are four types of culture gaps, each made up of seven norm pairs. First, there are what we call "task support norms" having to do with information sharing, helping other groups and concern with efficiency, such as "Support the work of other groups" versus "Put down the work of other groups." Second, there are "task innovation norms," which stress creativity, such as "Always try to improve" versus "Don't rock the boat." Third, we look at "social relationship norms" for socializing with one's work group and mixing friendships with business, such as "Get to know the people in your work group" versus "Don't bother." Finally, we examine "personal freedom norms" for self-expression, exercising discretion and pleasing oneself, such as "Live for yourself and your family" versus "Live for your job and career."

Culture gaps can be surveyed in a work group, a department, a division or an entire organization. By calculating the difference between the norms that are actually in force and those that should be, the four culture-gap scores are obtained. The larger the gap, the greater the likelihood that the current norms are hindering both morale and performance. If the assessed culture gaps are allowed to continue, work groups are likely to resist any attempt at change and improvement. Specifically, culture gaps materialize as an unwillingness to adopt new work methods and innovations, as a lack of support for programs to improve quality and productivity, as lip service when changes in strategic directions are announced and, in the extreme, as efforts to maintain the status quo at all costs.

Our use of the Kilmann-Saxton Culture-Gap Survey in numerous for-profit and no-profit organizations has revealed distinct patterns of culture gaps. For example, in some of the high-technology firms, lack of cooperation and information sharing across groups has resulted in large culture gaps in task support. In the automotive and steel industries, not rewarding creativity and innovation has resulted in large culture gaps in task innovation. In some social-service agencies in which work loads can vary greatly, large gaps in social relationships are found, indicating that too much time is spent socializing rather than looking to get the next job done. Finally, in extremely bureaucratic organizations, such as some banks and government agencies, large gaps in personal freedom are evident. Here, workers' sense of being overly confined and constrained lowers their performance and morale.

The most general finding to date is the presence of large culture gaps in task innovation. It seems that American industry is plagued by significant differences between actual and desired norms in this area—a condition that may relate directly to the frequently mentioned productivity problem in the United States. An industrial culture that pushes for short-term financial results is bound to foster norms that work against efforts at long-term improvement, regardless of what formal documents and publicity statements seem to advocate.

Do all employees of a corporation see the same culture gaps? Apparently not. The smallest culture gaps are found at the top of the organization's hierarchy. Managers believe their own publicity; they say that they reward creativity and innovation but seem to forget that their actions speak louder than their words. By contrast, cultural gaps are largest at the bottom of the hierarchy, where the gaps also reveal alienation and distrust. Here a common norm is: Don't trust management. In essence, workers see management as being up to no good, getting caught up in fads to fool and manipulate employees or thinking that the workers are too stupid to see what's behind management's latest whim.

Closing Gaps

Without a supportive culture, every action by top management will be discounted by the groups below—even top-down efforts to change the culture.

I have seen cases in which executives have tried dramatic changes in their own behavior coupled with symbolic deeds and fiery speeches in order to dictate a new culture to the company—but to no avail. Only when work-group members encourage one another to be receptive to overtures by management can the whole change program be successful. For example, various work groups might include such new norms as: Give management another chance; assume good intentions. Managers and consultants, therefore, have to work especially hard to encourage the work groups, including the executive groups, to meet one another halfway.

How can culture gaps be closed? How can an organization move its culture from the actual to the desired? Can a company be taken out of a culture rut and be put back on track for solving present and future problems? Will the organization survive this culture shock?

When the current culture is at least hopeful, the impact of survey results on workers is almost miraculous. In fact, some change from the actual to the desired norms can take place just by listing the new set of norms. Members start "playing out" the new norms immediately after they are discussed. But when the current culture is cynical, depressed and in a deep rut, the response to the survey results is quite different. Even when large gaps are shown or when a listing demonstrates the tremendous differences between actual and desired norms, employees seem apathetic and lifeless. They respond by saying that their work units cannot change for the better until the level of management above them and the rest of the company change. They believe that the external system is keeping them down.

Curiously, when I do a culture-gap survey at the next highest level, the very same argument is heard again: "We have no power to change; we have to wait for the next level to let us change; they have the power!" It is shocking, after conducting the culture-gap survey for an entire organization, to present the results to the top management group only to find the same feelings of helplessness. Here top management is waiting for the economy to change. In actuality, it is the corporate culture that is saying: Don't take on responsibility; protect yourself at all costs; don't try to change until everyone else has changed; don't lead the way, follow; if you ignore the problem, maybe it will go away.

This is the perfect example of a company in a culture rut, where the shock of realizing the discrepancy between actual and desired norms is just too great to confront. Instead, the organization buries its head and hopes everything will be sorted out by itself. Even in the face of strong evidence of a serious problem, time and time again I have witnessed this form of organizational denial—a much more powerful and perhaps destructive force than any case of individual denial. The group's power to define reality clouds everyone's better judgment. The bureaucratic culture "wins" again.

One large industrial organization asked me to present a three-day seminar to the chairman of the board, the chief executive officer and the 10 corporate officers on the topic of corporate culture. I suggested that a representative survey of culture gaps be conducted across all divisions in the company. In this way, I could report on the company's specific culture and thus generate a livelier and more interesting discussion than an abstract lecture would elicit. In a couple of weeks, the vice president for human resources called: "No, we better not do this," he said. "I don't think the executive group really wants to know what is going on in the company. Besides, we can't take the chance of surprising them with your survey results." Who is protecting whom?

Gaining control of the corporate culture is not only possible but necessary for today's organizations. As changes in corporate directions are planned, a new culture may have to replace the old culture—in one or more divisions or for the whole organization. But just as old cultures can become out-of-date and dysfunctional, the same can happen with new ones. Further changes in the organization's setting—and corresponding changes in strategy, structure and reward systems—can make any culture less functional than before. An important part of managing the corporate culture, therefore, is to continue monitoring and assessing norms. If the culture is not managed explicitly, it may be just a matter of time before the organization is once again disrupted. But if it is managed explicitly, the company can expect significant improvements in both morale and performance; it will be, in the best sense of the word, a cultured organization of employees.

Are You Corporate Cultured?

By Edgar H. Schein

Most of us live in organizations and must deal with them, but we continue to find it difficult to understand and justify much of what we observe and experience in our organizational life. Too much seems to be "bureaucratic" or "political" or simply "irrational." The concept of organizational culture holds promise for illuminating this confusing area. It is particularly relevant in understanding the mysterious and seemingly irrational things that go on in human systems.

The word "culture" has many meanings and connotations. When combined with "organization," the result will almost certainly be conceptual and semantic confusion.

The term "culture" should be reserved for the deeper level of basic assumptions and beliefs that are shared by members of an organization, that operate subconsciously, and that define in a basic "taken-for-granted" fashion an organization's view of itself and its environment.

These assumptions and beliefs are learned responses to a group's problems of survival in its external environment and its problems of internal integration. The assumptions come to be taken for granted because they solve those problems repeatedly and reliably.

Thus, what is meant by "culture" is a pattern of basic assumptions that have worked well enough to be considered valid and, therefore, taught to new members as the correct way to perceive, think and feel in relation to those problems.

These assumptions may be invented, discovered, or developed by a given group as it learns to cope with its problems of external adaptation and internal integration.

Unless we learn to analyze organizational culture accurately, we cannot really understand why organizations do some of the things they do and why leaders have some of the difficulties they have.

An examination of cultural issues at the organizational level is essential to a basic understanding of

what goes on in organizations, how to run them, and how to improve them.

Effects of culture on strategy. Many companies have found they can devise new strategies that make sense from a financial, product or marketing point of view, yet they cannot implement those strategies because they require assumptions, values and ways of working that differ from the organization's prior assumptions.

Action, for example, is a company that grew up and became successful by marketing a complex product to sophisticated customers.

When the company later developed smaller, simpler and less expensive versions of this product for a less sophisticated market, its product designers and marketing and sales divisions could not deal with the new customer type.

The sales and marketing people could not imagine what the concerns of the new, less knowledgeable customer might be; the product designers continued to assume they could judge product attractiveness themselves.

Neither group was motivated to understand the new customer type because, subconsciously, they tended to look down on such customers.

Failures of mergers, acquisitions and diversifications. When the management of a company decides to merge with or acquire another company, it usually carefully checks the financial strength, market position, management strength, and various other aspects of corporate health.

Rarely checked, however, are those aspects that might be considered "cultural": the philosophy or style of the company; its technological origins, which might provide clues as to its basic assumptions; and its beliefs about its mission and future.

Yet if culture determines and limits strategy, a cultural mismatch in an acquisition or merger is as great a risk as a financial, product or market mismatch.

Some years ago, for example, a large packaged-foods company purchased a successful chain of hamburger restaurants but, despite 10 years of concerted effort, could not make the acquisition profitable.

First, the company did not anticipate that many of the best managers of the acquired company would leave because they did not like the philosophy of the new parent company.

Instead of hiring new managers with experience in the fast-food business, the parent company assigned some of its own managers to run the new business.

These managers did not understand the technology of the fast-food business and hence were unable to use many of the marketing techniques that had proved effective in the parent company.

Finally, the parent company imposed many of the control systems and procedures that had historically proved useful for it—and consequently drove the operating costs of the chain too high.

The parent company's managers found that they could never completely understand franchise operations and hence could not get a "feel" for what it would take to run that kind of business profitably.

Failure to integrate new technologies. The introduction of any new technology into an occupation, organization or society can be seen as a culture change problem.

Occupations typically build their practices, values and basic self-image around their underlying technology.

Similarly, an organization that is successful because of its mastery of a given technology develops its self-image around that technology.

If the technology substantially changes, the organization or occupation not only must learn new practices but must redefine itself in ways that involve deep culture assumptions.

For example, with the introduction of sophisticated computerized information systems and automation, it becomes painfully obvious that in many crucial areas the subordinate knows more than the boss, or that groups who previously had no power now have a great deal.

People who are in power often anticipate such changes and realize the best way to avoid the loss of their own power is to resist the new technology altogether.

Even when such power issues are dealt with, the new technology carries its own occupational culture.

Only when change has begun do managers realize that the new technology is accompanied by a whole new set of assumptions, values and behavior patterns.

The realignment of status, power and working habits is clearly a major cultural change.

Intergroup conflicts within the organization. Groups form on the basis of physical proximity, shared fate, common occupations, common work experience, similar ethnic background or similar rank level.

Once a group acquires a history, it also acquires a culture.

If groups get into conflict with each other, that conflict is difficult to reduce—mainly because a group needs to maintain its identity, and one of the best ways of maintaining that identity is to compare and contrast it with other groups.

In other words, intergroup comparison, competition and/or conflict helps build and maintain intragroup culture.

If we view labor-management negotiations from this perspective, we can ask whether each group in the negotiation has developed a culture of its own, whether those cultures overlap enough to make mutual understanding possible, and, if not, how enough common culture could be established to make genuine negotiating or problem solving possible.

Negotiations in US companies seem to go faster and produce mutually more satisfactory solutions when there is a shared set of assumptions about the validity of the capitalist system, the rational-legal basis of authority, the openness of class structure, the Horatio Alger myth, and the value of the product or service being created by the organization.

Ineffective meetings and communication breakdowns in face-to-face relationships. Even the familiar daily problems of organizational life—the unproductive meeting, the difficulty of getting a point across to a subordinate during performance appraisal, the difficulty of communicating instructions clearly enough to ensure correct implementation, and so on—may be productively analyzed from the cultural perspective.

Instead of seeing communication breakdowns as the result of lack of clarity, defensiveness or semantics, we might recognize that such breakdowns often result from real differences in how people perceive and understand things because of their different cultural memberships.

Socialization failures. Every organization is concerned about the degree to which people at all levels "fit" into its structure.

Organizations will expend considerable effort in training, indoctrinating, socializing and otherwise attempting to ensure that the "fitting in" is not left to chance.

When the socialization process does not work optimally because the new member does not learn the culture of the host group, there are usually severe consequences.

At one extreme, if the new employee does not learn the pivotal or central assumptions of the organization, that employee usually feels alienated, uncomfortable and possibly unproductive.

Such feelings may even cause valued employees to leave the organization.

At the other extreme, if the employee is "oversocialized" in the sense of learning every detail of the culture, the result is total conformity, leading to an inability on the part of the organization to be innovative and responsive to new environmental demands.

Because an organization tends to be a conglomeration of subcultures but also has a total organizational culture if it has had enough of a history, the process of cultural learning for the newcomer is complicated and perpetual.

On first entering the organization, and subsequently with each major functional, geographical or hierarchical move, the person must learn new subcultural elements and fit them into a broader total view.

Productivity. As numerous studies of industrial work have shown, work groups form strong cultures.

Often such subcultures develop the assumption that work should be limited not by what one is able to do but by what is appropriate to do.

Productivity is a cultural phenomenon par excellence, both at the same-work-group level and at the level of the total organization.

Culture Helps People Cope with the External Environment

To understand the dynamics of culture, we must understand why basic assumptions arise and why they persist.

We must develop answers to such questions as:
• What does culture do?
• What functions does it serve?
• How does it originate, evolve and change?
• Why is it so difficult to change culture?

What culture does is to solve the group's basic problems of survival in, and adaptation to, the external environment and integration of its internal process to ensure the capacity to continue to survive and adapt.

There are four primary external issues.

Consensus on core mission, primary tasks, manifest and latent functions. Every new group or organization must develop a shared concept of its ultimate survival problem, from which is usually derived its most basic sense of core mission, or "reason to be."

In most business organizations, this hard definition revolves around the issue of economic survival and growth, which, in turn, involves the delivery of a necessary product or service to customers.

At the same time, society defines as part of the core mission the provision of jobs, so that members of the society have a way to make a living.

Every organization must define and fulfill its core mission or it will not survive. The mission typically also involves a deeper sense of *how* to survive in a given environment, where the answer to this question defines more discretely what the group ultimately views its identity to be.

At one company, for example, there was a debate around the question of whether to purchase a company in a different industry.

It was not only the economic considerations that were crucial, but deeper questions of "Who are we?" "What are we capable of?" and "What do we want to be?"

Consensus on means. The group cannot perform its primary task unless there is clear consensus on the means by which goals will be met.

How to design, finance, build and sell the product must be clearly agreed on.

From the particular pattern of these agreements, not only the style of the organization but also the basic design of tasks, division of labor, organization structure, reward and incentive systems, control systems and information systems emerge.

The skills, technology and knowledge that a group acquires in its effort to cope with its environment also become part of its culture if there is consensus on their use.

Collectively, all these skills, structure and processes define what can be thought of as the means for accomplishing the organization's goals and, as can be seen, these means constitute a large part of the culture if the group or organization has a long history.

The accomplishment of the organization's goals, even though they are directed toward the outside, requires the creation of a structure inside the group to make that accomplishment possible.

Consensus on criteria for measuring results. Once the group is performing, there must be consensus on how to judge its own performance in order to know what kind of remedial action to take when things do not go as expected.

If members of the group hold widely divergent concepts of what to look for and how to evaluate results, they cannot develop coordinated remedial action.

The potential complexity of achieving consensus of criteria was illustrated in an international refugee organization.

Field workers measured themselves by the number of refugees processed. Senior management paid more attention to the favorable attitudes of host governments because those governments financed the organization.

Senior management, therefore, checked every decision that was to be made about refugees with virtually every other department and several layers of management, to ensure the decision would not offend one of the supporting governments.

This, in turn, irritated the field workers, who felt they were usually dealing with crisis situations in which slowdowns might mean death for significant numbers of refugees.

Consensus on remedial and repair strategies. The final area of consensus crucial for external adaptation concerns what to do if a change in course is required and how to do it.

If information surfaces that the group is not on target—sales are off, profits are down, product introductions are late or the like—what is the process by which the problem is diagnosed and remedied?

These processes are not limited to problem areas. If a company is getting signals of success, does it decide to grow as fast as possible, does it develop a careful strategy of controlled growth, or does it take a quick profit and risk staying small?

Of particular importance, however, is the organization's response to "bad news" or information that threatens survival.

Responses to crises provide opportunities for culture building and reveal aspects of the culture that have already been built.

What we ultimately end up calling the culture of that group will be influenced both by its external adaptation processes and by its mode of building and maintaining itself: its processes of internal integration.

The internal integration systems are influenced by, and in turn influence, external adaptation.

Developing a common language and conceptual categories. To function as a group, the individuals who come together must establish a system of communication and a language.

The human organism cannot stand too much uncertainty or stimulus overload.

Categories of meaning that organize perceptions and thought, thereby filtering out what is unimportant while focusing on what is important, become not only a major means of reducing overload anxiety but also a necessary precondition for coordinated action.

In one organization, for example, the chairman often got angry with a member who was not contributing in group meetings and began to draw conclusions about the competency of that person.

The chairman assumed the silence meant ignorance, incompetence or lack of motivation.

The silent person, it turned out, was ready to make a presentation and was very frustrated because he was never called on to give it. He assumed he was not supposed to volunteer, and he began to believe his boss did not value him.

The danger was that both were setting up self-fulfilling prophecies. In this group, the absence of a common communication system undermined effective action.

Consensus on group boundaries; criteria for inclusion. If a group is to function and develop, one of the most important areas for clear consensus is the perception of who is "in" the new group and who is "out" or "not in" and by what criteria those decisions are made.

New members cannot really function and concentrate on their primary task if they are insecure about their membership, and the group cannot really maintain a good sense of itself if it does not have a way of defining itself and its boundaries.

As organizations age and become more complex, the problem of defining clear boundaries also becomes more complex. More people come to occupy boundary-spanning roles.

In a complex society, individual employees belong to many organizations, so that their identity is not tied up exclusively with any one organization.

Locating a "cultural unit" becomes more difficult since a given organization may really be a complex set of overlapping subcultures.

But consensus on criteria for membership is always one means of determine whether a cultural unit exists in any given group.

For instance, in the Action Company every new member of the technical or managerial staff must be interviewed by between five and 10 people, and only if that member is acceptable to the entire set is he or she offered a job.

If one asks what the interviewers look for, they often say, "We want someone who will fit in."

Once a person has been hired, if he fails in an initial job assignment the assumption is made that he is a competent person but was put in the wrong job.

In the Multi Company, education is a key criterion. Most of the young technical and managerial staff come from a scientific background, highlighting the assumption that, if one is to succeed in the company, one must understand the scientific base on which it was built.

Having an advanced degree, such as a doctorate, is a distinct advantage even if one is being hired into a marketing or managerial job.

Stratifications: consensus on criteria for differentiation of influence and power. A critical issue in any new group is how influence, power and authority will be allocated.

The process of stratification in human systems is typically not as blatant as the dominance-establishing rituals of animal societies, but is functionally equivalent in that it concerns the evolution of workable rules for managing aggression and mastery needs. Human societies develop pecking orders.

The easiest way to observe this process is to watch a new group, such as a committee or training group, in the early hours of its life.

Each person comes into the situation with very different prior or assumed status, and has varying degrees of power and authority attributed to him or her.

The process of group formation then involves a complex mutual testing around who will grant how much influence to whom, and who will seek how much influence from whom.

Peer relationships: consensus on criteria for intimacy, friendship and love. Every new group must decide simultaneously how to deal with authority problems and how to establish workable peer relationships.

Whereas authority issues derive ultimately from the necessity to deal with feelings of aggression, peer relationship, intimacy problems derive ultimately from the necessity to deal with feelings of affection, love and sexuality.

The leaders of Action, for example, strongly believed good decisions could be made only if everyone was encouraged to challenge authority and if peers were encouraged to debate very issue.

Needless to say, a climate of high conflict, intense competition among peers, and relatively low levels of intimacy developed.

Consensus on criteria for allocation of rewards and punishments. In order to function, every group must develop a system of sanctions for obeying or disobeying the rules.

The specific rewards and punishments, and the manner in which they are administered, constitute one of the most important cultural characteristics of a new organization.

In one market-oriented food company, for example, the norm developed that a manager who did his job competently could expect to be moved to another, generally bigger, project within approximately 18 months.

Managers who did not move every 18 months began to feel that they were failing.

In contrast, in the Action Company the norm was established that the designer of a product saw it through from beginning to end.

Therefore, a reward was defined as being allowed to stay with one's product through manufacturing and marketing to sales.

When studying the culture of an organization, one must investigate the reward system because it reveals fairly quickly some of the important rules and underlying assumptions in that culture.

Once one has identified what kinds of behavior are "heroic" and what kinds of behavior are "sinful" one can begin to infer the beliefs and assumptions that lie behind those valuations.

Corporate Leaders Help Embed Corporate Culture

The most powerful mechanisms for embedding and reinforcing culture are:

What leaders pay attention to, measure and control. One of the best mechanisms that founders, leaders, managers or even colleagues have available for communicating what they believe in or care about is what they systematically pay attention to.

Even casual remarks and questions that are *consistently* geared to a certain area can be potent as formal control mechanisms and measurements.

To illustrate, a consultant was told of a company that wanted him to help install a management development program. The consultant suggested to the president that he communicate his concern by paying attention to what was being done and by reinforcing it through the reward system.

The president announced that henceforth 50% of each senior manager's annual bonus would be contingent on what he or she had done to develop his or her own immediate subordinates during the past year.

He added that he himself had no specific program in mind but that each quarter he would ask each senior manager what had been done.

As it turned out, the subordinates launched a series of different activities, many of them pulled together from work that was already going on piecemeal in the organization: a coherent program was forged over a two-year period and has continued.

Other powerful signals that subordinates interpret for evidence of the leader's assumptions are what they observe does not get reacted to.

Leader reactions to critical incidents and organizational crises. When an organization faces a crisis, the manner in which leaders and others deal with it creates new norms, values and working procedures and reveals important underlying assumptions.

Crises also are significant in culture creation and transmission partly because the heightened emotional involvement during such periods increases the intensity of learning.

The assumption in Action that "we are a family who will take care of each other" comes out most clearly during periods of crisis.

When the company was in difficulty, the president became the strong and supportive father figure, pointing out to both the external world and the employees that the company had great strengths that would ensure future success, and that people should not worry about layoffs.

Deliberate role modeling, teaching and coaching. Founders and new leaders of organizations generally seem to know that their own visible behavior has great value for communicating assumptions and values to other members, especially newcomers.

There is one organization in which the president has made several videotapes outlining his explicit philosophy, and these tapes are shown to new members of the organization as part of their initial training.

However, there is a difference between the messages delivered from staged settings, such as when a president gives a welcoming speech to newcomers, and the messages received when a president is observed "informally." The informal messages are the more powerful teaching and coaching mechanism.

In the Action Company, the president made an explicit attempt to downplay status and hierarchy because of his assumption that good ideas can come from anyone.

He drove a small car, had an unpretentious office, dressed informally and spent many hours wandering among the employees at all levels getting to know them informally.

Criteria for allocation of rewards and status. Members of any organization learn from their own experience of promotions, performance appraisals, and discussion with the boss what the organization values and what the organization punishes.

Both the nature of the behavior rewarded and punished and the nature of the rewards and punishments themselves carry the messages.

An organization's leaders can quickly get across their own priorities, values and assumptions by consistently linking rewards and punishments to the behavior they are concerned with.

Criteria for recruitment, selection, promotion, retirement and excommunication. One of the most subtle yet most potent ways in which culture gets embedded and perpetuated is the initial selection of new members.

This cultural embedding mechanism is subtle because it operates unconsciously in most organizations.

Organizations tend to favor those candidates who resemble present members in style, assumptions, values and beliefs.

Such candidates are perceived to be the "best" people to hire and have characteristics attributed to them to justify their being hired.

Unless someone outside the organization is explicitly involved in the hiring, there is no way of knowing how much the current implicit assumptions are dominating recruiters' perceptions of the candidates.

Initial selection decisions for new members, followed by the criteria applied in the promotion system, are powerful mechanisms for embedding and perpetuating the culture, especially when combined with socialization tact designed to teach cultural assumptions.

Because the messages transmitted by these mechanisms are to a large extent implicit, conflicting messages can be sent.

Sometimes such messages result from unconscious conflicts in the message senders, and sometimes they result from conflicts among key leaders in what they believe, assume and value.

In either case, the messages are implicit, and it is therefore possible for conflicting assumptions to coexist in a group and for the group to accommodate to such inconsistencies and conflicts.

There are also secondary reinforcement mechanisms. These mechanisms are "secondary" because they work only if they are consistent with the primary mechanisms discussed above.

When they are consistent, they begin to build organizational ideologies and thus to formalize much of what is informally learned at the outset.

If they are inconsistent, they will either be ignored or will be a source of internal conflict.

But the operating cultural assumptions will always be manifested first in what the leaders demonstrate, not in what is written down or inferred from designs and procedures.

Organization design and structure. The design for the organization initially and the periodic reorganizations that companies go through thus provide ample opportunities for the founders/leaders to embed their deeply held assumptions about the task, the means to accomplish it, the nature of people, and the right kinds of relationships to foster among people.

Organizational systems and procedures. The most visible part of life in any organization is the daily, weekly, monthly, quarterly, and annual cycle of routines, procedures, reports, forms, and other recurrent tasks that have to be performed.

The origin of such routines is often not known to participants, or sometimes even to senior management, but their existence lends structure, predictability and concreteness to an otherwise vague and ambiguous organizational world.

If founders or leaders do not design systems and procedures as reinforcement mechanisms, they open the door to historically evolved inconsistencies in the culture, or weaken their own message from the outset.

Design of physical space, facades, buildings. This encompasses all the visible features of the organization that clients, customers, vendors, new employees and visitors would encounter.

The messages that can be inferred from the physical environment are potentially reinforcing of the leader's messages, but only if they are managed to be so.

Leaders who have a clear philosophy and style often choose to embody that style in the visible manifestations of the organization.

Stories about important events and people. As a group develops and accumulates a history, some of this history becomes embodied in stories about events and leadership behavior.

Since the message to be found in the story is often highly distilled or even ambiguous, however, this form of communication is somewhat unreliable.

Formal statements of organizational philosophy, creeds, charters. The final mechanism of reinforcement is the formal statement, the attempt by the founders or leaders to state explicitly what their values or assumptions are.

These statements highlight only a small portion of the assumption set that operates in the group and, most likely, highlight those aspects of the leaders' philosophy or ideology that lend themselves to public articulation.

Such public statements may have a value for the leader as a way of emphasizing special things to be attended to in the organization, as values around which to "rally the troops" and as reminders of fundamental assumptions not to be forgotten; but formal statements cannot be seen as a way of defining the culture of the organization.

At best, they cover a small, publicly relevant segment of the culture, those aspects that leaders find useful to publish as an ideology for the organization.

Leadership Is the Ability to Manage Culture

For the manager, the message is "give culture its due."

1) Do not oversimplify and do not confuse culture with other useful concepts, such as "climate," "values," or "corporate philosophy."

Culture operates at one level below these others and largely *determines* them.

Climate, values and philosophies *can* be managed in the traditional sense of management, but it is not at all clear whether the underlying culture can be.

But culture needs to be understood in order to determine what kinds of climate, values and philosophies are possible and desirable for a given organization.

2) Do not assume that culture applies only to the human side of an organization's functioning.

Culture determines not only the ways in which the internal system of authority, communication, and work is organized and managed but also the organization's most basic sense of mission and goals.

Focusing on how people relate to each other in the organization and labeling that aspect "the culture" can be a dangerous trap because it draws attention away from shared basic assumptions about the nature of the product, the market, the organization's mission, and other factors that may have far more influence on how effective the organization is ultimately.

3) Do not assume that culture can be manipulated like other matters under the control of managers.

Culture controls the manager—more than the manager controls culture—through the automatic filters that bias the manager's perceptions, thoughts and feelings.

As culture arises and gains strength, it become pervasive and influences everything the manager does, even his own thinking and feeling.

The point is especially important because most of the elements that the manager views as aspects of "effective" management—setting objectives, measuring, following up, controlling, giving performance feedback, and so on—are themselves culturally biased to an unknown degree in any given organization.

There is no such thing as a culture-free concept of management.

4) Do not assume that there is a "correct" or "better" culture, and do not assume that "strong" cultures are better than "weak" cultures.

What is correct or whether strength is good or bad depends on the match between cultural assumptions and environmental realities.

A strong culture can be effective at one point and ineffective at another point because external realities have changed.

5) Do not assume that all aspects of the culture are relevant to the effectiveness of the organization.

Any group with any history will have a culture, but many elements of that culture may be essentially irrelevant to that group's functioning.

Much of the time, therefore, the manager need not concern himself with culture issues; or, if problems of effectiveness arise, the manager must learn how to focus on only those cultural issues that are relevant.

Insight into the culture of one's own organization contributes another layer of explanation for why things do or do not work out.

When managers observe communication or problem-solving failures, when they cannot get people to work together effectively, they need to go beyond individual explanations.

The problem may not be their own lack of managerial skill or limitations in the personalities of the people involved.

Recognizing such cultural differences is essential so that the manager can explain how things can go wrong even if everyone has the same good intentions to make them work.

PART TWO

UNDERSTANDING THE EFFECTS OF CULTURE IN AN ORGANIZATION

SECTION I
THE EFFECTS OF CULTURE ON STRATEGY

If the corporate culture is incompatible with the business strategy, objectives will not be met. The three articles selected for this chapter illustrate what happens when the culture is out of sync with corporate strategies.

The first article, "The Use of Culture in Strategic Management," points out the problems inherent in cultural incongruence. This article provides an excellent discussion of leadership contribution, group commitment and barriers to change.

The second article, "Planning as Learning," emphasizes the importance of constant processing before, during and after strategic planning. The author emphasizes the need to make radical changes in strategy as a result of new information.

The third article, "Corporate Culture," issues some cautions about making major departures from traditional businesses. Several examples are cited of organizations which tried to venture too far from established markets and found that their corporate culture was not ready to support those changes.

The Use of Culture in Strategic Management

By Leonard R. Sayles and Robert V.L. Wright

Before changing the corporation's strategic direction, top management should be prepared to reshape the organizational culture to fit the new strategy. What's that? Change the culture? Can it be done?

Organizational culture should be an instrument of top corporate leadership. What we observe is the contrary. Corporations seek to execute new strategies—often to reflect profoundly changed external markets or technologies—but allow these plans to be subverted by a culture reflecting defunct strategies and retired leaders. While it may seem obvious to observe that culture must change if an organization is going to change, in most companies we know the inconsistencies are profound. While clearly unrealistic, many top executives expect to execute major new directions without changing these things that determine what people will actually do.

Why Culture?

Why has culture been rediscovered? Behavioral scientists have known for decades that what employees actually do, in contrast to what they are told, depends on their norms, values, and unstated beliefs as well as the infrastructure of procedures, incentives, and the division of labor. After all, the boss's words and presence occupy only a small part of the day. Further, most issues requiring action are ambiguous, even contradictory, and, with limited information, subordinates rely on their "instincts." And for the most part, this inner direction comes from the "culture," not from the subconscious. And that same culture is what will determine how successful will be the implementation of any change. And again, the significance of implementation, in supporting any planning initiatives, is widely understood, if not acted on.

From *Issues and Observations*, vol. 5, no. 4, November 1985. Reprinted by permission of the authors. All rights reserved.

Rediscoveries are not random, needless to say. Excellence was well explored by the Greeks centuries ago and by John Gardner (1961) somewhat more recently. But with growing sensitivity to Japanese competitive successes American executives were eager to be told by Peters and Waterman (1982) about the "new" excellence.

And culture is the answer to another anxiety. CEOs have made considerable investment in a number of sophisticated analytical tools designed to facilitate better planning, more rational resource allocation decisions, and to improve the quality of information flowing to headquarters. Yet often the results have been disappointing. Not surprisingly, then, it has been useful to have a culprit that frustrates good planning. And its name is culture; that's the drag, the source of resistance to change, to implementation.

The CEO's Contribution

Ironically, using culture as a scapegoat for failed planning just reverses cause and effect. The most important determinant of culture is the behavior of the chief executive. He or she is the one clearly responsible for shaping the motivations, commitments, and predispositions of all executives from senior managers to operators.

IBM for years personified the beliefs of Tom Watson; NASA was shaped by the personality and values of James Webb, although it was an extraordinarily diffuse organization. Irwin Miller changed dramatically a company, Cummins Engine, *and* a community to conform to his advanced ideas about culture and corporate responsibility. Hennessey transformed a sleepy Allied Chemicals, changing its culture and its name almost overnight. Hagerty molded Texas instruments to reflect his views of management, and Welch is transforming GE to conform to his beliefs about high technology.

One can't simply disregard history, but it is impressive to watch a strong-willed CEO cause an entire organization of a hundred thousand or even several hundred thousand employees to change its value and belief system. Organizations are, in fact, more manageable in an open society like the U.S. where we are not locked into a small number of heavily inter-dependent traditional values.

Most CEOs, however, do not see themselves as being able to influence culture, because of its vagueness or just because they are resigned to their heritage. Culture is often conceived of like charisma: you know it when you feel its influence, but can't do much about it. In truth, culture is manipulable and changeable.

Below, in identifying five major dimensions of organizational culture, we seek to make explicit the behavioral skills that contribute to the formation and maintenance of each. The dimensions or components of culture for the CEO to reshape and make congruent with strategy are these:
- relative diversity
- steepness of the hierarchy
- resource allocations and rewards
- degree of stability
- administrative practices

Diversity vs. Homogeneity

While by definition the existence of organizational culture presumes some uniformity, cultures differ in how much divergence they allow. For example, traditional (usually more rural) cultures have tended to favor enormous conformity, while modern industrial culture either allows for or actually encourages greater diversity within some common framework. Yet organizations also require some coherence, some sense of common purpose and membership.

Many corporations are highly homogeneous. Even though they may include a range of businesses participating in radically different industries and executing widely divergent strategies, they impress a set of values—and administrative practices reflecting these values—on everything. For example, organizations differ in what are perceived as predominant (most prestigious, important) functional capabilities. Historically, Westinghouse was thought of as an engineer's company; engineers got the top jobs and shaped the company. Their major competitor, GE, placed much more weight on marketing. But times change, and AT&T, for example, finds that its service-engineering tradition does not fill its need for a greater marketing orientation. There are companies that stress only finance in top management. Like pure conglomerates, the CEO professes no interest in operations and presumably

has no ability to understand the realities of production or technology or the market. (Further, there is great emphasis on pure number crunching. Qualitative ideas or more subjective data get ignored—if it can't be quantified it doesn't exist.)

The educational backgrounds, physical appearance, and interests of senior management represent another variable controlled by the CEO that shapes the sense of diversity or homogeneity. As in the past, without EEOC pressures (and still today with less clarity), some CEOs have a narrow view of the "right type" of manager. Such a CEO's associates will look and talk very similarly, and those without these requisite characteristics will presume that promotions to the top are best sought elsewhere. It hardly need to be said that good people come in a variety of shapes and sizes and that modern organizations require a diversity of talents. Regrettably, perhaps even inadvertently—on the basis of a small number of critical promotions—some CEOs give the impression of believing the contrary. This is unfortunate, not only in terms of fair play, but because such executives lose the use of one of the most important levers to change a culture: promoting those who are the most prominent "carriers" of the new culture.

More diverse organizations signal the acceptability of heterogeneity by making the business or functional background of those who get promoted less predictable. They also hire a certain number of outsiders, not just at the bottom rungs of career ladders, to bring divergent viewpoints.

Homogeneity of the work environment symbolizes that this is one company and there are legitimate needs to encourage corporate loyalty and mutual cooperation. But taken to an extreme, insistence on perfect consistency in the work environment in an otherwise diversified company—the "physicals" of office design and appearance—gives another message. Particularly in an historically individualist society like the U.S., extremes of uniformity can communicate "bureaucracy," suppression of the individual and his or her initiative, and consistency for its own sake—even when it is not functional. Inevitably this inhibits some free expression of ideas and willingness to experiment and to have form serve function. It also can put the individual in awe of the power and control of the organization, and the suspicion that individuals don't count and conformity is all. In one company, for example, after moving into several floors of a new New York City office building, the CEO had an assistant make regular tours of all offices. There had been a corporate "decorating" plan dictating number and style of wall decoration, placement as well as style of furniture, and a clear rule that nothing was to be left out on horizontal surfaces at the end of the work day. Violators spotted by the presidential assistant received sharply worded reprimands from the President.

The CEO also makes a conscious decision about how uniform is the administration, not just the environment. Must all businesses have similar internal structures and compensation plans even though they may run the gamut from risky, small, and entrepreneurial to large and mature? Diversity "complicates" administration and requires a tolerance for inconsistency and exception, but it also makes it possible to adapt situation to circumstance and stresses the recognition that different problems require different solutions, that different strategies require different policies and practices. The most common tendency is for the procedures that were necessary to operate the core or "Mother" business to be imposed on all other businesses including newly acquired businesses and diversifications.

Routines. Companies that are not highly diversified develop a set of interlocked routines, practices, and beliefs relating to the predominating business, technology, market or functional skill. These routines are most useful in carrying out their traditional and primary tasks, but they make it extraordinarily difficult to move into new strategies, activities, or technologies. These organizations discover that they can never be good at some line of business quite different from those they know, because they cannot create the unique environment necessary for that line of business to flourish. (But that environment may be creatable with an appropriate structure, reward system, and the technical expertise relevant to that industry and its technology.) For example, just recently Philbro Salomon considered a break-up of the firm because of the "natural incompatibility between the free-wheeling world of commodity trading and the consensus approach that is prevalent in the securities industry" (*New York Times*, 1984).

Most senior management is insensitive to or unaware of the constraints exercises by these embedded values, traditions, and technology, and only get some recognition of their power when the organization seeks to reach out to a new industry. At that point they discover they don't have what is called vaguely "know-how," can't seem to work with the "personalities" characteristic of that industry, feel uncomfortable with their way of "doing business," or find the newly acquired management intractable.

Moreover, many companies that are already highly diversified have carried over or developed piecemeal a set of routines, practices, and beliefs which are neither interlocked nor do they fit the diversity being managed. And they may not even be congruent with the beliefs or intentions of the current CEO, but simply reflect the value systems of predecessors.

Group commitments. The "diversity" dimension is also relevant to another critical trade-off that has to be made by senior management. Encouraging loyalty to the smaller group (a business unit, development project, or functional department) can produce extraordinary commitment and release great energies. (Small groups are among the most powerful motivators we know.) But as small group identification strengthens, loyalty to the large organization wanes. Ideally, the CEO wants both: unstinting energy devoted to winning small group objectives, but a willingness to collaborate across department or SBU "lines" and to share common resources with minimal fratricide.

Companies like Texas Instruments and IBM have fostered corporate-wide identification by seeking to become "total institutions." TI may be the more extreme. Almost everyone in management was hired just out of school; few come in from outside at higher levels. Social life revolves around the firm, and company sponsored recreation facilities (like the traditional IBM country clubs) help assure that on weekends and during vacations, employees interact with other employees. A host of educational, travel, and cultural programs are built around the corporation.

Such organizations, following the precepts of an enlightened founder, also often provide enormous employment security for employees. Employees learn that unless they are very unproductive or dishonest, they have something approximating lifetime employment. Just as important as job security is the recognition that the firm cares for them as individuals, that it is committed to them and will train and retrain them to take advantage of any latent skills, and that they can go upward as far as their ambitions and abilities allow. In such firms, as with the Japanese, one constantly hears that this is "my company" and there is the sense of reciprocity: "They really care about me and, in turn, I give them my loyalty."

To break down parochialism, CEOs can insist that effective managers shift the locus of their activity from the division or SBU that may have nourished their early career and promotions to a very different part of the corporation. For example, the head of Schlumberger made the controversial decision to shift successful managers from the core oil service business to the very different technologies incorporated in a newly-acquired semiconductor business (Auletta, 1984). These appear to be high risk decisions because executives who have been important in the success of one technology in one market are being shifted at relatively high levels of responsibility to what will be a strange environment. In the short run this may throw more problems on the CEO's desk.

Competitiveness and teamwork. Most managers are highly competitive with one another. This provides some of the motivation that leads to high performance. However, it can lead to problems if top management stresses competitiveness at the expense of all else. The costs include failure to cooperate in those areas where separate businesses intersect (and could complement one another), where they could gain economies of scale, or where they must use common corporate resources. Very high competitiveness can also encourage managers to devote scarce energy to injuring the reputation of other contenders for promotion, efforts that could be better spent on improving the business.

Top management sets the tone for both the degree and quality of competitiveness that will be encouraged or tolerated. Some CEOs make it clear that they expect cooperation, productive exchanges, and as we have said, even transfer executives from one business to another to develop a corporate-wide loyalty.

In part, the predisposition to extremely competitive turf battles is affected by the reward system. Successful companies like IBM sensibly promote good people rapidly in contrast to stressing length of service. However, very rapid rates of promotion for a few "stars," particularly given some of the limitations of managerial appraisal systems, can instill a gladiator mentality in which fast-track "comers" are encouraged to demolish their opposition, cut corners, and show fast results perhaps at the expense of solid, longer-run growth. They can provide an internal corporate "pressure cooker" atmosphere of distrust and self-aggrandizement. Worse yet, under such a climate information is perceived as power, and there are real incentives to withhold ideas and even to deceive colleagues. Thus competitive and technological information is poorly disseminated and the corporation gets less advantage from its widely dispersed operations and expert staff.

The Chief Executive has a tough job balancing the right amount of legitimate, motivating competitiveness—including generous rewarding of first-rate performance—with the need for a reasonable amount of cooperativeness among the senior ranks of the corporation and organizational solidarity. When competitiveness becomes extreme, openness and the sharing of resources and information decline to the detriment of the larger organization. Of course, in contrast, excessive emphasis on cooperation could decrease the strength of individual commitments to excellent performance.

"Steepness" of the Hierarchy

The culture of some organizations is very hierarchical as shaped by the senior management. Such a culture is maintained by great stress on formal, written memoranda; going through channels; and the discouragement of lateral and informal contacts.

Such organizations prohibit bypassing. Few people ever have contact with the CEO except immediate subordinates. Not only are there difficulties in exercising broadly-based leadership with that kind of isolation, but this pattern creates an extreme dependence on immediate supervision (with no way to get out from under and no way to find role models in, and counseling from, other managers).

To aid subordinates in understanding the thinking and values of senior management, a CEO in a less hierarchical firm can develop systems in which executives several levels below make presentations to top management and get questions and comments from top management—by-passing intermediate levels. They can even be encouraged to raise questions about current policies and directions. At a more informal level, CEOs can seek contacts that take the pulse of the organization and demonstrate their interest and goodwill. It is said that Fletcher Byrom, Koppers' former most successful CEO, purposely rode the local elevator to meet and see people, and he also hosted informal management development sessions that by-passed many levels.

In steeply hierarchical organizations, top management is satisfied not to have much intimate information about operations; financial data suffice. Lower levels then become concerned that their work is not understood or appreciated unless it shows up in the quarterly financials. In contrast, senior managers in flatter hierarchical firms make numerous visits and make it their business to be in a position to have some in-depth knowledge of operations. They use this "insertion" to provide themselves with some independent check of the decision-making capabilities of subordinate managers and to improve their confidence that operations are being well handled.

Hierarchically oriented firms are relaxed about the number of layers separating business heads from the work level. They allow these to multiply as managers get assistants to help with an overload, or as someone feels the need to create a promotion for an ambitious MBA who has no obvious next job. In contrast, other CEOs insist that every level must "add value," and they are constantly seeking to flatten the structure.

Most firms which stress the chain of command appear to be more concerned with absolute security than with effectiveness. There are many procedures for multiple approvals or sign-offs. Even executives with budgeted funding must seek higher level approval for expenditures over a minimal amount. Initiative and quick response time are only some of the costs incurred by these additional checks.

Given their rigid style of leadership, such steeply hierarchical firms also presume that all new ideas must originate at or near the top of the pyramid. Not only does this result in non-participating workers, with the attendant motivational losses, but creativity within middle management gets stifled. In particular, larger firms will normally have a "reservoir of entrepreneurial potential at operational levels" that can express itself in strategic initiatives for new products, technologies, or markets (Burgelman, 1984). But to go "against the grain" of the hierarchy and "manage upward" needs encouragement, even coddling, by the "culture."

Studies of highly contributing managers show that they are adept at flexing the system by negotiating with peers and superiors to get a new technology or procedure back on track. Rules get bent, routines altered, and resources redirected when these skillful middle managers build a new "mini" work flow system (Sayles, 1964; Kidder, 1981). More typically, and regrettably, middle and even upper level managers are reluctant to take on the "system." They do not take the initiative to get functional requirements or procedures modified to make them more complementary to the needs of specific strategies, products, or projects. They perceive the process of change as being interminable and the potential costs quite high relative to any benefits.

Open confrontation that challenges a senior's opinion or decision, the willingness to take unpopular positions, and the daring to make high-risk decisions do not occur readily in organizations with large and intimidating status differences between levels. In such organizations it is usually not even permissible to speak candidly about competitor strengths or to admit that a key business is not turning around. Ritualistic reassurances and mutual self-praise is more common than frank criticism.

Stressing the hierarchy thus means an emphasis on conformity and agreement. Open disagreement and conflicting opinions are discouraged because there is a rigid system for resolving these: appealing to the next level. A CEO can insist on a "completed staff work" approach in which real differences of opinion never reach the top. On the other hand, a CEO can show that he wants or at least tolerates legitimate differences of opinion.

In steeply hierarchical organization speaking out of turn can be costly, and subordinates learn to screen bad news. They are reluctant to speak openly and spontaneously on a new subject until they have received cues as to what is the appropriate position. One does not deviate very far from absolute deference to top managers; "yessing" is the preferred response.

In such organizations a great deal of effort is expended making sure that one is not responsible for any decision with the slightest risk attached. Responsibility for such decisions is shifted to subordinates (who have to take the "buck" that has been passed) or to a committee. Careful records are kept to be able to prove someone else is at fault should there be an embarrassing failure.

In contrast, other chief executives encourage divergent thinking, imaginative responses, and even "playing" with ideas. Messengers bearing bad news are not punished, and it is presumed that in a world filled with uncertainty, where initiative and quick response are valuable, a certain number of errors will be made. Candor is reinforced; deception or dissembling punished.

The CEO shapes this part of the culture directly and predictably by how he interacts with associates and subordinates. There is a direct relationship between his easily observed reactions to disappointments and contrary opinions and the degree to which the organization encourages openness and can deal expeditiously with major problems. In the same fashion, the CEO's ability to be self-critical and admit mistakes is a powerful symbol.

Organizations that seek to encourage reasonable amounts of risk taking and innovativeness inculcate these values by providing clear rewards for those who are vigorous, who assume responsibility and evolve innovative solutions to problems. And they minimize the penalties associated with failure (where such failure is not due to sheer incompetence), since they appear to accept the reality that a certain number of initiatives will not succeed because of unforeseeable events. Such organizations are willing to undertake a number of "experiments" and to support a variety of strategic initiatives on the assumption that certain ones will fail. They argue that there would not be big winners without this willingness to try.

Furthermore, organizational cultures oriented toward innovation and risk usually encourage the "middle level" initiatives we have referred to earlier in contrast to relying solely on a highly centralized master plan. They expect a certain number of surprises—good and bad—as a result of middle-level executives seeking to solve tough problems or challenges on their own, and thus putting themselves at risk. Most important, corporations that accept risk recognize that each of their component businesses and their associated strategies varies inherently as to risk. (And these differences in assumed risk ought to be reflected in reward potentials and thereby in heterogeneous compensation systems.)

Resource Allocations

In an enterprise economy, dollars are a critical determinant of culture. How they are allocated shapes perceptions and motivations about what can and should be done about priorities and relative status.

Though surprising, it is not unusual to see a CEO expecting major strategic activities to be added without changing budget allocations. A business unit might be expected to increase the frequency of new product introductions or to attain state-of-the-art manufacturing technology while its share of the corporate "pie" remains unchanged.

Such budget decisions are cues to managers as to what is being taken seriously by top management and what is rhetoric. They learn to shrug off new directions that are inconsistent with basic funding patterns.

The status system of the organization also gets shaped by such decisions. Increasing a unit's budget allocations means increasing its status. Such businesses find it easier to attain their objectives, not simply because of the cash but because self-confidence is bolstered along with the level of spontaneous cooperation offered by other groups. Managers who receive new funding for one of their initiatives also perceive such an allocation as a personal reward and, in turn, their motivation to make the new product, project, or process work becomes very high. They want to show that the confidence that has been expressed is well placed. Contrariwise, the "loser" in the budget process can become disheartened, and corporate life becomes more difficult. At times a self-sustaining spiral can develop in which poorer performance has led to reduced budgets, which in turn lowers performance still further. (At that point the "cash cow" may become hamburger.)

How lean and productive. The CEO also sets the pace and shapes perceptions of how "well off" the corporation is, how important it is to struggle and challenge oneself in contrast to taking life easy.

Organizations differ enormously in the degree to which management perceives itself as being hard working. While there may be jibes and some whining, executives respect the image of hard work when it is reflected by the top man. They resent silly meetings called for what appears to be the convenience or idiosyncracies of a CEO who can't sleep nights or prefers Sundays to Mondays. But they respond positively to an organization that prides itself on being hard driving, including coming early and staying late—when there is real reason.

At Intel, for example, presumably following the lead of the President, Vice Presidents sprint across the parking lot to be sure of arriving by 8 a.m., and top management is often observed meeting with employees at 5 a.m., because that is most convenient for the swing shift. All operations are "relentlessly analyzed in rigorous mutual criticism, dispensed at all levels" (*Wall Street Journal,* 1984).

This means the CEO has to be especially careful concerning his personal staff and corporate functions. They must be lean and growth must be vigorously checked. All modern organizations have the tendency to keep introducing more management specialists, and the specialists each justify their titles and status by seeking to increase the work they generate for others (and because they believe in their own "cause"). Without constant pruning and attention from top management, a bloating occurs which is demoralizing both because of what appears to be make-work, and also because of the sense of "waste"—of working to pay the overhead.

Rectitude and fiduciary responsibility. The CEO sets the standard for how corporate resources are used and reward given. At one extreme, the corporation and its resources can be conceived of as the personal property of the CEO and perhaps senior managers. In one very large corporation, for example, the corporate PR department devoted most of its efforts to getting good publicity for the President's wife. In turn, the President symbolized his beliefs by repeatedly engineering self-serving financial arrangements. Everyone in the company knew that everything revolved around the personal pleasures and prestige of the CEO. In such organizations, great emphasis is placed on ostentatious display that satisfies the desires of senior managers for continuous deference, luxury, and the use of the corporate jet. In contrast, James Webb, when he headed the U.S. space program, insisted on being driven in a quite aged car, and the executive dining room only had simple salads and sandwiches.

In companies seeking to get employees to conserve resources and to avoid seeing the company as a wealthy behemoth who will never miss various supplies "liberated" for home or personal use, there is great emphasis on scrupulous honesty. Symbolically, senior executives seek to err on the side of conservatism in how they handle the distinction between personal and organizational interests. Obviously, the size and number of "perks" and bonuses, and the opulence of senior management's surroundings, also communicate a great deal about the extent to which top management perceives itself as the *raison d'etre* of the organization or its fiduciary custodian.

A CEO seeking to emphasize change consonant with a new strategy will make sure that the reward system is in gear. For example, if managers are being urged to innovate and renew technology and infuse new products, it would be destructive to have bonuses weighted toward current performance or scale of operations. Yet such contradictory signals are more the rule than the exception.

Stability vs. Change

All organizations should balance stability and change; both are needed. Routinization fosters efficiency, while change is required to adapt to new challenges and to cope with disturbances that injure routines. Industry conditions, competitive strategies, the technology employed, and markets served also affect this balance. Turbulence in any or all of these areas pressures management to opt for more change; absence of such challenges tempts management to emphasize stability and efficiency, and sensibly so.

But there is a vast grey area for most organizations. Top management has much leeway in deciding how much encouragement to offer to those who would experiment with revisions of old approaches or to those who would make real structural innovations; and top management decides how much to punish those who would "rock the boat." As

noted above, the encouragement of change must be accompanied by the reward of risk taking (and by not excessively punishing failures for good cause, in contrast to failure for inaction).

Top management clearly signals by its own energetic stance (or lethargy), and by a wide variety of cues, how much it expects vigorous innovative endeavors, in contrast to ritualistic pleas for improvement and insistence on perfect order. Change-oriented organizations have a distinctive tempo; everything moves faster and more deliberately, in contrast to the slow-paced beat to which stability-oriented organizations "march."

Administrative Practices

A critical part of the inherited baggage for most CEOs is the procedures and policies that have been developed by key corporate functional groups like Finance, Accounting, and Human Resources. While in theory these are value free and derived from the professional disciplines of their fields, in practice most impose values of another time and reflect a uniform code of behavior for managers that may bear little relationship to the strategic directions contemplated by the CEO.

For example, the constraints of budget planning and the criteria for capital appropriation may require managers to redo and even change the numbers and assumptions that were built into their strategies. It is not unusual to find that an investment which is to be the centerpiece of a new strategic thrust endorsed by the CEO is undercut by a Finance VP who finds that it doesn't pass muster in terms of his discounted cash flow return formulas.

Reward systems and performance appraisal procedures may encourage behavior that was appropriate to earlier strategies but which is quite inconsistent with new thrusts. Also, we have seen CEOs eager to encourage more initiative and individual responsibility who blithely ignore the number of sign-offs or authorizations required for everything from expense accounts to minor capital expenditures (which have already been approved in business unit plans).

Even the emphasis on the accountant's "bottom line" communicates a great number of unintended messages. It tells managers that excellence in performance is irrelevant and that values such as personnel development and state-of-the-art technology have little career pay-off. Rather, paper profitability is the only accomplishment rewarded. Strategic goals take second place at best to hitting the monthly, quarterly, and annual profitability targets.

Regrettably, the typical CEO does not recognize how value-laden (predecessor-laden) administrative systems are. They ignore them as being too far away from the mainstream of decision making, or as simply mundane paper-pushing, and fail to realize what powerful motivators (and demotivators) are represented here.

Barriers to Culture Change

What a business does is as much, if not more, determined by the organizational culture in which it is immersed as it is by its strategic plan. This culture doesn't just "ooze up"; in large measure it is the product of the behavior of the CEO, whether past or current, and whether recognized or not. And CEOs who expect to change or revitalize their companies have to expect to spend much time and energy introducing compatible changes in the culture. They can't fall back on the more passive role of being the final arbiter or judge.

The job is especially difficult for two kinds of corporations: older, more mature ones facing new competitive threats and new technologies; and large diversified corporations with a newly-minted CEO. They are more likely to have incompatible infrastructures and culture than is the entrepreneurial, rapidly growing "high tech" firm in which dynamism, modest respect for hierarchical level, and leanness come with the industry, so to speak.

To make matters worse, the managers who must implement new strategies usually begin with skepticism. If they are at all experienced, they know that there have been many such ambitious plans in the past that have come and gone without leaving much of a trace, and it is likely that "this too shall pass."

Furthermore, there are enormous risks in seeking to implement major changes. Routines that produce efficiency get overturned, and many things that look good on paper fail miserably even after herculean efforts (Sayles, 1979). The executives that fail to make it work, if they really go all out to meet these new goals, often discover they have injured their reputations and careers. So managers look for excuses not to get committed. They are quick to pick up inconsistencies in the culture which indicate that top management doesn't really expect much or still lives in the past. All sorts of unintended cues can tell them that these new strategies are not much more than new paper tigers.

Many CEOs are handicapped themselves in tackling issues of culture because of some well-circulated myths and illusions:

- the belief one can set new directions and strategies for the organization without designing a complementing, supportive organizational infrastructure that will make those things happen
- the belief that functional groups—like accounting and human resource—can be left alone to design measurement and reward systems, among others, that have universal applicability
- the belief that good delegation requires top management to step so far back from operations that they only look at results, that is, bottom-line performance.

All of these beliefs and assumptions are flawed. Strategies are only as good as the structure that is erected to support and encourage them. Left to their own devices, functional groups design systems consistent with their own conception of what is required by abstract professional "principles" of good management. (Most of these presume there is a one-best-way, regardless of what strategy is being pursued.) Good delegation is a dynamic process of both involvement and providing autonomy, both depending on the strengths and performance of individual subordinates and the degree of uncertainty in the activities being managed.

One might fear that top management's reluctance to get involved in these determinants of culture reflects a conscious choice to avoid the onerous frustrations of internal management in favor of the more exciting and often more immediately gratifying activities in the external world. What has been called "paper entrepreneurship," asset redeployment, acquisitions, mergers, and buy-outs capture the imagination of CEOs to the detriment of leading the organization. But on reflection, such reluctance to manipulate culture is not that surprising. As long as there is no well-accepted way of translating strategy moves into culture change, CEOs are going to find that efforts to get their key subordinates to meet the new goals embodied in those ambitious new strategies often lead to little change in performance. And the more they exhort them to "do more," the more embittered can become the relationships.

There is almost always a tendency for trends to become more extreme. Great weight on quarterly financials induces a short-time perspective. In turn managers are encouraged to make conforming, even unrealistic, promises and eventually to cover up bad news and even distort the data. Internal competitiveness is accentuated and lateral communication repressed which further emphasizes the hierarchy. The process becomes self-feeding.

Also, most CEOs we have known would have a difficult time evaluating or characterizing the culture of their organizations or their style of leadership. There are a number of reasons. They receive little candid feedback unless they have been very fortunate in identifying a Board member or consultant who is both independent and perceptive and from whom counsel is welcome. Over the years, given their steady progression to a prestigious top management post, continuous positive reinforcement has given them some immunity to critical appraisals of their culture, their skills, and their corporate administrative system. Finally, most organizations have evolved gradually to their present culture, and since many of the parts are mutually consistent and familiar, most people have adapted and accommodated to that reality.

How Can the CEO Deal With Culture?

We have sought to argue that CEOs make, or at least influence profoundly, the cultures of their organizations. The major dimensions of culture we have described are mutable. This is not to say that there is some easy one-to-one correspondence between a decision and culture, or that the executive can order up the appropriate culture to implement his or her strategic choices. But culture does respond to and, in fact, mirrors the conscious and unconscious choices, behavior patterns, and prejudices of top management.

What makes culture a matter of conscious choice and not simply the result of everything that wasn't even intended? First is the recognition by top management that they're not the victims but the architects of the climate of the organization. Second is the ability to be self-conscious about what they do and how they do it.

Most important, the manager who would shape culture has to be able to deal with the organization's total infrastructure, with interrelationships and systems. It doesn't work to deal with management problems as though each were in a watertight compartment. It is foolish to say this is a compensation issue and that is an organization structure question. It is this compartmentalization that leads to all of the destructive inconsistencies that send out the messages management never intended.

To introduce change, one must work with the whole system, all the elements that shape the perceptions, beliefs, and reflexes of those who must carry out the strategy of the corporation. Neither handwriting nor delegation will do it; the CEO must do it.

The specific steps to be taken by the CEO to reshape his or her culture are these:
- Accept culture as an instrument of leadership, not as an impediment to leadership.
- Second, using trusted insiders or outsiders, get feedback on current action, on the implicit or explicit signals being communicated.
- Third, compare current actions and the resulting infrastructure with those infrastructural features that would be desirable to support and sustain new strategic directions. (To stimulate a critical assessment, it can be useful to ask what kind of culture would be ideal if one was starting from scratch. What kind of culture would one need to motivate and maintain the kinds of efforts necessary to cope with projected industries, markets, technologies, and competition?)

We have been talking about the culture of the corporation. Each business with a distinctive strategy within the corporation also requires a unique culture and resulting infrastructure. The CEO must not only tolerate but actually encourage a relevant degree of corporate heterogeneity. Operationally, this means encouraging business heads to propose and evaluate deviations from corporate-wide systems and practices. While such senior managers will have learned that it usually doesn't pay to try to prove to the Comptroller or the VP of Human Resources that the business has unique requirements, the CEO can reverse these expectations. But this requires the CEO to believe that each strategy requires its own cultural support system.

Summary and Conclusion

Sophisticated planning and changes in strategy by themselves don't produce performance changes, as many CEOs have learned to their dismay. It is implementation that counts and we have sought to show that the implementation is profoundly influenced by the design of the corporate culture or infrastructure. These shape the basic motivations, value, and behavior of the managers who must accomplish new objectives. While often ignored, CEOs have the choice of merely implicitly and randomly influencing their organization's culture on the one hand, or on the other hand seeking to systematically comprehend the influence of their behavior and decisions on what people believe and will do. The CEO sets the tempo, establishes the dominant values, and creates the climate which shapes what will be done, and how, with what zest, and toward what goals.

A CEO with ambitions for change embodied in soundly conceived and systematically worked-through strategic plans has only begun the task of turning around a faltering corporation. He must integrate these with compensatory and complementary changes in the corporate culture. Much of the latter represents vestigial remains of long-departed predecessors, their values and structures, plus corporate-wide administrative systems. The latter have been installed by key functional heads who are usually primarily interested in the integrity and consistency of their systems.

Many new strategies purport to encourage excellence. But excellence, if meant seriously, presumes a set of interlinked strategies to produce superior performance in technological innovation, manufacturing quality, market acceptance and penetration, and human resource development. This calls for a broad net of well-conceived and carefully implemented managerial actions that will not be executed in an environment which keeps reiterating deceptively simplistic financial targets. Concentrating on such targets for motivation is not unlike trying to help someone run a complex maze by telling them what the hidden treasure at the center looks like. Difficult, demanding management goals drop by the wayside in the rush to achieve winning numbers. Although excellence leads to superior financial performance, the road is a long, winding one. The CEO has to lead subordinates in learning to travel that road, as well as inspiring them to reach their destination.

References

Auletta, K. (1984, June 6, June 13). Profile, Jean Riboud (Parts I and II). *The New Yorker.*

Burgelman, R. (1984). Designs for corporate entrepreneurship in established firms. *California Management Review,* 26 (3), 154–166.

Gardner, J.W. (1961). *Excellence.* New York: Harper.

Kidder, T. (1981). *The soul of a new machine.* Boston: Little, Brown.

Wall Street Journal, February 4, 1983.

New York Times, May 23, 1984.

Peters, T., & Waterman, R. (1982). *In search of excellence.* New York: Harper.

Sayles, L. (1964). *Managerial behavior.* New York: McGraw-Hill.

Sayles, L. (1979). *Leadership: What effective managers really do and how they do it.* New York: McGraw-Hill.

Planning as Learning

By Arie P. de Geus

Some years ago, the planning group at Shell surveyed 30 companies that had been in business for more than 75 years. What impressed us most was their ability to live in harmony with the business environment, to switch from a survival mode when times were turbulent to a self-development mode when the pace of change was slow. And this pattern rang a familiar bell because Shell's history is similarly replete with switches from expansion to self-preservation and back again to growth.

Early in our history, for example, there was a burst of prosperity in the Far East and we dominated the market for kerosene in tins and "oil for the lamps of China." Survival became the keynote, however, when Rockefeller's Standard Oil snatched market share by cutting price. In fact, it was the survival instinct that led in 1907 to the joining of Royal Dutch Petroleum and the Shell Transport and Trading Company—separate businesses until then and competitors in the Far East. This, in turn, paved the way for Shell's expansion into the United States in 1911 with a new product, Sumatran gasoline—also a reaction to Standard Oil's activities.

Outcomes like these don't happen automatically. On the contrary, they depend on the ability of a company's senior managers to absorb what is going on in the business environment and to act on that information with appropriate business moves. In other words, they depend on learning. Or, more precisely, on institutional learning, which is the process whereby management teams change their shared mental models of their company, their markets, and their competitors. For this reason, we think of planning as learning and or corporate planning as institutional learning.

Institutional learning is much more difficult than individual learning. The high level of thinking among individual managers in most companies is admirable. And yet, the level of thinking that goes on in the management teams of most companies is considerably below the individual managers' capacities.

In institutional learning situations, the learning level of the team is often the lowest common denominator, especially with teams that think of themselves as machines with mechanistic, specialized parts: the production manager looks at production, the distribution manager looks at distribution, the marketing manager looks at marketing.

Because high-level, effective, and continuous institutional learning and ensuing corporate change are the prerequisites for corporate success, we at Shell* have asked ourselves two questions. How does a company learn and adapt? And, What is planning's role in corporate learning?

My answer to the first question, "how does a company learn and adapt," is that many do not or, at least, not very quickly. A full one-third of the Fortune "500" industrials listed in 1970 had vanished by 1983. And W. Stewart Howe has pointed out in his 1986 book Corporate Strategy that for every successful turnaround there are two ailing companies that fail to recover. Yet some companies obviously do learn and can adapt. In fact, our survey identified several that were still vigorous at 200, 300, and even 700 years of age. What made the difference? Why are some companies better able to adapt?

Sociologist and psychologist tell us it is pain that makes people and living systems change. And certainly corporations have their share of painful crises, the recent spate of takeovers and takeover threats conspicuously among them. But crisis management—pain management—is a dangerous way to manage for change.

Once in crisis, everyone in the organization feels the pain. The need for change is clear. The problem is that you usually have little time and few options. The deeper into the crisis you are, the fewer options remain. Crisis management, by necessity, becomes autocratic management. The positive characteristic of a crisis is that the decisions are quick. The other side of that coin is that the implementation is rarely good; many companies fail to survive.

Author's note: I use the collective expression "Shell" for convenience when referring to the companies of the Royal Dutch/Shell Group in general, or when no purpose is served by identifying the particular Shell company or companies.

The challenge, therefore, is to recognize and react to environmental change before the pain of a crisis. Not surprisingly, this is what the long-lived companies in our study were so well able to do.

All these companies had a striking capacity to institutionalize change. They never stood still. Moreover, they seemed to recognize that they had internal strengths that could be developed as environmental conditions changed. Thus, Booker McConnell, founded in 1906 as a sugar company, developed shipping on the back of its primary resource. British American Tobacco recognized that marketing cigarettes was no different from marketing perfume. Mitsubishi, founded in 1870 as a marine and trading company, acquired coal mines to secure access to ships' bunkers, built shipyards to repair imported ships, and developed a bank from the exchange business it had begun to finance shippers.

Changes like these grow out of a company's knowledge of itself and its environment. All managers have such knowledge and they develop it further all the time, since every living person—and system—is continuously engaged in learning. In fact, the normal decision process in corporations is a learning process, because people change their own mental models and build up a joint model as they talk. The problem is that the speed of that process is slow—too slow for a world in which the ability to learn faster than competitors may be the only sustainable competitive advantage.

Some five years ago, we had a good example of the time it takes for a message to be heard. One way in which we in Shell trigger institutional learning is through scenarios.[1] A certain set of scenarios gave our planners a clear signal that the oil industry, which had always been highly integrated, was no longer. That contradicted all our existing models. High integration means that you are more or less in control of all the facets of your industry, so you can start optimizing. Optimization was the driving managerial model in Shell. What these scenarios essentially were saying was that we had to look for other management methods.

The first reaction from the organization was at best polite. There were few questions and no discussion. Some managers reacted critically: the scenarios were "basic theory that everyone already knew"; they had "little relevance to the realities of today's business." The message had been listened to but it had not yet been heard.

After a hiatus of some three months, people began asking lots of questions; a discussion started. The intervening months had provided time for the message to settle and for management's mental models to develop a few new hooks. Absorption, phase one of the learning process, had taken place.

During the next nine months, we moved through the other phases of the learning process. Operating executives at Shell incorporated this new information into their mental models of the business. They drew conclusions from the revised models and tested them against experience. Then, finally, they acted on the basis of the altered model. Hearing, digestion, confirmation, action: each step took time, its own sweet time.

In my experience this time span is typical. It will likely take 12 to 18 months from the moment a signal is received until it is acted on. The issue is not whether a company will learn, therefore, but whether it will learn fast and early. The critical question becomes, "Can we accelerate institutional learning?"

I am more and more persuaded that the answer to this question is yes. But before explaining why, I want to emphasize an important point about learning and the planner's role. The only relevant learning in a company is the learning done by those people who have the power to act (at Shell, the operating company management teams). So the real purpose of effective planning is not to make plans but to change the microcosm, the mental models that these decision makers carry in their heads. And this is what we at Shell and others elsewhere try to do.

In this role as facilitator, catalyst, and accelerator of the corporate learning process, planners are apt to fall into several traps. One is that we sometimes start with a mental model that is unrecognizable to our audience. Another is that we take too many steps at once. The third, and most serious, is that too often we communicate our information by teaching. This is a natural trap to fall into because it's what we've been conditioned to all our lives. But teaching, as John Holt points out, is actually one of the least efficient ways to convey knowledge.[2] At best, 40% of what is taught is received; in most situations, it is only about 25%.

It was a shock to learn how inefficient teaching is. Yet some reflection on our own experience drove the point home. After all, we had spent nearly 15 man-years preparing a set of scenarios which we then transmitted in a condensed version in 2½ hours. Could we really have believed that our audience would understand all we were talking about?

Teaching has another disadvantage as well, especially in a business setting. Teachers must be given authority by their students based on the teachers' presumed superior understanding. When a planner presents the results of many man-years of looking at the environment to a management team, she is usually given the benefit of the doubt: the planner probably knows more about the environment than the management team she is talking to. But when the same planner walks into a boardroom to start teaching about the strategy of the company, her authority disappears. When you cannot be granted authority, you can no longer teach.

Fortified with this understanding of planning and its role, we looked for ways to accelerate institutional learning. Curiously enough, we learned in two cases that changing the rules, or suspending them, could be a spur to learning. Rules in a corporation are extremely important. Nobody likes them but everybody obeys them because they are recognized as the glue of the organization. And yet, we have all known extraordinary managers who got their organizations out of a rut by changing the rules. Intuitively they changed the organization and the way it looked at matters, and so, as a consequence, accelerated learning.

Several years ago one of our work groups introduced, out of the blue, a new rule into the corporate rain dance: "Thou shalt plan strategically in the first half of the calendar year." (We already had a so-called business planning cycle that dealt with capital budgets in the second half of the calendar year.)

The work group was wise enough not to be too specific about what it had in mind. Some operating companies called up and asked what was meant by "strategic planning." But the answer they got—that ideas were more important than numbers—was vague. Other companies just started to hold strategic planning meetings in the spring.

In the first year the results of this new game were scanty, mostly a rehash of the previous year's business plans. But in the second year the plans were fresher and each year the quality of thinking that went into strategic planning improved. So we asked ourselves whether, by having changed the rules of the game—because that's what the planning system is, one of the rules of the corporate game—we had accelerated institutional learning. And our answer was yes. We changed the rules and the corporation played by the new rules that evolved in the process.

A similar thing happened when we tried suspending the rules. In 1984 we had a scenario that talked about $15 a barrel oil. (Bear in mind that in 1984 the price of a barrel of oil was $28 and $15 was the end of the world to oil people.) We thought it important that, as early in 1985 as possible, senior managers throughout Shell start learning about a world of $15 oil. But the response to this scenario was essentially, "If you want us to think about this world, first tell us when the price is going to fall, how far it will fall, and how long the drop will last."

A deadlock ensued which we broke by writing a case study with a preface that was really a license to play. "We don't know the future," it said. "But neither do you. And though none of us knows whether the price is going to fall, we can agree that it would be pretty serious if it did. So we have written a case showing one of many possible ways by which the price of oil could fall." We then described a case in which the price plummeted at the end of 1985 and concluded by saying: "And now it is April 1986 and you are staring at a price of $16 a barrel. Will you please meet and give your views on these three questions: What do you think your government will do? What do you think your competition will do? And what, if anything, will you do?"

Since at that point the price was still $28 and rising, the case was only a game. But that game started off serious work throughout Shell, not on answering the question "What will happen?" but rather exploring the question "What will we do if it happens?" The acceleration of the institutional learning process had been set in motion.

As it turned out, the price of oil was still $27 in early January of 1986. But on February 1 it was $17 and in April it was $10. The fact that Shell had already visited the world of $15 oil helped a great deal in that panicky spring of 1986.

By now, we knew we were on to something: games could significantly accelerate institutional learning. That's not so strange when you think of it. Some of the most difficult and complex tasks in our lives were learned by playing: cycling, tennis, playing an instrument. We did it, we experimented, we played. But how were we going to make it OK to play?

Few managers are able to say, "I don't mind a little mistake. Go ahead, experiment," especially with a crisis looming. We didn't feel we could go to executives who run some of the biggest companies in the world and say, "Come on, let's have a little game." And in any case, board meetings have agendas, are fixed to end at a certain time, and require certain action to be taken. Still, within these constraints, we have found ways to learn by playing.

One characteristic of play, as the Tavistock Institute in London has shown, is the presence of a transitional object. For the person playing, the transitional object is a representation of the real world. A child who is playing with a doll learns a great deal about the real world at a very fast pace.

Successful consultants let themselves be treated as transitional objects. The process begins when the consultant says something like this to a management team: "We know from experience that many good strategies are largely implicit. If you let us interview people at various levels in your organization, we'll see whether we can get your strategy out on paper. Then we'll come back and check whether we've understood it."

Some weeks later the consultant goes back to the team and says: "Well, we've looked at your strategy and we've played it through a number of likely possibilities, and here is what we think will be the outcome. Do you like it?" The management team will almost certainly say no. So the consultant will say: "All right, let's see how we can change it. Let's go back to your original model and see what was built in there that produced this result." This process is likely to go through a number of iterations, during which the team's original model will change considerably. Those changes constitute the learning that is taking place among the team's members.

Like consultants, computer models can be used to play back and forth management's view of its market, the environment, or the competition. The starting point, however, must be the mental model that the audience has at the moment. If a planner walks into the room with a model on his computer that he has made up himself, the chances are slim that this audience will recognize this particular microworld. If the target group is a management team, the starting model must be the sum of their individual models. How can this be done?

One way is to involve team members in the development of a new common model and leave their individual models implicit. Alternatively, one can bring the individual models out in the open through interviews and make them explicit. In both approaches, computers can serve as transitional objects in which to store the common models that get built.

To most planners, one all-important aspect of these microworlds is counterintuitive: the probability that they have little relation to the real world. God seems to have told model builders that a model should have predictive qualities and that therefore it should represent the real world. In building microworlds, however, this is totally irrelevant. What we want to capture are the models that exist in the minds of the audience. Almost certainly,

these will not represent the real world. None of us has a model that actually captures the real world, because no complex reality can be represented analytically and a model is an analytical way of representing reality. Moreover, for the purpose of learning, it is not the reality that matters but the team's model of reality which will change as members' understanding of their world improves.

But why go to all this trouble? Why not rely on the natural learning process that occurs whenever a management team meets? For us at Shell, there are three compelling reasons. First, although the models in the human mind are complex, most people can deal with only three or four variables at a time and do so through only one or two time iterations.

Look, for instance, at current discussions about the price of oil. Nine out of ten people draw on a price-elasticity model of the market: the price has come down, therefore demand will go up and supply will eventually fall. Ergo, they will conclude, at some time in the future the price of oil must rise. Now we all know that what goes up must come down. But our minds, in thinking through this complex model, work through too few iterations, and we stop at the point where the price goes up. If we computerize the model of the person who stops thinking at the moment the price rises, however, the model will almost certainly show the price falling after its rise. Yet this knowledge would be counterintuitive to the very person (or persons) who built the model.

The second reasons for putting mental models into computers is that in working with dynamic models, people discover that in complex systems (like markets or companies) cause and effect are separated in time and place. To many people such insight is also counter-intuitive. Most of us, particularly if we are engaged in the process of planning, focus on the effect we want to create and then look for the most immediate cause to create that effect. The use of dynamic models helps us discover other trigger points, separated in time and place from the desired effect.

Lastly, by using computer models we learn what constitutes relevant information. For only when we start playing with these microworlds do we find out what information we really need to know.

When people play with models this way, they are actually creating a new language among themselves that expresses the knowledge they have acquired. And here we come to the most important aspect of institutional learning, whether it be achieved through teaching or through play as we have defined it: the institutional learning process is a process of language development. As the implicit knowledge of each learner becomes explicit, his or her mental model becomes a building block of the institutional model. How much and how fast this model changes will depend on the culture and structure of the organization. Teams that have to cope with rigid procedures and information systems will learn more slowly than those with flexible, open communication channels. Autocratic institutions will learn faster or not at all—the ability of one or a few leaders being a risky institutional bet.

Human beings aren't the only ones whose learning ability is directly related to their ability to convey information. As a species, birds have great potential to learn, but there are important differences among them. Titmice, for example, move in flocks and mix freely, while robins live in well-defined parts of the garden and for the most part communicate antagonistically across the borders of their territories. Virtually all the titmice in the U.K. quickly learned how to pierce the seals of milk bottles left at doorsteps. But robins as a group will never learn to do this (though individual birds may) because their capacity for institutional learning is low; one bird's knowledge does not spread.[3] The same phenomenon occurs in management teams that work by mandate. The best learning takes place in teams that accept that the whole is larger than the sum of the parts, that there is a good that transcends the individual.

What about managers who find themselves in a robin culture? Clearly, their chances of accelerating institutional learning are reduced. Nevertheless, they can take a significant step toward opening up communication and thus the learning process by keeping one fact in mind: institutional learning begins with the calibration of existing mental models.

We are continuing to explore other ways to improve and speed up our institutional learning process. Our exploration into learning through play via a transitional object (a consultant or a computer) looks promising enough at this point to push on in that direction. And while we are navigating in poorly charted waters, we are not out there alone.[4]

Our exploration into this area is not a luxury. We understand that the only competitive advantage the company of the future will have is its managers' ability to learn faster than their competitors. So the companies that succeed will be those that continually nudge their managers towards revising their views of the world. The challenges for the planner are considerable. So are the rewards.

Endnotes

1. Pierre Wack wrote about our system in "Scenarios: Uncharted Waters Ahead," HBR September–October 1985, p. 72 and in "Scenarios: Shooting the Rapids," HBR November–December 1985, p. 139.

2. John Holt, *How Children Learn*, rev. ed. (New York: Delacorte, 1983) and John Holt, *How Children Fail*, rev. ed. (New York: Delacorte, 1982).

3. Jeff S. Wyles, Joseph G. Kunkel, and Allan C. Wilson, "Birds, Behavior and Anatomical Evolution," *Proceedings of the National Academy of Sciences, USA*, July 1983.

4. Through MIT's Program in Systems Thinking and the New Management Style, a group of senior executives are looking at this and other issues.

Corporate Culture

From *Business Week*, October 27, 1980

Five years ago the chief executives of two major oil companies determined that they would have to diversify out of oil because their current business could not support long-term growth and it faced serious political threats. Not only did they announce their new long-range strategies to employees and the public, but they established elaborate plans to implement them. Today, after several years of floundering in attempts to acquire and build new businesses, both companies are firmly back in oil, and the two CEOs have been replaced.

Each of the CEOs had been unable to implement his strategy, not because it was theoretically wrong or bad but because neither had understood that his company's culture was so entrenched in the traditions and values of doing business as oilmen that employees resisted—and sabotaged—the radical changes that the CEOs tried to impose. Oil operations required long-term investment for long-term rewards; but the new businesses needed short-term views and an emphasis on current returns. Successes had come from hitting it big in wildcatting; but the new success was to be based on such abstractions as market share or numbers growth— all seemingly nebulous concepts to them. Too late did the CEOs realize that strategies can only be implemented with the wholehearted effort and belief of everyone involved. If implementing them violates employees' basic beliefs about their roles in the company, or the traditions that underlie the corporation's culture, they are doomed to fail.

Culture implies values, such as aggressiveness, defensiveness, or nimbleness, that set a pattern for a company's activities, opinions, and actions. That pattern is instilled in employees by managers' example and passed down to succeeding generations of workers. The CEO's words alone do not produce culture; rather, his actions and those of his managers do.

A corporation's culture can be its major strength when it is consistent with its strategies. Some of the most successful companies have clearly demonstrated that fact, including:

- International Business Machines Corp., where marketing drives a service philosophy that is almost unparalleled. The company keeps a hot line open 24 hours a day, seven days a week, to service IBM products.
- International Telephone & Telegraph Corp., where financial discipline demands total dedication. To beat out the competition in a merger, an executive once called former Chairman Harold S. Geneen at 3 a.m. to get his approval.
- Digital Equipment Corp., where an emphasis on innovation creates freedom with responsibility. Employees can set their own hours and working style, but they are expected to articulate and support their activities with evidence of progress.
- Delta Air Lines Inc., where a focus on customer service produces a high degree of teamwork. Employees will substitute in other jobs to keep planes flying and baggage moving.
- Atlantic Richfield Co., where an emphasis on entrepreneurship encourages action. Operating men have the autonomy to bid on promising fields without hierarchical approval.

But a culture that prevents a company from meeting competitive threats, or from adapting to changing economic or social environments, can lead to the company's stagnation and ultimate demise unless it makes a conscious effort to change. One that did make this effort is PepsiCo Inc., where the cultural emphasis has been systematically changed over the past two decades from passivity to aggressiveness.

Once the company was content in its No. 2 spot, offering Pepsi as a cheaper alternative to Coca-Cola. But today, a new employee at PepsiCo quickly learns that beating the competition, whether outside or inside the company, is the surest path to success. In its soft-drink operation, for example, Pepsi's marketers now take on Coke directly asking consumers to compare the taste of the two colas. That direct confrontation is reflected inside the company as well. Managers are pitted against each other to grab more market share, to work harder, and to wring more profits out of their businesses. Because winning is the key value at Pepsi, losing has its penalties. Consistent runners-up find their jobs gone. Employees know they must win merely to stay in place—and must devastate the competition to get ahead.

But the aggressive competitor who succeeds at Pepsi would be sorely out of place at J.C. Penney Co., where a quick victory is far less important than building long-term loyalty. Indeed, a Penney store manager once was severely rebuked by the company's president for making too much profit. That was considered unfair to customers, whose trust Penney seeks to win. The business style set by the company's founder—which one competitor describes as avoiding "taking unfair advantage of anyone the company did business with"—still prevails today. Customers know they can return merchandise with no questions asked; suppliers know that Penney will not haggle over terms; and employees are comfortable in their jobs, knowing that Penney will avoid layoffs at all costs and will find easier jobs for those who cannot handle more demanding ones. Not surprisingly, Penney's average executive tenure is 33 years while Pepsi's is 10.

These vastly different methods of doing business are but two examples of corporate culture. People who work at Pepsi and Penney sense that the corporate values are the yardstick by which they will be measured. Just as tribal cultures have totems and taboos that dictate how each member will act toward fellow members and outsiders, so does a corporation's culture influence employees' actions toward customers, competitors, suppliers, and one another. Sometimes the rules are written out. More often they are tacit. Most often, they are laid down by a strong founder and hardened by success into custom.

"Culture gives people a sense of how to behave and what they ought to be doing," explains Howard M. Schwartz, vice-president of Management Analysis Center Inc., a Cambridge (Mass.) consulting firm that just completed a study of corporate culture. Indeed, so firmly are certain values entrenched in a company's behavior that predictable responses can be counted on not only by its employees but by its competitors. "How will our competitors behave?" is a stock question that strategic planners ask when contemplating a new move. The answers come from assessing competitors' time-honored priorities, their reactions to competition, and their ability to change course.

Because a company's culture is so pervasive, changing it becomes one of the most difficult tasks that any chief executive can undertake. Just as a primitive tribe's survival depended on its ability to react to danger, and to alter its way of life when necessary, so must corporations, faced with changing economic, social, and political climates,

sometimes radically change their methods of operating. What stands in the way is not only the "relative immutability of culture," as the MAC study points out, but also the fact that few executives consciously recognize what their company's culture is and how it manifests itself. The concept of culture, says Stanley M. Davis, professor of organization behavior at Boston University and a co-author of the MAC study, is hard to understand. "It's like putting your hand in a cloud," he says.

Thomas J. Peters, a principal in McKinsey & Co., cites a client who believed it was imperative to his company's survival to add a marketing effort to his manufacturing-oriented organization. Because the company had no experts in marketing, it wanted to hire some. Consultants points out that this strategy would fail because all of the issues raised at company meetings concerned cost-cutting and production—never competition or customers. Rewards were built into achieving efficiencies in the first category, while none were built into understanding the second. Ultimately, the CEO recognized that he had to educate himself and his staff so thoroughly in marketing that he could build his own in-house team.

Similarly, American Telephone & Telegraph Co. is now trying to alter its service-oriented operation to give equal weight to marketing. Past attempts to do so ignored the culture and failed. For example, in 1961, AT&T set up a school to teach managers to coordinate the design and manufacture of data products for customized sales. but when managers completed the course, they found that the traditional way of operating—making noncustomized mass sales—were what counted in the company. They were given neither the time to analyze individual customers' needs nor rewards commensurate with such efforts. The result was that 85% of the graduates quit, and AT&T disbanded the school.

AT&T prides itself on its service operation, and with good reason. It provides the most efficient and broadest telephone system in the world, and it reacts to disaster with a speed unknown anywhere else. In 1975, for example, a fire swept through a switching center in lower Manhattan, knocking out service to 170,000 telephones. AT&T rallied 4,000 employees and shipped in 3,000 tons of equipment to restore full service in just 22 days—a task that could have taken a lesser company more than a year.

But costs for AT&T's service had been readily passed to customers through rate increases granted by public service commissions. Keeping costs down was thus never a major consideration. Now, however, since the Federal Communications Commission has decided to allow other companies to sell products in AT&T's once-captive markets, AT&T must change the orientation of its 1 million employees. In numbers alone, such a change is unprecedented in corporate history. Still, to survive in its new environment, Bell must alter its plans, strategies, and employee expectations of what the company wants from them, as well as their belief in the security of their jobs and old way of doing business.

To make the changes, Bell has analyzed its new requirements in exquisite detail that fills thousands of pages. It acknowledges its lack of skills in certain crucial areas: marketing, cost control, and administrative ability to deal with change. The company had rewarded managers who administered set policies by the book; today it is promoting innovators with advanced degrees in business administration. Once it measured service representatives by the speed with which they responded to calls; today they are measured by the number of problems they solve.

AT&T's New Role Model

Instead of its traditional policy of promoting from within, some new role models were hired from outside the company. Archie J. McGill, a former executive of International Business Machines Corp., was made vice-president of business marketing, for example. McGill is described by associates as an innovator who is the antithesis of the traditional "Bell-shaped man" because of his "combative, adversarial style." Just as IBM's slogan, "Think," encouraged its employees to be problem-solvers, McGill is hammering a new slogan, "I make the difference," into each of his marketers, encouraging them to become entrepreneurs. That idea is reinforced by incentives that pit salespeople against each other for bonuses, a system unknown at Bell before.

Even so, the changes are slow. Learning to become solution-sellers has produced "a tremendous amount of confusion" among Bell marketing people, reports one large corporate customer. For example, AT&T is "absolutely trapped" if a customer requests an extra editing part for its standard teletype system, he says. "If you want something they don't have, they tend to solve the problem by saying, 'Let's go out for a drink'."

Even McGill concedes that "anytime you have an orientation toward consulting [past practices] as opposed to being adaptive to a situation, change doesn't happen overnight." Bell's director of planning, W. Brooke Tunstall, estimates that it will take another three to five years to attain an 85% change in the company's orientation. Still, he insists, there

has already been "a definite change in mindset at the upper levels." The arguments heard around the company now concern the pace of change rather than its scope. Says Tunstall, "I haven't run into anyone who doesn't understand why the changes are needed."

The AT&T example clearly demonstrates the need for a company to examine its existing culture in depth and to acknowledge the reasons for revolutionary change, if changes must be made. As AT&T learned from its earlier attempt to sell specialized services, change cannot be implemented merely by sending people to school. Nor can it be made by hiring new staff, by acquiring new businesses, by changing the name of the company, or by redefining its business. Even exhortations by the chief executive to operate differently will not succeed unless they are backed up by a changed structure, new role models, new incentive systems, and new rewards and punishments built into operations.

A chief executive, for example, who demands innovative new products from his staff, but who leaves in place a hierarchy that can smother a good new idea at its first airing, is unlikely to get what he wants. In contrast, an unwritten rule at 3M Co., says one manager, is "Never be responsible for killing an idea." Similarly, if a CEO's staff knows that his first priority is consistent earnings growth, it will be unlikely to present him with any new product or service idea, no matter how great its potential, if it requires a long incubation period and a drag on earnings before it reaches fruition. At Pillsbury Co., for example, managers are afraid to suggest ideas for products that might require considerable research and development because they know that Chairman William H. Spoor is obsessed with improving short-term financial results, sources say.

The Real Priorities

One element is certain: Employees cannot be fooled. They understand the real priorities in the corporation. At the first inconsistency they will become confused, then reluctant to change, and finally intransigent. Indeed, consistency in every aspect of a culture is essential to its success, as PepsiCo's transformation into an archrival of Coke shows.

For decades, Coke's unchallenged position in the market was so complete that the brand name Coke became synonymous with cola drinks. It attained this distinction under Robert W. Woodruff, who served as chief executive for 32 years and is still chairman of the company's finance committee at age 90. Woodruff had an "almost messianic drive to get Coca-Cola [drunk] all over the world," says Harvey Z. Yazijian, co-author of the forthcoming book, *The Cola Wars*. So successful was Coke in accomplishing this under Woodruff—and later J. Paul Austin, who will retire in March as CEO—that Coca-Cola became known as "America's second State Dept." Its trademark became a symbol of American life itself.

"A real problem in the past," says Yazijian, "was that they had a lot of deadwood" among employees. Nevertheless, Coke's marketing and advertising were extremely effective in expanding consumption of the product. But the lack of serious competition and the company's relative isolation in its home town of Atlanta allowed it to become "fat, dumb, and happy," according to one consultant. Coke executives are known to be extremely loyal to the company and circumspect to the point of secrecy in their dealings with the outside world.

In the mid-1950s, Pepsi, once a sleepy New York-based bottler with a lame slogan, "Twice as much for a nickel, too," began to develop into a serious threat under the leadership of Chairman Alfred N. Steel. The movement gathered momentum, and by the early 1970s the company had become a ferocious competitor under Chairman Donald M. Kendall and President Andrall E. Pearson, a former director of McKinsey. The culture that these two executives determined to create was based on the goal of becoming the No. 1 marketer of soft drinks.

Severe pressure was put on managers to show continual improvement in market share, product volume, and profits. "Careers ride on tenths of a market share point," says John Sculley, vice-president and head of domestic beverage operations. This atmosphere pervades the company's nonbeverage units as well. "Everyone knows that if the results aren't there, you had better have your resume up to date," says a former snack food manager.

To keep everyone on their toes, a "creative tension" is continually nurtured among departments at Pepsi, says another former executive. The staff is kept lean and managers are moved to new jobs constantly, which results in people working long hours and engaging in political maneuvering "just to keep their jobs from being reorganized out from under them," says a headhunter.

Kendall himself sets a constant example. He once resorted to using a snowmobile to get to work in a blizzard, demonstrating the ingenuity and dedication to work he expects from his staff. This type of pressure has pushed many managers out. But a recent company survey shows that others thrive under such conditions. "Most of our guys are

having fun," Pearson insists. They are the kind of people, elaborates Sculley, who "would rather be in the Marines than in the Army."

Like Marines, Pepsi executives are expected to be physically fit as well as mentally alert: Pepsi employs four physical-fitness instructors at its headquarters, and a former executive says it is an unwritten rule that to get ahead in the company a manager must stay in shape. The company encourages one-on-one sports as well as interdepartmental competition in such games as soccer and basketball. In company team contests or business dealings, says Sculley, "the more competitive it becomes, the more we enjoy it." In such a culture, less competitive managers are deliberately weeded out. Even suppliers notice a difference today. "They are smart, sharp negotiators who take advantage of all opportunities," says one.

While Pepsi steadily gained market share in the 1970s, Coke was reluctant to admit that a threat existed. Yazijian says Pepsi now has bested Coke in the domestic take-home market, and it is mounting a challenge overseas. At the moment, the odds are in favor of Coke, which sells one-third of the world's soft drinks and has had Western Europe locked up for years. But Pepsi has been making inroads: Besides monopolizing the Soviet market, it has dominated the Arab Middle East ever since Coke was ousted in 1967, when it granted a bottling franchise in Israel. Still, Coke showed that it was not giving up. It cornered a potentially vast new market—China.

With Pepsi gaining domestic market share faster than Coke—last year it gained 7.5% vs. Coke's 5%—observers believe that Coke will turn more to foreign sales or food sales for growth. Roberto C. Goizueta, who will be Coke's next chairman, will not reveal Coke's strategy. But one tactic the company has already used is hiring away some of Pepsi's "tigers." Coke has lured Donald Breen Jr., who played a major role in developing the "Pepsi Challenge"—the consumer taste test—as well as five other marketing and sales executives associated with Pepsi. Pepsi won its court battle to prevent Breen from revealing confidential information over the next 12 months. But the company's current culture is unlikely to build loyalty. Pepsi may well have to examine the dangers of cultivating ruthlessness in its managers, say former executives.

Quite a different problem faces J.C. Penney today. Its well-entrenched culture, laid down by founder James Cash Penney in a seven-point codification of the company's guiding principles, called "The Penney Idea," has brought it tremendous loyalty from its staff but lower profits recently. Its introduction of fashionable apparel has been only partially successful because customers identify it with nonfashionable staples, such as children's clothes, work clothes, and hardware. It has also been outpaced in the low end of the market by aggressive discounters, such as K Mart Corp., which knocked Penney out of the No. 2 retailer's spot in 1976 and which has been gaining market share at Penney's expense ever since.

Penney's is proud that two national magazines cited it as one of the 10 best places to work in the nation, a claim that is borne out by employees. "Everyone is treated as an individual," notes one former executive. Another praises the company's "bona fide participative" decision-making process, and adds that Penney has "an openness in the organization that many large companies don't seem to achieve."

But Penney's paternalistic attitude toward its work force has meant that it always tries to find new jobs for marginally competent employees rather than firing them, says Stephen Temlock, manager of human resource strategy development. He concedes that some workers "expect us to be papa and mama, and aren't motivated enough to help themselves." The corollary of that, he admits, is that the company sometimes fails to reward outstanding performers enough.

Penney's entrenched culture makes any change slow, Temlock adds, but he insists that this solidity helps to maintain a balance between "an out-and-out aggressive environment and a human environment." Penney Chairman Donald V. Seibert believes that the company's problems have more to do with the retailing industry's endemic cyclicality than with company culture. Although he admits that he worries sometimes that the company is too inbred, he notes that it has brought in different types of people in the last several years as it entered new businesses, such as catalog sales and insurance.

Siebert adds that the company firmly believes that the principles of "The Penney Idea" will be relevant no matter how much the economic environment changes. "You can't say that there's a good way to modernize integrity," he emphasizes.

Seibert may be right. One competitor notes that the aggressive newcomers in retailing have profited from older retailers' mistakes, and thus have found shortcuts to growth. But, says this source, "the shortcuts are limited, and the newcomers' staying power has yet to be proven." Still, if the new threat continues, Penney's pace must speed up, and it must soon act more flexibly to protect itself; it may even have to abandon some of the customs that have grown up around its humanistic principles.

Another gentlemanly company found that it had to do just that to regain its leading position in banking. Chase Manhattan Bank had cruised along comfortably for years, leaning on the aristocratic image of its chairman, David Rockefeller. In the mid-1970s, however, Chase was jolted out of its lethargy by a sharp skid in earnings and a return on assets that lunged as low as 0.24% in 1976. Its real estate portfolio was loaded with questionable and sour loans, and its commercial lending department's reputation had been severely tarnished because high turnover of its lending officers and the resulting inexperience of those who replace them made the bank less responsive to customers. Some embarrassing questions about Chase's basic management practices began to be raised.

Rockefeller and a group of top executives, including Willard C. Butcher, now chief executive and chairman-elect, decided that the fault lay with a culture that rewarded people more for appearance than performance and that produced inbreeding and a smugness that made the bank loath to grapple with competitors. The typical Chase executive in those days was a well-groomed functionary who did not drive himself hard or set high standards for his own performance, banking analysts remember.

The first step toward change, Chase executives felt, was for the bank to define what it wanted to be. Early in 1977 it drew up a three-page mission statement that outlined the company's business mix. "We will only do those things we can do extremely well and with the highest level of integrity," the statement said. For Chase, this meant taking a hard look at some unprofitable parts of its business. Subsequently, it closed some 50 low-volume domestic branches in New York, and it began to turn away questionable loan business that it had accepted before.

The mission statement also spelled out specific targets for financial goals, such as return on equity and assets and debt-to-capital ratio. At the start, employees doubted that the company could meet these goals; one, for example, was a return on assets of 0.55% to 0.65%, more than double the 1976 figure.

Chase began a major effort to step up communications between top management and the rest of the staff. This was a departure from the old days, when decisions were simply handed down from the 17th-floor executive suite, says one former manager. The participation of all employees created a sense of "ownership" of the program by all, something consultant Robert F. Allen, president of the Human Resources Institute in Morristown, N.J., believes is essential to any long-lasting change.

Like AT&T, Chase promoted new role models, such as Richard J. Boyle, now a senior vice-president, who took over the bank's troubled real estate operations at age 32. Boyle, described as a "workaholic" with strong opinions and a willingness to make hard decisions, such as writing off floundering projects rather than carrying them on the company's books, is the antithesis of the old-style Chase banker, analysts say. To run commercial lending, the bank lured back James H. Carey, who had left Chase for Hambros Bank. "They put absolutely brilliant people in problem areas," remarks John J. Mason, banking analyst at Shearson Loeb Rhoades Inc.

Rewards for Performers

But tradition suffered: One-third of the bank's top executives were replaced by outsiders. Salaries and incentive payments were overhauled to provide greater rewards for top performers. And an advanced management course was started for promising young managers. The culture has been altered from its emphasis on style to a focus on performance. And now that employees' expectations of the company have changed, the new order is likely to prevail. But even Butcher, although pleased with the improvement, warns, "The danger is always that you become complacent."

Chase was able to effect the change in its culture under the aegis of its reigning leaders, Rockefeller and Butcher. But some companies find that the only way to solve problems is to bring in a new chief who can implement sweeping change. Yet even a new strongman can run up against a wall unless he understands the company's existing culture.

Dennis C. Stanfill, a corporate finance specialist, ran into just such problems when he took over as chief executive in 1971 at Twentieth Century-Fox Film Corp. Stanfill's aim was to balance the risks of the motion picture business with steady earnings from other leisure-time businesses, which he began acquiring. But he also insisted on running all of Fox's businesses, including the film operation, on an equal basis by keeping the corporate purse strings pulled tight—and in his hands.

What Stanfill overlooked was that creative people require a different kind of managing than do typical business employees. While the latter group can usually be motivated by using the carrot-and-stick approach, creative people are self-motivated. They will work as hard as needed to perform as perfectly as they can, because they identify their work not with the company but with themselves. What they want from their patron-managers, however, is applause and rewards for a good job, and protection when they bomb.

Stanfill violated those expectations when he refused to give Alan Ladd Jr., president of the film group, control over bonuses for his staff, which had produced such hits as *Star Wars*. From Stanfill's point of view, the decision was sound: In just three years he had erased a $125 million bank debt and brought the company into the black after it had been in default on its loans. He believed the traditional extravagances of the film company would keep the corporation on a shaky foundation. Indeed, he says, he wants "to keep the balance between show and business."

Not a 'Brokerage'

But the film company's response was predictable. Ladd quit to start his own operation, taking several key people with him. "In my opinion, Stanfill doesn't understand what motivates creative people," says Ladd. "You don't run a film business like a brokerage house."

Fox's directors quickly stepped in and demanded that Stanfill find a "name" replacement for Ladd. Stanfill has since picked Alan J. Hirschfield, who had been laid off by Columbia Pictures Industries Inc. and who has been praised by the industry for adding a creative spark to Fox this past year. But Stanfill now must make financial decisions jointly with Hirschfield.

Whether Stanfill will ever be comfortable in such a high-risk business remains questionable. One film industry analyst thinks not. He says: "Stanfill has never felt comfortable running an entertainment company. He is downside-risk-oriented on motion pictures, and didn't know why Ladd was so successful." If that is true, Stanfill could be on a collision course with Fox's implicit culture.

Stanfill may have recognized that the strategy he was imposing on Fox's film business, which produces 63% of the corporation's pretax operating earnings, violated its culture. But he obviously believed that it was necessary for the company's survival. He has not, however, changed Fox's culture. As more and more chief executives recognize the need for long-range strategies, they will have to consider the effects of these strategies on their companies. It may well be that CEOs must then decide whether their strategies must change to fit their companies' culture or the cultures must change to assure survival.

SECTION II
THE EFFECTS OF CULTURE ON STRUCTURE

Delayering is one of the newest terms to be applied to structural change in organizations. The basic idea is that current organizational structures are far too bureaucratic, rigid, formal and top-down oriented. Some American businesses have more than 15 layers of management, while more efficient and competitive firms operate with 5–7 layers.

Clearly, the concept of delayering makes sense, but again, the corporate culture often kills suggestions for more streamlined structures or defeats the intention of structural change.

In the first article selected for this section, "Restoring American Competitiveness: Looking for New Models of Organizations," Tom Peters proposes some radical ideas for creating more customer-oriented, innovative organizations.

In the second article, "How to Keep Ideas Moving," Jennifer Potter-Brotman discusses the effects of structure on innovation and the difference between influence and power within an organization.

In the third article, "Creating the 21st Century Organization," Nolan, Pollock and Ware, make an urgent and compelling case for moving from bureaucratic forms of organization to a more dynamic network form.

In the fourth article, "Decentralization: Rebuilding the Corporation," Marlene C. Piturro provides several examples and implications of structural changes in large organizations and discusses the dramatic differences that have occurred in the past several years in the ways we conceptualize how an organization should be shaped.

Restoring American Competitiveness: Looking for New Models of Organizations

By Tom Peters

Every day brings new reports of lousy American product or service quality, vis-a-vis our foremost overseas competitors. The news of buyers rejecting our products pours in from Des Moines; Miami; Santa Clara County, California; Budapest; Zurich; and even Beijing. Industry after industry is under attack—old manufacturers and new, as well as the great hope of the future, the service industry. Change on an unimagined scale is a must, and islands of good news—those responding with alacrity—are available for our inspection. But it is becoming increasingly clear that the response is not coming fast enough. For instance, even the near-freefall of the dollar does not seem to be enough to make our exports attractive or reduce our passion for others' imports.

"Competitiveness is a microeconomic issue," the chairman of Toyota Motors stated recently. By and large, I agree. There are things that Washington, Bonn, Tokyo, Sacramento, Harrisburg, and Albany can do to help. But most of the answers lie within—that is, within the heads and hearts of our own managers.

Needed: New Models

If we are to respond to wildly altered business and economic circumstances, we need entirely new ways of thinking about organizations. The familiar "military model"—the hierarchical, or "charts and boxes" structure—is not bearing up. It is a structure designed for more placid settings, and derived in times when you knew who the enemy was (not today's nameless or faceless Libyan terrorists or religious fanatics led by an old man in Teheran), and had time to prepare a response to your problems. (It took us Americans several years to gear up to win World War II—a luxury we can no longer afford in this era of nuclear capability.)

Likewise, peacetime economic wars of yore were marked by near certainty. Americans brought cheap energy to the fray, and were blessed by a vast "free trade" market at home. And for the first six decades of this century, we knew who our competitors were—a few big, domestic concerns. We knew where their leaders went to school, what cereals they ate for breakfast. Today, almost every U.S. industry has its competitors, from low-cost Malaysia to high-cost Switzerland, topped off by scores of tiny domestic competitors. Every industry now has—and keeps getting—new, unknown competitors. Moreover, the reality of exchange rates, interest rates, rates of inflation, prices of energy, and the ever-reconfigured microprocessor means that all of everything is up for grabs, unknown, constantly gyrating.

But remember that the American colonists broke away from their British masters in a war that featured the use of guerilla tactics. Popular mythology has it that the British insisted on lining up in rigid, straight-line formations to do battle, sporting bright red coats. By contrast, Ethan Allen and his fabled Green Mountain Boys eschewed formations, hid behind trees, and used their skill as crack shots while victoriously scampering through icy woods of the Hampshire Grants (now Vermont). Perhaps we again need organizations that evince the spunk and agility of the Green Mountain Boys rather than the formality of the British—a formality that was out of touch, then, with the new competitive reality in 18th century colonial wars and is out of touch, now, with the reality of the new economic wars.

Pictures, so it is said, are worth a thousand words. I believe that, and this article is devoted to describing two pictures, or "organizational maps." Neither looks much like a traditional organization chart; there is no square box at the top labeled "Chairman" (or "Vice-Chairman," or "Chief Executive Officer," or "President," and so on). Both charts break tradition in that they include customers, suppliers, distributors, and franchisees. The layouts are circular, moving from customers in toward the corporate chieftains at the circle's center. But beyond the circular scheme, the two bear little resemblance to one another.

Exhibit 1: The Inflexible, Rule-determined, Mass Producer of the Past

Let's begin with an assessment of Exhibit 1. Start with *a*, the corporate center/policy. This is the traditional, invisible, impersonal, generally out-of-touch corporate hub. The tininess of the circle representing the corporate center suggests both tightness and narrowness of scope; communication to the outside world (in or beyond the firm's official boundary) is usually via formal declaration—the policy manual or the multivolume plan, by and large determined on high—and communicated via the chain of command (i.e., downward). Within this tiny circle lie the "brains of the organization." It is here, almost exclusively, that the long-term thinking, planning, and peering into the future take place.

Exhibit 1
The Inflexible, Rule-determined, Mass Producer of the Past: All Persons Know Their Place

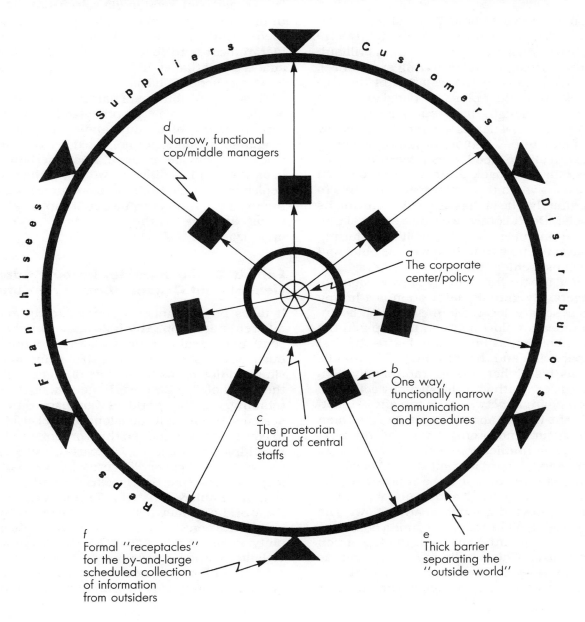

57

Move on to *b*—one-way, functionally narrow communication via rules and procedures. Most communication in this generic organization type is highly channeled (hence the straight line) and top-down (note the direction of the arrowheads). So, communication and "control" are principally via rulebook, procedure manual, union contract, or the endless flow of memos providing guidance and demanding an endless stream of microinformation from the line. Moreover, the communication rarely "wobbles" around the circle (look ahead to Exhibit 2 for a dramatic contrast); that is, the lion's share of the communicating is restricted to the narrow functional specialty (operations, engineering, marketing, etc.), more or less represented by the individual arrows.

Then comes *c*, the praetorian guard of central corporate staffs. The corporate center is tightly protected (note the thick line) by a phalanx of brilliant, MBA-trained, virgin (no line-operating experience), analysis-driven staffs. If the isolation of the corporate chieftains in their plush-carpeted executive suites were not enough, this group seals them off once and for all. It masticates any input from below (i.e., the field) into 14-color, desktop-published graphics, with all the blood, sweat, tears, and frustrated customer feedback drained therefrom. On those occasions when the senior team attempts to reach out directly, the staff is as good at cutting its superiors off ("Don't bother, we'll do a study of that marketplace—no need to visit") as it is at cutting off unexpurgated flow from below to the chief and his or her most senior cohorts.

Next, per *d*, are the functionally narrow cop/middle managers. My graphic description is a lumpy (substantial) square, located in the midst of the linear communication flow between the top and the bottom (the bottom, as in last and least—the first line of supervision and the front line). The middle manager, as his or her role is traditionally conceived, sits directly athwart the virtually sole communication channel between the top and the bottom. He or she is, first and foremost, the guardian of functional turf and prerogatives and the next block in the communication channel—remember that the praetorian guard was substantial block #1. The "cop" notion is meant to be represented by both the solidity of the block and its direct positioning in the downward communication flow. The middle manager is a filter of data, coming both from the bottom (infrequently) and from the top (much more frequently). The middle manager's job, as depicted here, is seen as vertically oriented (largely confined to the function in question and to passing things up and down) rather than horizontally oriented.

A thick, opaque barrier—*e*—marks the transition from the firm to the outside world of suppliers, customers, distributors, franchisees, reps, and so on. The barrier is very impermeable. Communication, especially informal communication, does not flow readily across it, either from the customer "in" or from the front line of the organization "out."

Which leads directly to the idea of *f*—formal "receptacles" from the scheduled collection of information from outsiders. Of course the old, inflexible organization does communicate with the outside world. But the communication tends to be formal, coming mainly from market research or from orderly interaction via salespeople. Both the timing and the format of the communication is predetermined. Even competitive analysis is rigid, hierarchical, and focused—a formal competitive analysis unit that audits known competitors, mainly on a scheduled basis.

These six attributes are hardly an exhaustive examination of the old-style organization, but they do capture many of its outstanding attributes and orientations—static, formal, top-down oriented, and rule-and-policy determined. It is orderly to a fault (a dandy trait in a different world). To be sure, this depiction is stylized and therefore somewhat unfair, but my observations argue that it captures a frightening amount of the truth in today's larger organizations.

Exhibit 2: The Flexible, Porous, Adaptive, Fleet-of-Foot Organization of the Future

It takes but a glance to appreciate the radically different nature of Exhibit 2—it's a mess! So, welcome to the real world in today's more innovative businesses: start-ups, mid-size firms, and the slimmed-down business units of bigger firms. To the world of The Limited, Benetton, or the Gap in retailing. To the world of Compaq, Sun Microsystems, or the ASIC divisions of Intel or Motorola in computer systems. To the world of steelmakers Worthington Industries, Chaparral, and Nucor. To the world of Weaver Popcorn, Johnsonville Sausage, Neutrogena, ServiceMaster, and University National Bank & Trust of Palo Alto, California. To the world of somewhat ordered chaos, somewhat purposeful confusion; the world, above all, of flexibility, adaptiveness, and action. Or to a new world violently turned upside down.

Begin with *a*—the new-look corporate guidance system, a vital vision, philosophy, set of core values, and an out-and-about senior management team (see *b* and *c* on page 59). First, the innermost circle depicting the corporate center in Exhibit 2 is obviously bigger than its counterpart in Exhibit 1. My point is frightfully difficult to describe. I pictured the traditional corporate center in Exhibit 1 as out of touch, shrivelled, formalistic, and ruled by very tight policy and a constraining rather than opportunistic plan, with contacts inside and outside the enterprise conveyed in written format, usually via brisk, impatient, and bloodless staffers (the praetorian guard). But the visual image that comes to mind for the center of Exhibit 2 is of a glowing, healthy, breathing corporate center. People from below regularly wander in without muss or fuss, and those at the top are more often than not out wandering. Customers and suppliers are as likely to be members of the executive floor (which, happily, doesn't really exist as a physical entity) as are the members of the senior team. But above all, the glow comes from management's availability, informality, energy, hustle, and the clarity of (and excitement associated with) the competitive vision, philosophy, or core values. Rule here is not written,

Exhibit 2
The Flexible, Porous, Adaptive, Fleet-of-Foot Organization of the Future:
Every Person Is ''Paid'' to Be Obstreperous, a Disrespecter of Formal Boundaries,
to Hustle and to Be Engaged Fully with Engendering Swift Action, Constantly Improving Everything

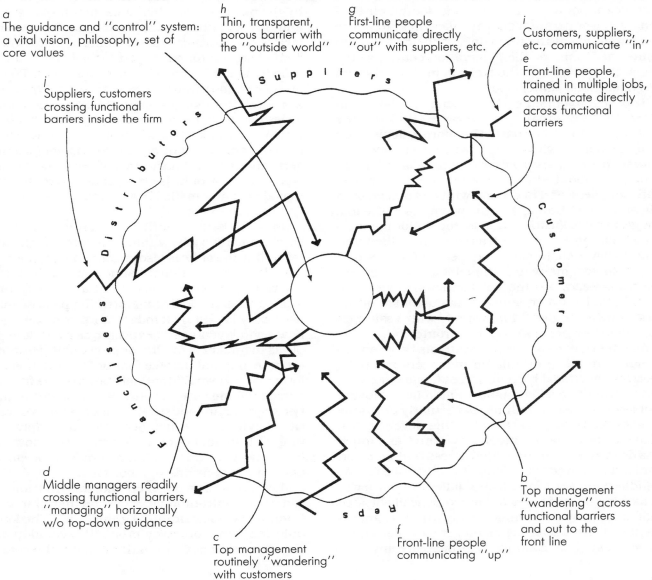

a
The guidance and ''control'' system: a vital vision, philosophy, set of core values

h
Thin, transparent, porous barrier with the ''outside world''

g
First-line people communicate directly ''out'' with suppliers, etc.

i
Customers, suppliers, etc., communicate ''in''

e
Front-line people, trained in multiple jobs, communicate directly across functional barriers

j
Suppliers, customers crossing functional barriers inside the firm

d
Middle managers readily crossing functional barriers, ''managing'' horizontally w/o top-down guidance

c
Top management routinely ''wandering'' with customers

f
Front-line people communicating ''up''

b
Top management ''wandering'' across functional barriers and out to the front line

but by example, by role model, by spirited behavior, and by fun—the vigorous pursuit of a worthwhile competitive idea, whether the firm is a bank, local insurance agency, or superconductor outfit.

Next, as previously anticipated, comes b—top management "wandering" across functional barriers and out to the front line in the firm. First, all the communication lines in Exhibit 2 are portrayed as zigzagging and wavy, with reason: To be as flexible and adaptive as required by tomorrow's competitive situation demands the wholesale smashing of traditional barriers and functional walls, both up and down and from side to side. So, this particular wavy line not only depicts the chief and his or her senior cohorts wandering about, but it shows them purposefully disrespecting those functional spokes (in fact, there are no formal functional spokes in this organization chart). And, of course, the even more significant point is that the chiefs' (and their lieutenants') wandering regularly takes them to where the action is—at the front line, in the distribution center at 2 a.m., at the reservation center, at the night clerk's desk, in the factory, in the lab, or on the operations center floor.

Top management's "somewhat aimless ambling," as I like to call it, is not just restricted to the inside portion of the chart. Therefore, c depicts top management "wandering" with customers. Of course, the primary point is that top management is out and about—hanging out in the dealerships, with suppliers, and in general with customers, both big and small. But, again, the waviness of the line suggests a clarification; that is, the senior management visit here is not restricted to the stilted, formal, "visit a customer a day" sort of affairs that mark all too many traditional top-management teams. Instead, it is the semi-unplanned visit; the drop-in to the dealer, supplier, or customer; or the largely unscheduled "ride around" with a salesperson on his or her normal, daily route.

As important as any of the contrasts between Exhibits 1 and 2 is d—middle managers routinely crossing functional barriers and managing horizontally without specific top-down guidance. Moving fast to implement anything, particularly engaging in fast-paced new product and service development, demands much faster, much less formal, and much less defensive communication across traditional organization boundaries. Thus, the chief role for the middle manager of the future (albeit much fewer in number than in today's characteristically bloated middle-management ranks) is horizontal management rather than vertical management. The latter, as suggested in Exhibit 1, principally involves

guarding the sanctity of the functional turf, providing any number of written reasons why function x is already overburdened and can't help function y at this particular juncture. In the new arrangement, the middle manager is paid proactively to grease skids between functions; that is, to be out of the office working with other functions to accomplish, not block, swift action taking. Once more, the zigzag nature of the line is meant to illustrate an essential point: Communication across functional barriers should be natural, informal, proactive, and helpful, not defensive and not preceded by infinite checking with the next layer(s) of management.

Perhaps the biggest difference involves e—frontline people, trained in multiple jobs, also routinely communicating across previously impenetrable functional barriers. The frontline person in Exhibit 1 has not only been cut off from the rest of the world by the button-down chieftains, praetorian guards, and turf-guarding middle managers, but also by a lack of training and cross-training, a history of not being listened to, and a last layer of cop—an old-school, Simon Legree, first-line supervisor. The role of the new-look frontline person sets all this on its ear. First, he or she is "controlled" not by a supervisor, middle management, or procedure book, but rather by the clarity and excitement of the vision, its daily embodiment by wandering senior managers, and extraordinary level of training, the obvious respect she or he is given, and the self-discipline that almost automatically accompanies exceptional grants of autonomy.

Not only is the frontline person encouraged to learn numerous jobs within the context of the work team, but she or he is also encouraged, at the frontline, to cross functional boundaries. Only regular frontline boundary crossing, in a virtually uninhibited fashion, will bring forth the pace of action necessary for survival today. More formally, in the new regime you would expect to see frontline people as members of quality or productivity improvement teams that involve four or five functions. Informally, you would routinely observe the frontline person talking with the purchasing officer, a quality expert, or an industrial engineer (who she or he called in for advice, not vice versa) or simply chatting with members of the team 75 feet down the line—always at work on improvement projects that disdain old divisions of labor/task.

Move on to f and g, which take this frontline person two nontraditional steps further. First, f—frontline people communicating "up." The key to unlocking extraordinary productivity and quality improvements lies within the heads of the persons who live with the task, the persons on the firing line. Thus, in the new-look organization it becomes more commonplace for the frontline person to be communicating up, perhaps even two or three levels of management up (and one prays that there are no more than that in total) or all the way to the top on occasion.

And then—virtually unheard of outside sales and service departments today—the "average" person, per g, will routinely be out and about; that is, frontline people communicating directly with suppliers, customers, etc. Who is the person who best knows the problem with defective supplier material? Obviously, it's the frontline person who lives with it eight hours a day. With a little bit of advice and counsel from team members, and perhaps some occasional help from a middle manager (and following a bunch of perpetual training), who is the best person to visit the supplier—yes, take on a multi-day visit that includes discussions with senior supplier management? Answer: It's again obvious—the first-line person or persons who suffer daily at the scene of the supplier's crime.

Now let's turn to the boundary, h—a thin, transparent permeable barrier to the outside world. This is yet another extraordinary distinction between the old-look and the new-look outfit. Recall Exhibit 1: The external barrier was thick, impermeable, and penetrated only at formal "receptacles." The new barrier is thin and wavy. Both the thinness and the imprecision are meant to suggest that there will be regular movement across it, in both directions. Frontline people, and senior people without prior notification, will be heading out with only semi-planned routines. Likewise, "external" colleagues will be regularly hanging out inside the firm (see i and j below). To be sure, the firm does exist as a legal entity: It is incorporated, and people are on its payroll. But more than any other factor, the idea of the firm turned inside out—the tough, recalcitrant hide that separates it from "them" (customers, suppliers, etc.) ripped off—is the image I'm trying to convey. NIH (not invented here) is no longer tolerable. The firm must be permeable to (that is, listen to with ease and respect and act upon) ideas from competitors, both small and large, foreign and domestic; from interesting noncompetitors; from suppliers, customers, franchisees, reps, dealers, frontline people, and suppliers' frontline persons; and from joint venture partners. It must become virtually impossible to put one's finger on the outside organization boundary. Flow to and fro, by virtually everyone, all the time, and largely informally (i.e., leading to fast improvement without muss, fuss, and memos) must become the norm.

Next we move to i—customers, suppliers, etc., communicating (talking, hanging out, and participating) "in." The movement from adversarial to new nonadversarial/partnership relationships with outsiders of all stripes is one of the biggest shifts required of American firms. Right now, the big (or small) business organization is typically the site of unabated warfare: top management versus lower management, management versus the union, function versus function, and—relative to outsiders—company versus customers, company versus franchisees, company versus dealers and, above all, company versus suppliers. This must stop—period. Cleaning out the bulk of the distracting praetorian guard and middle management will obviously help, but achieving an attitude of partnership is at the top of the list of requirements, truly "living" a permeable organizational barrier. Customers and suppliers (and their people at all levels) must be part of any new product or service design teams. Even more routinely, customers, suppliers, franchisees, and reps ought to be part of day-to-day productivity and quality improvement teams. Once again, to compete today means to improve constantly, to invest fast; stripping away the impermeable barriers is the sine qua non of speedy implementation.

Which leads directly to i—suppliers, customers, etc., crossing functional barriers to work, and help, inside the firm. The idea of i was fine and dandy, but not enough. Customers shouldn't just be in the firm; they must be part of its most strategic internal dealings. The supplier shouldn't be shunted off to the purchasing person. Rather, he should be working with cost accountants, factory or operations center people, marketing teams, and new product and service design teams. Moreover, the wavy line suggests that the communication will be informal, not stilted.

There is no doubt that Exhibit 2, taken as a whole, appears anarchic. To a large extent, this must be so. To move faster in the face of radical uncertainty (competitors; energy, money, and currency costs; revolutionary technologies; and world instability) means that more chaos, more anarchy is required.[1] But that is only half the story. Return to Exhibit 2, idea a—the corporate guidance system in the new-look firm. Recall my halting effort to describe it as a glowing sun, an energy center. In fact, the control in Exhibit 2 may be much tighter than in the traditional Exhibit 1 organization. Instead of a bunch of stilted, formalistic baloney and out-of-touch leaders, the new control as noted is the energy, excitement, spirit, hustle, and clarity of the competitive vision that emanates from the corporate center. So when the newly empowered frontline person goes out to experiment—for example, to work with a supplier or with a multifunction team on quality or productivity improvement—she or he is, in fact, *tightly* controlled or guided by the attitudes, beliefs, energy, spirit, and so on, of the vital competitive vision. Moreover, that frontline person is extraordinarily well trained, unlike in the past, and remarkably well informed (for example, almost no performance information is kept secret from his or her). So, it's not at all a matter of tossing people out into a supplier's operation and saying, "We gotta be partners, now." The frontline person "out there" is someone who has seen senior management face to face (and smelled their enthusiasm); a person who has served on numerous multifunction teams; a person whose learning and training is continuous; a person who has just seen last month's divisional P&L in all its gory (or glorious) detail, following a year-long accounting course for all frontline "hands." Thus, there can be an astonishingly high degree of controlled flexibility and informality, starting with the frontline and outsiders, in our new-look (Exhibit 2) organization. But there is also an astonishing amount of hard work required—perpetually clarifying the vision, living the vision, wandering, chatting, listening, *and* providing extraordinary and continuous training, for example—that must precede and/or accompany all this. So, perhaps "purposeful chaos," or something closely akin, is the best description of the Exhibit 2/new-look firm.

The ultimate point that underlies this brief contrast between and description of the two models is the nonoptional nature of the Exhibit 2 approach. Americans are getting kicked, battered, and whacked about in industry after industry. We must change, and change fast. The two charts discussed here are radically different, and although I'm not sure that Exhibit 2 is entirely "correct," I am sure that the radical difference between the two is spot on.

Endnotes

1. See R.C. Conant and R.W. Ashby, "Every Good Regulator of a System Must be a Model of That System." *International Journal of Systems Science*, 1970, 1(2), 89–97. There is a compelling theoretical as well as pragmatic basis for the idea. In 1970, Conant and Ashby posited the Law of Requisite Variety, which has become the cornerstone of information theory. In layman's terms, it means that you have to be as messy as the surrounding situation. In a volatile world, we must have more sensors, processing information faster and leading to faster (and by definition more informal) action taking.

How to Keep Ideas Moving

By Jennifer Potter-Brotman

Early winners in the corporate competitiveness game are managers who stimulate innovation by influencing rather than controlling others. They know how to streamline the decision-making process, generate a constant flow of fresh ideas, and keep projects moving toward effective completion.

The Crumbling Hierarchy

Rarely, however, can an organization expect to foster innovation and be market responsive by having its people report up and delegate down a lengthy, rigid chain of command.

Realizing this, many companies are restructuring. They are trimming layers of management, moving staff functions to the line, and redefining reporting relationships at all levels. At the same time, they are asking managers to spend time outside their own spheres of activity and to share information, ideas, opinions, and knowledge with colleagues throughout the organization. Companies are linking peers formally, by developing work teams across functions, departments, and units, and informally, through peer networks as a way to pool creativity and reach higher quality decisions.

These new structures and relationships create enormous pressures for individuals. In traditional hierarchies most problems are solved according to well-defined procedures. Decisions often are made unilaterally, projects implemented by direction, and relationships formed and nurtured based on leadership, loyalty, and obedience. In the new flattened structures authority is less important, and procedures for working successfully in a peer group are either unfamiliar or confusing. Managers whose success has come from wielding authority wonder how, with fewer subordinates, more demands, and less clarity, they can accomplish their jobs.

Their question is well founded, but from years of research, observation of companies and managers in change, and many painful lessons, an answer has emerged. When success depends on obtaining

cooperation from those over whom one has no direct control, managers must behave differently. They must adopt new attitudes and learn and apply new skills. Specifically, they must learn to influence effectively.

The Influence Factor

Recognizing the essential role that successful peer relationships and the ability to influence play in effective modern management is not new, but never has it been more important. Author Stan Davis touched on this in Matrix more than a decade ago. He wrote that authority and responsibility long had been separated and that the organization chart should reflect this. At about the same time, Professor John Kotter of the Harvard Business School observed that successful business leaders are masters of influence. They can energize people over whom they have little or no direct authority to help accomplish critical objectives.

The Forum Corporation in 1977 initiated the first in-depth study of influence in business organizations. This continuing research tracks major changes in business, studies the impact of these changes on the management process, and seeks to provide insight into the role influence plays in helping companies and individuals cope with change. The most important conclusions the study reaches are that effective influence management requires

- changing organizational and personal values;
- providing individuals with skills and tools through training;
- incorporating a process for building, using, and sustaining influence by directly connecting it to organizational strategy.

Value Change

Corporate hierarchies are breeding grounds for profound cynicism. Managers often get squeezed between the vertical lines and develop a rather narrow belief that, first and foremost, you protect yourself and your turf. This and other traditional values embodied in authority and the hierarchical management process—such as not taking risks, putting individual unit goals ahead of team objectives, and having absolute control of decisions—are ineffective in today's more horizontal organizations. But old beliefs don't die easily.

In a recent client assignment, a classic case of value conflict arose. The firm's senior marketing executive thought the new team spirit in his organization was wonderful. He bragged about his personal commitment to the company and was a talking billboard for closer peer relationships and task-force management. Unfortunately his boasting was only lip service. His claim that he valued consensus decision making was tentative at best. When pressure to make a decision mounted, he found it difficult to share the power. His coworkers felt manipulated and not part of the process. They sensed no real role in shaping results and had trouble supporting the executive's course of action.

Such difficulty in allowing participation is understandable. Workplace changes present situations and events that people have not encountered before and for which no familiar models exist. On project teams, for example, people must grapple with a lack of clear guidelines and precedents, a confusion of roles and responsibilities, and the conflicts that inevitably arise. Without training and reinforcement of new values, the attitudes, morale, and performance of workers eventually will be affected adversely.

Skill Training

Individuals who want to learn to influence more effectively must understand how to manage in new contexts and apply appropriate behaviors. This requires skills that may be unfamiliar, perhaps because they have not been required or considered urgent in authoritarian settings. More horizontal organizations require skills such as sparking peers' interest in working together and leading groups to establish ground rules for cooperation.

Some influence skills, such as tapping the diverse talents of others and encouraging a free flow of ideas, are clearly oriented to conceptual, interactive, and creative thinking. Others are more logical, linear, and analytical, such as applying the rational criteria on which decisions will be based.

Strategic Alignment

Even when they succeed in changing individual values and make a commitment to retrain managers, many companies find that results still come slowly or not at all. People stay on their turf, ideas aren't generated, projects grind to a halt in midstream, and cost overruns abound. The company then misses market opportunities, frequently because management has failed to provide an organizational context that encourages and reinforces business-unit collaboration. Management hasn't given lower level employees a strong sense of team membership, hasn't made clear a mission statement emphasizing the importance of integrating unit strategies, and hasn't created an incentive system for rewarding cross-unit participation.

Laying the groundwork for peer relationships is vital to fostering innovation. The most creative organizations are not those with the greatest number of high-level "thinkers" on staff. Rather, they are firms that adopt agile structures, motivate their employees to act in a more entrepreneurial fashion, encourage managers to create their own opportunities, and support innovation in a way that ensures alignment with company direction.

The Influence Process

Success in a project-team and task-force efforts requires a management process comprising three critical steps:
- building influence by creating the structure under which the team will function and bringing in the appropriate players;
- using influence to reach high-quality decisions;
- sustaining influence in order to implement those decisions.

Values inherent in this process include supporting and helping others, demonstrating commitment in a way that gets others to share power for the sake of team goals, and earning others' trust. The person who can influence effectively not only knows specific practices and behaviors but, more importantly, manages and leads the process.

Building Influence

Everyone encounters problems they can solve only with the assistance of colleagues. When such challenges arise, you must know how your coworkers will respond when you ask them for help. By building influence, you and your peers will be willing to go the extra mile to cooperate with each other. Rarely will you feel that you must go it alone, and you will find it easier to convince others to take risks and implement decisions.

A key to building influence is the ability to create ground rules where none exist and to act as a catalyst that brings the group together and sets it moving in the right direction. Through the use of influence, the rules developed by group members who want to design the way they will work together offset the lack of structure in many peer groups. On project teams, for example, the group will define roles and clarify responsibilities for all participants. When the group does this, it establishes the foundation for cooperation. Building influence, therefore, helps the manager make current and future peer relationships work more effectively.

Using Influence

Once a manager builds the structure for influence, the challenge is to reach high-quality decisions. At the core of using influence is sharing power—specifically sharing control so that the group sorts out its ideas, concerns, and conflicts in a logical and analytical manner.

We've all attended meetings in which a suggestions comes out of left field that is badly timed, has little or no apparent merit, and contradicts everything on which the group has agreed. An authoritarian group leader would ignore the outburst and move the meeting along to another subject. A leader who uses influence effectively, however, would ask the troublemaker to test the idea against what the group thinks.

Sharing power also means fostering divergent thinking and generating ideas. Most people believe that only the most creative should try out new ideas. A leader, however, need not be particularly creative in order to stimulate others to expand their thinking.

Imagine that you must make a critical decision quickly. One of your peers proposes a plan that is sound, straightforward, and, while perhaps a bit conservative, will succeed. Another's proposal is off the wall. It offers a radical solution peppered with interesting ideas that if fleshed out, however, just might work. You can play it safe and go with the first proposal because it's clear and won't cause conflict. Or you can accept the second proposal and agree to work with the person who submitted it.

The manager who uses influence effectively helps create a climate that urges individuals to present ideas without fear of criticism or pressure for specific results. This, in turn, gives people a greater sense

of reward. No matter how many restraints in an organization, there is always room for creativity.

Sustaining Influence

Building and using influence have little value if the manager can't sustain that influence. This requires the manager to establish mutual trust within the peer group. The manager must learn to trust others' judgment, the reliability of their information, and their execution of decisions. Members of the peer group will trust the manager in return.

Frequently during the project team's efforts a group member will be ready to present his or her suggestions, only to have another member ask for major modifications. What should the presenter do? Someone with hierarchical ideals would stall the other person and appeal to a high-level manager for advice, direction, and possible mediation. But the ability to influence offers a different approach. To ensure continued commitment, the challenged group member would call a meeting of the group and ask whether requests for last-minute changes make sense.

Managers, then, establish trust by proving they can get people to commit themselves to decisions long enough to carry them out and by remaining flexible should emerging factors necessitate change. Those who are able to influence most successfully can manage situations and remain flexible in their thinking and keen in their perceptions.

A Final Word

Companies caught in the turbulence of our rapidly changing business environment must bring the right people together in the right way in order to foster innovation, reach informed and high-quality decisions, and implement projects in a timely, cost-effective manner. Influence plays an important role in helping this occur, but top management must set the tone. Unless an organization creates a climate that places a high value on interdependence between people, departments, and divisions, innovation will suffer, productivity will lag, and, on the bottom line, market share and profitability likely will falter.

Creating the 21st Century Organization

By Richard L. Nolan, Alex J. Pollock and James P. Ware

The bureaucratic hierarchy form used by most organizations today is obsolete. The 21st century organization structure is a network form, which is more effective for coping with key facets of the emerging competitive environment.

We are aware that declaring the bureaucratic hierarchy obsolete is an extremely strong statement, but our conclusion is based on our work with companies that are in the process of successfully transforming themselves into viable 21st century global competitors. Companies that simply modify or attempt to improve on the bureaucratic hierarchy form continue to fall short of becoming globally cost-competitive, market-driven, and/or achieving a lasting competitive advantage. These failures are in contrast to those companies that pursue these same objectives within the context of network organization forms.

Two years ago, we hypothesized that modern Information Technology (I/T) was changing organizational forms.[1] We explored the concept of organizations as open systems of information and knowledge that have been dramatically affected by changes in the economics of computing and communications technologies. We suggested that information technology, in combination with significant changes in the competitive business environment, would lead to the development of diamond-shaped network organizations, and that I/T Architecture is a powerful new tool for designing effective organizations.

The purpose of this issue of *Stage by Stage* is to extend our discussion about what 21st century organizations will look like, report on observations about network organizations, and suggest what senior executives must do now to begin the process of transforming their businesses into 21st century corporations.

The Need for Diamond-Network Organization Structures

In 1986 we suggested that the common journalistic plea to move from bureaucracies to entrepreneurial styles was oversimplified and misplaced, that (as argued by Henry Mintzberg) both bureaucracies and entrepreneurial forms of organization can be successful adaptations to their respective environments.[2] The complex, hierarchical bureaucracy succeeds when the environment demands high degrees of specialization but the pace of change is slow; entrepreneurial forms succeed by adjusting rapidly to dynamic environments—but only when the business requires relatively simple information and few specialized disciplines.

But what about environments, such as those we observe today and expect for the 1990s (let alone the 21st century), that demand both complex coordination of multiple specializations *and* rapid adjustment to shifting markets, competition, and technology? What is needed is a new structure—one enabled by the ability to manipulate, create, store, and communicate knowledge and information both rapidly and inexpensively: the network organization. This new organizational structure combines the strengths of both bureaucracies and entrepreneurial forms (see Figure 1).

The fundamental issue is how to combine increased specialization with flexibility and rapid response capability. These two important organizational goals are often in conflict. Specialization means achieving deep knowledge of many different disciplines, each exploding with new knowledge, research, data, ideas, and theories. Large organizations must exploit specialization in all the basic functions of the firm—scientific research, marketing, manufacturing, computing technology, finance, social science and economics, and management and organization. In contrast, the dynamic, entrepreneurial organization pulls its diverse parts together quickly in response to opportunity, often ignoring the complexities embedded in the various

Figure 1
Organization Forms and Environmental Demands

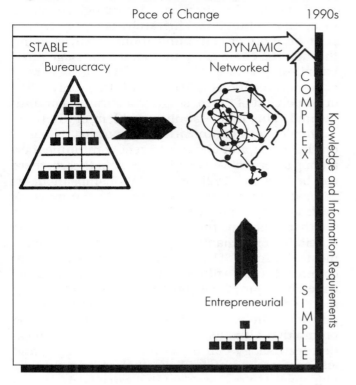

specialized disciplines in order to get the job done. "Quick and dirty" prevails over "doing it right" because of the importance of being nimble in the market.

The challenge of simultaneously achieving these two organizational goals has generated a good deal of interest and discussion, both within Nolan, Norton and with our clients. We remain convinced of the importance of networking for solving the strategic need for dynamic, flexible organizations that can cope with complexity and diversity.

Others share our interest in network organizations. Robert Eccles and Dwight Crane of the Harvard Business School have recently published a provocative study of network organizational structures in investment banks.[3] Netmap International, a consulting firm based in San Francisco, has built a software tool for diagnosing and interpreting networking relationships in management groups. Peter Drucker, in a recent issue of *Harvard Business Review,* suggested that the organization of the future:

    . . . will be knowledge-based, . . . composed largely of specialists who direct and discipline their own performance . . . . It will be what I call an information-based organization.[4]

The Fundamental Differences of the Network Form

The four basic components of organizations are tasks, people, technology, and systems. Each of these components is treated differently in a network organization form than in a bureaucratic hierarchy or entrepreneurial form.

Tasks—The *jobs* in a network organization are more abstract and less well-defined than those in a bureaucracy. In the factories of Industrial Age organizations, jobs were standardized and precisely defined so blue collar workers on the assembly line could easily be trained to complete their work at acceptable levels of productivity and quality. In the offices of Information Age organizations, much of the work is unpredictable, highly diverse, and information-intensive. The network organization depends on its knowledge workers to attack and solve problems on a day-to-day basis; many of the tasks cannot be fully defined in advance because the environment is so complex, dynamic, and unpredictable.

People—While a bureaucracy reduces its dependence on individual initiative by defining formal job descriptions and procedures for handling problems, a network creates an organizational context in which individuals can exercise a great deal of freedom, initiative, and creativity to solve unanticipated problems. Where a bureaucracy narrowly focuses people, a network broadly leverages them. The skills required for successful performance in a network entail such characteristics as interdependent problem solving, curiosity, commitment to quality, need for achievement, and an ability to work well with other people. The basis of networks is knowledge workers; the orientation is professionals in contrast to middle managers. The skill sets and mindsets of knowledge workers are substantially different from those of middle managers.

Technology—In functional hierarchies, technologies were introduced to perform physical work in the factories more efficiently, and to automate high volume, routine office work, such as order entry or invoicing functions. In the network organization form, these applications are still important, but the emphasis shifts toward the use of information technology in more robust and sophisticated ways.

The technologies in use in network organizations provide support primarily to knowledge workers. Two years ago we discussed the impact that computing and communications technologies have on information acquisition, processing, and storage; on communications costs and possibilities; and on management decision-making. Information technology is also changing the way individuals work, and the way they relate to each other and to the organization's suppliers and customers. With information technology, work can be done at almost any place (not just on company premises), at any time (not just 8 to 5), with any set of workers (not just those in the company or in the country).

Systems—Systems are the structured processes that enable organizations to perform purposeful work. They specify and promulgate goals, define and monitor the execution of tasks, and maintain communications to motivate and monitor performance.

In the bureaucratic hierarchy, systems are generally functionally oriented, with major system groups for Accounting, Marketing, Manufacturing, and Personnel. Within each functional group, there are well-defined subgroups. For example, in Accounting, there would be application systems for Payroll, Accounts Receivable, Accounts Payable, General Ledger, and Capital Budgeting.

As the network organization emerges, these traditional applications are no longer adequate. New management systems must provide the flexibility to enable geographically dispersed workers to work together as teams. During a project, team performance must be measurable so that key resource decisions can be executed. Once a given project is completed, the systems must support the efficient formation of other teams. The systems must also be able to measure and monitor overall productivity and capital formation, even in a dynamic, project-oriented context.

Reward systems must also be changed to pay people for overall contribution and to motivate them to work in a network environment. Most existing reward systems provide narrow incentives for making a network organization form successful.

Networks Look and Function Differently

Networks are webs of interrelationships organized to carry out the tasks of projects. Networks are dynamic and organic; as the marketplace environment changes, the network changes. This changing organic form is in direct contrast to the more stable pyramid form of the functional hierarchy.

Networks function differently from bureaucratic hierarchies along a number of key dimensions.

Relationships—Multiple direct relationships are the essence of a network. Under the established principles in a functional hierarchy of one boss for every subordinate and a span of control of six to 12

subordinates for every manager, the number of direct relationships in a functional hierarchy is the number of people minus one. Accordingly, communication in a functional hierarchy is highly dependent on indirect communications—that is, going through the chain of command. If a message must pass through six levels, and the average accuracy of communications is 70 percent, then only $(.70)^6$ or 12 percent of the message is accurately communicated. This is the familiar problem of filtering.

The network organization, in contrast, is based on the concept of allowing direct communication among all organizational members. In theory, there can be $[n \times (n-1)/2]$ direct relationships in an organization of n members. Although the network deals better with the problem of filtering, it creates another problem: the problem of chaos from the possibility of so many people being able to communicate directly. The dilemma of organizational communication—filtering versus chaos—is illustrated in Figure 2. Of course, the time and energy required for members of an organization to maintain active links with all other members would be prohibitive, although information and communication technology can make these links easier and less costly to maintain. Nevertheless, communication chaos is a real problem that must be dealt with if the network organization form is to flourish.

Figure 2
Number of Relationships as a Function of Members of the Organization

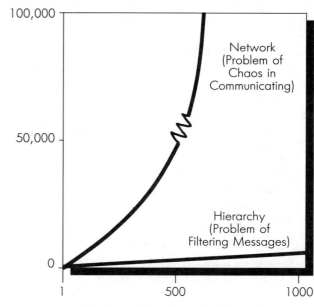

Number of People in the Organization

Number of Bilateral Communication Possibilities

No large organization will be purely a network (just as no large organization is purely a bureaucratic hierarchy). All existing organizations are made up of combinations of various structural types. In the transition from dominant hierarchy structures to network structures, we see active, change-oriented networks "floating" over operations which are carried out and controlled by more traditional hierarchy forms. It is also common to see other forms, such as ventures, simultaneously coexisting within the network context.[5]

The Digital Equipment Corporation case study featured in this issue of *Stage by Stage* is indicative of diverse organizational forms. Some parts of Digital—particularly those with longer-term planning responsibilities—are clearly more "network-like," while other parts are more bureaucratic in terms of their procedures, emphasis on individual accountabilities, and management control practices.

Levels—Networks typically have fewer reporting levels than do functional hierarchies. Network organizations, filled primarily with knowledge workers and supported by computing and communications technologies, do not need armies of middle managers to assemble, process, and report on management control information. Knowledge workers prefer to work more independently; they often resist and resent explicit direction and control from superiors. In fact, the whole concept of "level" is anathema to many knowledge workers, and is actually dysfunctional to their productivity.

Span of Control—The conventional wisdom in a bureaucracy is that a manager can effectively manage six to 12 subordinates. This number is limited by his or her ability to communicate with subordinates and keep track of their activities. When we consider the power of electronic communications and record-keeping, and new developments like artificial intelligence and decision support systems, relative to the face-to-face communications characteristic of hierarchical organizations, the traditional assumptions governing span of control break down.

Peter Drucker has suggested that we redefine "span of control" as "span of communication"[6] and recognize that information technologies have completely changed the rules of the game in terms of how many subordinates a manager can handle, what kinds of communications are necessary to maintain control over organizational activities, and how teams of professionals work together to solve organizational problems. Overreliance on traditional hierarchical assumptions about span of control can severely constrain an organization's ability to

cope with the complexity and rates of change so common in today's business environment.

Functional Specialization—Industrial Age bureaucracies typically contain functional hierarchies. The functional organization structure brings together specialists in each area required by the business—engineering, manufacturing, sales, finance, personnel, etc. Clustering specialists by function is based on assumptions of economies of scale and standardization, which in turn creates boundaries.

The shortcoming of this approach is that it creates what David Norton has called "functional gridlock."[7] Each function develops its own way of getting the job done, and the total organizational goals are often obscured. Walls build up between functional units, and not only is communication inadequate, but individual careers typically proceed up only one functional ladder. The net result is lack of understanding across functional boundaries and, commonly, mutual distrust.

In network organizations, the information flows freely across departmental boundaries at lower levels as well as senior levels, so the required information gets to the right places for action more quickly. Networks rely on the knowledge and ideas of organizational members, who directly contact the people they need to work with to get required information or commitments.

Permeable Boundaries—Another feature that distinguishes network organizations from bureaucracies is the nature of the boundaries between networks and their environments, and between parts of the organization itself. In a bureaucracy, the boundaries are clear and well understood; you are either "in" or "out"—there is little middle ground. Relationships with suppliers are generally defined by contracts that spell out in detail not only purchase order specifications, but terms of payment, legal liabilities, and so on. Negotiations are typically at arms length. The objective is to minimize the costs of materials or services to be acquired, consistent with performance requirements.

In a network environment, in contrast, it is often difficult to determine where the buyer organization stops and the supplier begins. While the contractual terms binding supplier and customer together are often just as well-defined as in the bureaucratic context, the relationship is generally very different. The relationship is seen as a symbiotic one, in which the two parties are mutually dependent on each other.

Boundaries in a network context are intersected by electronic media. Electronic purchase ordering, invoicing, and payments are increasingly common. While these arrangements have helped to increase responsiveness, improve product deliveries, and reduce in-process inventories, they also introduce new kinds of managerial and organizational challenges.

Professor James Cash of the Harvard Business School poses this example to make the point: A European commercial airline orders replacement parts by electronic mail from a United States manufacturer, who in turn instantly translates the order into an electronic request for components from a subcontractor in the Far East. The entire transaction is completed in a matter of seconds; yet it involves three corporations in three countries and raises challenging questions about legal commitments, financial obligations, taxation policies, and the issue of exporting jobs from one economic entity to another.[8]

The "permeability" of network boundaries affects individual roles as well. Networks frequently bring members of two or more organizations into direct contact with each other in the context of joint design teams, alliance projects, or customer/supplier projects. For example, one major automobile manufacturer now outsources a significant portion of its engineering design work to major vendors, who are networked into the engineering design teams and use the same CAD/CAM technologies as the inside engineers, thereby enabling rapid transmittal of design work. In effect, the vendor engineers are part of the manufacturer's network, even though they are located in other cities and are paid by the vendor. Networking technologies make this kind of arrangement not only practical but effective.

Successful network organizations encourage and support professional relationships between their knowledge workers and colleagues in other organizations, sometimes even those working for competitors. These networks can be a powerful source of information, ideas, and even future employees or alliance partners, and constitute a very important resource.

Internal Boundaries—Boundaries between functions, line and staff, or segmenting geographic territories may also be crossed more readily at all levels of an effectively functioning network organization. Information does not necessarily follow the formal, hierarchical command structure. Rather, information flows through the organization in branching patterns, with frequent "crosswalks" across functions. Informed decisions can be made and implemented at lower levels, and the pace of decision-making and organizational action can be much faster.[9]

These cross-functional network information flows lead naturally to more complex interpersonal relationships. In a bureaucracy, there are formal procedures for bringing specialized skills to bear on problems and issues. Some specialists are usually viewed as advisors, at best, and are often perceived by other specialists as interfering with the "real" work of the organization.

In a network organization, by contrast, relationships develop among workers with problems and workers with the skills to assist in solving those problems. Knowledge workers develop influence based on their knowledge, expertise, and ability to contribute to solutions, rather than on bureaucratic sources of power such as formal authority, procedural requirements, or budgetary approval. The *relationship* network is more efficient in bringing together the diverse skills required for solving new problems than any preconceived information path could be.

Vertical Integration—Network organizations may also have a different orientation toward vertical integration. In the Industrial Age mindset, the ultimate objectives is to control maximum resources and achieve dominance of the marketplace. The epitome of this perspective was Ford Motor Company's River Rouge plant, where iron ore was unloaded at one end of the facility, and completed automobiles came out the other end. Today, natural resources such as raw materials and energy, while still important, are actively traded in international markets, and are no longer the source of competitive advantage that they once were. In today's complex, dynamic business environment, strategy points more toward the smaller, flexible network organization buying and selling resources in various markets, rather than the vertically integrated bureaucracy.

This difference in strategy is precisely the reason that the automobile manufacturer cited earlier has chosen to outsource not only the manufacturing of many of its subassemblies, but much of its engineering design work as well. And that particular manufacturer is not unique. As *Fortune Magazine* reported several months ago, Toyota, which outsources 70 percent of its parts, has a profit per car 36 percent higher than General Motors, which outsources only 30 percent of its parts.[10] Today, a network of vendors, raw materials suppliers, and professional services can often be assembled more quickly and less expensively than a vertically integrated organization, while also providing greater flexibility for the future.

We believe that the Apple Company is an exemplar of network organization. In his book *Odyssey*,

John Sculley, CEO of Apple, reflects a shift in attitude toward vertical integration. He views Apple as a company that is happy to support the development of new partner companies—Apple calls them "spin-outs"—like software developers and distributors that will help to create, nurture, and expand the total market. Sculley believes that the dynamic, turbulent business environment creates a wealth of opportunities. He suggests that a network of small, dynamic companies with ongoing ties to each other can most effectively create and meet market needs and maintain an exciting, motivating, and professionally challenging environment for all members of the organizations involved:

> Because we believe that interdependencies—networks of smaller companies—are a major source of strength, we are spinning out from the Apple mothership new ideas, new business directions in the form of new companies. . . .
>
> The ultimate aim is to expand the network further than it has gone. In the future we envision a federation of companies spun out of the mothership in such fields as systems products and in markets like engineering or industrial training.
>
> . . . large corporations are only capable of doing a few things at any one time. All the resources and focus of the corporation are directed toward those few things. If you want to do something else, you don't have the corporation working for you—you have the bureaucracy and expenses of the company working against you. . . .
>
> Our spinouts will remain a vital part of the *network of interdependencies* [emphasis added] around which the third-wave corporation garners its strength and flexibility.[11]

Multidisciplinary teams—Effective network organizations build and rely on cross-disciplinary teams that are judged on the basis of the results they produce, rather than on how well they follow predetermined procedures. As Tracy Kidder showed in *The Soul of a New Machine*,[12] a team of committed individuals working together can accomplish more than traditional functional organizational units. Paul Lawrence and Jay Lorsch, in their classic study of organizational structure and effectiveness,[13] demonstrated that organizations that measure and reward performance based on results, rather than on following formal procedures, are much more effective in dynamic, complex environments. Bureaucracies,

focused on forms and procedures, stability, and predictability, tend to reward skills and behaviors that are far more focused on individual accountability and on "following the rules."

Career development strategies must also be different in network organization. Where career ladders in bureaucratic organizations are typically vertical, in networks they are most productively cross-functional. "Fast trackers" in network organizations are encouraged to build their careers by operating in diverse environments typically involving financial, operating, and global responsibilities. As we noted in our original article in 1986, network organizations require "distributed leadership"—a pattern of many specialists making interconnected decisions and taking their own initiative to address problems as a team, rather than waiting to be told what to do.

Different Style—Networks also require a different style of operation, or what has commonly been referred to as "culture." First and foremost, workers in a network organization must be flexible. They participate in changing subnetworks to carry out diverse projects, often working on several different projects at the same time. Second, workers must adopt a problem-solving mode of behavior guided by an ethic of doing what's "right." In contrast, the familiar bureaucratic response of "not my job" is not the norm in a network organization.

Third, the autonomy of doing what's "right" must be blended with a mutual respect for the actions and ideas of others. Frequently, there will be overlap in attacking problems and widely different approaches employed. Individuals must resolve most of these conflicts themselves if the network organization is to function effectively. If mutual respect is absent, the conflict of overlapping and multiple approaches for problem-solving can lead to breakdowns in the network organization.

Fourth, network organizations require the nurturing of knowledge workers in pursuing professional excellence and functioning as teams. Quality is an important ethic within a network organization culture, creating peer group motivation through its emphasis on doing things as effectively as possible.

These differences in operating style also mean a very different role for managers, requiring a different set of managerial skills. With many knowledge workers who are capable of setting their own goals and working with very little direct supervision, the traditional autocratic management style is not only unnecessary, but can actually be counterproductive in a network structure. Rather, the role of the network manager is to lead, coordinate, facilitate team-building, and support the knowledge workers.

These attributes of style are intangibles, and are difficult to manage formally. Nevertheless, our experience indicates that their presence is essential to the migration to a network organization. In the past, and even still today, we have observed that many companies attempt to achieve this different style under the heading of "culture change programs."

Recommendations for Action

Adaptation of the bureaucratic form of organization to the functional hierarchy has served business organizations well for over 100 years (and government, military, and the church for over 2000 years). But it will not be adequate to carry competitive businesses into the 21st century. The 21st century competitive environment will be global, fast, flexible, complex, and volatile.

The emerging network organization structure has fundamental features that are more attuned to the new environment. It is much less developed in terms of proven management principles and practices than the bureaucratic hierarchy. Nevertheless, we believe the core features of the network appear more promising, and are well worth the time investment of executive teams.

In our work with companies that are managing their transformations to 21st century corporations, we recommend that the executive team develop an action program consisting of the following items:

Action Item #1—Baseline the company's position in migrating toward the network organization.

We are only 12 years away from the 21st century. Successful companies are already operating with emergent network organizations. These network structures have often evolved in spite of functional hierarchies, and are supported by rich information technology infrastructures. Executive management must recognize the existence of these "shadow" network organizations and begin to help them move explicitly toward the more comprehensive, formal, and effective set of network practices and structures described here.

Action Item #2—Develop an inventory of the desirable cultural attributes of the network organization and strive to reinforce these attributes in all aspects of the management process.

Style and culture are absolutely critical to the flourishing of a network organization structure. Many of the desirable attributes of a network culture are directly counter to the values and operating style of a bureaucracy, and will not be adopted by the organization without significant, explicit senior management support.

At the same time, however, "culture change" programs alone will not provide the needed stimulus for change. Formal organizational tools, such as job descriptions, compensation systems, management controls, and communication processes—and their supporting information systems—must also be modified to support the culture change initiatives. Ultimately, however, executive sponsorship for the needed changes, and active executive leadership through personal example, is what makes the difference.

Action Item #3—Initiate an aggressive core systems renovation effort. Core systems enable an organization to perform complex work in a controlled manner. Today's organizations have evolved to the point where thousands of people cooperate in applying billions of dollars of financial resources, millions of horsepower of energy, billions of MIPs,[14] and gigobytes of computer memories to produce and distribute the highly sophisticated goods and services that make up our modern economy. This achievement is no trivial matter; and complex, functioning systems for resource allocation and control make it all possible.

It would be sheer folly to think that any fundamental change in organizational practices will take place until we are able to supplant existing systems capabilities with better alternatives.

Nevertheless, existing core systems are old and obsolete; they were designed for the bureaucratic hierarchy. An important, and first, step to creating 21st century organizations is to migrate core systems to new designs that enable organizations to perform work efficiently and effectively within the network organization form. This migration is so complex, and the risk of loss of control is so great, that the migration cannot be accomplished in one "fell swoop" nor in one major strategic program; it is multiprogram, multifaceted, and multiyeared.

Thus, transformation from bureaucratic hierarchies to network structures is a major, multidimensional effort—one that will take many years to accomplish, and in a sense will never be complete. Transformation involves change in all the key elements of an organization—tasks, people, technologies, and management systems. We have observed that the more successful companies are focusing on making this process manageable by "chunking" their network structure into five major components (operations, people, accountability, markets, and the technology infrastructure) and building world-class systems to support each. Our Nolan Norton Institute is now initiating multiclient research programs intended to facilitate the design, architecting, and implementation of these core systems. We plan to report on the progress of these research activities in subsequent issues of *Stage by Stage.*

Notes

1. Richard Nolan and Alex Pollock, "Organization and Architecture, or Architecture and Organization," *Stage by Stage*, Volume 6, Number 5, September–October, 1986.
2. *Structure in Fives: Designing Effective Organizations,* Prentice-Hall, 1983.
3. Robert G. Eccles and Dwight E. Crane, "Managing Through Networks in Investment Banking," *California Management Review,* Fall 1987.
4. "The Coming of the New Organization," *Harvard Business Review,* January–February 1988, Volume 66, Number 1.
5. See Nolan and Kelvie on venture organization forms, *Stage by Stage*, Volume 6, Number 5, July–August, 1986.
6. "Playing the Information-Based 'Orchestra,'" *Wall Street Journal,* May 22, 1986.
7. "Breaking Functional Gridlock: The Case for a Mission-Oriented Organization," *Stage by Stage*, Volume 8, Number 2, 1988.
8. Personal conversation. See also "IS Redraws Competitive Boundaries," by James I. Cash and Ben Konnsynski, *Harvard Business Review,* Volume 63, Number 2, March–April, 1985.
9. For an obvious contrast, and a powerful example of the limitations of bureaucratic organizations, see David Norton's description of the decision-making processes at Hierarchic Manufacturing, contained in *Stage by Stage*, Volume 8, Number 2, 1988.
10. *Fortune,* February 15, 1988.
11. *Odyssey,* by John Sculley, with John Byrne, Harper & Row, 1987, pp. 391–394.
12. Avon Books, New York, 1981.
13. Paul Lawrence and Jay W. Lorsch, *Organization and Environment,* Harvard Business School Division of Research, Boston, MA, 1967.
14. MIPs are "millions of instructions per second"—a term used to express the computation power of computers.

Decentralization: Rebuilding the Corporation

By Marlene C. Piturro

"Managers had better assume that the skills, knowledge, and tools they will have to master and apply 15 years hence are going to be different and new.... And only they themselves can take responsibility for the necessary learning and relearning, and for directing themselves."

Peter F. Drucker
A.M.A. Course Catalog, 1986

It used to be easy to visualize what a company should look like—it should be shaped like a pyramid, with the CEO on top. Power, responsibility, decision-making authority, and money trickled down from the man at the summit, who ran things with a firm hand.

Present that scenario to most modern managers, and they would be horrified. This rapidly disappearing structure is at odds with a pervasive trend toward decentralization—assigning greater responsibility to a company's separate business units.

Involvement and Innovation

Arlene Johnson, vice-president of programs at Catalyst, a New York-based research and advisory organization that helps corporations foster the career and leadership development of women, sees most companies either working toward decentralization or adjusting to the changes wrought by it.

Johnson explains: "I see the move toward decentralization as a way for managers to be closer to the action. There is less tolerance for hierarchy, and more power, autonomy, and entrepreneurial spirit further down the line than ever before. Decentralization is appropriate for our times. There's an increasingly competitive climate for business, a need to penetrate global markets, a need for more involvement of employees at all levels, and a desire by people to feel responsible and involved with what they're doing."

Reprinted by permission of the publisher from *Management Review*, August 1988. © American Management Association, New York. All rights reserved.

"In the upper echelons the opportunities are really exciting. While before each company had only one CEO, in a decentralized company there's a chance for 50 or even more people to be CEOs of their own, smaller businesses. It leads to a lot more innovation."

Johnson emphasizes the importance of separating the concept of decentralization from geography: "It's entirely possible to either have a centralized organization with sites all over the world, or a decentralized organization all in one place. It's a question of reorganizing accountability rather than where you are physically."

She believes a more decentralized organization creates an environment where there's freedom for experimentation and innovation. For example, trying out innovative human resources policies, such as extended parenting leave, part-time work, work at home, and job sharing, will be easier at a company that's made up of many small businesses. "Trying something on a small scale is relatively risk-free for a big company. If the experiment is successful, other parts of the organization may adopt it," Johnson says.

How does working in a decentralized environment affect employees' opportunities for upward mobility? Johnson comments: "From a career-advancement point of view, decentralization can be a double-edge sword. Every manager is closer to bottom-line responsibility, so success and failure are more readily visible than in a centralized company. You need to be a risk-taker if you want to succeed in a highly decentralized organization."

Decentralizing at Clairson

Clo Ross, administrative vice-president of Clairson International, a manufacturer of household and commercial wire storage products, sits near the top of a "lean and mean" corporate structure composed of herself and two other corporate vice-presidents reporting to a CEO.

Clairson, with its headquarters in Ocala, Florida, employs approximately 1,700 employees. Its

74

Should You Decentralize MIS?

Just when people get comfortable using PCs and tying into a mainframe for most functions, their company decides to decentralize management information systems (MIS) by placing MIS personnel in end-user departments.

Cost considerations are a big factor here, and a move to decentralize MIS should never be taken lightly. think of having 50 computer systems in a decentralized company instead of one MIS department serving the whole organization, not to mention the headaches of integrating all the systems so they can communicate with each other.

Pepsico, Incorporated, based in Purchase, New York, presents an interesting example of MIS decentralization. The soft drink giant has been decentralized for years. Its corporate culture revolves around being close to each division's business, so putting MIS people with end-users was a natural move.

What made the decision even easier was that many available computer products are PC-based, and these tools work better in a smaller environment than in a centralized one. Local area networks (LANs) make it possible for end-users in the divisions to stay in touch at a reasonable cost.

There are several advantages to decentralized MIS departments: faster response to requests for new applications, testing and delivery of new products, and the availability of MIS people who are close to your business, hence better able to meet your needs. The downside is the lack of integration with central programs and mainframe capabilities.

household products division has nine locations in Ocala and one in Reno, Nevada, and the commercial products division has facilities in Georgia, Florida, Nevada, California, and Iowa.

Ross explains how Clairson functions: "The presidents of the two major divisions . . . go through a planning cycle each spring to devise next year's business strategy and a three- to five-year plan. Then they meet with our executive committee for several days, during which the next year's budgeting and action plans are hammered out.

"Once the plans have been finalized and reviewed by the CEO, the presidents are off to the races. They have lots of autonomy in how they run their businesses. Every month there's a financial meeting at which their numbers are reviewed. As long as things are good, we keep our hands off. If there's a downturn or a problem, corporate gets more involved until things turn around."

Ross claims things weren't always this way at Clairson. For a long time, the company was a highly centralized, "seat-of-the-pants" operation where all policies and procedures were set by the CEO. After a period of rapid growth leading to the development of many different products and locations, management pushed the decision-making process as far down as possible. Ross explains: "Now we're much looser. We treat people as responsible adults by

creating an environment where they aren't closely monitored. We have no audit control or quality control inspectors—we expect each employee to be responsible for what he or she is doing."

In addition to granting employees autonomy in decision making, the company has been flexible in allowing "local" control of various administrative functions. Benefits, compensation review, affirmative action, and equal employment opportunity compliance, however, remain centralized.

While decentralization has been successful at Clairson, there have been difficulties as well. "We pay a certain price because we're decentralized," Ross explains. "Communication is critical, so once a month we [the corporate vice-presidents] travel to the plants and listen to everyone. Nothing can replace face-to-face contact, but it's really difficult when you have many locations. We spend three full days a month just listening to our workers, and it's time well spent."

According to Ross, the change at Clairson didn't happen overnight. *In Search of Excellence* [Peters and Waterman, Harper & Row, 1982] had a profound influence on our thinking, she says. "We realized

Handling Affirmative Action and Other HR Functions

The consensus among human resources interviewees for this article is that certain programs influenced by federal regulation should be kept centralized. Affirmative action, equal employment opportunity, and similar programs should be monitored by headquarters, although a certain amount of discretion should be granted to the divisions as to how they meet those goals. Human resources personnel become critical here—they've got to ensure that corporate policies are implemented in the divisions without seeming to mandate headcounts.

Decentralization places human resources personnel in a new role. They are no longer staff, but internal consultants to a division or line of business. Human resources people can get closer to the bottom line by working with, teaching, and learning from line managers. In addition, an assignment to a client group rather than corporate headquarters can be exciting and challenging.

Many companies also are finding that centralizing other functions works well. Certain issues require particularly careful consideration before their control passes into divisional hands: dealing with unions, executive compensation, leadership and succession planning, and the performance appraisal process. Fringe benefits have proven to be a gray area. Some companies relish divisional autonomy in responding to the needs of employees. Others prefer to consolidate their benefits packages because of the planned 1989 phase-in of Section 89 of the Internal Revenue Service Code (Welfare Discrimination Testing) which will make it more difficult to offer a tailor-made benefits package to one division. Aggregating benefits will make sense in terms of compliance, but may cause problems with divisions seeking autonomy in benefits planning.

that it was time for a revolution in American industry. There was such a decline in productivity that we needed something to reverse that trend."

Restructuring at General Foods

In contrast, when General Foods, the giant food and beverage company, was acquired by Phillip Morris in 1985, there were bound to be unavoidable changes. "The General," as the company is known by its employees, underwent a major decentralization and downsizing in 1987.

Randy Kautto, director of human resources for General Foods-U.S.A., one of the three companies created by the restructuring, feels "very positively" about the restructured company and its leadership. "Erven Shames [CEO and president] instinctively has led this restructuring in a very appropriate way. He's provided clear, decisive leadership, and there's consistency between his behavior and what he says. That's what we strive for throughout the organization."

Kautto continues: "We knew there would be many changes in the way we operate, so we established grass-roots task forces on a number of issues, such as decision making, rewards, and business strategy. In the near future we'll be evaluating how our first year under decentralization went, particularly our rules about decision making. For example, the question of who has the ability to decide which advertising agency we use will come up. The issue is how much autonomy managers have."

Unlike some other companies, General Foods has kept employee benefits, investments, overall business strategy, human resources policy, and compensation centralized. However, it has maintained a "hands-off" policy regarding benefits and day-to-day operations with some of the companies it has acquired.

Career Paths: A Major Issue

Kautto raises an issue discussed consistently by managers in decentralized companies: What happens to career paths? Decentralization clearly puts staff people, such as human resources, research, legal, and finance, closer to their company's businesses, but this breaks the tie to corporate that existed in a centralized or matrix organization. Line managers also are affected; the path to the top is no longer clear-cut.

He comments: "We're going to have to redefine career paths, particularly for people who feel responsible not only to their businesses but to their colleagues throughout the organization and their industry. It's much more difficult to keep up-to-date professionally when there's not a direct link with

---

A Restructuring Veteran Shares Her Thoughts

Peggy Braden Moore, an attorney who has practiced in New York, California, and Connecticut, has experienced both sides of the restructuring issue. As counsel, she has represented management, and she also has been an employee of a *Fortune* 500 company that went through several reorganizations.

Moore recounts her experience: "It was a schizophrenic feeling being both counsel to top management and one of the affected employees. Policies may sound neutral, but when they're applied to you, it's different." She explains the rationale companies use to restructure: "Corporate headquarters doesn't generate income, it provides service. Top managers begin to perceive corporate as a cost center and want to cut costs by cutting staff, but whether this makes sense in the long run is debatable.

"At my company, as dollar figures climbed for in-house counsel, management would say, 'There's too much corporate overhead. Let's allocate these costs to the divisions.' Management would look at the cost (salaries and benefits) of in-house litigation and decide to cut staff and give the work to outside firms. But if $2 million in legal fees were incurred, then the $200,000 for staff salaries began to look like a bargain. That's what produced a cycle of centralization/decentralization. The net result for me was that each time the company restructured, I got more work without the commensurate raise in title or salary. After the third restructuring, I left."

According to Moore, the relocation that often accompanies decentralization also can be tough on employees. "Companies do sophisticated studies using demographics and information on housing and schools, but the goal is to find a place with well-educated workers and a high rate of unemployment that will welcome any employer," she says. "One location where we moved as part of decentralization was a farming community. Employees would work their farms in the early morning, work for us nine to five, and continue to farm in the evening. What they earned at the plant wasn't enough to sustain them."

Moore concludes: "No one takes into account the disastrous impact frequent restructuring have on employees. It seems companies move in five- to seven-year cycles, in which they go from centralized to decentralized and then back again. It's upsetting, not to mention expensive."

---

corporate. While restructuring has worked very well, we are assessing its impact."

Will decentralization serve to make businesses more formidable competitors that can move more quickly and aggressively than centralized companies? Or will it be just another managerial fad?

As with all management strategies, decentralization is no panacea, nor is it appropriate to all corporations. When decentralization provides clear accountability, builds greater expertise at all levels of staff, concentrates resources in each business as the level needed for competitive success, and simplifies decision making, it should be used to further management's goals.

SECTION III
THE EFFECTS OF CULTURE ON STAFFING

Perhaps the greatest cultural change in the past decade for large North American companies has been the move in philosophy ''from bigger is better'' to ''lean and mean.'' In one recent survey, almost 60% of large firms reported a reduction in force in the last eighteen months. These reductions have a major impact on organizational norms, expectations and values.

This section focuses on downsizing and how it has affected the work environment in organizations. In the first article, ''Downsizing: Results of a Survey by the American Management Association,'' Eric Greenberg shares his finds regarding this issue in different sizes and types of industries.

In the second article, ''Downsizing: the Ultimate Human Resource Strategy,'' Appelbaum, Simpson, and Shapiro discuss the changes in the North American psyche with regard to employment: job security is a thing of the past. This article includes ten steps for downsizing.

In the third article, ''The Downside of Downsizing,'' Anne Fisher suggests ways to deal with the survivors of restructuring and emphasizes the importance of communication norms during times of transition.

In the fourth article, ''Running Lean, Staying Lean,'' Robert Tamasko emphasizes the need to exercise constant vigilance in managing a company's size. In this article, he reveals the insidious role the culture plays when streamlined structures return to mid-level bloat.

In the final article in this section, ''The New Employment Contract,'' Chris Lee shares several examples that demonstrate how changes in the corporate culture have resulted in a new relationship between employer and employee.

Downsizing: Results of a Survey by the American Management Association

By Eric Rolfe Greenberg

News that will bring welcome relief to many personnel professionals is that the recent wave of downsizing by American corporations has crested, according to data collected by the American Management Association in July 1987. Although nearly half of the 1,134 survey respondents said they had undergone a reduction in force in the 18 months from January 1986 through June 1987, only 17.4% told of plans to downsize in the next 12 months.

Although the number of companies downsizing will decrease, the survey found, the number of jobs lost per company in forthcoming force reductions will remain relatively constant. The average number of jobs lost in each downsizing action in the past was 362; the average per reduction to come will be 356.

Corporate size and business type proved to be important variables in the AMA sample (see Exhibit 1). Nearly six out of ten large firms, defined as those with more than $500 million in annual sales, reported a reduction in force in the past 18 months, with an average of 2,770 employees (or 8.9% of the workforce) let go. Half of the sample's mid-sized firms (those with sales of between $50 and $500 million) downsized, costing an average of 125 jobs (or 11.1% of the firms' employees). Among small firms (those with less than $50 million in annual sales), 40% reduced their workforces with an average of 39 workers (or 13.6% of the firms' employees) terminated.

Manufacturing concerns were hit harder than service companies. Fifty-seven percent of the manufacturers in the sample reported a recent downsizing effort, compared with 37.6% of the service providers. Within the latter category, non-profit firms proved more secure for workers than profit-making organizations: Just 30.1% of the

Exhibit 1
Corporate Size (in Sales) and Business Type of Organizations Responding to the American Management Association Downsizing Survey

| Business Type | Annual Sales | | | |
	Large (+$500M)	Mid-size ($50 to $500M)	Small (Under $50M)	No Answer
Manufacturing	56	139	162	8
Service (for profit)	61	96	153	24
Service (nonprofit)	12	81	163	8
Other	25	47	80	12
No answer	1	0	2	4
TOTALS:	155	363	560	56

nonprofits downsized, compared with 43.1% of the for-profit service companies.

Policy and Philosophy

Respondents were asked to choose one of the following three policy statements on job security:
- Profitability is more important than job security; realities of the marketplace control the company's ability to offer employment.
- Job security is important, and the company will make reasonable efforts to retain employees during economic downturns.
- Job security is important for morale and productivity; the company will do anything it can to avoid layoffs.

As anticipated, the middle course proved most popular: 53.5% of survey respondents agreed that they would make "reasonable efforts" to avoid reductions in force when business slows down. But nearly twice as many respondents (29.6) checked the third option—"the company will do anything it can to avoid layoffs"—as the first (16.0).

Companies live by their philosophies. The 515 companies that actually downsized in the previous

18 months gave markedly different answers than did companies untouched by workforce reductions (see Exhibit 2).

Exhibit 2
Responding Organizations' Position on Job Security

Company Policy on Job Security	Respondents That Downsized in Previous 18 Months	Respondents That Did Not Downsize in Previous 18 Months
Profitability more important than job security	24.1%	9.2%
Company will make "reasonable efforts" to retain employees	56.3%	51.0%
Company will do anything possible to avoid layoffs	18.8%	38.5%
No answer	0.8%	1.3%

The middle ground holds in both sample segments, but at the ends the responses vary widely. Perhaps the most informative single figure is the following: Nearly 20% of the companies that would do "anything possible to avoid layoffs" nevertheless turned to workforce reductions.

Smaller companies proved more committed to avoiding layoffs than larger ones: A third of the sample's small firms would do their utmost to avoid layoffs, compared with 25.6% of the mid-size companies and 23.2% of the large ones. And nonprofit service companies were most firm in their resistance to downsizing, with 46.2% checking the "anything possible to avoid layoffs" option, compared with 23.1% of the for-profit service concerns and 25.2% of the manufacturing firms.

Offers of Assistance

Respondents were given a checklist of services that companies often provide to discharged workers. The services ranged from early retirement incentives, which proved the most popular tactic, through job redeployment loans and benefit extensions to renegotiation of union contracts, reported by only a handful of respondents. Significant results for each service follow:

1. *Early-retirement incentives.* Forty-five percent of the survey respondents that downsized in the period studied offered such incentives to exempt workers, and 31.3% offered them to nonexempts. Among all respondents, large firms are twice as likely to offer early retirement to both managers and hourly workers, and manufacturers led the service sector in offering such incentives by a narrow margin (33.7% vs. 28.3%).

2. *Job redeployment/retraining opportunities.* Among respondents that actually downsized, managers were as likely to receive deployment and retraining offers as hourly workers. Just over 35% of respondents that had downsized afforded such services to both exempts and nonexempts. However, retraining has proven far more popular with large companies: Two-thirds of them would retrain hourly workers in future force reductions, compared with one-third of the small firms.

3. *Job-sharing and part-time employment.* A far more attractive option for hourly workers than for managers, job-sharing plans for nonexempts were used by 31.1% of the firms that downsized. Just 18.3% of respondents offered the option for exempt personnel. For managers, job sharing is a far livelier option among service companies. One-fourth of the service organizations polled would plan job sharing for exempt workers in any future force reductions; only 15.1% of the manufacturing firms would do so.

4. *Voluntary lack-of-work programs.* A comparatively new entry in the lists, lack-of-work programs (in which employees voluntarily take "no work no pay" days while continuing to receive pay for days on which they do work) were organized for hourly workers by 30% of companies that downsized, and for managers by 18.3%. The data offered no substantial difference in the popularity of such programs among large and small companies, although manufacturers proved more likely than service organizations to organize such a program.

5. *Outplacement services.* Selectivity was an issue in this category. The questionnaire asked if outplacement services would be offered to selected levels or job categories, or across the board to exempts and/or nonexempts. Respondents proved far more likely to offer outplacement aid to selected categories of managers; 40.5% said they would do so, compared with 26.2% who said they would offer outplacement to all managers. Where hourly workers are concerned, the figures reverse: A fourth of all respondents would offer outplacement aid to all exempts, while just 16.5% would help only selected nonexempts.

6. *Exemption of severance pay beyond normal policy provisions.* Managers received more of such benefits than did hourly workers when workforces

were reduced. Forty percent of the respondents that downsized extended severance pay beyond normal limits for their terminated managers; only 27.2% did so for hourly workers. Among all respondents, a third would extend severance pay for managers, compared with 21.4% that would do so for nonexempts.

7. *Extension of health benefits.* The gap closes in this category when compared with severance pay policies, but managers still receive greater consideration than do hourly workers. Among companies that downsized, 41.9% extended health benefits for their terminated managers, compared with 32.8% that did so for hourly workers. Similar gaps occur everywhere in the sample whether it is viewed in terms of corporate size or in relation to business activity (although the gap is larger among manufacturers).

8. *Salary reductions across the board.* When companies consider this option, they do so both for managers and for hourly workers in nearly equal degree. Among the whole sample, 25.9% of respondents would impose salary reductions for exempt workers, and 23.2% would seek pay reductions for nonexempts. Those that have actually downsized favor the tactic slightly less: 22.9% report salary reductions for managers, while 20% have them for hourly workers.

9. *Union-management committees on force reductions.* Just 8.1% of sample respondents would form such a committee to deal with downsizing. Manufacturers are no more sanguine about the prospects than are service firms; 13.6% of large companies would organize such a committee, but only 5.7% of small firms would do so.

10. *Renegotiation of union agreements.* Few respondents would choose to open this particular Pandora's box. Overall, only 12.3% of the sample would enter renegotiation to deal with imminent downsizing. Large firms and manufacturing concerns would be twice as likely as others to begin

union negotiations anew, but in no segment does the number rise above 18% of the sample.

Downsizing: Ready or Not?

Preparedness is a different issue altogether from the specific actions that companies might or might not take in a downsizing phase. The AMA questionnaire put the question directly: "In your estimation, how well prepared is your organization to deal with a major downsizing and outplacement effort?" Just over half of the respondents said they were well prepared for a workforce reduction, but nearly as many (43.6%) said they were not (see Exhibit 3).

Exhibit 3
Responding Organizations' Degree of Preparedness for Downsizing

Degree of Preparedness for Downsizing	Respondents That Downsized in Previous 18 Months	Respondents That Did Not Downsize in Previous 18 Months
Very well prepared	14.2%	8.9%
Well prepared	51.1%	36.6%
Not well prepared	38.7%	37.4%
Badly prepared	5.4%	14.6%

Obviously, experience is the best teacher: Two-thirds of the companies that downsized consider themselves well prepared for another round, while less than half of the firms with no recent downsizing believe they are prepared for the event. In addition, nearly 30% of companies that reduced workforces in the past 18 months plan another downsizing effort in the coming year—far more than the 46 firms in the sample that have not downsized in the past but plan to do so.

Downsizing: The Ultimate Human Resource Strategy

By Steven H. Appelbaum, Roger Simpson and Barbara T. Shapiro

Human resource management is a dynamic system which strives to manage the careers of people through the phases of time. As part of its strategic efforts, the company must monitor for environmental changes and adapt to them simultaneously, and it must adjust to employees' needs at different points in their careers. This attempt to find a balance between the internal and external spheres of an organization demands constant reassessments in so far as company objectives or strategies are concerned.

As such, a downsizing project is but one of many responses open to the company in its attempt to gain an edge or maintain its performance level. Even then, post-implementation monitoring and evaluation are two important determinants of success. It will not help the company who has gone through a successful downsizing process to lose the battle because of apathy and lack of constant readjustments. Proactive management equals long term commitment and adaptability. This is a key element in the human resource management strategy for effectiveness via the medium of downsizing. This article sets out, in detail, certain steps that can be undertaken which will contribute to the successful implementation of downsizing.

Introduction

In the aftermath of the recession from the 1970s a new reality has taken root within the North American psyche with regard to employment—job security is a thing of the past. Cost and other competitive considerations on both a national and international level have induced companies to stay "lean and mean" in order to maintain a better balance between effectiveness and efficiency. As such, the concept of job security and the counter-effect of employee loyalty has eroded. What implications

Reprinted by permission of *Business Quarterly*, published by the School of Business Administration, University of Western Ontario.

this has to the future of employee-employer relations remains to be seen.

This article will examine the issue of downsizing and suggest a strategic model which management can use to incorporate the many considerations related to downsizing into its strategic planning process. Essentially the responsibility of all management levels, its inception and development must necessarily originate from top management—its implementation largely the concern of the human resources division. In this instance, the role of the human resource manager becomes especially crucial since downsizing, in the final analysis, deals with and revolves around the employees in an organization.

Downsizing is the (systematic) reduction of a workforce by an employer in a variety of ways—usually as a result of some external considerations such as losses, cashflow difficulties and technological changes. Techniques used may include hiring freezes, early retirement programs, transfers and terminations, with variations on each.[1]

Coined originally in reference to scale-downs in car sizes by automobile manufacturers, downsizing was applied to the process of cutbacks when businesses and government agencies began making major reductions to their employee base as a response to recessionary pressures.[2]

Causes of Downsizing

The need for downsizing may be influenced by many factors, such as:

- Acquisitions and mergers leading to excess personnel once operations have been consolidated.
- Technological innovations resulting in productivity improvements with less human intervention.
- International competition leading to product and employee redundancy.
- Slow economic growth and a rapidly changing market-place resulting in the need to be cost competitive.

The biggest single culprit, however, can be traced to the recession of the late '70s and early '80s. Until then, most employers had recognized the cyclical nature of the economy (hence, businesses) and had accepted the periodic existence of surplus employees. From time to time, most employers have had to cut staff—but often on a temporary basis until some crisis is over. The recession ended that.

When the purse strings become tighter and employers began looking at the possibility of cost reductions, employees were an accessible target since they were within management's sphere of control as well as comprising a major proportion of production costs. Companies went on crash diets in search of greater efficiency. With the slimming process went the idealism of the benignly Parkinsonian past—to be replaced by a rude introduction to the tough new world of bare knuckle competition.[3] Downsizing became a new permanent philosophy with employers realizing that they can get by with less.

Meanwhile, public sector streamlining came as a result of pressure from taxpayers, who, feeling the pinch of higher taxes, called for cutbacks and reductions in services. Connected to this was an ever-growing national deficit which led to both public and political demands for spending curtailment. Such demands culminated in changes to the underlying employment structure of people delivering the services.[4]

In some U.S. companies, the strong performance of the dollar in the international money markets has also contributed to the necessity of downsizing. Kodak, for instance, which earns 20% of its revenues abroad, has taken a beating because of exchange rates—cutting about 9% of its Rochester workforce through layoffs and early retirement programs. This, in turn, led to major repercussions on the economy of Rochester which was a major Kodak town.[5]

Effects of Downsizing

With the increase in downsizing, major repercussions on both a macro and micro level usually follow. On a societal front, it has increased the pressure on the unemployment and welfare programs as the number of unemployed have grown. On a more personal level, downsizing has had a traumatic effect on the individuals concerned. Many cases of individual depression/hardship—not only in an economic sense—have been reported, especially in terms of lost confidence through the loss of their old job and their inability to get another one. This has been hardest on older persons who lost jobs in the last few years of their working lives, often after many years of service to one employer.

Similarly, the impact on "survivors" has been just as traumatic.[6] Increases in the levels of stress, conflict and role ambiguity along with dissatisfaction with supervisors and co-workers and decreases in job satisfaction do not augur well for the company—leading to possible decreases in the level of co-ordination and motivation within the workplace and hence, performance of the organization. Findings have reported that after the downsizing has occurred, the organization goes into a depressed state—with a general tendency to be very lethargic. After an initial upsurge in productivity, survivors settle into a condition of fearful expectancy.[7]

Not all the effects are negative, however—increased efficiency and cost competitiveness are two common results. Less bureaucracy and a more streamlined chain of command within management have led to increased flexibility and speed in decision-making. In essence, reductions in the number of managers have led not only to increased cost efficiency but also to a more effective organizational decision and control structure—with overall improvements in job satisfaction.[8]

From a cost perspective downsizing can be very expensive, but the long term benefits can be very substantial. Dupont, for example, spent $125 million in the first quarter of 1985 but expects to save $230 million each year. Union Carbide spent $70 million for an estimated annual recurring savings of $250 million. Clearly with such costs, long term staff reductions are required to recover the initial outlay. Herein lies the necessity of developing a downsizing effort which would be in alignment with the company's strategic plans.

Downsizing and Strategic Planning

The need for and experiences with downsizing have led to the realization that a better integration of human resource planning into a corporation's strategic planning processes is necessary for a company to remain effective and efficient—i.e., competitive. Downsizing has provided many painful lessons—especially in human costs—where companies have allowed organizational planning to fall out of alignment with the realities of the marketplace. Many of these companies' planning activities were not sufficiently proactive to allow for timely and strategic responses to changing conditions. More and more companies are developing strategies that clearly link human resources to long term market and organizational considerations.[9] Similarly, strategic planning has moved from the confines of top management to incorporate operational level contributions as a way of decreasing uncertainty and increasing control. Line managers now often formulate and implement policy with fewer guidelines and more flexibility.[10] In essence, although strategic planning is still recognized as the key to successful restructuring and survival, it must have as an adjunct human resource planning.

An interesting development emerging from the downsizing experiences concerns the target groups involved. Along with employees at the operational levels, middle and even senior management have also been targeted for streamlining. Advances in information technology and the need to be more responsive have moved the chief executive closer to the forefront of things—thus eliminating the need for multiple layers of middle management. Some companies have eliminated several management layers totally and now have new leaner organizations with a more effective staff support, larger spans of control and fewer organizational levels.[11] The result has been greater residual efficiency.

Implementation Experiences

It would do well to remember at this point that companies do not exist in a vacuum—rather they function within a large societal framework with accountabilities to various legal and labor-relations constituencies, not to mention the company's policies and employees as well. As such, downsizing attempts should also be planned and implemented with this in mind. Many companies have reacted quickly and traditionally by cutting what they considered to be expendable functions such as planning and public affairs. Others adopted a more cautious approach and went through planning exercises before making any cuts. Regardless of orientation, there is consensus that varying degrees of regulation, industrial characteristics and diversified markets militate against neat, all-inclusive theories of reorganization. However, no matter what the circumstances are surrounding a downsizing effort, certain steps can be undertaken which would help contribute to its successful implementation. Before a model for downsizing is presented, a capsule summary of ten steps needed in this process is provided to yield a quick cursory view of this complex and intricate process. These steps are common to some organizations and do not have supporting documentation described in the model.

Ten Steps for Downsizing

Step One: Develop a plan and manage it—HR must lead.

From a conceptual standpoint, it would be helpful to have a downsizing plan. Some points to consider: how large the problem is, what skills are involved; whether your company is in a hiring mode or not; and the hiring situation in the surrounding community.

It is important not to fall into the trap of automatically thinking of terminations and layoffs. That may force you into a situation where you will have to develop a termination plan. Look at other options first. It is a lot easier to influence management to consider the other options in the beginning stages as opposed to when they lock (themselves) into a position.

Step Two: Define the future organization.

If a total closedown is anticipated, the future organization, of course, would be described as being "zero." If the business is to continue, this step would entail defining the new business level that is anticipated and describing the positions that would be needed (i.e., the types of jobs, number of jobs and skills required).

Step Three: Define the affected groups.

During this step, you are basically assessing what groups are involved, or affected, by whatever kind of transition you are planning. If some form of future organization is anticipated, it is the difference between the present staff and the staff of the future organization.

Step Four: Identify the people who will need placement.

Guidelines to follow: (1) if a job or group(s) is eliminated, the incumbents will become a surplus; and (2) if a group is reduced, those with the least seniority will become surplus but "critical skills" will be protected. In terms of item No. 2, there is a justification process.

Step Five: Plan for staffing the future organization.

Things to consider: (1) job incumbents keep their jobs if the job will continue as is; (2) employees with the most seniority (if qualified and possessing critical skills) will be included in the new group if the old group is to be reduced; (3) plan staffing of unfilled jobs (presumably, those created as a result of firing "documented poor performers"); and (4) analyze your demographics (age, sex, race, etc.), and then adjust the staff.

Step Six: Create placement opportunities.

This step is not one that has to be sequential—it can be done throughout the process. Its purpose is to soften the impact of downsizing. "Inside" strategies that you can use include early retirement incentives, termination of "documented poor performances"; anticipatory "banking" of jobs (this relates to openings that become available once jobs freeze); openings at another location; and incentives for voluntary separation.

"Outside" strategies include soliciting placement opportunities at other companies (including vendors you use for supplies) and outplacement.

Step Seven: Develop process facilitators.

To help facilitate the downsizing process it is important to communicate with employees (share the bad information and the good; employees are going to do what they think is best for them regardless); involve both the line and HR function; have an empathetic, pro-active management; and emphasize the individual. Examples of this activity include résumé preparation workshops, interview coaching, and employee counseling.

Step Eight: Allow reasonable time for placements.

Time is a big factor in determining whether your plan will work. If the boss comes in and says, "We've got to close down the plant. Reduce staff by 30% effective August 1st," you might as well start your layoff/termination program. You need to think in terms of three months at a minimum between notification and termination. Results should be monitored in case a "course correction" is called for.

Step Nine: Terminate or layoff, if necessary.

Early in the process, you should at least think about the possibility of terminations and/or layoffs. If you get into a termination mode, you have to be in a position to get from a placement list to a termination list.

Step Ten: Provide for a healthy, smaller organization.

To ensure the health of the future organization, good people should be retained during and after the reduction and your mission should be redefined. In terms of the former recommendation, employee recognition and career planning should be emphasized to build in the idea of "continuity of career."

Model for Downsizing

Although downsizing is a major strategic initiative for a company, it must have as an adjunct human resource planning. It cannot be implemented efficiently without the continuous participation and involvement of the human resource personnel. In effect, the role of the personnel manager becomes a crucial one since downsizing deals with and revolves around the employees in an organization. The attached model, while recognizing the importance of other factors crucial to the organization's success, is mainly concerned with people and as such, emphasizes the issue of downsizing from a human resource orientation. In point of fact, downsizing may be regarded as the ultimate personnel management experience.

The strategic human resource model is not complete in every detail; but it does, however, outline the principal steps that management—and the human resource manager in particular—would be involved in during the process. Exhibit 1 outlines this general model for downsizing (in modular form), the objectives, criteria (i.e. standards), responsibilities and considerations to be accounted for in a downsizing project.

Exhibit 1
Downsizing Model*

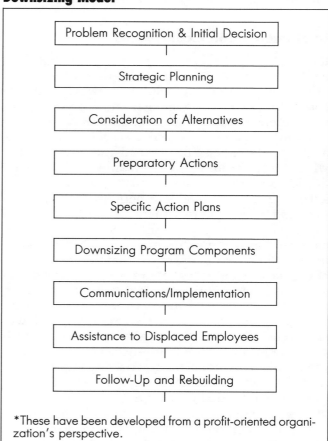

Problem Recognition & Initial Decision

Strategic Planning

Consideration of Alternatives

Preparatory Actions

Specific Action Plans

Downsizing Program Components

Communications/Implementation

Assistance to Displaced Employees

Follow-Up and Rebuilding

*These have been developed from a profit-oriented organization's perspective.

Step One: Problem Recognition and Initial Decision
The first step in a downsizing project is to recognize the need for it, that the problem is not some temporary aberration of the marketplace, but a permanent state of affairs. As such, an analysis of all factors relevant to the performance of the organization should be done before the decision to cutback is made. Standards of performance below that of contemporaries' or the existence of alternative investments which would improve performance given acceptable risk may be a signal for action. Such a decision would be the responsibility of service management and the various functional advisers.

Considerations
1. Has a thorough evaluation of the business been conducted?
2. Do the results indicate a long term downward trend?
3. Is there a particular element (unit, division, department) of the business that is performing significantly better or worse than others?
4. Does the analysis indicate a major reason for the trend—for example, lower productivity, excessive labor costs, technological changes?

The impact of the recession and a lack of proactive planning shocked many companies into realizing that they had grown fat, become less cost-competitive and hence, were vulnerable to competition. This led to a more proactive orientation—with increased awareness of and information-gathering on all factors and trends affecting the company. Once the need for downsizing is recognized the strategic implications must be analyzed.

Step Two: Strategic Planning
To ensure that the company stays within its strategic course, a review of its short and long term goals—in light of the downsizing decision—is called for. The strategic ramifications of such an action must be well understood. Certain areas of interest include future market possibilities, size and nature of the company, impact on the company's various constituencies, impact on the employees in question, impact on the competition, and cost and impact on the future profitability of the company. The best possible qualitative and quantitative information on the strategic impact should be obtained. Decisions to eliminate services and functions should be based on a positive assessment of their worth, not a reactive one. Finally, strategic plans should include realistic projections of human resource

needs for goal attainment. Such are the responsibilities of senior management and the board of directors.

Considerations
1. Have all priorities been re-examined?
2. Is a senior human resource representative a full member of the strategic planning committee?
3. Has there been adequate consideration of alternatives?
4. Was the planning conducted using well-balanced and objective analyses of the options?
5. Is there a clear corporate commitment to the new strategic direction outlined for the company?
6. Has the timing been considered? For example, will employees be released in a trickle, wave or flood?
7. Has it been approved by the board of directors?
8. Has an appropriately staffed executive team been created to oversee the downsizing process?

Top management support and commitment is a crucial precondition towards the successful development and implementation of any downsizing effort. The integration of human resource planning into a company's strategic and operational plans is equally crucial since any strategic revision must consider the future employment needs of the organization. One of the key steps to successful downsizing lies in defining the future organization—that is, defining the new business level to be anticipated and describing the positions that would be needed (for example, the types of jobs, number of jobs and skills required).[12] By managing people as a crucial resource within the entire organizational system, human resource planning helps give an organization strategic direction.

Step Three: Alternative Considerations
This step ensures that all possible alternatives to downsizing have been considered. Since terminations are expensive and may result in long term inability to attract the right people when the business picks up again, the company is advised to proceed carefully. Companies need to avoid falling into the trap of automatically thinking of terminations and layoffs; they need to examine other options (related to downsizing or otherwise) before locking themselves into a certain position.[13] Therefore, management needs to examine all other cost-effective alternatives to see whether these alternatives are strategically compatible with the long term goals and objectives of the company. This becomes the responsibility of all senior management and functional heads.

Considerations
1. Has consideration been given to cutting non-personnel costs, such as: postponing capital expenditure decisions, energy conservation, leasing rather than buying capital equipment, speeding up order systems to reduce inventories, budget reductions (for travel, education, memberships, etc.) and sale of unprofitable assets?
2. Has consideration been given to other downsizing alternatives, such as: a hiring freeze, pay and benefits freeze, reductions in pay and benefits, voluntary retirement, more hours/less pay and attrition?
3. If a voluntary retirement program has been considered, is the compensation in terms of pensions, cash payments reasonable?
4. Is the voluntary retirement offer likely to attract the employees the company wishes to let go, or will it also encourage key employees to quit?
5. If key personnel are lost through a voluntary retirement program, what contingency plans does the company have for replacing them?
6. Is a succession plan a key element?

This is a key step and clearly of strategic importance. As a major downsizing effort is expensive and not easily reversible, a thorough review of alternatives is necessary before the decision to cutback is made. Similarly, downsizing alternatives themselves must be carefully considered. In particular, voluntary retirement programs, if open-ended and generous enough to be of serious consideration, may end up encouraging those the company wishes to retain to leave, while not encouraging those it wishes to leave to go! Dupont, for example, had an open-ended program designed to cut some 6,500 employees but twice that number left, including 400 employees who had to be kept on the job until successors could be trained.[14] AT&T experienced a similar reaction to this process.

Step Four: Preparatory Actions
These contribute to the smooth implementation of the downsizing program and minimizes the risk of potential problems. In essence, management should ensure that their plans conform to all laws and regulations. As well, management should review all collective agreements with unions to decide on a strategy for dealing with them. A communication plan should be developed in order to deal with notifications to employees—both affected and unaffected—as well as to customers, suppliers, investors and communities so affected. These preparatory efforts are "process facilitators"—part of an empathetic, proactive management.[15] An analysis of these employees to be affected should be carried out in order to develop appropriate compensation plans, notice and follow-up action. A downsizing task force should be created with a clear mandate to resolve the issue within broad approved policies. This task force should include, as a minimum, the CEO, personnel manager, chief financial officer, chief operating officer (or plant manager), legal counsel and a pension and benefits consultant. Although these tasks are a collective responsibility, the role of the human resource manager is an important determinant of success.

Considerations
1. Has a legal advisor been consulted and retained?
2. Is there any legal impediment to the proposed action in terms of contractual obligations, timing, compliance to government regulations, etc.?
3. Has a tactical approach for dealing with unions been developed?
4. Has a communications policy been decided in terms of who will be notified and when?
5. Has a public relations strategy been decided?
6. Has personnel analyzed the groups and individuals affected? What relevant information is being provided to the planning group?

The development of such preparatory action will help determine the ease with which any downsizing effort can be implemented. In particular, communication linkages—both internal and external—should help reduce some degree of uncertainty and resistance to the changes, and, hence, increase acceptance.

Step Five: Specific Action Plans
The objective here is to ensure that strategic decisions have been translated adequately into tactical plans covering all aspects of the problem. Comprehensive action plans should be prepared to avoid issues "falling through the cracks." The downsizing task force has the responsibility of deciding on what to do where, when, how and with whom.

Considerations
1. Have the affected employees been identified? Have appropriate selection criteria been used—such as job analysis, performance appraisals, division profits, realistic forecasts and human resource planning model-outputs?
2. Have key employees to be retained been identified?
3. Has a decision been reached on whether terminations will take place individually or in groups?

4. Has a specific plan been developed to deal with employees to be terminated in terms of ongoing support and placement opportunities? Will there be job search assistance, counseling, job search workshops, communications with other potential employers, block advertising and outplacement services?
5. What of those employees targeted for termination who pose a security risk (e.g., theft, sabotage, property damage)? How does the organization minimize such potentially negative reactions?
6. Has a program been designed to reassure non-terminated employees for the purpose of restoring morale and reducing possible drops in productivity?
7. For those to be terminated, have seniority, critical skills, succession plans, and poor performance which has been documented been taken into account?
8. Has responsibility for termination action been delegated to the individual(s) who will do the job?
9. Has training and preparation been given to the "terminators" to reduce the stress factor on them?
10. Has an appropriate compensation program been developed and costed for each affected employee concerning the total downsizing effort?
11. Has the implementation timing of the plan been decided on?

Companies downsizing should form task forces to develop strategies and tactics.[16] An early step may be to retain legal counsel to advise on the myriad number of laws and regulations. Affected groups must be defined and people needing placement determined.[17] Employees might initially be identified on a unit to unit basis, but some may be valuable and should be retained. Key variables to consider may be possession of critical skills, qualifications and seniority. Similarly, employees to be terminated should be identified. Computer simulation models reflecting current and future manpower needs may be used to facilitate this process.[18] Although low performers should be the first to go, there is literary consensus that low performance should not be given as a reason for broad downsizing. In the final analysis, these decisions will have to be undertaken within the broader framework of the organization's strategic plans.

The creation of various programs such as job search workshops, placement services and counseling designed to ease the impact of downsizing, can help by reducing the demoralizing effect of layoffs and terminations. Equally important will be those efforts geared at maintaining morale and productivity levels among those retained by the company. To this end, reassurance and closer communications between the human resource manager and employee(s) concerned may be imperative. An interesting extension of this was practiced by Monsanto to help facilitate its downsizing project.[19] Through extensive interaction and exchanges between the Human Resources Department and employees, management was able to gain a better understanding of what employees wanted and were concerned about. This, in turn, provided management with an expanded range of alternatives for dealing with them.

Step Six: Downsizing Program Components
Essentially a check on the previous step, this ensures that people affected are dealt with in a humanistic and equitable manner and in accordance with all laws and agreements. The company should attempt to reduce the stress on management and employees as far as possible through the provision of an adequate program of financial compensation, moral support and job relocation assistance. An equitable plan will minimize the damage to the corporation's reputation and ensure that future generations of employees will not be negatively influenced by the current situation. This is the primary responsibility of the human resource manager and chief financial officer—albeit with the approval of the CEO and board of directors.

Considerations
1. Has the company researched compensation plans used by other companies in similar situations and used them as a basis for measuring the effectiveness of the company plan?
2. Is the company plan equitable in terms of financial compensation, given the company's situation? Does it recognize length of service, the likelihood of re-employment, pension rights, unused vacation allowance, temporary continuance of benefits packages (life and health insurance), legal rights, contracts and agreements and government regulations?
3. Has a program been established to provide counseling, relocation assistance, outplacement services, etc.? What are the eligibility requirements for these—universal or selective?
4. Has the company contained information on government training programs, unemployment insurance, etc., for the information of affected employees?

5. Have key employees whom the company wishes to retain been identified and notified under conditions of strict confidentiality?

6. Have these key employees been reassured as to their value to the company? What other efforts have been made to rebuild confidence, support and trust?

Going beyond the creation of "process facilitators," these considerations are designed to soften the disruption of cutbacks through the provision of fair and considerate remuneration, both economic and non-economic, to terminated and non-terminated employees. Although surviving employees must be reassured, they should not be informed of the decision in advance, unless absolutely necessary, to avoid leakages and possible disruptive behavior. Research has revealed mixed outcomes when it comes to this. On the one hand, some feel that to forewarn the company's constituencies (e.g., union) too early is equivalent to forearming them.[20] Since this is an area where a prescriptive approach is not reasonable, management must decide on the basis of the individual circumstances.[21] Similarly, severance payments depend upon the specifics of the situation (company's profitability, type of plan, etc.). The company, however, must meet both the statutory (provincial and federal) and common law requirements as well.

Step Seven: Communication/Implementation
Although communication is an extremely important component throughout the downsizing process, it becomes especially crucial towards the end. Termination announcements, especially, must be both timely and effective. This step ensures that adequate communication is made to all affected individuals at the appropriate time. Termination plans should be kept confidential until the decided time for action. Actual announcements should be to groups of employees, not individuals. These should be kept factual and short. After the initial announcement, however, a meeting between the human resource specialists and individuals should be called to explain briefly to each person his/her severance pay, benefits accrued and, where applicable, pension package. Such is the responsibility of the taskforce and terminations personnel. Meanwhile, the human resource department should prepare for these announcements in addition to the personal details for each of the affected employees.

Considerations
1. Has the planning been conducted in sufficient

secrecy so as to avoid the negative effects of the internal "grapevine"?

2. Are all announcements to be carried out simultaneously or in accordance with a pre-determined plan?

3. Have communications to those affected been made in an unambiguous manner?

4. Are the reasons for downsizing clearly communicated emphasizing the company's (economic) predicament as the factor, not individual performance?

5. Have the general terms and conditions of the decision been clearly communicated? When will it take effect?

6. Will there be written confirmation following the announcements outlining the severance arrangements?

7. Are employees aware of the on-going support programs available?

Essentially the hardest part of the process, it is also the shortest. Those responsible for terminating activities will be under a great deal of stress as they terminate friends and colleagues often after many years of working together. Announcements should be short and concise. The announcer should ideally be a line manager with authority to release employees. The simultaneous announcement of terminations will help reinforce the message that "economic necessity" rather than "individual performance" is the sole reason for termination. The general terms and conditions of the decision along with information of support programs should be announced. The manager should avoid any personalized discussions during the initial announcements since the objective here is to emphasize the collective impact of the problem. Individual meetings will come later. Finally, extra security measures should be undertaken to avoid any potentially negative reactions in the immediate aftershock of the termination if this is felt to be necessary.

Step Eight: Assistance to Displaced Persons
To ensure that the trauma of separation is minimized as much as possible, various programs to assist displaced employees should be put into effect. Counseling seminars, job search workshops and placement services are especially important now. Such attempts to reduce the impact of the cutbacks on a personalized level will help both the affected employees and the company to adjust to the changes. As such, it is an important part of the healing process for the company—not to mention the preservation of its reputation as a responsible employer within the employee and general community.

Basically the responsibility of human resource management, these programs must have the support of senior management to be effective.

Considerations
1. Will there be counseling seminars? job search workshops?
2. Will selected employees be offered outplacement services?
3. Will space be made available where employees can go to prepare their résumés, applications? Will there be secretarial assistance? For how long?
4. Will relocation counselors be provided?
5. Will references be provided?

The aforementioned are but a few of the activities which the company may want to consider. Many other alternatives are available for helping terminated employees. The selection of specific programs will depend on the situation in question.

Step Nine: Follow-up and Rebuilding
To ensure the successful continuation of the organization, focus must now fall on those remaining in it. The productivity and morale of surviving employees have to be maintained at a high level during and after the cutbacks. Management should work actively on re-building confidence, support and trust in them. Similarly, the company must actively rebuild its image in the community. As many communities are directly (and indirectly) affected by downsizing, a public relations program designed to rebuild confidence is essential. Public Relations and Personnel play a key integrative role here.

Considerations
1. Does the company actively counsel retained employees to reaffirm their value to the company?
2. Is there an effort to clarify new roles and responsibilities so that attitudes change from reactive to proactive?
3. What of training or re-training programs for survivors based on their new responsibilities and identified need?
4. Has the company developed a broad public relations plan which outlines its reasons for downsizing and intentions in the foreseeable future?

This is an important part of the process. The same amount of time and effort that was spent on the actual staff reduction must now be devoted to rebuilding confidence, support and trust. Management must be visible, honest and supportive during this highly unstable period.[22] Communication will facilitate this reassurance process. Particular attention must be paid to the remaining employees since they are now the best performers, the ones who stand the best chance of getting a new job if they chose to leave.[23] It is equally necessary that survivors are immediately notified of their retention with undue emphasis on the fairness of treatment for those departing and the organization's future potential.[24] Above all, management must deal openly and honestly with all questions including the possibility of future terminations. A new strategic plan should be "planned for" at this juncture to address the future.

Equally important is the need for re-building the company's image in both the local community where it is located as well as the broader community of shareholders, customers, suppliers, competitors, financial institutions and the business world in general. Since much of a business' successful continuation depends on the confidence it inspires in the community, a very careful public relations plan is required to explain the company's point of view and to build renewed confidence in its future potential.

References/Endnotes

1. Ellig, Bruce, "Pay Policies while Downsizing the Organization: A Systematic Approach," in *Personnel,* May–June, 1983.
2. Levine, Charles, "Retrenchment, Human Resource Erosion and Role of the Personnel Manager," in *Public Personnel Management,* Fall, 1984.
3. Nielsen, John, "Management Layoffs Won't Quit," in *Fortune,* October 28, 1985.
4. Levine, *Op. Cit.*
5. Nielsen, *Op. Cit.*
6. Kiechel, Walter, "Managing a Downsized Operation," in *Fortune,* July 22, 1985.
7. *Ibid.*
8. Luce, Sally, "Human Resource Policy under Pressure: Learning from Restraint," in the *Canadian Business Review,* Spring 1983.
9. McDowall, Duncan, "Restructuring the Organization: Sharp Cuts and New Directions," in *Canadian Business Review,* Autumn 1985.
10. *Ibid.*
11. Luce, *Op. Cit.*
12. Jenkins, Robert, "Downsizing: Is it Possible to Reduce Staff Without Layoffs?", New Orleans, ASPA, June 1986.
13. *Ibid.*
14. Nielsen, *Op. Cit.*
15. Jenkins, *Op. Cit.*

16. Bullock, K., Stephenson, T. and Kellogg, "Downsizing: Opportunities and Dilemmas," in *Cost and Managemant,* July–August 1985.
17. Jenkins, *Op. Cit.*
18. Ellig, *Op. Cit.*
19. Jenkins, *Op. Cit.*
20. Bullock, *Op. Cit.*
21. Lippitt, Gordon and Ronald, "Human Downsizing: Organizational Renewal versus Organizational Depression," in *Advanced Management Journal,* Summer 1984.
22. Bullock, *Op. Cit.*
23. Kiechel, *Op. Cit.*
24. Adamson, B. and Axsmith, Murray, "Managing Large-scale Staff Reductions," in *Business Quarterly,* Summer 1983.

Bibliography

Ames, Charles, "Downsizing Your Company to Meet New Realities," in *Industry Week,* February 18, 1985.

Axsmith, M. and Adamson, B., "Managing Large-scale Staff Reductions," in *Business Quarterly,* Summer 1983.

Bullock, K., Stephenson, T. and Kellogg, "Downsizing: Opportunities and Dilemmas," in *Cost and Management,* July–August 1985.

Campbell, Alan, "Can Service Reorganization Reorganize the Low Prestige of the Public Service?" in *Public Management,* February 1978.

Carter, Craig, "Fewer Frills, Less Space to Reduce Costs" in *Chain Store Age Executive,* December 1980.

Drucker, Peter, "Planning for 'redundant' workers" in *Personnel Administrator* (reprinted from the *Wall Street Journal,* September 25, 1989).

Ellig, Bruce, "Pay Policies While Downsizing the Organization: A Systematic Approach," in *Personnel,* May–June 1983.

Fletcher, Mike, "How to Reduce Employee Dissatisfaction While Downsizing," in *Industrial Management,* May–June 1983.

Greenhalgh, L., "Maintaining Organizational Effectiveness During Organizational Retrenchment," in *Journal of Applied Behavioral Science,* Volume 18, No. 2, 1982.

Grescoe, Paul, "Why MacMillan Bloedel's Close Shave with Disaster is Over (knock on wood)," in *Canadian Business,* September 1983.

Jenkins, Robert, "Downsizing: Is it Possible to Reduce Staff Without Layoffs?", New Orleans, ASPA, pp. 110–111.

Kiechel, Walter, "Managing a Downsized Operation," in *Fortune,* July 22, 1985.

Levine, Charles, "Retrenchment, Human Resource Erosion and Role of the Personnel Manager," in *Public Personnel Management,* Fall 1984.

Lippitt, Gordon and Ronald, "Human Downsizing: Organizational Renewal versus Organizational Depression," in *Advanced Management Journal,* Summer 1984.

Luce, Sally, "Human Resource Policy under Pressure: Learning from Restraint," in *Canadian Business Review,* Spring 1983.

McDowall, Duncan, "Restructuring the Organization: Sharp Cuts and New Directions," in *Canadian Business Review,* Autumn 1985.

Mosena, D.R., "Downsizing Gracefully," in *American Planning Association,* January 1984.

Nielsen, John, "Management Layoffs Won't Quit," in *Fortune,* October 28, 1985.

O'Hanlon, Thomas, "Less Means More at Firestone," in *Fortune,* October 20, 1980.

Smith, M.E., "Shrinking Organizations, a Management Strategy for Downsizing," in *Business Quarterly,* Winter 1982.

Tauper, Y.D. and Ertl, J.J., "Incentives to Retirement," in *Employee Relations Law Journal,* Summer 1984.

Van Sumeren, M., "Organizational Downsizing: Streamlining the Healthcare Organization," in *Healthcare Financial Management,* January 1986.

The Downside of Downsizing

By Anne B. Fisher

"There were a couple of months where we sat around and worried all day," says a former CBS employee recalling the network's cost-cutting drive last spring. "Then we started to worry that we were worrying too much, so we went back to work for ten minutes. Then somebody would call up and say, 'Did you see the papers this morning? Are you getting laid off?' So we'd go back to worrying again."

Does this sound familiar? Do people around your office seem more detached than they used to be? Do they come up with fewer bright ideas? Do they spend a lot of time murmuring in the corridors or in each other's offices, and clam up when someone walks past?

If so, they are suffering from a widespread ailment. Call it middle-management malaise or the leaner-and-meaner blues. Its cause: the dismissal of more than a million Americans from management and professional jobs over the past five years.

The malady needn't be fatal. Many companies have come through a restructuring in strapping shape, and their experiences provide some surprising lessons in motivating the survivors. Executives should be prepared, for example, to train particular energy on matters that may seem insignificant or irrelevant—a wildly improbable rumor or some burned-out light bulbs in the hallway.

Too often, say many middle managers, senior executives won't even recognize the malady, or they dismiss it with remarks like "What's everybody sniveling about? They still have jobs, don't they?" But nervousness and gloom cost money, which some companies have tried to estimate. In last year's second half, when Bell & Howell was buffeted in a three-way takeover skirmish and reports of impending layoffs flew, sales representatives in the field spent half their time on the phone with pals at headquarters in Chicago trying to keep up with the gossip, and everybody else was too distracted and dispirited to work much. Bell & Howell executives figure that the resulting drop in productivity

may have dragged the company's profits for the half down as much as 11%, or $2.1 million.

Nor are the costs of discontent always a once-and-done thing. Consider Bethlehem Steel's experience. The company began hacking away at its 89,000-person work force in 1980 and by the end of 1987 had chopped it in half and then some, to 33,400. Amid all the fear and confusion, the United Steelworkers of America in 1984 had no trouble signing up many of the remaining salaried employees at Bethlehem's plants. Until then only one plant, in Lackawanna, New York, had a number of white-collar union members, and productivity there was "notoriously bad," says a former Bethlehem executive. He adds: "So now the company is saddled with about 700 salaried unionized employees at other locations."

Managers by the thousand have joined a union called Me First. A survey of about 1,000 readers by *Industry Week* magazine last June reported that 60% of middle managers say they are less loyal to their employers than five years ago. Another study, by the management consulting firm Hay Group, says that in 1979 almost three-quarters of middle managers were optimistic about their chances for advancement. By the end of 1987, mainly because of layoffs and restructurings they had seen, only about one-third still thought their futures looked sunny.

That sense of diminishing expectations naturally makes employees far more willing to jump ship if the opportunity arises. Says William Morin, chairman of Drake Beam Morin, a New York-based outplacement firm: "The old cradle-to-grave psychological contract—'If I work hard, the company will take care of me'—is absolutely gone." He notes that 15 years ago a manager worked for an average of only two companies in his or her career. Today the average is closer to seven and appears to be rising.

The decline in dedication has particular resonance for any company undergoing or planning a job-slashing overhaul. Consultants, pundits at business schools, and beleaguered managers agree on one point: You are not going to get gung-ho performance from a bunch of scared, resentful, mistrustful people. "No matter how good your strategy is," warns consultant Michael Cooper of the Hay Group, "if your employees don't get behind it, you will keep on losing market share to Japanese and Western European companies, where employee commitment is generally still quite high." Put another way, how companies cope with motivating the remaining troops could make the difference between ending up leaner and more competitive and just ending up leaner.

The first and most crucial point to remember is that employees can't embrace the new strategy if they don't know what it is. Sometimes, as when Ford began to recast itself in 1980, there's a self-evident goal: survival. A longtime Ford executive observes, "When you've just reported a $1.5 billion net loss, nobody wonders why you have to cut back." Usually, however, the reasons for a structuring are murkier. "The toughest thing to explain is why you see a need to trim your sails when your markets are booming," says James Baughman, a former Harvard business school professor who is manager of corporate organization, executive compensation, and management development at General Electric. His job for the past seven years has included explaining why Chairman Jack Welch sold more than 200 businesses, spent $11 billion to buy 300 new ones, closed 73 plants and facilities, and lowered the head count by more than 100,000, to 302,000.

Now GE is shrinking its defense businesses in anticipation of a less hawkish mood in Washington over the next few years. Says Baughman: "When you do something like this, morale does suffer because employees ask, 'Why now, when things are going so well?' The thing you must keep emphasizing is that you're making changes because of market realities—not whims, caprices, or internal politics. Everything has to be clearly tied to a specific advantage you expect to gain in the marketplace, whether it's now or three years from now."

Consultants, who are building a tidy business advertising panicky managers on how to inform and inspire jittery employees, say that top management must get out there and communicate a compelling vision of the future. This vision should explain exactly where Ostrich Corp. is headed and precisely how it plans to get there.

Top managers who won't or can't articulate a vision are fairly common and cause much bitterness. One seasoned middle manager, kept in the dark by his bosses about the purpose and extent of a staff cutback in his department, took a couple of star performers with him when he was dismissed. Says he: "Employees are not little children. They are adults who can handle information. If you feed people all kinds of lies and evasions, naturally they will resent you." Be as honest as you possibly can, say those who've been there. If you don't know something, or you do know but SEC rules or other legal constraints have momentarily sealed your lips, come out and say that. Silence is the worse policy.

A frank and continuous flow of information can keep the rumor mill from spinning out of control and enable workers to concentrate on business. AT&T, which has shed 66,000 staffers in the past four years, learned that the hard way. Top management began a series of missteps by confiding to Wall Street security analysts that the company was planning massive job cuts. The analysts, always a gabby group, put the word out, and many AT&T employees read all about it in the newspapers before their bosses had a chance to fill them in. That brought business to a screeching halt for weeks, while people speculated about what was coming next. Amid the uncertainty, at least two middle managers killed themselves.

Once the layoffs began, gossip—fueled by fear and untempered by any insights from the brass—ran wild. Says a former AT&T manager: "No on in top management stepped forward and said the rumors weren't true. Nobody told us anything official at all, in fact. So the grapevine went berserk." AT&T has been striving ever since to divert people's attention back to their work, but it isn't easy. Burke Stinson, a district manager at headquarters in New York, says wistfully, "We've tried a lot of things, but morale around here is still unacceptably low."

In the effort to communicate what's really going on, technology can be handy. Ford maintains an in-house television network to broadcast a steady stream of up-to-the-minute company news plus talks from Chairman Donald Petersen. Bethlehem Steel during its drastic downsizing beamed a constantly updated electronic newsletter to every employee within peering distance of a computer terminal.

The medium of choice is a series of personal appearances by a real live senior manager, preferably one who can and will field questions from the crowd. Choose these emissaries carefully. At BankAmerica, where the payroll has shrunk by 24,000 since 1984, the personnel department made executives audition for the part.

"You can't give people mush," says Robert Beck, executive vice president for human resources. "You have to be willing to say, 'Look, we have to tighten our belts now because we had too many shipping loans,' and so on. At the same time, though, you don't want somebody out there stressing doom and gloom. We had one senior VP who would go out and try to discuss things with the troops, and word came back, 'Hey, don't send this guy again, he's pouring gasoline on the fire, everybody's all upset.' So we didn't send him anymore." Beck gave would-be ambassadors two chances to practice their spiels. Anyone who came across, he says, as "condescending or evasive or too pessimistic" got other assignments for the duration.

In-person pep talks can be particularly tonic when your company's uncertain fate keeps turning up in the newspapers, day after suspense-filled day. Says a former Bell & Howell manager who had a ringside seat for last year's takeover drama: "Management does look foolish, and employees do get jumpy, if the top people are closemouthed while everybody outside is yakking away."

Salomon Brothers' plan to close down its municipal finance department last October leaked to the press on a Friday. The New York *Times* printed the story on Saturday, which put a crimp in the weekends of everyone in the department. Chairman John Gutfreund wasted no time in calling a mass meeting on the trading floor first thing Monday morning. That clearly had a calming effect, especially when those who were departing realized what munificent severance packages they'd be taking with them. Notes one insider, a trifely enviously: "Some of these people don't have to think about looking for another job until five years from now." The morale-boosting message to those who remained: We will be shrinking a bit, but don't worry, we're not trying to hide anything, and we'll still treat you well.

Let's suppose you've conceived a brilliant market-driven strategic vision and explained it in clear and ringing terms to every last employee in the company, from the boardroom to the mail room. You've been as frank as you could be, you've tried to answer everybody's questions, you've even responded to what's turned up in the media. Can you stop talking now? No. The companies whose restructurings have caused the least disruption in morale and productivity are those whose managers, top and middle, have kept right on preaching the new gospel long after the last layoffs ended and the rumors died down. Says GE's James Baughman: "You know you're there when the boss is explaining the situation and employees start interrupting him to explain it to *each other*. I've seen this in some places at GE, but in general we aren't there yet."

Crucial as communication is, how employees bounce back from a restructuring depends on a few other things too. Actions speak louder than words. Above all, say managers who have been through the downsizing mill, the people being let go must be treated with respect, kindness, even solicitude. That sounds idealistic, but in practice it is less a matter of human decency than of hard-nosed pragmatism, because the employees who remain will be watching closely to see how the laid-off are treated. Notes a Midwestern manufacturing company manager who had had to lay off a number of people: "If you're nasty to the people who are leaving, morale takes a terrible dive because those who stay conclude that they're working for a bunch of sadistic idiots."

A sure, and common, way to create this disastrous conviction is to conduct wholesale massacres. Horror stories abound. To take just one: When BHP Petroleum was cutting back its oil and gas operations in Houston a couple of years ago, the company called a meeting of the entire staff. Each employee was given an envelope with A or B written on it. Then the B's were sent to another room—and told they were being laid off. "A mass firing is always humiliating and dehumanizing," says a Houston headhunter who helped some of the refugees find new jobs. Have the courtesy—and the guts—to lay people off in private, one by one.

While you're at it, try not to gloat. One reason morale and productivity sank so low at AT&T was that many managers, in letting people go, conveyed the message, "I'm still needed around here and you're not. Nyah, nyah, nyah." Muses AT&T's Stinson: "Some managers do tend to keep their own ego candle lit by blowing out somebody else's."

Some quite talented people won't work alongside a boss like that. Star managers—the ones you want to keep, the ones you're counting on to help you realize the aforementioned brilliant market-driven strategy—are often remarkably softhearted creatures, easily unnerved by signs of unwonted managerial meanness. Since they are also the most readily employable elsewhere, they may wander off just when you need them most.

In the past few years, companies and consulting firms have amassed a formidable body of hard-won knowledge on how to keep stars in a downsizing. Money helps, and many newly restructured enterprises have offered bonuses, raises, stock options, or some combination of the three to handpicked squads of indispensable players. Money by itself, though, is rarely sufficient: Your competitors have it too. What stars really want is to be told that, yes, the company has a fantastic future, and if they just stick around, their own opportunities will be fabulous as well. "The most common mistake is to assume these people already know how much top management values them," observes Richard Belous, a labor economist at the Conference Board in Washington, D.C. "The fact is, they often *don't* know that. Someone has to explicitly tell them."

Arco's experience bears out that observation. When the oil company cut its work force by 6,000 in the summer of 1985, nobody at headquarters in Los Angeles mentioned to any of the most-valued managers that there might be good reasons to hang tight. As a result, when generous severance deals were offered all around, several stars took the package and ran. Their startling departures, says a manager who is still there, cause "an awful lot of extra drain and strain" at an already grim-enough moment.

Beyond the immediate problem of replacing him or her, a top-notch manager's defection can reverberate for years because future stars—stars-in-training, as it were—begin to eye the exits too. "The perception is, if top management can't persuade *him* there's a future here, maybe I shouldn't hang around either," explains a former West Coast bank manager who flew the coop when his boss did. "If you let people get the idea that the company is not just cutting back but is sinking into mediocrity, morale really goes to hell."

That threatened to happen at First Boston recently. After months of market losses, profit declines, layoffs, and assorted other upheavals, the Wall Street firm saw Bruce Wasserstein and Joseph Perella, the stars of its still robust mergers and acquisitions department, walk out to start their own shop. In mid-April seven stars of the leveraged buyout business quit to form a company of their own. First Boston's managing directors got busy giving energetic pep talks aimed at boosting spirits generally and at keeping future stars from joining their erstwhile chiefs' new ventures. Some staffers have listened and taken to wearing T-shirts to work that read: "Just Say No to Wasserstein Perella & Co." Demand for the shirts quickly out-stripped supply.

T-shirts may seem trivial, but consider a bit of industrial psychology that consultants say is often overlooked. First formulated by University of Utah professor Frederick Herzberg, the concept is known among academics as motivation-hygiene theory. The gist: In a time of much change and uncertainty, seemingly minuscule matters take on inordinate importance in people's minds. Litter in the employee parking lot, a lack of towels in the men's room, a small rip in the carpet that's been there for years—such are the things people start to dwell on when their overall faith in their superiors is shaky. Conversely, a modest pat on the back—an extra day of vacation, a really rip-roaring company party—can be enough to cheer people up and make them feel like working harder. "All kinds of details become highly charged symbols," says Randall Dunham, a University of Wisconsin industrial psychologist who counsels companies with debilitating morale problems. "So managers have to be almost overly aware of all the little stuff."

In one company that called on Dunham for advice, annual-job-performance evaluations that in previous years had come around like clockwork were suspended, without explanation, in the midst of a draconian downsizing. The decision signified nothing much, except that senior people were extremely busy just then, and management saw the lapse as no big deal. But employees, spooked by the usual lurid rumors, spent countless nonproductive hours fretting about *what it meant*. The entire staff was "a nervous wreck," Dunham recalls, and stayed that way until management, astonished by all the fuss, cleared up the mystery.

Severely morale-damaged companies may want to try a radical route back to health. A program called transformational leadership is the brainchild of Noel Tichy, who teaches organizational behavior at the University of Michigan's business school. Over the past 20 years Tichy has numbered Exxon, Chase Manhattan, Du Pont, Union Carbide, Citibank, and a dozen other huge companies among his consulting clients. He is now working with IBM. What sets his method apart is its emphasis on recognizing people's emotional response to change and loss. Tichy believes that a restructuring, replete with widespread layoffs, affects middle managers and their employees in much the same way as a death in the family or a divorce. "Unless you acknowledge a certain period of mourning as being normal and legitimate," he says, "you won't be able to do a new beginning properly."

In Tichy's workshops, employees are encouraged to get their grief out in the open. Only afterward do they progress to serene contemplation of the new order. The process seems to raise morale and bolster people's commitment, but it works best if management participates too. And therein, says Tichy, lies the rub: "Most managers are scared to death of emotion. It's a lot easier to put on a macho act and come across as a heartless cost cutter. But if you can't do the 'soft' stuff, as well as the tough stuff, you'll never get people's total support."

Tirelessly explaining what's happening, tactfully dismissing the departing, stroking star survivors, paying attention to minutiae, maybe even baring your soul—all of this and getting the actual work done, and with fewer people to do it? The trimming and reshaping of American corporations makes unprecedented demands on senior executives and on the dwindling number of managers in the middle.

"What we're talking about," says a consultant, "is all the normal traits of highly skilled management, only intensified." Or, as a mid-level executive at a *Fortune* 500 company puts it: "The good thing is that these days, if you're doing your job right, you haven't got *time* to worry about whose head will roll next." He's only half joking.

Running Lean, Staying Lean

By Robert M. Tomasko

Even with great attention to running a lean field organization and managing it with well-selected and trained general managers, the Roman empire crumbled. Some blame it on repeated onslaughts from leaner and meaner competitors from the north. Others say it was due to a bloated, high-overhead headquarters in Rome. Corporate empires, too, will crumble eventually if continuous attention is not paid to managing a company's size. Staying downsized can be a lot harder than getting there.

The slash-and-burn approach to streamlining may produce significant overhead reductions in the near term. And a combination of fear and adrenaline might even keep the survivors on a common course for awhile. But sustainable downsizing, in many cases, requires a complete rethinking of the logic behind a corporation's organization. It will also require use of computer networking and tools such as expert systems, as they are developed.

Most important, though, are the changes needed in human resource management. Career paths will need to change direction, performance appraisals must acquire teeth, and pay systems must eliminate their management bias. And paradoxically, to insure continual productivity improvements, more attention, not less, must be given to providing job security for employees of downsized organizations.

Networks, Not Conglomerates

To keep a business operating through a streamlined organization over the long haul requires lowering the walls between line and staff and among the various operating divisions. In addition, streamlined organizations must lower barriers to the outside world. In times of rapidly growing markets, limited production capacity, and plenty of business for all comers, it made a great deal of sense to put as many parts of the business under one roof as possible.

This was the era of vertical integration when Ford, the car builder, made its own steel and Greyhound, the bus company, built its own buses. The key to economic success and competitive outflanking was to own as many of the resources that went into the business as possible.

This era has ended for many industries. Companies now operate in a period of vertical disintegration, where competitive advantage comes to those not wedded to one source of supply or technology, where attempts to build corporate size through acquisitions of dubious synergy are no longer rewarded by the stock market. Organizations will resemble spider webs more than pyramids.

Lewis Galoob Toys Inc. does not look like a big company. To some observers it is a very alien form of business creature, but it did sell over $50 million worth of toys in 1985. The ideas for the toys are purchased from independent inventors or large entertainment businesses. Engineering and design work is handled by outside contractors. The builders of the toys themselves are selected by evaluating bids from the many toy manufacturers based in Hong Kong. These businesses in turn have most of the actual work done across the border in labor-cheap mainland China. Common carrier freight lines bring the finished toys to the U.S. where they are sold through a network of commissioned representatives.

The Galoob staff number a little more than 100, not even enough to include an accounts receivable department; revenue collecting is also contracted out. What does the Galoob company do? It managers a network of relationships. It is what the dean of the University of California at Berkeley's business school, Raymond Miles, calls "a switchboard instead of a corporation."

One of Galoob's competitors, Worlds of Wonder, the meteoric seller of Teddy Ruxpin talking bears and Lazer Tag, reached over $300 million in sales in less than two years of existence. With no time or desire to build a corporate bureaucracy, it adopted an organization network similar to Galoob's. It hired executives like Stephen Race, who typifies the new breed of general manager that is cropping up in more and more streamlined corporations. He learned flexibility and independence while a management consultant. One day he would be trying to influence a rust-bowl manufacturer to focus more on marketing than manufacturing, and the next he would be flying to Brazil to help a clothing maker improve profitability. This background also taught him skills useful in influencing people who work for different bosses in different companies. This skill is vital when one has to manage networks of contractors instead of subordinates.

Solar System

These "solar system organizations," as some observers call them, have outside suppliers orbiting around a small central corporate nerve center. They may not become *the* organization of the future, but they certainly will be among the types that add value without adding clutter. Companies like Worlds of Wonder and Galoob are in businesses where sales can shift as rapidly as the roller coasters their young customers ride; for them it can make good strategic sense not to get overcommitted to fixed assets.

This style of operating also makes sense for those who want to be driven by customer pull, not factory push. It has enabled consumer products companies like 315-person Minnetonka, Inc. (Softsoap and Calvin Klein's Obsession) to challenge and occasionally out-innovate giants like Procter & Gamble. It works when a careful analysis of value added and comparative advantage is done. This sort of planning has convinced many consumer electronics firms to leave the factory to someone else and focus their organization-building in marketing, sales, and distribution. Sometimes one company's low value added is another's high: California-based Flextronics concentrates on manufacturing, procurement, and customer service for electronics firms with complementary skills.

To get enough popular Teddy Ruxpin dolls built quickly enough, Worlds of Wonder had to make some in its competitors' factories. And this new twist to corporate networking is not limited to toy makers. To meet heavy demand, Chrysler is having some of its full-size cars built at an idle American Motors Corporation plant in Kenosha, Wisconsin. Lee Iacocca has decided it is better to rent a competitor's plant than build one he may have to shut down. Moves like this, and greater reliance on suppliers to preassemble the components they provide, are helping to build what Iacocca's lieutenant, Harold Sperlich, calls a company with enough mass

to be efficient, but small enough to be manageable. Ford has been following a similar strategy. Its president has decided to manage size as well as market share and be willing to "live with some shortage of our ability to get our full share in a peak year."

Make or Buy?

Giving up complete self-sufficiency may be hard for some companies, but for many it will be the only way to stay downsized. To preserve some of Du Pont's cutbacks the company is starting to buy rather than develop all its own technologies. A number of established companies have found it is useful to develop close relationships with embryonic "Silicon Valley-like" firms already at the state of the art in technologies they are interested in, and contract with them to do research and product development. This strategic partnering (in which the small outfits receive money not otherwise easily available to fund their growth) is more effective than trying to duplicate their innovative environments in the larger company. Also, it often yields better results than directly purchasing these start-ups, a move that too often drives the creative talent elsewhere.

Better Dead Than Alive

The corporate raider's traditional call to action, "This company is worth more dead than alive," could be better stated this way: Many individual businesses under a broad corporate umbrella will not be alive and kicking until their superstructure is killed off. Some companies have had a history of not letting this superstructure form: Hewlett-Packard, Johnson & Johnson, and 3M.

Others, such as Campbell Soup, have used a reorganization to limit its influence. Bankers Trust New York Corporation, long a typical banking miniconglomerate, has become one of the leading corporate investment banks by narrowing its scope, selling off its consumer branches, and focusing its organization on what it does best. Eastman Kodak has capitalized on its 10-percent workforce reduction, which included cutting its top management slots by 25 percent, by making a major overhaul in its basic organizational design. This historically integrated company was broken into 17 smaller, autonomous business units as a response to its chief executive's objective of finding a way to "make a big company act like a small company."

"How big is too big?" is a question many executives are starting to ask. The best answer is the usual, "It all depends," although some guidelines are starting to emerge. According to Alonzo McDonald, former president of Bendix, "When it comes to motivating people, you hit diseconomies of scale early." For some companies this has meant limiting divisions to 10,000 people, factories to 1,000, and offices to 100. While these numbers are arbitrary and need to be determined company by company, the principle behind them is not. Ralph Cordiner, who reorganized General Electric in the 1950s, felt it was important to keep a decentralized unit small enough that a good manager could get his arms around it.

Peter Drucker has taken this advice and expanded it a little, saying that the rule is that a small group of executives, "four or five maybe, can still tell without having to consult charts, records, or organization manuals who the key people are in the unit, where they are, what their assignments are and how they perform, where they came from, and where they are likely to go."

Even in Europe, the intellectual home of corporate bureaucracy, companies are starting to search for ways to prune back overgrown structures. To help arrest profit and market share declines, West Germany's global air carrier Lufthansa is planning early retirement and deployment strategies to allow it to eliminate management layers. The object is to build a company of profit centers around groups of interrelated air routes, instead of running Lufthansa as one worldwide, tightly integrated system.

Another German firm, Siemens, has already moved farther along on these same lines. For many years it has been known as "Ma Siemens," Germany's largest privately owned bureaucracy. Now, under the activist leadership of a new chief executive, large—but, in the European style, layoff-less—staff reductions have been made over a several-year period. To make use of the possibilities they offered, considerable management attention then went into creating meetings and other forums to bring together the managers and staff who develop Siemens products with those who sell and market them.

Who Needs Pruning?

Of course, some companies have always managed to stay lean. The innovative French resort operator, Club Mediterranee, follows IBM's rotation scheme as it continually moves generalist staff (but of the carefully specified "Club Med mold") between headquarters and field, as well as among its vacation villages.

Another French business also illustrates how a company can become big without becoming bureaucratic. Carrefour S.A., the $6-billion pioneer of the hypermarket concept (gargantuan stores selling food and other goods), keeps its company expanding and its organization lean by decentralizing as many functions as possible to their stores. A headquarters staff of less than 20 (including secretaries) guides the business. Almost half these people are involved in the human resource management function, one of the key ways Carrefour keeps control and insures consistency in its operations. Only one layer of management is between the central office and stores—a tier of regional managers. Each of these has, at most, five assistants.

Continual attention to employee training at all levels is what makes the lean structure work. In a typical year two out of every three workers receive some form of training; Carrefour spends more than 2 percent of its payroll costs on these programs. Providing the training is a responsibility of managers at all levels, not that of a separate staff development bureaucracy.

Individual departments within Carrefour's hypermarkets are fun as profit centers. The best-performing department in a given specialty throughout the Carrefour system, say casual clothing or frozen foods, is expected to play a key role in managing that specialty on a company-wide basis. This requires that, in addition to being responsible to a store manager for its own profit plan, this clothing or food unit will also help other clothing or food department managers select merchandise, train staff, and develop business plans. The lateral networks created by this cross-company interchange help tie what can easily become a very fragmented business together, and help maintain the small headquarters staffing over the long run.

'Soft' Controls

While it may seem that companies like Club Med and Carrefour are very decentralized, in fact the opposite is true. They stay lean by actually having more central control over their far-flung stores and resorts than do some companies that keep tens of thousands of employees all at one location. But they substitute "soft" controls (focused cultures, carefully selected employees, mandatory training) for the "hard" ones (staff, supervisors, systems). These companies all seem to manage by mission. At Carrefour, all employees are told they have responsibilities in four areas: people, merchandise, money, and assets. Job descriptions are built around these areas; training programs are keyed to teach the skills needed to perform in each; and performance reviews provide regular report cards on how well each is handled.

Across the Atlantic, Frederick Smith, founder of Federal Express, achieves similar results by making videos so he can be seen by his package carriers across the U.S. He continually emphasizes the importance to Federal Express customers of the boxes and envelopes they are handling. By stressing how critical the contents of these packages are to their recipients, he has turned what could be a routine delivery job into something that has an important mission attached to it. And this, along with an investment in a state-of-the-art information network, has allowed him to run Federal Express with far fewer managers than would be otherwise needed to provide the same consistently high level of service.

In addition to maintaining their lean management structures, companies that stay streamlined well into the 1990s will have found ways to keep the size and scope of their headquarters staffs in check. The experiences of Carrefour and others indicate this is possible, but it does requires some creative organizational redesign. A key to managing staff resources effectively is treating them less like overhead and more like actual businesses. Some companies have carried this philosophy further and found ways to turn overhead into profit.

In the past several years, an increasing number of companies, including Control Data, Morgan Stanley & Company, Parsons Brinckerhoff, Polaroid, Security Pacific National Bank, Union Carbide, and Xerox have turned carefully selected headquarters staff functions into businesses that sell their wares outside the home company. Control Data provides personnel services to other businesses for a fee, Parsons' public relations department has become an accredited advertising agency, and Xerox sells logistics and distribution services to customers of its reprographic equipment. Companies have several objectives in mind when doing this:

- Lowering overhead costs;
- Making profits;
- Building a broader staff service than their own company can afford alone;
- Bringing more of a customer orientation to their headquarters staff; and
- Retaining high performers by adding new challenges to their jobs.

The objective of all these reconfigurations of the corporation is to increase management's value added while decreasing management costs. Paul Strassman, former strategy planner at Xerox, calculates that American management productivity is fairly weak. His measures of return on management indicate the managements of most U.S. companies are barely paying their own way. The purpose of steps such as corporate networking, vertical dis-integration, selling staff services, and buying instead of making is to increase this kind of return significantly.

Human Resource Planning, Not Personnel Administration

Maryann Keller, an automobile industry analyst, has had many opportunities to compare the Japanese and American ways of managing. She notes, "The Japanese regard cost control as something you wake up every morning and do. Americans have always thought of it as a project. You cut costs 20 percent and say: 'Whew! That's over.' We can't afford to think that way anymore." This warning certainly applies to downsizing as well. Without making changes in the way the size and shape of corporations are managed, it will be business as usual and mid-level bloat will return. These are partially people issues, but the job is far bigger than the scope of the traditional personnel function. Issues in organizational planning involve power and strategy more than good relationship-building and administrative procedure.

Staying streamlined requires, in most companies, a strengthened human resources function.

This does not necessarily imply a bigger staff department, but more attention being paid to human resources management by senior executives and line managers. Planning and monitoring the size and shape of a company is a general management responsibility, not something that can be delegated easily to a staff unit. It is something that needs to be closely related to the business planning process.

In recent years there has been considerable talk, and minimal action, about the importance of closely integrating human resources and strategic planning. In most companies it is unrealistic to expect the initiative for this to come from the personnel experts, though they certainly have a valuable role to play in the linkup. Leadership on this, if it is going to be kept from being just another staff-talking-to-other-staff activity, has to start at the top. Much of the detailed planning is also best left to senior line managers, some of whom will have had experience working in the human resources function at some point in their careers.

As they prepare to stay downsized over the long haul, it can make sense for some firms to move the training function out of the personnel area and group it with other culture-building and control units such as finance, information systems, and communications.

Even with redeployments such as these, there is still plenty the human resources group can do to keep the company downsized. Here are a few of the key action areas:

• *Make it hard to get hired.* Develop detailed selection criteria for new recruits that take into account their fit with the overall company culture as well as the requirements of the job. Deliberately understaff: Use contractors and part-time employees as buffers to even the swings of cyclical businesses. Continually look for ways, short of hiring people, to get low value-added work done.

• *Make it hard for poor performers to stay.* Put real teeth in the performance review process. Adopt a single simple system that can be applied from top to bottom of the company. See that it evaluates a small number of performance targets that are linked to each job's mission. Also ensure that how a person accomplishes a job is rated as well as what is accomplished. Obtain relevant inputs to the process by having managers rated by their subordinates and staff by their internal customers, as well as by their bosses. Use the results of the reviews primarily to improve performance, not to distribute salary increases.

• *Slow down the upward-only fast track.* Design career paths that cover more horizontal territory than vertical, that include more functional specialties than hierarchial levels. Try to keep people out of mid-level and senior staff jobs until they have had some experience in the line organization. Limit appointments to key line executive positions to managers who have spent some of their careers in the human resource function. Do not assume all good performers will stay for their entire careers; over-invest in training.

• *Keep the pay system from building excess management back into the company.* Adjust aspects of the compensation and job evaluation systems that lead to bloated management organizations. Look hard at two-track pay scales—but be sure the non-management side applies to all staff professionals, not just R&D types. Consider applying skill-based pay to staff workers; examine the possibility of customizing your job evaluation criteria to match the skills essential to your company's basis of competition.

Providing Job Security: The Downsizing Paradox

Downsizing is clearly a shock to most of a company's employees. They may have built expectations over many years of service that they had proved themselves, passed some sort of tenure point, and now had jobs for life. Breaking the bargains, spoken or implicit, that were formed has been one of the most wrenching aspects of downsizing—and one of the most disruptive. James Olson, AT&T's chairman, asks: "Do you know how tough it is asking people to support your strategy when you know you can't promise all of them jobs when this is over?" Olson certainly has an uphill battle to fight, as do other companies trying to build commitment to a new strategy at the same time as they face continuing staff reductions. At General Electric, CEO John Welch has had to eliminate one-quarter of GE's jobs. For the 350,000 remaining he has redefined what it means to work at GE: "The job of the enterprise is to provide an exciting atmosphere that's open and fair, where people have the resources to go out and win. The job of the people is to take advantage of this playing field and put out 110 percent. . . . The people who get in trouble in our company are those who carry around the anchor of the past."

Welch's view is a good statement of the way the employer-employee bargain is being redefined in many downsized businesses. Planned downsizers, like GE, as well as companies that have been less focused in their reductions, have a sometimes elongated period of transition and consolidation to go through while reshaping their organizations, systems, and strategies. Strong leadership from the top of the company, like that Welch provides, is essential to moving effectively through this period. But at the close of this period, many companies may find it advantageous to rethink something paradoxical to the ideas of downsizing: managing the company to provide as high a degree of job security as possible for those remaining. At post-downsized Apple Computer, temporary help is used to staff up to 10 percent of jobs. Michael Ahearn, Apple's staffing manager, says: "If we bring someone on board full time, there is an implied obligation that the job won't disappear."

Sony of America vice-president Samadi Wade provides a Japanese-eye view of what happens when workers and managers are continually concerned about how long their jobs will last: ". . . I understand why some American companies fail to gain the loyalty and dedication of their employees.

Employees cannot care for an employer who is prepared to take their livelihood away at the first sign of trouble."

Of course, IBM is one of the American companies that has taken this point of view to heart. It defends its costs and inconveniences by citing concrete benefits to its business, such as its ability to cut two-thirds of the cost of product manufacturing through the skill and smarts of its workforce. They maintain these achievements would have been impossible without the productive and committed workforce that their full-employment practices help produce.

Other employers committed to providing employment security, like the Lincoln Electric Company, cite the same benefits occurring for the same reasons.

Many U.S. manufacturers have found the secret to getting continual productivity improvement is making sure the people who you expect to deliver it know that in doing so they are not paving their way to an unemployment line. This is a view that applies in the office as well as the factory, to staff professionals and middle managers as well as assembly workers. And it is one that companies concerned about staying streamlined, not just temporarily lean, can do much worse than to consider.

Balanced Attention to All the Corporation's Constituencies

Many private-sector executives have become as skilled at balancing competing interest groups as seasoned members of Congress. Most know that the myth of the company as a short-term profit maximizer is just that, and that they must constantly respond to multiple constituencies. Coping with the sometimes conflicting demands of government regulators, unions, employees, supplier cartels, local communities, Wall Street, shareholders, retirees, and customers requires statesmanship coupled with a strong sense of direction. This sense of direction, their view of the company's overall mission, is something that cannot be learned in business school. Executives develop, personalize, and pull together teams to support it throughout their careers. As a management tool a sense of direction is critical as companies try to ensure their futures. Getting by through playing off competing interests may make for an exciting career, but will not necessarily build a business that will prevail. This kind of corporate gamesmanship is doomed to failure because what may be in the immediate best interests of one constituency will not always

even serve this group, let alone the others, over the long haul.

Through most of the 1960s and 1970s the stock market rewarded companies that maintained strong growth rates—often through unrelated acquisitions—and achieved ever-increasing earnings, even if the latter were generated by the underinvesting in base businesses. Sticking to one's knitting was considered dull, and usually went unrewarded. By the mid-1980s the piper had to be paid.

Many companies had lost their competitive advantage to more focused overseas rivals, and inflated corporate structures were strangling both profits and good ideas for the future. And the always short-term-oriented stock market switched to favor value generated by lean companies having equity returns better than any nearby safer alternative. The restructuring this has led to has caused more turmoil than many industries have seen since the Depression. Some companies with clear missions and purposes are taking advantage of it to reposition themselves to provide sustainable value for their customers. Others' reactions are more keyed to immediate fears of corporate raiders and today's price of capital. They are still leaving themselves open to being tossed around by the concerns of the moment.

Mission-driven businesses, like Apple Computer, Chrysler, TRW, and Xerox, are no strangers to restructuring or the downsizing that frequently accompanies them. But through careful planning and follow-through they have built organizations that are stronger, not just smaller. While not losing sight of the stock market, they also have not ignored their employees' needs. Corporate missions are built on the interrelated needs of all the constituencies mentioned before. To the extent those of one group must be emphasized for a time, a "correction" in corporate attention will eventually occur and provide attention to the requirements of the others. These companies work hard to avoid the bitter criticism of one veteran oil company manager: "We used to be a community . . . . Now it's clear there is only one important group—the shareholders." Planned downsizers, while reacting to immediate pressures, are preparing for future challenges by not forgetting the employees they will have to count on to meet them.

A Demographic Kicker

The demographics of the 1980s have been a challenge for many companies and managers. The post-war baby boom generation reached middle management age just at a time when restructuring-driven downsizing eliminated many of the positions they hoped to move into. Companies that have responded to this by pruning back their organizations *and* working hard to provide job security for those selected to remain will be one step ahead of the others in having loyal and committed people to deal with the demographics of the 1990s.

While the U.S. workforce grew by 2.6 percent in the 1970s, this rate will slow to 1.1 percent by 1995. The coming of management age of the "baby bust" generation will lead to shortages, not continued surpluses. Companies will be running lean because they have to, not because they want to reduce overhead. These shortages already have reached industries dependent on workers just entering the labor market. In many regions of the U.S. the minimum wage is something to laugh at. While redeployment of the aging baby boom workers will absorb some of the slack and making better use of women, minorities, and retirement-age managers will also help a little, the going will not be easy for many companies.

The New Employment Contract

By Chris Lee

Once upon a time, the working world was a predictable place. You went to work for a company and were more or less adopted into a stable system. You worked hard, but were well rewarded for your efforts. Because you were loyal to The Company, you earned regular promotions, an increasingly better standard of living and a secure future.

A fairy tale? By today's standards, yes. During the last five years, former bastions of job security—*Fortune 500* companies, banks, utilities—have downsized, restructured and merged themselves into radically different shapes. Managers and professionals who were once almost guaranteed employment, if not regular promotions, have lost their jobs. Meanwhile, the survivors struggle to adapt to a shifting environment.

The result of these changes, according to some observers, has been a rending of the "employment contract" between companies and their employees. To be sure, the traditional expectations shared by employer and employee usually were not formalized by an unbreakable, written document. But there was an implicit agreement about the way the game would be played. The employee provided loyalty, dependability and a fair day's work in exchange for a fair day's pay, a shot at the boss's job and a secure future.

Today, few—if any—companies can assure current or future employees of career stability, advancement or even a job. Employers are reacting with uncertainty, while employees are reacting by suing employers for unjust termination or by quitting and remaining on the job. Social scientists are reacting by decreeing that the problem deserves more study. All the players realize the rules of the game have changed. But no one can be sure what will replace them.

There's been a lot of discussion here about the old and new employment contract—what it was and what it's becoming. In our [company], we've said,

'If you do a good job, you'll be taken care of.' Now, we find we can't fulfill that contract, that implied understanding that has been ingrained in our culture.

J.E. Reller
General Manager, Staffing Technologies
Control Data Corp.

Control Data Corp., well known for its progressive employee-relations policies, is one of a handful of major corporations that demonstrates its commitment to job security. Although it never *guaranteed* no layoffs, it designed a "rings of defense strategy" in 1980 to protect permanent, full-time employees. The rings of defense guarantee that before employees lose their jobs, overtime will be eliminated, work subcontracted to outside vendors will be brought inside, supplemental or temporary employees will be laid off, and attrition will be encouraged through hiring restrictions and early retirement.

When the double whammy of the computer slump and increased competition hit CDC, however, the rings of defense collapsed. The trickle of layoffs that began in 1985 rapidly turned into a flood that swept away nearly half the work force by the middle of this year.

Today the slimmed-down company faces a collection of daunting tasks: outplacing employees, reassuring survivors, and rethinking its paternal approach to job security and employee development. "We're trying to help people understand that no one—no company, no government entity—can guarantee employment," says Reller. "High-tech companies like us have been on a rapid growth curve, with multiple opportunities for everyone. Now we're experiencing real trauma trying to adjust to no change—growth has declined, promotions have declined, raises have declined."

CDC is examining its changing employment contract against the backdrop of deeply held principles that emphasize its commitment to employee security and development. "We're in the process of trying to evaluate changes at CDC with these principles in mind," explains Joe McGregor, general manager of human resources planning. "We're working to figure out what will be in the 'new' contract. It's evolving; we're not yet sure ourselves what is going to happen."

Through its strategic planning process, CDC is trying to answer two abiding questions: Where are we now, and where are we going? According to McGregor, thoughts thus far center on a few new realities, including the shift from a growing to a shrinking mode and the switch from a permanent to a temporary, flexible work force. But perhaps the dominant truism for CDC—and every other business—is that stability and predictability have turned into change and uncertainty.

Control Data may be one of the few organizations looking carefully at the changes wrought in the employment contract in the wake of the past few eventful years, but it certainly is not alone in resorting to massive work-force paring. Over the past five years, at least 13 million jobs have been eliminated in the United States, according to a *Forbes* magazine estimate. The Bureau of Labor Statistics puts the toll of lost executive, managerial and administrative jobs over the same period at 500,000.

Like the body counts of a war half a world away, distant news of yet another massive layoff or corporate downsizing has lost its power to stun. But the shock waves resulting from the upheavals in the corporate landscape ripple throughout the work force, creating a cumulative effect that can only be estimated.

The key issue in American industry today is not just downsizing as such, but the effect downsizing has on the consolidation of the company, the decentralization of authority, on managerial systems, and on the morale and performance of the streamlined work force.

Jerome M. Rosow
President
Work in America Institute

A symposium sponsored by the Work in America Institute last spring examined the impact of downsizing and restructuring on American business. In his keynote address, Rosow characterized the massive downsizings of the past few years as "the ripping apart of a social contract" between companies and their employees. Top HR executives at several leading companies explained why they're cutting back their work forces and what they're doing to avoid sacrificing the survivors' morale and commitment.

Prior to the turbulence of the past few years, professionals at General Electric were practically assured of job security, while the company was assured of employee loyalty. "That bond has been broken in the '80s," said Frank Doyle, senior vice president of corporate relations at GE. But he described his company's "delayering" in terms of a new social contract that can benefit both employee and employer.

For the company, Doyle explained, the payoff for breaking that bond is increased flexibility and efficiency in fulfilling its "fundamental economic mission—producing goods and services at the best quality and lowest possible cost. We will perform that mission better if we take steps not only to reshape the management structure, but to extend to employees that same kind of dynamic flexibility we've begun to demonstrate as employers."

What will that flexibility mean to GE employees? According to Doyle, more versatile jobs, the chance to use a broader base of skills and greater participation in decision making.

At AT&T, known for "cradle-to-grave careers," three downsizings in as many years produced a huge culture shock. Hal W. Burlingame, senior vice president of personnel, told the symposium audience that the cutbacks, totaling about one-third of AT&T's work force, followed several other major upheavals: divestiture, deregulation and the revolution in communication technologies. Initially, AT&T stuck to the old rules—even though it was in a whole new ball game.

"The business that built itself into an institution by creating universal service for telephone customers tried to create a universal approach to its people," Burlingame explained. "That mind-set strongly influenced some of our decisions in the early days of downsizing. We began to realize that our concept of fairness and equity, where everyone was treated the same and we had no formal means of differentiating effectively between individuals or skills when we made cuts in the work force, was not always the most fair for the business or its people. Not was it appropriate in terms of the markets we were addressing.

"As we became more market-focused," he continued, "we realized that we had to devise ways of holding onto the 'critical skills' people—both management and occupational—who would serve us in the future."

In 1986, when the third downsizing took place, AT&T changed its approach. This time, people who were "keepers" were told they had been selected to stay. People who were at risk knew they were at risk. Through it all, AT&T learned to look at human resource management in strategic terms, Burlingame said. "And that is the most effective way to build a new relationship between AT&T and the people who comprise it.''

The experiences of these corporate giants raise more questions than they answer about the new employment contract. Having made the decision to shrink your work force, how do you make sure essential employees don't cut and run? Can you expect to engender a sense of loyalty and commitment from employees once you've ''broken faith''? What kinds of payoffs will employees value in place of traditional job security?

While companies in the throes of major change struggle to find answers, social scientists have discovered that their corporate soul-searching is justified. Recent studies that track the impact of new workplace realities across organizations have uncovered some alarming trends.

Job satisfaction for middle managers has dropped so precipitously that it is now close to the abysmal levels reported by clerical and hourly workers, proclaims a report from the Center for Management Research in Wellesley, MA. Citing a recent Hay Group/Yankelovich/Clancy Shulman study, this report also points to a decrease in commitment to The Company, diminished career aspirations, and a dwindling sense of job security, particularly among mid-managers and professionals.

These findings echo those of a 1984 Opinion Research Corp. report, ''Supervision in the '80s: Trends in Corporate America.'' ORC, which has been sampling employee attitudes since 1970, uncovered an emerging paradox: While most employees remain highly satisfied with their jobs, their opinions of their companies are steadily declining. ORC found these attitudes hold true across employee classifications: managerial, supervisory, professional, clerical and hourly workers. At the same time, when ORC asked employees if they are committed to their companies' growth and success, at least seven out of 10 said they are.

These seeming contradictions, ORC's report concludes, indicate that employee commitment is out there, but it is not being effectively mobilized. To do so, ORC recommends that organizations:

- Understand employee work values. Management must know what employees value in their jobs in order to tailor rewards to these values.
- Let employees know what the standards of job performance are.
- Tie performance to rewards and clearly communicate the links between them to employees.
- Provide effective performance evaluations.
- Give supervisors and managers the tools they need to manage—training in communication and appraisal skills, support from management for their actions, authority consistent with their responsibilities and reasons to be committed to the organization.

Our national resource, which is also our national problem, is an almost unbelievably large number of educated, motivated and competitive people striving to achieve both traditional and nontraditional kinds of success. Traditionally, they want increasing amounts of responsibility, money, power, status—all the things that come with promotion. Nontraditionally, they also want their work to expand their minds, fulfill their souls and encourage their personal growth—all the things that come from unending challenge. Unfortunately, there aren't all that many such jobs around; and, as the numbers show, it's not going to get much better.

Judith Bardwick
The Plateauing Trap

The ''national resource'' to which Bardwick refers is, of course, the much-examined baby boom. This bulge in the demographic python has been straining the institutional resources—schools, colleges, hospitals—of this country since the 1950s. Now the squeeze play is on in the workplace. The fact that the boomers' entry into management ranks corresponded with an era of downsizing and decreasing opportunities only exacerbates the impact of both. Clearly, the fact that more people are competing for scarcer promotions demands some changes in the ''growth potential'' clause of the employment contract.

''Most of the baby boomers have gone as far as they will go in management and will stay in their present jobs another 30 years or so,'' wrote Peter Drucker in an essay in *The Wall Street Journal* in 1985. In order to create a better match between their career aspirations and reality, he continued, ''we will have to redesign managerial and professional jobs so that even able people will still be challenged by the job after five or more years in it. . . . We will have to heap responsibility on people in junior positions. And, above all, we will have to find rewards and recognition other than promotion—more money, bonuses, extra vacations . . . and so on. In the meantime, however, an entire generation has grown up for whom promotion is the only 'real' satisfaction and failure to get one every year or two is equivalent to being a 'loser.' ''

How are employers reacting thus far? some have begun to explore a new direction in career development, one in which the primary responsibility for an individual's career belongs to the individual, not the career development specialist form corporate human resources.

Control Data is just beginning to incorporate this change in emphasis into its orientation program for newly hired employees. It also plans to create a career-management center that will help individuals map out their options—examine their values, update their skills, anticipate career shifts in the future—before they are displaced or simply decide they are misplaced in their current jobs. "Before, we never said, 'Your career is your responsibility,' " says Reller. "Now, our feeling is that 70 percent of the future is the employee's responsibility and maybe 30 percent or less is the company's. We want them to think about that."

Tod White, president of Blessing-White, a consulting company in Princeton, NJ, that specializes in career development, says the old idea of a tidy career path is obsolete, particularly in large companies. "There are fewer rungs [on the career ladder], more qualified and competent 25- to 35-year-olds, and more competition for fewer slots," he says. At the same time, the volume of change—downsizing, restructuring, acquisitions—has increased exponentially. In many organizations, he points out, the people are the same, but all the rules have changed. Increasingly uncertain and anxious employees are asking, "What does all this mean for my career?"

In fact, more employees are more likely to get stuck in jobs they have outgrown. They become dissatisfied, quit their jobs or, perhaps even worse for the organization, quit and remain on the job.

"It's up to the individual to find new kinds of job satisfaction," says White. "The individual has to take the initiative. But it behooves the organization to help employees deal with those concerns. If employees are anxious and confused, the organization is not getting the productivity it needs." He sees the new direction in career development as a partnership between the individual, his or her manager and the organization. Managers play a central role by answering some tough questions about the individual's future in the organization, but it's still incumbent on the individual to *ask* the questions.

Sam Campbell, a principal with Kearney Campbell & Associates, a consulting firm based in Prescott, WI, agrees with White's assessment of shifting career development strategies. "I think there's a really healthy part to this," he says. "In the past, too many people were lulled into complacency about their careers and career planning. Now, they realize they have to think more about their careers. The superior performers always did."

Campbell, who recently retired from Honeywell after more than 20 years in human resources, knows whereof he speaks. He was one of the primary movers behind the company's jobs and relationships studies. (See "The Honeywell Studies: How Managers Learn to Manage," *Training*, August 1985.) "[Successful managers] told us, 'There are other people just as competent as I am. I just wanted it more.' We called these people self-initiators. Three forces were at work in their careers: self-initiation, boss-initiation and organizational initiation."

Honeywell researchers concluded that an individual's boss needs to act as a mentor, trainer and coach, and the organization needs to sponsor some kind of developmental activities. But according to Campbell, self-initiation was by far the most important factor. "If that didn't happen, none of the rest mattered."

Until fairly recently, the primary unwritten contract in the American workplace offered material well-being and the status of being a breadwinner in exchange for a limited commitment to jobs that were often dull and unrewarding. But it is clear that this kind of contract will not be adequate for a high-discretion/high-expressivism workplace."
Daniel Yankelovich
and John Immerwahr
Work in the 21st Century

Expressivism is the term Yankelovich and Immerwahr use to identify the values of what often is called the "new work force." These are the baby boomers who want intangible rewards from their jobs, such as the chance to express themselves and fulfill their potential as individuals. "Those who adhere to the values of expressivism place great emphasis on autonomy and freedom of choice, reacting uneasily to most forms of rigid hierarchy and to lack of involvement with decision making that affects their lives," the authors explain.

In *Work in the 21st Century*, the authors report on research conducted by the Public Agenda Foundation that explored people's "core relationships" to work. The findings lead Yankelovich and Immerwahr to conclude that the philosophy of expressivism is on the rise and that it will continue to increase. "Our survey shows that expressivist jobholders . . . are much more likely to want freedom about how to do their work, and they are much more concerned with creativity. They are also less concerned with economic security."

A yearning for autonomy, individuality and self-expression. It all sounds as though the values of the "new work force" were custom-designed to match the demands of the new contract being drafted by today's lean and mean workplace.

Other researchers, however, call the idea of the new work force a "myth." Charles Hughes, co-founder of the Center for Values Research Inc. in Dallas, has been collecting data on employee values for 15 years. In his data base of half a million people, he says, "I see very slight changes in values. The data does not support any dramatic change."

Hughes classifies the majority (60 to 70 percent) of the work force into two types: conformist, characterized by the traditional work ethic and loyalty to the organization, and tribalistic, characterized by a desire for security and a preference for paternalistic management.

Where does this leave the idea of the brave new work force? "Oh, the new age is coming," he says, "but slowly, very slowly. Values vary tremendously by location. If you go to a plant in Tuscaloosa, you'll find plenty of people with tribalistic values; go to Bell Labs and you'll find zero. People who are talking about [the new work force] today are not collecting data. They might be talking to managers or vice presidents, but not to workers on the third shift in a factory."

David Jamieson, president of Los Angeles-based Jamieson Consulting Group, has been monitoring the impact of the changing work force on organizations for several years. He thinks the downsizings and restructurings of the last five years have *forced* people to think in new terms. "People look at their working environment and they see that the old trust and loyalty no longer carry any weight. They are reexamining their security needs in light of their value needs."

In Jamieson's view, the members of the new work force do not see themselves as powerless victims in the evolving employer-employee relationship equation. "The employer used to be able to say, 'Here's your salary; your soul is ours.' We're past that now." People know that a company is unlikely to meet their security needs, so the company's ability to meet their "value needs" becomes proportionately more important. Traditionally, employees scrutinized employers in terms of the job, salary and location offers, Jamieson says. Now the employer's offerings of flexible benefits, continuing education, training, child care and other benefits that meet lifestyle needs have become more important trade-offs.

"Employees have become more critical shoppers, and they are shopping for the best 'contract,'" he says. "They have begun to draft the contract in terms of: 'I am leasing my behavior to the organization. What do I want in return?'"

Given economic uncertainties, a growing number of people are finding their smartest career "buy" may be in a small company, where they have the chance to be a bigger fish in a smaller pond, develop a wider range of skills and maintain greater flexibility in career options.

David Birch, author of *Job Creation in America: How Our Smallest Companies Put the Most People to Work* (Free Press, 1987), and a team of researchers at MIT spent seven years mapping out the changing landscape of American business by tracking trends in a data base of 5.6 million companies. He credits small companies (those with fewer than 100 employees) and start-ups with most of the 9 million new jobs created since 1980. This leads him to conclude that small companies are the most vital part of our economy today.

Small companies, although volatile and uncertain by nature, actually offer better odds for job security than large ones, he contends. "The *Fortune 500* have wiped out jobs equivalent to the entire state of Massachusetts since 1980."

We need to erect 'secure bridges' over which workers can safely traverse the path from one job or occupation to the next. A sense of well-being and security, necessary for most workers, would then derive from the knowledge that the bridge is there, rather than from assurances that their jobs are for life. If you know that there is in place a well-defined procedure by which you can move from one job to another without significant sacrifice, you will be just as secure as if granted some form of permanency.

David Birch
Job Creation in America

While Birch thinks individuals need to be responsible for their own careers and security, he argues for a social policy that would establish some sort of middle ground between what he calls "a rampant laissez-faire approach" and a guaranteed job for life. He likens the idea of secure bridges to other types of security already in place in American life: "We offer security at the beginning of a career (guaranteed public education) and at the end (in the form of Social Security) but nothing in the middle. If we are to hold our present pace and remain competitive, we must now concentrate on the middle."

Secure bridges for employees, he says, start with knowledge of "what's out there." Individuals must continually reassess their skills in light of potential career shifts and stay abreast of the demand in the marketplace. Computerized job-listing services, such as those now used by some of the building trades, would be one way to help people track changing supply and demand in the labor market.

Birch is not alone in advocating the need to re-examine and change existing systems of employment support. Pat Choate, senior policy analyst at TRW, advanced the concept of Individual Training Accounts (ITAs) several years ago in *Retooling the American Work Force,* a policy study written for the Northeast-Midwest Congressional Coalition in 1982. Choate's approach mimics Individual Retirement Accounts. It would create an interest-bearing account to which both employee and employer contribute. Like an IRA, it would be vested in the individual, not the job. Employees who are laid off would be able to draw upon the account to pay for retraining and relocation.

Another essential plank in the new security bridge would be outplacement support for employees who lose their jobs. Judging by the rapid increase in the number of consulting firms offering outplacement services, this one is already in place. The Association of Outplacement Firms has quadrupled its membership since 1982, and the outplacement industry has boosted its revenues from $15 million to $350 million over the past decade. At this point, many companies routinely offer outplacement assistance to managers and professionals; some provide help to lower-level layoff victims as well.

Birch characterizes both outplacement and ITAs as "American" solutions that help employees help themselves between jobs. Rather than the European model of government-funded security—which too frequently amounts to long-term unemployment payments—these are private solutions, he told *Training.* The jointly funded ITA and the employer-paid outplacement contract are options that form bridges rather than barriers to new jobs.

Nevertheless, says Birch, what it still comes down to is individual effort. "I saw a motorcyclist the other day whose black leather jacket said, 'Yea, though I walk through the valley of the shadow of death, I will fear no evil, for I'm the toughest mother in the valley.' That's what it's all about. Who will get jobs in the future? Those who are well-trained and willing to out-compete others for jobs."

Capitalism, then, is by nature a form or method of economic change and not only never is but never can be stationary.

Joseph Schumpeter
Capitalism, Socialism and Democracy

This year, *Forbes* magazine celebrated its 70th anniversary with a special issue trumpeting the "creative destruction" necessary for progress in our capitalist system. Much of the issue ended up as a tribute of sorts to Schumpeter, a German economist who died in 1950. His theory, *Forbes* explains, rests on the radical notion "that the market perfection of classical economics—in which suppliers are small, numerous and powerless—is less important to prosperity than a society's willingness to change."

Schumpeter's theories have enjoyed a resurgence recently, according to *Forbes,* now that "entrepreneurs, the agents of painful change, are heroes, while bureaucrats and stay-put managers are suspect. . . . Change, however, is painful to many and disquieting to many more. Democratic governments have to protect the victims of change without stopping the process of economic evolution. The difficult trick is to find ways of treating the unemployed and the underskilled with compassion, without thwarting the wrenching change through which capitalism renews itself."

Whether it's creative destruction or just plain old Brand-X destruction, employers undeniably are in the middle of it. As they ride the current wave of change into the 21st century, many are struggling to balance the requirements for success in a changing economic system against the needs of their employees. Birch outlines the stakes in this high-risk new environment: "However we go about creating security, it must foster—not inhibit—mobility and do so in a way that provides the individual worker with a sense of control over his or her destiny. Moreover, we have to get on with it quickly, for events have a way of overtaking us. As increasing numbers of workers are threatened by the process of change, more will demand that we either slow the pace or create more secure bridges for them to cross. Since we cannot win by slowing down, the alternative is clear enough.

SECTION IV
THE EFFECTS OF CULTURE ON MANAGEMENT STYLE

There are many training programs on management style. Most of these programs revolve around some form of interpersonal communications training based on the Carkhuff model developed in the late 60's.

Recently, many training departments have used Ken Blanchard's paradigm for Situational Leadership as the foundation for enriching management style. In Blanchard's model the manager must decide whether to direct, coach, support or delegate based on the motivation and competence of an individual for a particular situation. Even though the effectiveness of this approach is dependent on the responsive and initiative skills which Carkhuff operationalized earlier, it is a strong model which stresses the importance of thinking about who the employee is before choosing how to relate to that person.

Unfortunately, the problem with most training programs is that they don't account for the impact of the culture on style. In fact, the corporate culture exerts the strongest influence on management style. Therefore, unless the culture is compatible with human resource development thrusts, there will be little or no change in management style over the long term.

This section contains three articles which were selected because of the insights they provide on the effect of the corporate environment on style.

In the first article, Andrall Pearson suggests that organizations build "muscle" through a combination of being tough minded and people oriented. Pearson raises several questions that facilitate a deeper understanding of the cultural norms effecting style.

In the second article, Luthans differentiates between "successful" managers and "real" managers. He points out that in some organizations, managers can be successful independent of their effectiveness. The reason for this, of course, is that successful managers may be more astute at capitalizing on the dysfunctional norms of the organization, while effective managers are more interested in getting the job done even if that means going against organizational politics (cultural norms).

In essence, although not explicitly stated, effective management style depends on the ability of the manager to relate and plan in a thinking environment.

Muscle-build the Organization

By Andrall E. Pearson

Most top managers know they should be doing a better job of building the superior organization they want. They may not, however, know what more successful managers are doing—or how to do it themselves. And while most would agree that their business's success hinges on the quality of its people, very few executives are willing to adopt the tough, aggressive approach to managing people that's required to produce a dynamic organization.

The hard truth is, only an aggressive approach can make a big difference, quickly. But it has its costs: at least initially, managers have to be willing to sacrifice continuity for a thorough shake-up. Nevertheless, most top-notch companies have been through the experience; it's what transformed the company into an outstanding organization. And once the transformation has taken place, things can settle down without a loss of momentum.

In my 15 years with PepsiCo and 20 years of consulting for other corporations, I have seen that "winners"—IBM, Hewlett-Packard, Marriott, Avery International, among others—emphasize "people development" as the way to "muscle-build" their organizations. By stressing the identifying and grooming of talent at every level, these companies eventually create a huge gulf between themselves and their competitors. They also hold on to most of their best managers even through other companies may recruit them aggressively.

If you think you do a good job of managing people, try stepping back and asking yourself the following questions. They're a solid indication of whether people development is your company's number one daily priority.

Do you maintain consistent, demanding standards for everyone in your company—or are you willing to tolerate a mediocre division manager, an uneven sales force, a weak functional department head?

What are your hiring standards? Are you bringing in people who can upgrade the quality of your company significantly, or are you just filling holes? Are you willing to leave a vacancy open until you find an outstanding candidate—for months, if necessary?

Are you hiring *enough* people? Does your organization have sufficient depth—a bank of talent to draw on—or do you sometimes promote people you know will never really produce outstanding results?

How effective is each area of your company at identifying high-potential managers and developing them quickly? Are promising people rotated carefully to expose them to different problems and functions?

Do you know specifically where your organization's biggest performance problems are? Are you taking steps to solve them, or are you looking the other way?

Do you make measurable progress each year in the quality of your senior management group and in the people heading each functional area? Are you generating clearly better quality executives and backups—not just people whose bosses assert are better managers?

As the above questions suggest, traditional approaches to people development—like promotion from within based chiefly on job tenure—are no longer good enough. A company that uses experience as its primary criterion for advancement is encouraging organizational hardening of the arteries—especially if that experience came in an undemanding environment. Businesses today need better, brighter managers with a broader repertoire of skills—a repertoire people cannot master by working their way up the steps of a one-dimensional career ladder. Mergers and acquisitions, new technology, price pressures, and the information explosion all require a stronger and more savvy management team, people who can innovate and win in an uncertain future.

Ironically, as the need for more capable managers has heightened, the talent pool has shrunk. More and more of the most promising future business leaders are choosing the service industries—Wall Street, consulting, and smaller entrepreneurial companies—rather than moving into the big manufacturing enterprises.

These trends all call for upgrading the organization: strengthening your company's entire management group from top to bottom and attracting and preparing future leaders through new approaches—in effect, muscle building. For most companies, I believe that this aggressive approach is the only way to make a business live up to its potential.

Muscle building an organization requires five separate but interrelated steps:

1. Set higher performance standards for everyone—*and keep raising the standards.* Recognize that performance can always be improved, and cultivate a spirit of constructive dissatisfaction with current performance among all executives and managers.
2. Develop managers through fresh assignments and job rotation; keep everyone learning. Don't let high-potential people stay in the same position or the same functional area too long.
3. Adjust every facet of the work environment—corporate culture, organizational structure, policies—to facilitate and reward managers' development, rather than thwart the upgrading effort (as many formal systems do).
4. Infuse each level of the company with new talent. Bring in seasoned managers to solve organizational problems, to serve as backups for management succession, and to lead by example.
5. Use the personnel department as an active agent for change. Make personnel executives partners in the upgrading process. Expect as much from them as from the other top managers.

Let's look at each step in more detail.

Keep Raising Standards

The heart of any management upgrading process is the establishment of higher performance standards across the board. This responsibility rests with the top manager—the CEO or division general manager, depending on the company. If you're a senior manager and you delegate this task, you will convey the message that managerial development is not really that important, and every manager will set different standards.

Raising performance goals entails analyzing the company's current situation (where you are today versus where you want to be), establishing higher expectations (ways of bridging the gap), selling the entire management team on the upgrading process, and developing an action plan.

Step one is the situation analysis—looking at every important position in the company and asking, "What do we expect of this job? How should this position be moving our business forward? How close does the incumbent come to meeting the idea?" In other words, you will be judging people against the company's mission and priorities. This questioning will indicate where the organization's weak links are and will give you a good sense of which executives already have high standards and which are most skillful at developing other people. The way to get started is to sit down with your top executives—division managers and key staff leaders—and ask these reviewers to assess everyone who reports to them. You should also ask them how they could enhance their *own* performance.

Here are some of the questions you should explore:

Who are our best performers, and how are we going to make them even better? How can we stretch them and accelerate their professional growth?

Which senior managers and department heads tolerate marginal performance? Which do not emphasize enough their people's development?

Where are our biggest performance problems, and what are we going to do about them? (You cannot build muscle in your organization unless you are willing to replace marginal performers.)

Which groups of managers (e.g., marketing managers, operations managers) have the necessary mix of talents and skills to achieve more ambitious goals? Who in each group is promotable, and who is not?

For example, I'd be interested to find out specifically what each manager did this year to change the *results* of his or her unit. I'd look for measurable things like formulating or implementing a new competitive strategy, successfully launching a new product, or quickly cutting costs in a downturn. I'd be less interested in plans a manager has for the future, or a laundry list of routine programs he or she implemented, or personal characteristics like how smart someone is—all of which are difficult to relate to better performance.

I'd also be interested in how each manager compares with people the reviewer regards as future stars. Usually, people are better at comparing and ranking subordinates than at measuring someone's performance in a vacuum. By comparing people with star performers, you start to set higher standards and expectations. And if a unit has no stars (or only a few), you can also start to enrich the mix of talent there.

With a fix on each manger's current performance and development needs, you can then take a look at each executive's potential. A single question asking how far each person can advance measured by the number of job layers) will usually start a lively and productive discussion, especially when a manager is ranked as high-potential yet has remained in the same job for four or five years.

You should repeat your questioning with all important department heads. Ideally, you should gather in-depth information on at least two or three levels of people under you. Your personal involvement is the best way to galvanize top managers into action—into recognizing your commitment to big changes in the way the organization operates. In implementing a management upgrading process at PepsiCo, I developed firsthand knowledge of the strengths and weaknesses of well over 100 executives. Going through this process, unit by unit and manager by manager, is obviously hard work, but there is no easy way to establish and enforce tougher performance standards and focus everyone's attention on management development.

I should add that the work is not only time-consuming but also emotionally charged. It leads to heated discussions, especially early on, when standards are likely to differ widely. Using elaborate performance-appraisal forms and systems, as most companies do, is easier, but these systems are usually a triumph of form over substance—an annual exercise to be gotten over with quickly. A simple, informal, face-to-face approach is what's needed to boost performance. You must be willing to engage in frank, tough-minded discussions of each manager's weaknesses—and you must convince each person to use equal candor with subordinates.

You are likely to find that many executives are initially either unwilling or unable to give you useful staff evaluations. For example, a division manager might say that everyone in the division is doing a pretty good job. If this happens, you will have to bear down and force the manager to draw distinctions—say, to identify who the single best performer is. It is also helpful to ask the executive to categorize the managers into four groups, from poor to superior, and then ask for a specific plan for the people in each group. Always focus first on the bottom group. The manager should specify who should be replaced, who should be reassigned, and when these decisions will be implemented.

Rooting out the poorest performers will foster a climate of continual improvement. If everyone in the bottom quartile is replaced, the third quartile becomes the new bottom group and the focus of subsequent improvement efforts.

The human tendency to avoid confrontation allows companies to fall into the trap of complacency and subpar performance. Upgrading the organization, by contrast, requires managers to make tough decisions: to fire some people, demote or bypass others, and tell poor performers where they stand. No one enjoys delivering bad news, but good managers will understand how critical it is to the company's long-term success—particularly if the CEO personally sets the example.

Some managers might object that this relentless scrutiny—and the inevitable firings—will demoralize employees. My experience suggests precisely the opposite. Top performers relish the challenge of meeting ever higher goals. What does demoralize them is a climate that tolerates mediocrity; under such circumstances, they may slow down their work to the tempo of the organization—or they may leave the company.

After you have completed your preliminary situation analysis, you are ready to formulate the specific actions you will take over the next 9 to 12 months to muscle-build your organization. What are your goals for each key manager and each department? What are the implications of those plans for recruiting and job assignments? This action plan sets the stage for a more demanding and results-oriented environment, one in which measurable progress will occur.

In my experience, focusing on a limited number of high-impact results, conducting comparative evaluations, and separating current performance from potential will produce far better effects than focusing on personal traits, making exhaustive MBO lists, or using rigorous forms.

The analysis, of course, does not stop here but should become an ongoing process, a day-to-day questioning. What's working well? Where can we improve? Over time, you may wish to supplement your face-to-face interviews with surveys to gather this kind of information.

Worship Success and Potential

The situation analysis is the cornerstone of your upgrading effort. Having identified how well your managers and divisions are performing, you are now in a position to determine how best to deploy your people. If you want to grow fast and improve fast, you have to develop people fast. And the secret to that is to produce challenging, fresh, *taxing* assignments.

It goes without saying that you want to put the best qualified person into each important job (and to move marginal performers aside so they don't block new talent). What may be less obvious is that you want to keep every high-potential manager constantly challenged and learning. Make sure that talented people don't stay in one job too long. Most people need about a year to master a new assignment; after four years, they're usually just repeating what they've already done, and they may go to sleep on the job. In most companies, people work in a single area for years, moving slowly and ponderously up the career ladder. By the time they reach senior positions, many have run out of steam—they've become "deadwood."

Just reassigning a top performer isn't enough. You don't want a talented person simply to repeat the same experience in a different region or at a somewhat higher level. You need to round out executives' experience through challenging new assignments that will give them a broader business viewpoint. Entirely different positions can accomplish this—for example, moving someone from domestic operations to international, putting a manager in a new functional area, or letting a high achiever engineer a turnaround.

At PepsiCo, we thought nothing of making the CFO of Frito-Lay a general manager of Pepsi-Cola in Canada, or promoting the North American Van Lines CEO to head up corporate planning, or putting a good, hands-on Pepsi marketing vice president into restaurant operations. We tried to make sure that every division president served in at least two operating divisions and in at least one staff assignment (not just in line jobs). We also moved promising managers into our best run divisions to minimize business disruptions and expose them to better work environments.

Large companies should rotate their managers through different divisions both to keep them challenged and to help the organization prepare future leaders who understand its many facets. Companies that have a number of smaller divisions or a significant international business can easily move people around like this. Managers in these enterprises have many opportunities to be tested and to learn in freestanding situations at lower risk.

Decisions about reassignments are best made once a year as part of the annual performance review, not on a piecemeal basis throughout the year. Making a series of moves at one time allows you to consider the needs of the whole organization and to deploy your entire pool of talent most productively. Also, when assignments are shuffled all at once, the company has time to settle down and assimilate the changes. In the real world, of course, you will also be faced with a few piecemeal decisions, but that doesn't negate the approach.

The aim of rearranging things is to make the best corporate use of all your managers, instead of asking each business unit to do the best it can with existing resources. To be sure, you take some chances when you bypass traditional channels of promotion. Moving someone to an entirely new division is not without risks: the new unit may resent your interference, or—worse—a person may fail in the new job.

To prevent resentment and resistance, don't just foist your selections on your operating people. Take particular care when implementing this portion of the upgrading process, and choose candidates whose odds of succeeding in a new division are high. Operating managers must realize that these people are top performers and not someone another area wanted to get rid of. You should also give your operating managers veto power over candidates, or give them a slate to choose from. Eventually, they will accept and support "corporate musical chairs" as they realize they're getting better qualified people for their openings.

If you promote on the basis of potential and not just on experience, you're bound to make some mistakes. The safest route is to promote someone already in the department rather than an outsider with less experience in the function. But you'll never shake up the organization enough if you stick to safe choices. If you see one of your assignments not working out, face it quickly, and try to find another slot for the person. Over time you'll learn which jobs require pertinent experience (there are some) and which ones don't (there are many of these).

There is one other risk in rotating people throughout a company. You are running a business, after all, not a finishing school for executives. Continuity and experience are important in building relationships and relevant skills. The priorities shouldn't be one-sided in either direction. The company needs a balance. Avoid moving people so much that you destroy continuity and nobody really gets developed, but also be as careful as you can to keep people from getting stale.

Unclog the Organization

The way a corporation is organized and runs can either facilitate or thwart the upgrading process. Unfortunately, organizations often become so complicated over time that some of the things I've recommended here simply won't work. If companies have tightly drawn "empires," for example, they'll have difficulty transferring executives across divisions. For that reason, a new emphasis on people development often calls for a complete transformation of the work environment.

Consider the ways in which a multilayered organizational structure can impede performance. With broken-up jobs, no one has clear-cut responsibility or a feeling of ownership and as a result, people may sit back and wait for the group to solve problems. It's difficult to assess individual performance. Decision-making mechanisms can be so complicated that people dissipate all their energy simply trying to get a question answered.

For reasons like these, a slow-moving, bureaucratic environment usually flushes talented people out the door faster than it brings them in. Innovators can't thrive in a highly centralized organization. If you want more original thinking, you have to decentralize responsibility throughout the company and get rid of red tape. Give people the freedom to stick their necks out and to take independent action.

Here are four suggestions for creating a climate conducive to executive development:

1. Keep your organizational structure as simple as possible. With fewer layers, there can be more individual responsibility, less second-guessing, clearer decision making, and greater accountability for results.
2. Break down organizational barriers. Emphasize that managers are corporate assets rather than the property of a single division or function.
3. By the same token, formally encourage cross-fertilization. Expose your best managerial prospects to top functional leaders. Some companies conduct reviews where all the senior marketing vice presidents, for example, evaluate prospects for marketing posts. In other corporations, the executives attend personnel reviews in other divisions.
4. Finally, make sure that every unit is rewarding its best achievers appropriately. This may sound obvious, but most businesses do a poor job of relating pay to performance. Sometimes better performers receive larger raises than less promising people (personnel policies or other factors don't always encourage this), but the differences may be so slight that they're demotivating. Nothing frustrates high-potential people more than hearing a lot of praise at their reviews and then learning that their efforts won't be rewarded accordingly. In the more demanding work environment you're creating by muscle building, it's especially important to peg pay to performance.

Create a Nucleus of Leaders

If you want to make sweeping improvements in your organization, you'll have to bring in fresh talent. The upgrading steps I've described are all crucial, but they take time to implement and bear fruit. An essential ingredient in the process is to bring in several high performers *quickly*—to fill important posts and to develop a talent pool you can draw on for promotions later.

Simply deciding to look outside the company for the next two or three openings isn't the answer. That's like trying to empty the ocean with a thimble; you'll never get anywhere. You may also be tempted to bring in new talent only at the entry level, especially if your employees tend to make their careers in your company. But are your present managers capable of supervising top performers? I recommend that you introduce new people at the highest levels of your organization and let the upgrading trickle down.

In a large, decentralized enterprise, the best way to start this talent infusion is to hire a group of proven managers without having any particular jobs in mind for them. (In football, this is called drafting for talent, not for position.) Ultimately, these people will be fed into the system as openings occur, but initially they can work directly for you or another senior person on special projects—assuming the role of in-house consultants. They can be assigned to divisions or functions that are in particular need of help, or to new endeavors. The important point is that proficient managers will be in place (setting an example for others) and learning about your company (preparing for more specific assignments).

This approach worked well at PepsiCo, where we brought in seven "floaters" over a three-year period. Within nine months, they were all working in key jobs, and five of them eventually ended up running big divisions. As another example, we felt we had too few promotable individuals in our food-service division, so we wanted to build a broader bank of talent. We considered 200 food-service executives, interviewed 50 of them, and brought in the best two we could find. Within two years, one was running a division and the other held an important operating position. Ernie Breech had similar success at Ford when he brought in the "whiz kids" (including Robert McNamara and Tex Thornton).

As these examples show, you can bring in people with assorted backgrounds or you can concentrate on a single area, like corporate finance. Your goal may be to get the best financial people you can find and give them a group of divisions to follow. They will not only make important contributions as in-house consultants but usually an operating unit will snap them up quickly, and they'll end up serving as a division CFO or even running a unit or company themselves.

Hiring people to serve as general resources may sound like an expensive proposition. But the cost is almost certainly less than you would pay for a consultant to handle the same special projects, and this method promises a significant impact on the upgrading process. Also, a cost-conscious CEO can usually eliminate enough low-impact current jobs or managers to pay for the floaters.

Eventually, you'll be able to focus your recruiting at the lower levels of management. Here as elsewhere, you must make the commitment to work consistently and effectively to develop the best staff possible. This goal usually means emphasizing campus recruiting—year after year, at the best schools—rather than just hiring people from other companies. It means that recruiting must be a top-management priority.

Make Personnel a Partner

You can't improve an entire organization by yourself. As you would expect, you certainly need the support of all your executives and managers. As you might not expect, your other partner in the process is the personnel department. I'll talk about each of these in turn.

Muscle building an organization is impossible without the active involvement of your line managers. But how do you convince a busy general manager to shoulder a new set of responsibilities? You need to do more than express your own commitment to the upgrading process: you have to be unrelenting in your emphasis on people development.

Make it clear that you are asking executives to do more than just preside over annual reviews. (And if you feel someone isn't emphasizing even this part of the process enough, try attending a couple of review sessions with subordinates.) Every time you see or call a manager, you should stress your interest in the key people and their individual performance. Ask specific questions. What has been done about the marginal production manager? What progress has there been in the Cleveland office? What projects is the new recruit working on? After a few run-throughs, the answers will be ready before you ask the questions.

You can deepen your executives' involvement in other ways, for instance, by asking them to showcase their "comers" at periodic business reviews or to nominate people to serve on special task forces. You should also make time for observing the best people in action during your field visits.

Commitment from line managers often doesn't come easily; you have to create it, nurture it, even push it. You're asking them to rethink their job priorities and make more difficult decisions. The personnel department can be a valuable ally in this effort and serve as a burr under the saddle of resistant managers.

Personnel people are often seen as peripheral to the real action in a company—a group of paper shufflers who develop benefits packages, collect evaluation forms, and process paychecks. But these activities are not their most important reason for being. Outstanding personnel people can be a force for positive change in the organization. They can help ensure that line managers handle their people responsibilities properly, and they can help the whole company make the best possible use of its assets.

Unfortunately, business leaders rarely recognize the potential of the personnel function, so they often fail to staff the department with high-caliber people. Their low expectations then become a self-fulfilling prophecy.

Personnel executives can facilitate organizational muscle building in several ways:

- They can push executives to make consistent, demanding evaluations of their subordinates. This might include, for example, pointing out differences between a criticism-shy manager's performance appraisals and other managers' evaluations of their people, and giving advice on how to deliver bad news in an appropriate way.
- They can force managers to take action on marginal performers (reassignment, coaching, allowing time for improvement) and insist that poor performers be replaced.
- They can help search out the best people in the company and the best slot for each person. They can encourage executives to take risks on high-potential prospects. (Superior personnel executives, plugged into every part of the company, are especially valuable here.) One of the most offbeat, successful deployment decisions we made at PepsiCo, for example, was to shift our trucking company president to head up the corporate staff. Another success involved appointing an international division area vice

president as chief of restaurant operations and marketing. Our corporate personnel vice president spearheaded both moves; if he hadn't prodded neither would have happened.

- They can encourage executives to focus on results and *heap* rewards on the best performers. (Some personnel systems set rigid limits on compensation, so pay increases average out, and no one is motivated.)

If you want valuable assistance from your personnel department, you will probably need brighter, more highly skilled personnel executives than you may have now. The good news is that if you give personnel more responsibility and integrate it with other executive functions, you should attract better people.

The Full-Court Press

The five-step upgrading process I advocate is undeniably a huge undertaking. It requires time, energy, money, and possibly the restructuring of the entire company—in short, a full-court press.

You can't achieve the results I'm talking about by implementing just one part of the processor by working to improve your organization gradually. Nor can you hire a few MBAs or a new marketing vice president and expect the organization to change to its roots. A piecemeal or incremental approach won't foster the broad-based involvement, ownership, and conviction that make real progress; you'll move one step forward, one step back, and you'll never get off dead center. Your goal is to advance.

Some CEOs may feel that management muscle building is not worth the effort it takes. As is true with other improvement programs, the companies most in need of upgrading will probably be the ones least likely to attempt it. Many company chiefs who have implemented a systematic people-development program, however, have told me that it became the most rewarding part of their jobs. Muscle building makes a difference on the bottom line, in the company's strategic success, and in the way people feel when they come to work in the morning—including the CEOs.

Successful vs. Effective Real Managers

By Fred Luthans

What do *successful* managers—those who have been promoted relatively quickly—have in common with *effective* managers—those who have satisfied, committed subordinates and high performing units? Surprisingly, the answer seems to be that they have little in common. Successful managers in what we define as "real organizations"—large and small mainstream organizations, mostly in the mushrooming service industry in middle America—are not engaged in the same day-to-day activities as effective managers in these organizations. This is probably the most important, and certainly the most intriguing, finding of a comprehensive four-year observational study of managerial work that is reported in a recent book by myself and two colleagues, titled *Real Managers.*[1]

The startling finding that there is a difference between successful and effective managers may merely confirm for many cynics and "passed over" managers something they have suspected for years. They believe that although managers who are successful (that is, rapidly promoted) may be astute politicians, they are not necessarily effective. Indeed, the so-called successful managers may be the ones who do not in fact take care of people and get high performance from their units.

Could this finding explain some of the performance problems facing American organizations today? Could it be that the successful managers, the politically savvy ones who are being rapidly promoted into responsible positions, may not be the effective managers, the ones with satisfied, committed subordinates turning out quantity and quality performance in their units?

This article explores the heretofore assumed equivalence of "successful managers" and "effective managers." Instead of looking for sophisticated technical or governmental approaches to the

performance problems facing today's organizations, the solution may be as simple as promoting effective managers and learning how they carry out their jobs. Maybe it is time to turn to the real managers themselves for some answers.

And who are these managers? They are found at all levels and in all types of organizations with titles such as department head, general manager, store manager, marketing manager, office manager, agency chief, or district manager. In other words, maybe the answers to the performance problems facing organizations today can be found in their own backyards, in the managers themselves in their day-to-day activities.

The Current View of Managerial Work

Through the years management has been defined, as the famous French administrator and writer Henri Fayol said, by the functions of planning, organizing, commanding, coordinating, and controlling. Only recently has this classical view of managers been challenged.[2] Starting with the landmark work of Henry Mintzberg, observational studies of managerial work have found that the normative functions do not hold up. Mintzberg charged that Fayol and others' classical view of what managers do was merely "folklore."[3]

On the basis of his observations of five CEOs and their mail, Mintzberg concluded that the manager's job consisted of many brief and disjointed episodes with people inside and outside the organization. He discounted notions such as reflective planning. Instead of the five Fayolian functions of management, Mintzberg portrayed managers in terms of a typology of roles. He formulated three interpersonal roles (figurehead, leader, and liaison); three informational roles (monitor or nerve center, disseminator, and spokesman), and four decision-making roles (entrepreneur, disturbance handler, resource allocator, and negotiator). Although Mintzberg based this view of managers on only the five managers he observed and his search of the literature, he did ask, and at least gave the beginning of an answer to, the question of what managers really do.

The best known other modern view of managerial work is provided by John Kotter. His description of managers is based on his study of 15 successful general managers. Like Mintzberg, Kotter challenged the traditional view by concluding that managers do not so simply perform the Fayolian functions, but rather spend most of their time interacting with others. In particular, he found his general managers spent considerable time in meetings getting and giving information. Kotter refers to these get-togethers as "network building." Networking accomplishes what Kotter calls a manager's "agenda"—the loosely connected goals and plans addressing the manager's responsibilities. By obtaining relevant and needed information from his or her networks, the effective general manager is able to implement his or her agenda. Like Mintzberg, Kotter's conclusions are based on managerial work from a small sample of elite managers. Nevertheless, his work represents a progressive step in answering the question of what managers do.

Determining What Real Managers Do

The next step in discovering the true nature of managerial work called for a larger sample that would allow more meaningful generalizations. With a grant from the Office of Naval Research, we embarked on such an effort.[4] We used trained observers to freely observe and record in detail the behaviors and activities of 44 "real" managers.[5] Unlike Mintzberg's and Kotter's managers, these managers came from all levels and many types of organizations (mostly in the service sector—such as retail stores, hospitals, corporate headquarters, a railroad, governmental agencies, insurance companies, a newspaper office, financial institutions, and a few manufacturing companies).

We reduced the voluminous data gathered from the free observation logs into managerial activity categories using the Delphi technique. Delphi was developed and used during the heyday of Rand Corporation's "Think Tank." A panel offers independent input and then the panel members are given composite feedback. After several iterations of this process, the data were reduced into the 12 descriptive behavioral categories shown in Exhibit 1. These empirically derived behavioral descriptors were then conceptually collapsed into the four managerial activities of real managers:

1. *Communication.* This activity consists of exchanging routine information and processing paperwork. Its observed behaviors include answering procedural questions, receiving and disseminating requested information, conveying the results of meetings, giving or receiving routine information over the phone, processing mail, reading reports, writing reports/memos/letters, routine financial reporting and bookkeeping, and general desk work.

2. *Traditional Management.* This activity consists of planning, decision making, and controlling. Its observed behaviors include setting goals and objectives, defining tasks needed to accomplish goals, scheduling employees, assigning tasks, providing routine instructions, defining problems, handling day-to-day operational crises, deciding what to do, developing new procedures, inspecting work, walking around inspecting the work, monitoring performance data, and doing preventive maintenance.

3. *Human Resource Management.* This activity contains the most behavioral categories: motivating/reinforcing, disciplining/punishing, managing conflict, staffing, and training/developing. The disciplining/punishing category was subsequently dropped from the analysis because it was not generally permitted to be observed. The observed behaviors for this activity include allocating formal rewards, asking for input, conveying appreciation, giving credit where due, listening to suggestions, giving positive feedback, group support, resolving conflict between subordinates, appealing to higher authorities or third parties to resolve a dispute, developing job descriptions, reviewing applications, interviewing applicants, filling in where needed, orienting employees, arranging for training, clarifying roles, coaching, mentoring, and walking subordinates through a task.

4. *Networking.* This activity consists of socializing/politicking and interacting with outsiders. The observed behaviors associated with this activity include non-work-related "chit chat"; informal joking around; discussing rumors, hearsay and the grapevine; complaining, griping, and putting others down; politicking and gamesmanship; dealing with customers, suppliers, and vendors; attending external meetings; and doing/attending community service events.

These four activities are what real managers do. They include some of the classic notions of Fayol (the traditional management activities) as well as the more recent views of Mintzberg (the communication activities) and Kotter (the networking activities). As a whole, however, especially with the inclusion of human resource management activities, this view of real managers' activities is more comprehensive than previous sets of managerial work.

Exhibit 1
The Activities of Real Managers

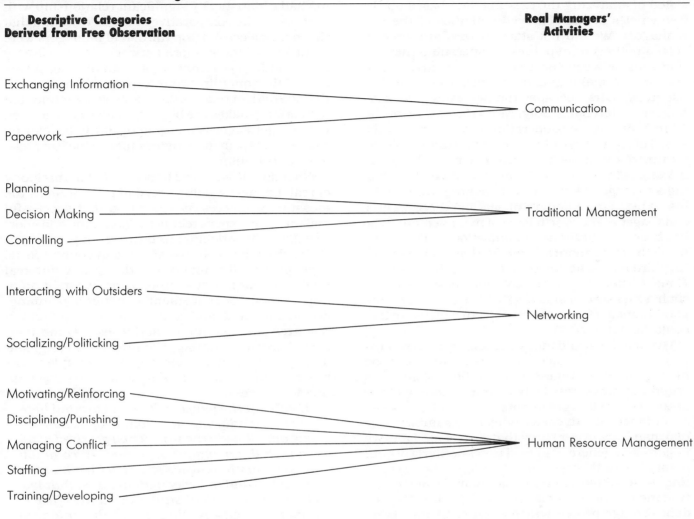

Descriptive Categories Derived from Free Observation	Real Managers' Activities
Exchanging Information	Communication
Paperwork	
Planning	Traditional Management
Decision Making	
Controlling	
Interacting with Outsiders	Networking
Socializing/Politicking	
Motivating/Reinforcing	Human Resource Management
Disciplining/Punishing	
Managing Conflict	
Staffing	
Training/Developing	

After the nature of managerial activity was determined through the free observation of the 44 managers, the next phase of the study was to document the relative frequency of these activities. Data on another set of 248 real managers (not the 44 used in the initial portion of this study) were gathered. Trained participation observers filled out a checklist based on the managerial activities at a random time once every hour over a two-week period. We found that the real managers spend not quite a third of their time and effort in communication activities, about a third in traditional management activities, a fifth in human resource management activities, and about a fifth in networking activities. This relative frequency analysis based on observational data of a large sample provides a more definitive answer to the question of what real managers do than the normative classical functions and the limited sample of elite managers used by Mintzberg and Kotter.

How the Difference Between Successful and Effective Real Managers Was Determined

Discovering the true nature of managerial work by exploding some of the myths of the past and extending the work of Mintzberg and Kotter undoubtedly contributes to our knowledge of management. However, of more critical importance in trying to understand and find solutions to our current performance problems is singling out successful and effective managers to see what they really do in their day-to-day activities. The successful-versus-effective phase of our real managers study consisted of analyzing the existing data based on the frequencies of the observed activities of the real managers. We did not start off with any preconceived notions or hypotheses concerning the relationships between successful and effective managers. In fact, making such a distinction seemed like "splitting hairs" because the two words are so often used interchangeably. Nevertheless, we decided to define success operationally in terms of the speed of promotion within an organization. We determined a success index on a sample of the real managers in our study. It was calculated by dividing a manager's level in his or her organization by his or her tenure (length of service) there.[6] Thus, a manager at the fourth level of management, who has been with his or her organization for five years, would be rated more successful than a manager at the third level who has been there for 25 years. Obviously, there are some potential problems with such a measure of success, but for our large sample of managers this was an objective measure that could be obtained.

The definition and measurement of effectiveness is even more elusive. The vast literature on managerial effectiveness offered little agreement on criteria or measures. To overcome as many of the obstacles and disagreements as possible, we used a combined effectiveness index for a sample of the real managers in our study that represented the two major—and generally agreed upon—criteria of both management theory/research and practice: (1) getting the job done through high quantity and quality standards of performance, and (2) getting the job done through people, which requires their satisfaction and commitment.[7]

We obviously would have liked to use "hard measures" of effectiveness such as profits and quantity/quality of output or service, but again, because we were working with large samples of real managers from widely diverse jobs and organizations, this was not possible.

What Do Successful Real Managers Do?

To answer the question of what successful real managers do, we conducted several types of analyses—statistical (using multiple regression techniques), simple descriptive comparisons (for example, top third of managers as measured by the success index vs. bottom third), and relative strength of correlational relationships.[8] In all of these analyses, the importance that networking

played in real manager success was very apparent. Of the four real manager activities, only networking had a statistically significant relationship with success. In the comparative analysis we found that the most successful (top third) real managers were doing considerably more networking and slightly more routine communication than their least successful (bottom third) counterparts. From the relative strength of relationship analysis we found that networking makes the biggest relative contribution to manager success and, importantly, human resource management activities makes the least relative contribution.

What does this mean? It means that in this study of real managers, using speed of promotion as the measure of success, it was found that successful real managers spent relatively more time and effort socializing, politicking, and interacting with outsiders than did their less successful counterparts. Perhaps equally important, the successful real managers did not give much time or attention to the traditional management activities of planning, decision making, and controlling or to the human resource management activities of motivating/reinforcing, staffing, training/developing, and managing conflict. A representative example of this profile would be the following manager's prescription for success:

"I find that the way to get ahead around here is to be friendly with the right people, both inside and outside the firm. They get tired of always talking shop, so I find a common interest—with some it's sports, with others it's our kids—and interact with them on that level. The other formal stuff around the office is important but I really work at this informal side and have found it pays off when promotion time rolls around."

In other words, for this manager and for a significant number of those real managers we studied, networking seems to be the key to success.

What Do Effective Real Managers Do?

Once we answered the question of what successful managers do, we turned to the even more important question of what effective managers do. It should be emphasized once again that, in gathering our observational data for the study, we made no assumptions that the successful real managers were (or were not) the effective managers. Our participant observers were blind to the research questions and we had no hypothesis concerning the relationship between successful and effective managers.

We used the relative strength of correlational relationships between the real managers' effectiveness index and their directly observed day-to-day activities and found that communication and human resource management activities made by far the largest relative contribution to real managers' effectiveness and that traditional management and—especially—networking made by far the least relative contribution.[9]

These results mean that if effectiveness is defined as the perceived quantity and quality of the performance of a manager's unit and his or her subordinates' satisfaction and commitment, then the biggest relative contribution to real manager effectiveness comes from the human oriented activities—communication and human resource management. A representative example of this effectiveness profile is found in the following manager's comments:

"Both how much and how well things get done around here, as well as keeping my people loyal and happy, has to do with keeping them informed and involved. If I make a change in procedure or the guys upstairs give us a new process or piece of equipment to work with, I get my people's input and give them the full story before I lay it on them. Then I make sure they have the proper training and give them feedback on how they are doing. When they screw up, I let them know, but when they do a good job, I let them know about that too."

This manager, like our study of real managers in general, found that the biggest contribution to effectiveness came from communicating and human resource management activities.

Equally important, however, was the finding that the least relative contribution to real managers' effectiveness came from the networking activity. This, of course, is in stark contrast to our results of the successful real manager analysis. Networking activity had by far the strongest relative relationship to success, but the weakest with effectiveness. On the other hand, human resource management activity had a strong relationship to effectiveness second only to communication activity), but had the weakest relative relationship to success. In other words, the successful real managers do not do the same activities as the effective real managers (in fact, they do almost the opposite). These contrasting profiles may have significant implications for understanding the current performance problems facing American organizations. However, before we look at these implications and

suggest some solutions, let's take a look at those real managers who are both successful and effective.

What Do Managers Who Are Both Successful and Effective Do?

The most obvious concluding question is what those who were found to be both successful and effective really do. This "combination" real manager, of course, is the ideal—and has been assumed to exist in American management over the years.

Since there was such a difference between successful and effective managers in our study, we naturally found relatively few (less than 10% of our sample) that were both among the top third of successful managers and the top third of effective managers. Not surprisingly, upon examining this special group, we found that their activities were very similar to real managers as a whole. They were not like either the successful or effective real managers. Rather, it seems that real managers who are both successful and effective use a fairly balanced approach in terms of their activities. In other words, real managers who can strike the delicate balance between all four managerial activities may be able to get ahead as well as get the job done.

Important is the fact that we found so few real managers that were both successful and effective. This supports our findings on the difference between successful and effective real managers, but limits any generalizations that can be made about successful and effective managers. It seems that more important in explaining our organizations' present performance problems, and what to do about them, are the implications of the wide disparity between successful and effective real managers.

Implications of the Successful versus Effective Real Managers Findings

If, as our study indicates, there is indeed a difference between successful and effective real managers, what does it mean and what should we do about it? First of all, we need to pay more attention to formal reward systems to ensure that effective managers are promoted. Second, we must learn how effective managers do their day-to-day jobs.

The traditional assumption holds that promotions are based on performance. This is what the formal personnel policies say, this is what new management trainees are told and this is what every management textbook states *should* happen.

On the other hand, more "hardened" (or perhaps more realistic) members and observers of *real* organizations (not textbook organizations or those featured in the latest best sellers or videotapes) have long suspected that social and political skills are the real key to getting ahead, to being successful. Our study lends support to the latter view.

The solution is obvious, but may be virtually impossible to implement, at least in the short run. Tying formal rewards—and especially promotions—to performance is a must if organizations are going to move ahead and become more productive. At a minimum, and most pragmatically in the short run, organizations must move to a performance-based appraisal system. Managers that are effective should be promoted. In the long run organizations must develop cultural values that support and reward effective performance, not just successful socializing and politicking. This goes hand-in-hand with the current attention given to corporate culture and how to change it. An appropriate goal for cultural change in today's organizations might simply be to make effective managers successful.

Besides the implications for performance-based appraisals and organizational culture that came out of the findings of our study is a lesson that we can learn from the effective real managers themselves. This lesson is the importance they give and effort they devote to the human-oriented activities of communicating and human resource management. How human resources are managed—keeping them informed, communicating with them, paying attention to them, reinforcing them, resolving their conflicts, training/developing them—all contribute directly to managerial effectiveness.

The disparity our study found between successful and effective real managers has important implications for the performance problems facing today's organizations. While we must move ahead on all fronts in our search for solutions to these problems, we believe the activities basic to the effective real managers in our study—communication and human resource management—deserve special attention.

Endnotes

1. The full reference for the book is Fred Luthans, Richard M. Hodgetts, and Stuart Rosenkrantz, *Real Managers*, Cambridge, MA: Ballinger, 1988. Some of the preliminary material from the real managers study was also included in the presidential speech given by Fred Luthans at the 1986 Academy of Management meeting.

Appreciation is extended to the co-authors of the book, Stu Rosenkrantz and Dick Hodgetts, to Diane Lee Lockwood on the first phase of the study, and to Avis Johnson, Hank Hennessey and Lew Taylor on later phases. These individuals, especially Stu Rosenkrantz, contributed ideas and work on the backup for this article.

2. The two most widely recognized challenges to the traditional view of management have come from Henry Mintzberg, *The Nature of Managerial Work*, New York: Harper & Row, 1973; and John Kotter, *The General Managers*, New York: Free Press, 1982. In addition, two recent comprehensive reviews of the nature of managerial work can be found in the following references: Colin P. Hales, "What Do Managers Do? A Critical Review of the Evidence," *Journal of Management Studies*, 1986, 23, pp. 88–115; and Stephen J. Carroll and Dennis J. Gillen, "Are the Classical Management Functions Useful in Describing Managerial Work?" *Academy of Management Review*, 1987, 12, pp. 38–51.

3. See Henry Mintzberg's article, "The Manager's Job: Folklore and Fact," *Harvard Business Review*, July–August 1975, 53, pp. 49–61.

4. For those interested in the specific details of the background study, see Luthans, Hodgetts and Rosenkrantz (Endnote 1 above).

5. The source that details the derivation, training of observers, procedures, and reliability and validity analysis of the observation system used in the real managers study is Fred Luthans and Diane L. Lockwood's "Toward an Observation System for Measuring Leader Behavior in Natural Setting," in J. Hunt, D. Hosking, C. Schriesheim, and R. Stewart (Eds.) *Leaders and Managers: International Perspectives of Managerial Behavior and Leadership*, New York: Pergamon Press, 1984, pp. 117–141.

6. For more background on the success portion of the study and the formula used to calculate the success index see Fred Luthans, Stuart Rosenkrantz, and Harry Hennessey, "What Do Successful Managers Really Do? An Observational Study of Managerial Activities," *Journal of Applied Behavioral Science*, 1985, 21, pp. 255–270.

7. The questionnaire used to measure the real managers' unit quantity and quality of performance was drawn from Paul E. Mott's *The Characteristics of Effective Organizations*, New York: Harper & Row, 1972. Subordinate satisfaction was measured by the Job Diagnostic Index found in P.C. Smith, R.M. Kendall, and C.L. Hulin's

The Measurement of Satisfaction in Work and Retirement, Chicago: Rand-McNally, 1969. Subordinate commitment is measured by the questionnaire in Richard T. Mowday, L.W. Porter, and Richard M. Steers' *Employee-Organizational Linkages: The Psychology of Commitment, Absenteeism, and Turnover,* New York: Academic Press, 1982. These three standardized questionnaires are widely used research instruments with considerable psychometric back-up and high reliability in the sample used in our study.

8. For the details of the multiple regression analysis and simple descriptive comparisons of successful versus unsuccessful managers, see Endnote 6. To determine the relative contribution the activities identified in Exhibit 1 made to success, we calculated the mean of the squared correlations (to approximate variance explained) between the observed activities of the real managers and the success index calculated for each target manager. These correlation squared means were then rank ordered to obtain the relative strengths of the managerial activities' contribution to success.

9. The calculation for the relative contribution the activities made to effectiveness was done as described for success in Endnote 8. The statistical and top third-bottom third companies that was done in the success analysis was not done in the effectiveness analysis. For comparison of successful managers and effective managers, the relative strength of relationship was used; see *Real Managers* (Endnote 1) for details.

SECTION V
THE EFFECTS OF CULTURE ON QUALITY

Quality has become an obsession for most North American companies in the last decade. Certainly, those companies which have been successful attribute a large share of their cause for survival and growth to the focus on quality. And yet, in many organizations, making quality the norm is still a difficult process. More than any other factor, the corporate culture influences the degree to which quality programs are accepted and ingrained in the "way we do business."

The first article, "Injecting Quality into Personnel Management," demonstrates how the quality improvement process extends beyond products to every aspect of the business. In this selection, Clay Carr discusses how quality control concepts can be applied to the human resource function.

In the second article, "The House of Quality," Hauser and Clausing trace how the quality "movement" has grown over the past 20 years. The authors point out that the foundation of the house of quality is the belief that products should be designed to reflect customers' desires and tastes. This belief reflects the beginning of a whole new culture change initiative that involves the formation of thinking relationships with customers which result in a psychology of interdependence.

The final article in this section is "Competing on the Eight Dimensions of Quality." The author, David Garvin, describes the need for strategic quality management and proposes eight critical dimensions that can serve as a framework for strategic analysis: performance, features, reliability, conformance, durability, serviceability, aesthetics, and perceived quality.

Injecting Quality into Personnel Management

By Clay Carr

According to Philip Crosby, in his book by the same name, quality is free. That's probably true. What certainly is true is that quality is *big*.

This isn't news to most people. Ever since American manufacturers discovered that Japanese products weren't selling in the United States solely—or even mainly—because they were cheap, quality has become a watchword of American industry.

The latest, and probably most spectacular sign of this is the escalation of automobile warranties to six and seven years, as well as appliance manufacturers' extended money-back guarantees to their consumers. And it's everywhere: turn a stone, and you'll find someone preaching quality under it; reach in a nest, and you'll find this month's new book on quality.

Please don't misunderstand me. As a consumer, I welcome this new emphasis on quality. As an American, I'm frankly glad to see that some companies are again caring about building high-quality, durable products. Nor is this emphasis superficial. I recently heard an economist estimate that about 2% of the inflation rate for several years should be discounted, because product quality had improved enough for products to be genuinely worth that additional amount.

Still, there are problems. All too many quality programs are a flash in the pan, albeit a showy flash. All too few organizations understand what Peters and Austin espoused in *A Passion for Excellence*: [t]he heart of quality is not technique. It is a commitment by management to its people and product—stretching over a period of decades and lived with persistence and passion . . . .''

In human resources (HR), there's another problem. Most books on quality deal with quality in manufacturing. It's assumed that you're producing a product, and that the normal repertoire of statistical tools can be applied to it.

Certainly there are operations in any personnel department that are production oriented. Making record changes, for instance, is very close to a production operation—particularly in a large office. The normal statistical quality control procedures can be applied to them.

Similarly, quality circles (or similar tactics) can be used to attack out-of-control processes and bring them back within bounds.

All this can be done and should be done. The problem, though, is that it doesn't attack any of the really bottom-line operations of a typical HR office: recruiting, job evaluation, training, policy setting, labor relations and so on. Few of these activities lend themselves to statistical quality control in any meaningful way.

This doesn't mean there aren't any methods that will measure the quality of these operations. There are. A specialist who provides a range of HR services to a department can be evaluated by sending a questionnaire on his or her performance to a sample of supervisors. The same technique can be used to measure the satisfaction of employees, supervisors or both groups with the treatment they receive when they visit the personnel office.

The problem is that such techniques as these measure others' evaluation of the HR endeavor. That's important, but it can't substitute for the promotion and evaluation of quality in the eyes of those engaged in the endeavor itself.

How do we do that?

Four Quality Control Concepts Apply to Personnel Activities

First, there are four concepts from more formal quality control that can be directly applied to HR activities—even if that application is somewhat different from product quality. These four concepts include:

- Quality is important.
- Continual improvement is a way of life.
- Do away with scrap and rework.

• You can't inspect quality in.

Second, the greatest payoff for quality in HR and similar staff activities comes from following two guides that, superficially, appear to have nothing to do with quality.

1) Quality is important.

The first requirement for quality in the HR office is exactly the same as the first requirement for it anywhere else. The head of the office must care, must fully and honestly care, to produce a quality product. He or she must pass this passion on to key personnel—not just in words, programs and slogans, but in day-by-day decision making.

The person in charge must be able to honestly say, "We . . . know that quality improvement must be continuous without regard to short-term objectives and goals."[1] Then the department head must embody this in decisions, time after time after time.

He or she must protect employees and give them the time to do it right the first time—when operating management is pressuring them for quick results. He or she must return less-than-quality work until it's done right, even when bored to tears with the routine. The department head must recognize employees who do quality work—even when their extra time and care, in the short run, may make them less popular with managers.

2) Continual improvement is a way of life.

Japanese quality control is something beyond statistical quality control, as important as that may be. It includes a constant emphasis on *improvement*.[2]

This is one of the key meanings, for instance, of quality circles. Their *method* is grass-root participation in the process of management. Their *goal* is constant improvement.

Attuned as we Americans are to the big and spectacular, it's all too easy for us to overlook the effect of small but constant improvement. Just as the entire history of the universe can be reduced to the interaction of a very few forces and particles, an organization can be transformed over time by the impact of dozens and hundreds of these small improvements.

Again, there's no precise measurement. We can't say, "We're 3.5% more effective this year than we were last year." But we can notice processes going more smoothly and quickly and results that are observably better.

That, too, is quality.

3) Do away with scrap and rework.

There are two other concepts that can be applied even more directly and specifically to major HR processes than the two previously discussed. The first of these concepts is the idea that scrap and rework should be reduced—or done away with entirely.

Scrap is a product or products that are totally unusable. Rework is a product that must have one or more operations repeated on it before it can be used. In a production operation, these are significant costs. They are also clear signs of lack of quality. The scrap and rework rates are two of the most commonly tracked aspects of production.

Although you may not think of it, we have scrap and rework in HR activities. Assuming that we never, well, *almost* never, produce something that has to be 100% redone, let's refer to our application as cutting down on rework.

When do we encounter rework? We face it when:

• The HR office has almost finished renegotiating a new health plan and suddenly discovers a provision that would raise costs at least 5% for the coming year and must be renegotiated.
• The orientation training is found to be confusing to new employees and has to be revised.
• The profile used to identify candidates for a branch chief position turns up candidates completely unacceptable to management and has to be redone.
• A job analyst helps a manager establish a position that, it turns out, the staffing function can't find candidates for.

We usually call these mistakes errors in judgment, but they're exactly the same thing the folks on the production line call rework. They're products that weren't good enough for their intended use—didn't meet specifications—and had to be reworked: There's no significant difference between them and rework.

Why does it make a difference what we call them? Well, if we start looking at them as rework, we might begin to think of them as avoidable and look for ways to prevent them.

For instance, we might start by computing the amount of time it takes to do each instance of rework. On the line, rework is often expressed as a percentage of production; in the HR office, we might more usefully convert it into a percent of the total productive time spent. We might ask what percentage of the productive time of the individuals involved it took to:

• Renegotiate the health plan
• Redo the orientation
• Rework the profile
• Rework the position.

The point is we substitute a systematic way of looking at mistakes or rework for a haphazard one.

I'm not suggesting this is a new way of blaming those who make the mistakes. That has no place in an effective quality assurance program. Until they've surfaced, though, it's impossible to see if there's a remedy for them.

When an HR activity is repeated many times, the actions requiring rework may start to fall into identifiable patterns. Even if there aren't enough repetitions for statistical techniques to be used, the patterns can be analyzed for causes and then reduced or eliminated.

4) You can't inspect quality in.

It's true that in contemporary quality control "you can't inspect quality into a product." Here's what Kaoru Ishikawa, one of Japan's foremost experts on quality control, says about inspection: "[I]nspectors are unnecessary personnel who reduce the overall productivity of a company. They are not making anything. Inspection is necessary because defects and defectives exist. If defects and defectives disappear, inspectors become unnecessary. . . . [R]esponsibility for quality assurance rests with the producers. . . . [I]f the line worker who is responsible for a particular product is given the task of self-inspection, feedback is instantaneous and action can be taken immediately. The latter approach ensures a sharp reduction in the number of defectives."[3]

Fine, you say, but what's that got to do with personnel management? After all, we don't inspect products.

No? What is it when a supervisor or senior specialist "reviews" the work of a junior staffer? Isn't the process exactly the same?

The idea of reviewing work is so deeply ingrained in HR activities—indeed, in almost all paperwork activities—that we lose sight of what it really is. It's really inspection; it contributes nothing. It really takes the responsibility for quality work away from the originator.

It can also have another, even more serious result. If an employee knows someone else is inspecting his or her work, the employee may be tempted to slack off a little on his or her own review, knowing the formal reviewer will catch anything the employee may miss. If there's some degree of anonymity, so you don't know just whose work you're reviewing, the temptation will surely become irresistible.

As Ishikawa and others have pointed out, the Japanese succeed at quality assurance because they *trust* their people. They do not believe they need to watch (review, inspect) them constantly. This is perhaps a lesson that can be transported across cultures.

These are four general quality concepts that can be applied to HR activities. We can treat quality as important; we can strive for constant improvement; we can reduce scrap and rework; and we can reduce inspection to sampling. Each of these concepts can pay off for us in increased efficiency and effectiveness. Each of these should be built into our thinking and our managing.

True quality in HR activities, however, begins somewhere else.

Virtually all thought about quality begins with the assumption that quality is the correct manufacture and steady improvement of a given product.[4] As accurate as this assumption is on the production line, it's not really accurate in the HR arena. Our products aren't givens. In fact, choice of what to produce is often very significant. And that changes what quality means.

Quality Means First Choosing to Do the Right Thing

If *what* you do is a critical question, quality means first of all choosing to do the right things, and then doing them in the right order.

Doing the right thing. We've become so accustomed to a production-line model of quality assurance that it may seem strange even to speak of "doing the right thing" as an intrinsic factor in quality. Yet how can it be otherwise?

Quality, as the word is most often used, is a characteristic of *efficient* processes. Efficient production results from a high *rate* of output with a minimum of *scrap* and *rework* or, alternatively, a high rate of output times a high percentage of acceptable output.

Although efficiency is important in a personnel office, effectiveness is the name of the game. Efficiency is important to the extent that it represents the cost-effective production of worthwhile (effective) results. It's the results that count.

Thomas Gilbert uses the word "competent" to describe a person or activity that produces a valuable result at a reasonable cost: "Roughly speaking, *competent* people are those who can create valuable results without using excessively costly behavior. . . . Imagine the 'world's greatest' team of bridge builders working smoothly to create the most beautiful and nearly indestructible bridge at the lowest possible cost. Is the team competent? The distinction between competence and efficiency would be very clear if we should learn that our 'world's greatest' team built the bridge across the wrong river. Obviously, efficient behavior applied in the wrong direction can be even more incompetent than bumbling efforts in the right directions."[5]

In personnel management, a quality result is first of all a *competent* result, in Dr. Gilbert's sense.

Just what does this mean? It means that a product can only be a quality product if it is first of all the right product. For example:

The goal of any referral system is for a supervisor to make a good selection. A system that provides him or her with a number of highly qualified candidates from which to make this selection is a quality system. It's also helpful if it's an efficient system, with few inspections and little or no rework—but this is clearly a secondary consideration.

The purpose of an instance of training is to create or increase a capability in trainees. If they possess this capability when they finish training, it has been quality training. If the trainer was interesting, used effective examples, and kept the class moving, so much the better. None of this, however, will substitute for a quality result.

The point is straightforward: For many HR activities, the choice of the goal—the choice of *what* to do—is so important that no amount of improvement in the *how* can offset a poor choice. Put more formally, the efficiency with which an action is carried out can never itself create an effective action.

This is a key difference from production-oriented quality control, and one that's overlooked at great peril. If we spend our time tweaking the efficiency factors to the neglect of effectiveness, we'll produce (in Dr. Gilbert's terms) only highly efficient incompetence.

Items Must Be Accomplished in Their Correct Priority

Doing things in the right order. That we can choose what to do means the first requirement of quality is to do the right thing—not a less effective action. The second requirement stems from the same roots and is just as necessary. We need to do the right thing—not something with a lower priority.

On a production line, there are differences in the kinds of steps that are taken. Some steps are important for further processing; until they're done, other steps can't be done. You can't paint a door until it's installed.

Some steps are critical; if they're not done right the entire product may fail. If you leave out the playback head on a VCR, the entire system is useless.

Some steps are demanding; it's difficult to get them right. Attaching the leads to a microchip without breaks, shorts or foreign particles takes concentration and skill.

But *every* step must be performed, whether it's required for further steps; whether it's critical; or whether it's demanding. There may be freedom to schedule when it's performed, but never whether.

HR work isn't like that. If you work in a personnel office like the ones I'm used to, there's never enough time to get everything done that should be done. The day-to-day imperatives of recruiting, training, negotiating, *et al.* must be met. Consultation and advice need to be given. Mid- and long-range planning need to be done. Customers need to be visited. *Ad infinitum.*

The second requirement of HR quality is that time be allocated to activities in the right priority. And this, also, is a true quality requirement.

The first requirement says that no matter how efficient an action is it can't be a quality action if it's ineffective. The second requirement goes even further. It says that no matter how efficiently and effectively an action is done it will never be a quality action if the time could have been spent on a higher-priority task.

Again, this is an intrinsic part of true quality. For instance, it is quality to:

- Rework an interoffice memo three or four times to get the wording just perfect when the recruiting plan is only half done
- Check and recheck the data used for a report projecting hiring for a year, with a known error of at least 20%, when health insurance payouts are running 10% over estimates
- Draw up an ambitious organizational development scheme when 40% of the supervisors haven't had even the basic supervisory training?

How could any of these actions be a quality action in any meaningful way? They couldn't. But do the accounts sound unfamiliar? Has it been that long since you saw a similar low-priority action lavished with such meticulous attention?

This ties in directly with one of the important findings of the past decade or so. Many people used to think that effective performers did the same things as poor performers, but did them better. There's a lot of evidence now that this isn't true. Top performers generally not only do better but *different*; they allocate their time in accordance with different priorities.

One problem with misallocation of priorities is that the individual may be quite busy, performing efficiently and producing a visible result. Judged in terms of the product in isolation, it's a competent result. But it's the wrong result—and for this reason can never be a high-quality result.

Actually, time can be misallocated in two different ways. First, the individual may simply be doing a lower-priority task. The third example above, planning a bold organizational development venture when supervisors aren't being adequately trained, is this kind of poor quality. Second, the individual may be doing a necessary task, but spending time "doing it perfectly" that could have been used for higher priority work. Getting the memo or the report "just so" in the examples above represents this kind of misplaced priorities.

Like so many things in life, quality in HR activities is a question of where you focus. Because the quality assurance movement has grown up in a manufacturing environment—where the product is set and the process is what we focus on—it can't be applied directly to HR activities. We can, however, take key ideas from this environment and apply them.

- We can emphasize quality work and insist on it.
- We can promote constant improvement.
- We can reduce scrap and rework.
- Perhaps most importantly, we can reduce inspection, i.e., review.

The truth is, though, that none of these actions individually or in concert can produce a quality action. In the HR business, a quality action is first of all a *competent* action. It is purely and simply doing the right thing.

We may produce a low-quality result by doing the wrong thing. We may produce it by doing something with a lower priority than what we should be doing. Either way, we haven't produced a quality result—and no amount of attention to the quality of the process will make it one.

There is perhaps a final moral buried in this. Bureaucracy has been described as the triumph of process over product, of means over ends. Identifying quality solely with process is a subtle but most effective way of promoting this dislocation of effort. Identifying quality first with the result is a way of counteracting it.

Endnotes

1. Poling, H.A., president and chief operating officer, Ford Motor Co., on the first page of testimonials to Kaoru Ishikawa in Mr. Ishikawa's *What Is Total Quality Control? The Japanese Way.* (tr. David J. Lu) Prentice Hall: Englewood Cliffs, NJ, 1985.
2. Imai, Masaaki, *Kaisen*. Random House: New York, NY, 1986. (Kaisen is the Japanese word for improvement.)
3. Ishikawa, Kaoru, *Ibid*. pp. 77–78. This is only a small part of Dr. Ishikawa's objection to inspection, but it is the part most relevant to HR activities.
4. Two of my favorite books on quality are something of an exception to this. *I Know It When I See It* and *Theory Why?*, both by John Guaspari, deal with quality in a broader context. Both are published by Amacom: New York, NY, in 1985 and 1986 respectively.
5. Gilbert, Thomas, *Human Competence*. McGraw Hill: New York, NY, 1978, pp. 17 and 73. *Theory Why?*, by Guaspari, also deals with the relationship between quality (efficiency) and effectiveness.

The House of Quality

By John R. Hauser and Don Clausing

Digital Equipment, Hewlett-Packard, AT&T, and ITT are getting started with it. Ford and General Motors use it—at Ford alone there are more than 50 applications. The "house of quality," the basic design tool of the management approach known as quality function deployment (QFD), originated in 1972 at Mitsubishi's Kobe shipyard site. Toyota and its suppliers then developed it in numerous ways. The house of quality has been used successfully by Japanese manufacturers of consumer electronics, home appliances, clothing, integrated circuits, synthetic rubber, construction equipment, and agricultural engines. Japanese designers use it for services like swimming schools and retail outlets and even for planning apartment layouts.

A set of planning and communication routines, quality function deployment focuses and coordinates skills within an organization, first to design, then to manufacture and market goods that customers want to purchase and will continue to purchase. The foundation of the house of quality is the belief that products should be designed to reflect customers' desires and tastes—so marketing people, design engineers, and manufacturing staff must work closely together from the time a product is first conceived.

The house of quality is a kind of conceptual map that provides the means for interfunctional planning and communications. People with different problems and responsibilities can thrash out design priorities while referring to patterns of evidence on the house's grid.

What's So Hard About Design

David Garvin points out that there are many dimensions to what a consumer means by quality and that it is a major challenge to design products that satisfy all of these at once.[1] Strategic quality management means more than avoiding repairs for consumers. It means that companies learn from customer experience and reconcile what they want with what engineers can reasonably build.

Before the industrial revolution, producers were close to their customers. Marketing, engineering, and manufacturing were integrated—in the same individual. If a knight wanted armor, he talked directly to the armorer, who translated the knight's desires into a product. The two might discuss the material—plate rather than chain armor—and details like fluted surfaces for greater bending strength. Then the armorer would design the production process. For strength—who knows why?—he cooled the steel plates in the urine of a black goat. As for a production plan, he arose with the cock's crow to light the forge fire so that it would be hot enough by midday.

Today's fiefdoms are mainly inside corporations. Marketing people have their domain, engineers theirs. Customer surveys will find their way onto designers' desks, and R&D plans reach manufacturing engineers. But usually, managerial functions remain disconnected, producing a costly and demoralizing environment in which product quality and the quality of the production process itself suffer.

Top executives are learning that the use of interfunctional teams benefits design. But if top management *could* get marketing, designing, and manufacturing executives to sit down together, what should these people talk about? How could they get their meeting off the ground? This is where the house of quality comes in.

Consider the location of an emergency brake lever in one American sporty car. Placing it on the left between the seat and door solved an engineering problem. But it also guaranteed that women in skirts could not get in and out gracefully. Even if the system were to last a lifetime, would it satisfy customers?

In contrast, Toyota improved its rust prevention record from one of the worst in the world to one of the best by coordinating design and production decisions to focus on this customer concern. Using the house of quality, designers broke down "body durability" into 53 items covering everything from climate to modes of operation. They obtained customer evaluations and ran experiments on nearly every detail of production, from pump operation to temperature control and coating composition.

Decisions on sheet metal details, coating materials, and baking temperatures were all focused on those aspects of rust prevention most important to customers.

Today, with marketing techniques so much more sophisticated than ever before, companies can measure, track, and compare customers' perceptions of products with remarkable accuracy; all companies have opportunities to compete on quality. And costs certainly justly an emphasis on quality design. By looking first at customer needs, then designing across corporate functions, manufacturers can reduce prelaunch time and after-launch tinkering.

Exhibit I compares start up and preproduction costs at Toyota Auto Body in 1977, before QFD, to those costs in 1984, when QFD was well under way. House of quality meetings early on reduced costs by more than 60%. *Exhibit II* reinforces this evidence by comparing the number of design changes at a Japanese auto manufacturer using QFD with changes at a U.S. automaker. The Japanese design was essentially frozen before the first car came off the assembly line, while the U.S. company was still revamping months later.

Exhibit I
Startup and preproduction costs at Toyota Auto Body before and after QFD

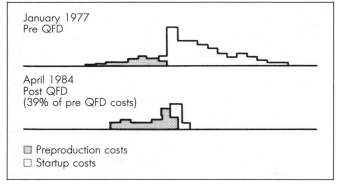

January 1977
Pre QFD

April 1984
Post QFD
(39% of pre QFD costs)

☐ Preproduction costs
☐ Startup costs

Building the House

There is nothing mysterious about the house of quality. There is nothing particularly difficult about it either, but it does require some effort to get used to its conventions. Eventually one's eye can bounce knowingly around the house as it would over a road map or a navigation chart. We have seen some applications that started with more than 100 customer requirements and more than 130 engineering

considerations. A fraction of one subchart, in this case for the door of an automobile, illustrates the house's basic concept well. We've reproduced this subchart portion in the illustration "House of Quality," and we'll discuss each section step-by-step.

Exhibit II
Japanese automaker with QFD made fewer changes than U.S. company with QFD

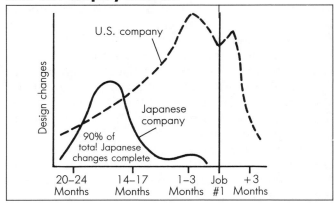

What do customers want? The house of quality begins with the customer, whose requirements are called customer attributes (CAs)—phrases customers use to describe products and product characteristics (see *Exhibit III*). We've listed a few here; a typical application would have 30 to 100 CAs. A car door is "easy to close" or "stays open on a hill"; "doesn't leak in rain" or allows "no (or little) road noise." Some Japanese companies simply place their products in public areas and encourage potential customers to examine them, while design team members listen and note what people say. Usually, however, more formal market research is called for, via focus groups, indepth qualitative interviews, and other techniques.

CAs are often grouped into bundles of attributes that represent an overall customer concern, like "open-close" or "isolation." The Toyota rust-prevention study used eight levels of bundles to get from the total car down to the car body. Usually the project team groups CAs by consensus, but some companies are experimenting with state-of-the-art research techniques that derive groupings directly from customers' responses (and thus avoid arguments in team meetings).

CAs are generally reproduced in the customers' own words. Experienced users of the house of quality try to preserve customers' phrases and even clichés—knowing that they will be translated simultaneously by product planners, design engineers, manufacturing engineers, and salespeople.

Exhibit III
Customer attributes and bundles of CAs for a car door

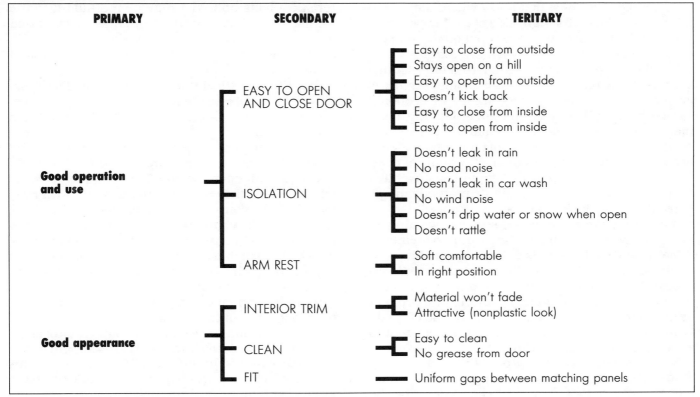

PRIMARY	SECONDARY	TERITARY

Good operation and use
- EASY TO OPEN AND CLOSE DOOR
  - Easy to close from outside
  - Stays open on a hill
  - Easy to open from outside
  - Doesn't kick back
  - Easy to close from inside
  - Easy to open from inside
- ISOLATION
  - Doesn't leak in rain
  - No road noise
  - Doesn't leak in car wash
  - No wind noise
  - Doesn't drip water or snow when open
  - Doesn't rattle
- ARM REST
  - Soft comfortable
  - In right position

Good appearance
- INTERIOR TRIM
  - Material won't fade
  - Attractive (nonplastic look)
- CLEAN
  - Easy to clean
  - No grease from door
- FIT
  - Uniform gaps between matching panels

Of course, this raises the problem of interpretation: What does a customer really mean by "quiet" or "easy"? Still, designers' words and inferences may correspond even less to customers' actual views and can therefore mislead teams into tackling problems customers consider unimportant.

Not all customers are end users, by the way. CAs can include the demands of regulators ("safe in a side collision"), the needs of retailers ("easy to display"), the requirements of vendors ("satisfy assembly and service organization"), and so forth.

Are all preferences equally important? Imagine a good door, one that is easy to close and has power windows that operate quickly. There is a problem, however. Rapid operation calls for a bigger motor, which makes the door heavier and, possibly, harder to close. Sometimes a creative solution can be found that satisfies all needs. Usually, however, designers have to trade off one benefit against another.

To bring the customer's voice to such deliberations, house of quality measures the relative importance to the customer of all CAs. Weightings are based on team members' direct experience with customers or on surveys. Some innovative businesses are using statistical techniques that allow

customers to state their preferences with respect to existing and hypothetical products. Other companies use "revealed preference techniques," which judge consumer tastes by their actions as well as by their words—an approach that is more expensive and difficult to perform but yields more accurate answers. (Consumers say that avoiding sugar in cereals is important, but do their actions reflect their claims?) Weightings are displayed in the house next to each CA—usually in terms of percentages, a complete list totaling 100% (see *Exhibit IV*).

Exhibit IV
Relative-importance weights of customer attributes

BUNDLES	CUSTOMER ATTRIBUTES	RELATIVE IMPORTANCE
EASY TO OPEN AND CLOSE DOOR	Easy to close from outside	7
	Stays open on a hill	5
ISOLATION	Doesn't leak in rain	3
	No road noise	2
	A complete list totals	100%

Will delivering perceived needs yield a competitive advantage? Companies that want to match or exceed their competition must first know where they stand relative to it. So on the right side of the house, opposite the CAs, we list customer evaluations of competitive cars matched to "our own" (see *Exhibit V*).

Ideally, these evaluations are based on scientific surveys of customers. If various customer segments evaluate products differently—luxury vs. economy car buyers, for example—product-planning team members get assessments for each segment. Comparison with the competition, of course, can identify opportunities for improvement. Take our car door, for example. With respect to "stays open on a hill," every car is weak, so we could gain an advantage here. But if we looked at "no road noise" for the same automobiles, we would see that we already have an advantage, which is important to maintain.

Marketing professionals will recognize the right-hand side of *Exhibit V* as a "perceptual map." Perceptual maps based on bundles of CAs are often used to identify strategic positioning of a product or product line. This section of the house of quality provides a natural link from product concept to a company's strategic vision.

How can we change the product? The marketing domain tells us what to do, the engineering domain tells us how to do it. Now we need to describe the product in the language of the engineer. Along the top of the house of quality, the design team lists those engineering characteristics (ECs) that are likely to affect one or more of the customer attributes (see *Exhibit VI*). The negative sign on "energy to close door" means engineers hope to reduce the energy required. If a standard engineering characteristic affects no CA, it may be redundant to the EC list on the house, or the team may have missed a customer attribute. A CA unaffected by any EC, on the other hand, presents opportunities to expand a car's physical properties.

Any EC may affect more than one CA. The resistance of the door seal affects three of the four customer attributes shown in *Exhibit VI*—and others shown later.

Engineering characteristics should describe the product in measurable terms and should directly affect customer perceptions. The weight of the door will be *felt* by the customer and is therefore a relevant EC. By contrast, the thickness of the sheet metal is a part characteristic that the customer is unlikely to perceive directly. It affects customers only by influencing the weight of the door and other engineering characteristics, like "resistance to deformation in a crash."

In many Japanese projects, the interfunctional team begins with the CAs and generates measurable characteristics for each, like foot-pounds of energy required to close the door. Teams should avoid ambiguity in interpretation of ECs or hasty justification of current quality control measurement practices. This is a time for systematic, patient analysis of each characteristic, for brainstorming. Vagueness will eventually yield indifference to things customers need. Characteristics that are trivial will make the team lose sight of the overall design and stifle creativity.

Exhibit V
Customers' evaluations of competitive products

BUNDLES	CUSTOMER ATTRIBUTES	RELATIVE IMPORTANCE
EASY TO OPEN AND CLOSE DOOR	Easy to close from outside	7
	Stays open on a hill	5
ISOLATION	Doesn't leak in rain	3
	No road noise	2

CUSTOMER PERCEPTIONS — Worst 1 2 3 4 5 Best

OUR CAR DOOR
COMPETITOR A'S
COMPETITOR B'S

Exhibit VI
Engineering characteristics tell how to change the product

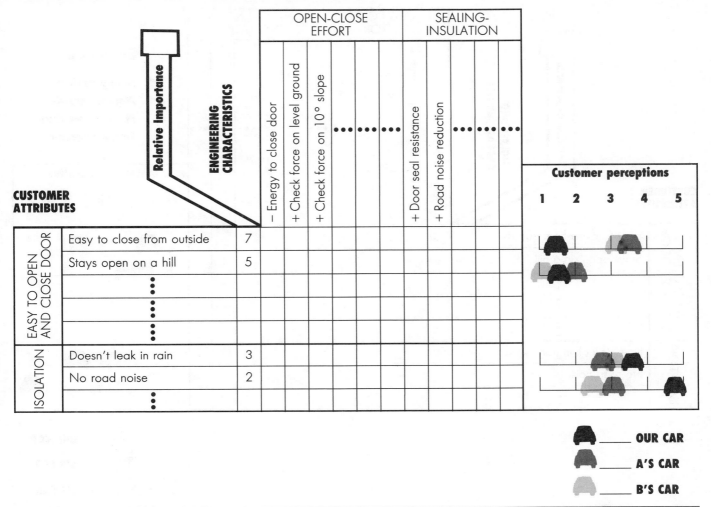

How much do engineers influence customer-perceived qualities? The interfunctional team now fills in the body of the house, the "relationship matrix," indicating how much each engineering characteristic affects each customer attribute. The team seeks consensus on these evaluations, basing them on expert engineering experience, customer responses, and tabulated data from statistical studies or controlled experiments.

The team uses numbers or symbols to establish the strength of these relationships (see *Exhibit VII*). Any symbols will do; the idea is to choose those that work best. Some teams use red symbols for relationships based on experiments and statistics and pencil marks for relationships based on judgment or intuition. Others use numbers from statistical studies. In our house, we use check marks for positive and crosses for negative relationships.

Once the team has identified the voice of the customer and linked it to engineering characteristics, it adds objective measures at the bottom of the house beneath the ECs to which they pertain (see *Exhibit VIII*). When objective measures are known, the team can eventually move to establish target values—ideal new measures for each EC in a redesigned product. If the team did its homework when it first identified the ECs, tests to measure benchmark values should be easy to complete. Engineers determine the relevant units of measurement—foot-pounds, decibels, etc.

Incidentally, if customer evaluations of CAs do not correspond to objective measures of related ECs—if, for example, the door requiring the least energy to open is perceived as "hardest to open"—then perhaps the measures are faulty or the car is suffering from an image problem that is skewing consumer perceptions.

Exhibit VII
Relationship matrix shows how engineering decisions affect customer perceptions

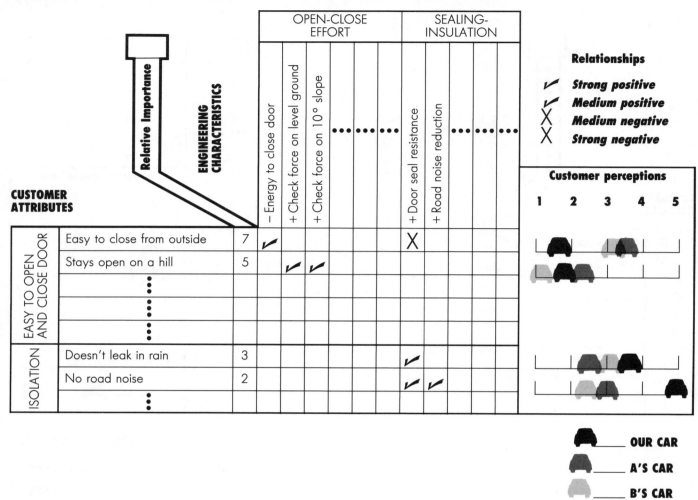

How does one engineering change affect other characteristics? An engineer's change of the gear ratio on a car window may make the window motor smaller but the window go up more slowly. And if the engineer enlarges or strengthens the mechanism, the door probably will be heavier, harder to open, or may be less prone to remain open on a slope. Of course, there might be an entirely new mechanism that improves all relevant CAs. Engineering is creative solutions and a balancing of objectives.

The house of quality's distinctive roof matrix helps engineers specify the various engineering features that have to be improved collaterally (see *Exhibit IX*). To improve the window motor, you may have to improve the hinges, weather stripping, and a range of other ECs.

Sometimes one targeted feature impairs so many others that the team decides to leave it alone. The roof matrix also facilitates necessary engineering trade-offs. The foot-pounds of energy needed to close the door, for example, are shown in negative relation to "door seal resistance" and "road noise reduction." In many ways, the roof contains the most critical information for engineers because they use it to balance the trade-offs when addressing customer benefits.

Incidentally, we have been talking so far about the basics, but design teams often want to ruminate on other information. In other words, they custom-build their houses. To the column of CAs, teams may add other columns for histories of customer complaints. To the ECs, a team may add the costs of servicing these complaints. Some applications

Exhibit VIII
Objective measures evaluate competitive products

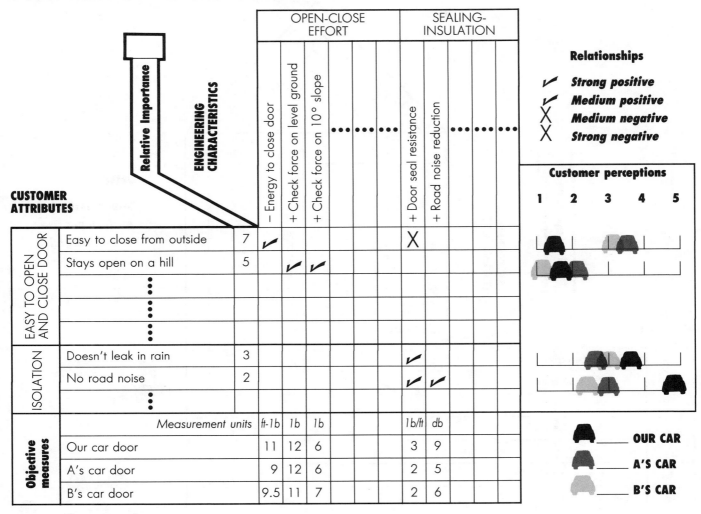

CUSTOMER ATTRIBUTES		Relative Importance	OPEN-CLOSE EFFORT				SEALING-INSULATION			
			− Energy to close door	+ Check force on level ground	+ Check force on 10° slope		+ Door seal resistance	+ Road noise reduction		
EASY TO OPEN AND CLOSE DOOR	Easy to close from outside	7	✓				X			
	Stays open on a hill	5		✓	✓					
ISOLATION	Doesn't leak in rain	3					✓			
	No road noise	2					✓	✓		
Objective measures	Measurement units		ft-lb	lb	lb		lb/ft	db		
	Our car door		11	12	6		3	9		
	A's car door		9	12	6		2	5		
	B's car door		9.5	11	7		2	6		

Relationships
✓ Strong positive
✓ Medium positive
X Medium negative
X Strong negative

Customer perceptions
1 2 3 4 5

____ OUR CAR
____ A'S CAR
____ B'S CAR

---

add data from the sales force to the CA list to represent strategic marketing decisions. Or engineers may add a row that indicates the degree of technical difficulty, showing in their own terms how hard or easy it is to make a change.

Some users of the house impute relative weights to the engineering characteristics. They'll establish that the energy needed to close the door is roughly twice as important to consider as, say, "check force on 10° slope." By comparing weighted characteristics to actual component costs, creative design teams set priorities for improving components. Such information is particularly important when cost cutting is a goal. (*Exhibit X* includes rows for technical difficulty, imputed importance of ECs, and estimated costs.)

There are no hard-and-fast rules. The symbols, lines, and configurations that work for the particular team are the ones it should use.

Using the House

How does the house lead to the bottom line? There is no cookbook procedure, but the house helps the team to set targets, which are, in fact, entered on the bottom line of the house. For engineers it is a way to summarize basic data in usable form. For marketing executives it represents the customer's voice. General managers use it to discover strategic opportunities. Indeed, the house encourages all of these groups to work together to understand one another's priorities and goals.

Exhibit IX
Roof matrix facilitates engineering creativity

Relationships

↙ **Strong positive**
↙ **Medium positive**
✗ **Medium negative**
✗ **Strong negative**

Customer perceptions

	1	2	3	4	5

OUR CAR
A'S CAR
B'S CAR

CUSTOMER ATTRIBUTES		Relative Importance	–Energy to close door	+Check force on level ground	+Check force on 10° slope		+Door seal resistance	+Road noise reduction	
EASY TO OPEN AND CLOSE DOOR	Easy to close from outside	7	↙				✗		
	Stays open on a hill	5		↙	↙				
	⋮								
ISOLATION	Doesn't leak in rain	3					↙		
	No road noise	2					↙	↙	
	⋮								
Objective measures	Measurement units		ft-1b	1b	1b		1b/ft	db	
	Our car door		11	12	6		3	9	
	A's car door		9	12	6		2	5	
	B's car door		9.5	11	7		2	6	

OPEN-CLOSE EFFORT | SEALING-INSULATION

ENGINEERING CHARACTERISTICS

The house relieves no one of the responsibility of making tough decisions. It does provide the means for all participants to debate priorities.

Let's run through a couple of hypothetical situations to see how a design team uses the house.

• Look at *Exhibit X*. Notice that our doors are much more difficult to close from the outside than those on competitors' cars. We decide to look further because our marketing data says this customer attribute is important. From the central matrix, the body of the house, we identify the ECs that effect this customer attribute: energy to close door, peak closing force, and door seal resistance. Our engineers judge the energy to close the door and the peak closing force as good candidates for improvement together because they are strongly, positively

Exhibit X
House of quality

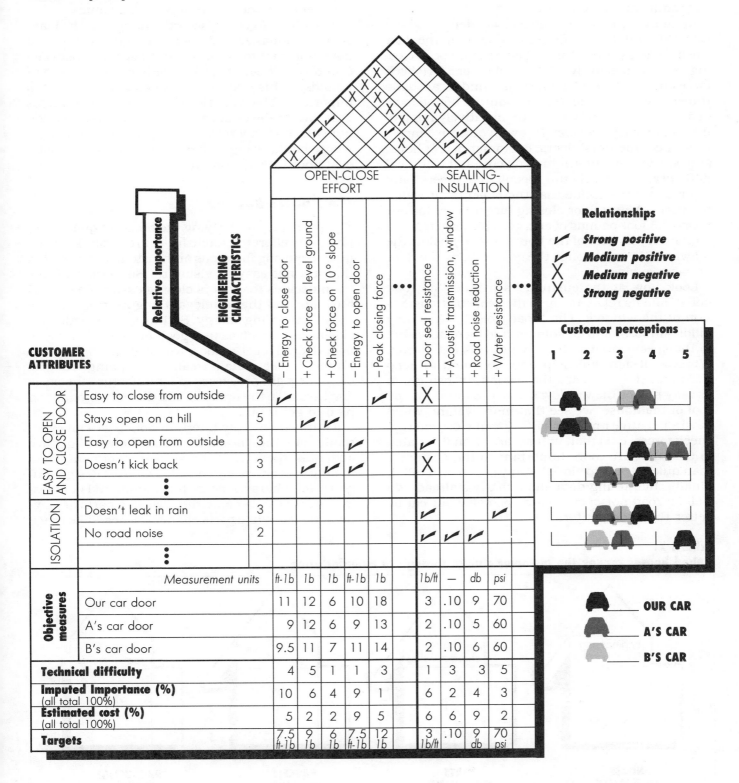

CUSTOMER ATTRIBUTES		Relative Importance	− Energy to close door	+ Check force on level ground	+ Check force on 10° slope	− Energy to open door	− Peak closing force	+ Door seal resistance	+ Acoustic transmission, window	+ Road noise reduction	+ Water resistance
EASY TO OPEN AND CLOSE DOOR	Easy to close from outside	7	✔				✔	X			
	Stays open on a hill	5		✔	✔						
	Easy to open from outside	3				✔		✔			
	Doesn't kick back	3		✔	✔	✔		X			
ISOLATION	Doesn't leak in rain	3						✔			✔
	No road noise	2						✔	✔	✔	
Objective measures	Measurement units		ft-lb	lb	lb	ft-lb	lb	lb/ft	—	db	psi
	Our car door		11	12	6	10	18	3	.10	9	70
	A's car door		9	12	6	9	13	2	.10	5	60
	B's car door		9.5	11	7	11	14	2	.10	6	60
Technical difficulty			4	5	1	1	3	1	3	3	5
Imputed Importance (%) (all total 100%)			10	6	4	9	1	6	2	4	3
Estimated cost (%) (all total 100%)			5	2	2	9	5	6	6	9	2
Targets			7.5 ft-lb	9 lb	6 lb	7.5 ft-lb	12 lb	3 lb/ft	.10	9 db	70 psi

ENGINEERING CHARACTERISTICS

OPEN-CLOSE EFFORT

SEALING-INSULATION

Relationships

✔ **Strong positive**
✔ **Medium positive**
X **Medium negative**
X **Strong negative**

Customer perceptions
1 2 3 4 5

OUR CAR
A'S CAR
B'S CAR

related to the consumer's desire to close the door easily. They determine to consider all the engineering ramifications of door closing.

Next, in the roof of the house, we identify which other ECs might be affected by changing the door closing energy. Door opening energy and peak closing force are positively related, but other ECs (check force on level ground, door seals, window acoustic transmission, road noise reduction) are bound to be changed in the process and are negatively related. It is not an easy decision. But with objective measures of competitors' doors, customer perceptions, and considering information on cost and technical difficulty, we—marketing people, engineers, and top managers—decide that the benefits outweigh the costs. A new door closing target is set for our door—7.5 foot-pounds of energy. This target, noted on the very bottom of the house directly below the relevant EC, establishes the goal to have the door "easiest to close."

Look now at the customer attribute "no road noise" and its relationship to the acoustic transmission of the window. The "road noise" CA is only mildly important to customers, and its relationship to the specifications of the window is not strong. Window design will help only so much to keep things quiet. Decreasing the acoustic transmission usually makes the window heavier. Examining the roof of the house, we see that more weight would have a negative impact on ECs (open-close energy, check forces, etc.) that, in turn, are strongly related to CAs that are more important to the customer than quiet ("easy to close," "stays open on a hill"). Finally, marketing data show that we already do well on road noise; customers perceive our car as better than competitors'.

In this case, the team decides not to tamper with the window's transmission of sound. Our target stays equal to our current acoustic values.

In setting targets, it is worth noting that the team should emphasize customer-satisfaction values and not emphasize tolerances. Do not specify "between 6 and 8 foot-pounds," but rather say, "7.5 foot-pounds." This may seem a small matter, but it is important. The rhetoric of tolerances encourages drift toward the least costly end of the specification limit and does not reward designs and components whose engineering values closely attain a specific customer-satisfaction target.

The Houses Beyond

The principles underlying the house of quality apply to any effort to establish clear relations between manufacturing functions and customer satisfaction that are not easy to visualize. Suppose that our team decides that doors closing easily is a critical attribute and that a relevant engineering characteristic is closing energy. Setting a target value for closing energy gives us a goal, but it does not give us a door. To get a door, we need the right parts (frame, sheet metal, weather stripping, hinges, etc.), the right processes to manufacture the parts and assemble the product, and the right production plan to get it built.

If our team is truly interfunctional, we can eventually take the "hows" from our house of quality and make them the "whats" of another house, one mainly concerned with detailed product design. Engineering characteristics like foot-pounds of closing energy can become the rows in a parts deployment house, while parts characteristics—like hinge

Exhibit XI
Linked houses convey the customer's voice through to manufacturing

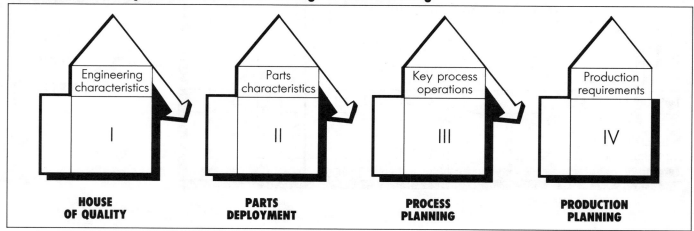

properties or the thickness of the weather stripping—become the columns (see *Exhibit XI*).

This process continues to a third and fourth phase as the "hows" of one stage become the "whats" of the next. Weather-stripping thickness—a "how" in the parts house—becomes a "what" in a process planning house. Important process operations, like "rpm of the extruder producing the weather stripping" become the "hows." In the last phase, production planning, the key process operations, like "rpm of the extruder," become the "whats," and production requirements—knob controls, operator training, maintenance—become the "hows."

These four linked houses implicitly convey the voice of the customer through to manufacturing. A control knob setting of 3.6 gives an extruder speed of 100 rpm; this helps give a reproducible diameter for the weather-stripping bulb, which gives good sealing without excessive door-closing force. This feature aims to satisfy the customer's need for a dry, quiet car with an easy-to-close door.

None of this is simple. An elegant idea ultimately decays into process, and processes will be confounding as long as human beings are involved. But that is no excuse to hold back. If a technique like house of quality can help break down functional barriers and encourage teamwork, serious efforts to implement it will be many times rewarded.

What is also not simple is developing an organization capable of absorbing elegant ideas. The principal benefit of the house of quality is quality in-house. It gets people thinking in the right directions and thinking together. For most U.S. companies, this alone amounts to a quiet revolution.

Endnote

1. David A. Garvin, "Competing on the Eight Dimensions of Quality," HBR November–December 1987, p. 101.

Competing on the Eight Dimensions of Quality

By David A. Garvin

U.S. managers know that they have to improve the quality of their products because, alas, U.S. consumers have told them so. A survey in 1981 reported that nearly 50% of U.S. consumers believed that the quality of U.S. products had dropped during the previous five years; more recent surveys have found that a quarter of consumers are "not at all" confident that U.S. industry can be depended on to deliver reliable products. Many companies have tried to upgrade their quality, adopting programs that have been staples of the quality movement for a generation: cost of quality calculations, interfunctional teams, reliability engineering, or statistical quality control. Few companies, however, have learned to *compete* on quality. Why?

Part of the problem, of course, is that until Japanese and European competition intensified, not many companies seriously tried to make quality programs work even as they implemented them. But even if companies *had* implemented the traditional principles of quality control more rigorously, it is doubtful that U.S. consumers would be satisfied today. In my view, most of those principles were narrow in scope; they were designed as purely defensive measures to preempt failures or eliminate "defects." What managers need now is an aggressive strategy to gain and hold markets, with high quality as a competitive linchpin.

Quality Control

To get a better grasp of the defensive character of traditional quality control, we should understand what the quality movement in the United States has achieved so far. How much expense on quality was tolerable? How much "quality" was enough? In 1951, Joseph Juran tackled these questions in the first edition of his *Quality Control Handbook,*

a publication that became the quality movement's bible. Juran observed that quality could be understood in terms of avoidable and unavoidable costs: the former resulted from defects and product failures like scrapped materials or labor hours required for rework, repair, and complaint processing; the latter were associated with prevention, i.e., inspection, sampling, sorting, and other quality control initiatives. Juran regarded failure costs as "gold in the mine" because they could be reduced sharply by investing in quality improvement. He estimated that avoidable quality losses typically ranged from $500 to $1,000 per productive operator per year—big money back in the 1950s.

Reading Juran's book, executives inferred roughly how much to invest in quality improvement: expenditures on prevention were justified if they were lower than the costs of product failure. A corollary principle was that decisions made early in the production chain (e.g., when engineers first sketched out a product's design) have implications for the level of quality costs incurred later, both in the factory and the field.

In 1956, Armand Feigenbaum took Juran's ideas a step further by proposing "total quality control" (TQC). Companies would never make high-quality products, he argued, if the manufacturing department were forced to pursue quality in isolation. TQC called for "interfunctional teams" from marketing, engineering, purchasing, and manufacturing. These teams would share responsibility for all phases of design and manufacturing and would disband only when they had placed a product in the hands of a satisfied customer—who remained satisfied.

Feigenbaum noted that all new products moved through three stages of activity: design control, incoming material control, and product or shop-floor control. This was a step in the right direction. But Feigenbaum did not really consider how quality was first of all a strategic question for any business; how, for instance, quality might govern the development of a design and the choice of features or options. Rather, design control meant for Feigenbaum mainly preproduction assessments of a new design's manufacturability, or that projected manufacturing techniques should be debugged through pilot runs. Materials control included vendor evaluations and incoming inspection procedures.

In TQC, quality was a kind of burden to be shared—no single department shouldered all the responsibility. Top management was ultimately accountable for the effectiveness of the system; Feigenbaum, like Juran, proposed careful reporting of the costs of quality to senior executives in order to ensure their commitment. The two also stressed statistical approaches to quality, including process control charts that set limits to acceptable variations in key variables affecting a product's production. They endorsed sampling procedures that allowed managers to draw inferences about the quality of entire batches of products from the condition of items in a small, randomly selected sample.

Despite their attention to these techniques, Juran, Feigenbaum, and other experts like W. Edwards Deming were trying to get managers to see beyond purely statistical controls on quality. Meanwhile, another branch of the quality movement emerged, relying even more heavily on probability theory and statistics. This was "reliability engineering," which originated in the aerospace and electronics industries.

In 1950, only one-third of the U.S. Navy's electronic devices worked properly. A subsequent study by the Rand Corporation estimated that every vacuum tube the military used had to be backed by nine others in warehouses or on order. Reliability engineering addressed these problems by adapting the laws of probability to the challenge of predicting equipment stress.

Reliability engineering measures led to:

Techniques for reducing failure rates while products were still in the design stage.

Failure mode and effect analysis, which systematically reviewed how alternative designs could fail.

Individual component analysis, which computed the failure probability of key components and aimed to eliminate or strengthen the weakest links.

Derating, which required that parts by used below their specified stress levels.

Redundancy, which called for a parallel system to back up an important component or subsystem in case it failed.

Naturally, an effective reliability program required managers to monitor field failures closely to give company engineers the information needed to plan new designs. Effective field failure reporting also demanded the development of systems of data collection, including return of failed parts to the laboratory for testing and analysis.

Now, the proponents of all these approaches to quality control might well have denied that their views of quality were purely defensive. But what else was implied by the solutions they stressed—material controls, outgoing batch inspections, stress tests? Perhaps the best way to see the implications of their logic is in traditional quality control's most extreme form, a program called "Zero Defects." No other program defined quality so stringently as an absence of failures—and no wonder, since it emerged from the defense industries where the product was a missile whose flawless operation was, for obvious reasons, imperative.

In 1961, the Martin Company was building Pershing missiles for the U.S. Army. The design of the missile was sound, but Martin found that it could maintain high quality only through a massive program of inspection. It decided to offer workers incentives to lower the defect rate, and in December 1961, delivered a Pershing Missile to Cape Canaveral with "zero discrepancies." Buoyed by this success, Martin's general manager in Orlando, Florida accepted a challenge, issued by the U.S. Army's missile command, to deliver the first field Pershing one month ahead of schedule. But he went even further. He promised that the missile would be perfect, with no hardware problems or document errors, and that all equipment would be fully operational 10 days after delivery (the norm was 90 days or more).

Two months of feverish activity followed; Martin asked all employees to contribute to building the missile exactly right the first time since there would be virtually no time for the usual inspections. Management worked hard to maintain enthusiasm on the plant floor. In February 1962, Martin delivered on time a perfect missile that was fully operational in less than 24 hours.

This experience was eye-opening for both Martin and the rest of the aerospace industry. After careful review, management concluded that, in effect, its own changed attitude had assured the project's success. In the words of one close observer: "The one time management demanded perfection, it happened!"[1] Martin management thereafter told employees that the only acceptable quality standard was "zero defects." It instilled this principle in the work force through training, special events, and by posting quality results. It set goals for workers and put great effort into giving each worker positive criticism. Formal techniques for problem solving, however, remained limited. For the most part, the program focused on motivation—on changing the attitudes of employees.

Strategic Quality Management

On the whole, U.S. corporations did not keep pace with quality control innovations the way a number of overseas competitors did. Particularly after World War II, U.S. corporations expanded rapidly and many became complacent. Managers knew that consumers wouldn't drive a VW Beetle, indestructible as it was, if they could afford a fancier car—even if this meant more visits to the repair shop.

But if U.S. car manufacturers *had* gotten their products to outlast Beetles, U.S. quality managers still would not have been prepared for Toyota Corollas—or Sony televisions. Indeed, there was nothing in the principles of quality control to disabuse them of the idea that quality was merely something that could hurt a company if ignored; that added quality was the designer's business—a matter, perhaps, of chrome and push buttons.

The beginnings of strategic quality management cannot be dated precisely because no single book or article marks its inception. But even more than in consumer electronics and cars, the volatile market in semiconductors provides a telling example of change. In March 1980, Richard W. Anderson, general manager of Hewlett-Packard's Data Systems Division, reported that after testing 300,000 16K RAM chips from three U.S. and three Japanese manufacturers, Hewlett-Packard had discovered wide disparities in quality. At incoming inspection, the Japanese chips had a failure rate of zero; the comparable rate for the three U.S. manufacturers was between 11 and 19 failures per 1,000. After 1,000 hours of use, the failure rate of the Japanese chips was between 1 and 2 per 1,000; usable U.S. chips failed up to 27 times per thousand.

Several U.S. semiconductor companies reacted to the news impulsively, complaining that the Japanese were sending only their best components to the all-important U.S. market. Others disputed the basic data. The most perceptive market analysts, however, noted how differences in quality coincided with the rapid ascendancy of Japanese chip manufacturers. In a few years the Japanese had gone from a standing start to significant market shares in both the 16K and 64K chip markets. Their message—intentional or not—was that quality could be a potent strategic weapon.

U.S. semiconductor manufacturers got the message. In 16K chips the quality gap soon closed. And in industries as diverse as machine tools and radial tires, each of which had seen its position erode in the face of Japanese competition, there has been a new seriousness about quality too. But how to translate seriousness into action? Managers who are now determined to compete on quality have been thrown back on the old questions: How much quality is enough? What does it take to look at quality from the customer's vantage point? These are still hard questions today.

To achieve quality gains, I believe, managers need a new way of thinking, a conceptual bridge to the consumer's vantage point. Obviously, market studies acquire a new importance in this context, as does a careful review of competitors' products. One thing is certain: high quality means pleasing consumers, not just protecting them from annoyances. Product designers, in turn, should shift their attention from prices at the time of purchase to life cycle costs that include expenditures on service and maintenance—the customer's total costs. Even consumer complaints play a new role because they provide a valuable source of product information.

But managers have to take a more preliminary step—a crucial one, however obvious it may appear. They must first develop a clear vocabulary with which to discuss quality as *strategy*. They must break down the world quality into manageable parts. Only then can they define the quality niches in which to compete.

I propose eight critical dimensions or categories of quality that can serve as a framework for strategic analysis: performance, features, reliability, conformance, durability, serviceability, aesthetics, and perceived quality.[2] Some of these are always mutually reinforcing; some are not. A product or service can rank high on one dimension of quality and low on another—indeed, an improvement in one may be achieved only at the expense of another. It is precisely this interplay that makes strategic quality management possible; the challenge to managers is to compete on selected dimensions.

1. Performance

Of course, performance refers to a product's primary operating characteristics. For an automobile, performance would include traits like acceleration, handling, cruising speed, and comfort; for a television set, performance means sound and picture clarity, color, and the ability to receive distant stations. In service businesses—say, fast food and airlines—performance often means prompt service.

Because this dimension of quality involves measurable attributes, brands can usually be ranked objectively on individual aspects of performance. Overall, performance rankings, however, are more difficult to develop, especially when they involve benefits that not every consumer needs. A power shovel with a capacity of 100 cubic yards per hour will "outperform" one with a capacity of 10 cubic yards per hour. Suppose, however, that the two shovels possessed the identical, capacity—60 cubic yards per hour—but achieved it differently: one with a 1-cubic-yard bucket operating at 60 cycles per hour, the other with a 2-cubic-yard bucket operating at 30 cycles per hour. The capacities of the shovels would then be the same, but the shovel with the larger bucket could handle massive boulders while the shovel with the smaller bucket could perform precision work. The "superior performer" depends entirely on the task.

Some cosmetics wearers judge quality by a product's resistance to smudging; others, with more sensitive skin, assess it by how well it leaves skin irritation-free. A 10-watt light bulb provides greater candlepower than a 60-watt bulb, yet few customers would regard the difference as a measure of quality. The bulbs simply belong to different performance classes. So the question of whether performance differences are quality differences may depend on circumstantial preferences—but preferences based on functional requirements, not taste.

Some performance standards *are* based on subjective preferences, but the preferences are so universal that they have the force of an objective standard. The quietness of an automobile's ride is usually viewed as a direct reflection of its quality. Some people like a dimmer room, but who wants a noisy car?

2. Features
Similar thinking can be applied to features, a second dimension of quality that is often a secondary aspect of performance. Features are the "bells and whistles" of products and services, those characteristics that supplement their basic functioning. Examples include free drinks on a plane, permanent-press cycles on a washing machine, and automatic tuners on a color television set. The line separating primary performance characteristics from secondary features is often difficult to draw.

What is crucial, again, is that features involve objective and measurable attributes; objective individual needs, not prejudices, affect their translation into quality differences.

To many customers, of course, superior quality is less a reflection of the availability of particular features than of the total number of options available. Often, choice is quality: buyers may wish to customize or personalize their purchases. Fidelity Investments and other mutual fund operators have pursued this more "flexible" approach. By offering their clients a wide range of funds covering such diverse fields as health care, technology, and energy—and by then encouraging clients to shift savings among these—they have virtually tailored investment portfolios.

Employing the latest in flexible manufacturing technology, Allen-Bradley customizes starter motors for its buyers without having to price its products prohibitively. Fine furniture stores offer their customers countless variations in fabric and color. Such strategies impose heavy demands on operating managers; they are an aspect of quality likely to grow in importance with the perfection of flexible manufacturing technology.

3. Reliability
This dimension reflects the probability of a product malfunctioning or failing within a specified time period. Among the most common measures of reliability are the mean time to first failure, the mean time between failures, and the failure rate per unit time. Because these measures require a product to be in use for a specified period, they are more relevant to durable goods than to products and services that are consumed instantly.

Reliability normally becomes more important to consumers as downtime and maintenance become more expensive. Farmers, for example, are especially sensitive to downtime during the short harvest season. Reliable equipment can mean the difference between a good year and spoiled crops. But consumers in other markets are more attuned than ever to product reliability too. Computers and copying machines certainly compete on this basis. And recent market research shows that, especially for young women, reliability has become an automobile's most desired attribute. Nor is the government, our biggest single consumer, immune. After seeing its expenditures for major weapons repair jump from $7.4 billion in fiscal year 1980 to $14.9 billion in fiscal year 1985, the Department of Defense has begun cracking down on contractors whose weapons fail frequently in the field.

4. Conformance

A related dimension of quality is conformance, or the degree to which a product's design and operating characteristics meet established standards. This dimension owes the most to the traditional approaches to quality pioneered by experts like Juran.

All products and services involve specifications of some sort. When new designs or models are developed, dimensions are set for parts and purity standards for materials. These specifications are normally expressed as a target or "center"; deviance form the center is permitted within a specified range. Because this approach to conformance equates good quality with operating inside a tolerance band, there is little interest in whether specifications have been met exactly. For the most part, dispersion within specification limits is ignored.

One drawback of this approach is the problem of "tolerance stack-up": when two or more parts are to be fit together, the size of their tolerances often determines how well they will match. Should one part fall at a lower limit of its specification, and a matching part at its upper limit, a tight fit is unlikely. Even if the parts are rated acceptable initially, the link between them is likely to wear more quickly than one made from parts whose dimensions have been centered more exactly.

To address this problem, a more imaginative approach to conformance has emerged. It is closely associated with Japanese manufacturers and the work of Genichi Taguchi, a prizewinning Japanese statistician. Taguchi begins with the idea of "loss function," a measure of losses from the time a product is shipped. (These losses include warranty costs, nonrepeating customers, and other problems resulting from performance failure.) Taguchi then compares such losses to two alternative approaches to quality: on the one hand, simple conformance to specifications, and on the other, a measure of the degree to which parts or products diverge from the ideal target or center.

He demonstrates that "tolerance stack-up" will be worse—more costly—when the dimensions of parts are more distant from the center than when they cluster around it, even if some parts fall outside the tolerance band entirely. According to Taguchi's approach, production process 1 in the *Exhibit* is better even though some items fall beyond specification limits. Traditional approaches favor production process 2. The challenge for quality managers is obvious.

Incidentally, the two most common measures of failure in conformance—for Taguchi and everyone else—are defect rates in the factory and, once a

Exhibit
Two approaches to conformance

In the following graphs, shaded areas under the curves indicate items whose measurements meet specifications. White areas indicate items not meeting specifications.

Production process 1

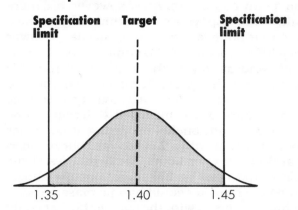

In production process 1 (favored by Taguchi), items distribute closely around the target, although some items fall outside specifications.

Production process 2

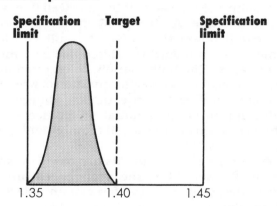

In production process 2 (favored in traditional approaches), items all distribute within specifications, but not tightly round the target.

Source: L.P. Sullivan, "Reducing Variability: A New Approach to Quality," *Quality Progress*, July 1984, p. 16.

product is in the hands of the customer, the incidence of service calls. But these measures neglect other deviations from standard, like misspelled labels or shoddy construction, that do not lead to service or repair. In service businesses, measures of conformance normally focus on accuracy and timeliness and include counts of processing errors, unanticipated delays, and other frequent mistakes.

5. Durability

A measure of product life, durability has both economic and technical dimensions. Technically, durability can be defined as the amount of use one gets from a product before it deteriorates. After so many hours of use, the filament of a light bulb burns up and the bulb must be replaced. Repair is impossible. Economists call such products "one-hoss shays" (after the carriage in the Oliver Wendell Holmes poem that was designed by the deacon to last a hundred years, and whose parts broke down simultaneously at the end of the century).

In other cases, consumers must weigh the expected cost, in both dollars and personal inconvenience, of future repairs against the investment and operating expenses of a newer, more reliable model. Durability, then, may be defined as the amount of use one gets from a product before it breaks down and replacement is preferable to continued repair.

This approach to durability has two important implications. First, it suggests that durability and reliability are closely linked. A product that often fails is likely to be scrapped earlier than one that is more reliable; repair costs will be correspondingly higher and the purchase of a competitive brand will look that much more desirable. Because of this linkage, companies sometimes try to reassure customers by offering lifetime guarantees on their products, as 3M has done with its videocassettes. Second, this approach implies that durability figures should be interpreted with care. An increase in product life may not be the result of technical improvements or the use of longer-lived materials. Rather, the underlying economic environment simply may have changed.

For example, the expected life of an automobile rose during the last decade—it now averages 14 years—mainly because rising gasoline prices and a weak economy reduced the average number of miles driven per year. Still, durability varies widely among brands. In 1981, estimated product lives for major home appliances ranged from 9.9 years (Westinghouse) to 13.2 years (Frigidaire) for refrigerators, 5.8 years (Gibson) to 18 years (Maytag) for clothes washers, 6.6 years (Montgomery Ward) to 13.5 years (Maytag) for dryers, and 6 years (Sears) to 17 years (Kirby) for vacuum cleaners.[3] This wide dispersion suggests that durability is a potentially fertile area for future quality differentiation.

6. Serviceability

A sixth dimension of quality is serviceability, or the speed, courtesy, competence, and ease of repair. Consumers are concerned not only about a product breaking down but also about the time before service is restored, the timeliness with which service appointments are kept, the nature of dealings with service personnel, and the frequency with which service calls or repairs fail to correct outstanding problems. In those cases where problems are not immediately resolved and complaints are filed, a company's complaint-handling procedures are also likely to affect customers' ultimate evaluation of product and service quality.

Some of these variables reflect differing personal standards of acceptable service. Others can be measured quite objectively. Responsiveness is typically measured by the mean time to repair, while technical competence is reflected in the incidence of multiple service calls required to correct a particular problem. Because most consumers equate rapid repair and reduced downtime with higher quality, these elements of serviceability are less subject to personal interpretation than are those involving evaluations of courtesy or standards of professional behavior.

Even reactions to downtime, however, can be quite complex. In certain environments, rapid response becomes critical only after certain thresholds have been reached. During harvest season, farmers generally accept downtime of one to six hours on harvesting equipment, such as combines, with little resistance. As downtime increases, they become anxious; beyond eight hours of downtime they become frantic and frequently go to great lengths to continue harvesting even if it means purchasing or leasing additional equipment. In markets like this, superior service can be a powerful selling tool. Caterpillar guarantees delivery of repair parts anywhere in the world within 48 hours; a competitor offers the free loan of farm equipment during critical periods should its customers' machines break down.

Customers may remain dissatisfied even after completion of repairs. How these complaints are handled is important to a company's reputation for quality and service. Eventually, profitability is likely to be affected as well. A 1976 consumer survey found that among households that initiated complaints to resolve problems, more than 40% were not satisfied with the results. Understandably, the degree of satisfaction with complaint resolution closely correlated with consumers' willingness to repurchase the offending brands.[4]

Companies differ widely in the approaches to complaint handling and in the importance they attach to this element of serviceability. Some do their best to resolve complaints; others use legal gimmicks, the silent treatment, and similar ploys to rebuff dissatisfied customers. Recently, General Electric, Pillsbury, Proctor & Gamble, Polaroid, Whirlpool, Johnson & Johnson, and other companies have sought to preempt consumer dissatisfaction by installing toll-free telephone hot lines to their customer relations departments.

7. Aesthetics

The final two dimensions of quality are the most subjective. Aesthetics—how a product looks, feels, sounds, tastes, or smells—is clearly a matter of personal judgment and a reflection of individual preference. Nevertheless, there appear to be some patterns in consumers' rankings of products on the basis of taste. A recent study of quality in 33 food categories, for example, found that high quality was most often associated with "rich and full flavor, tastes natural, tastes fresh, good aroma, and looks appetizing."[5]

The aesthetics dimension differs from subjective criteria pertaining to "performance"—the quiet car engine, say—in that aesthetic choices are not nearly universal. Not all people prefer "rich and full" flavor or even agree on what it means. Companies therefore have to search for a niche. On this dimension of quality, it is impossible to please everyone.

8. Perceived Quality

Consumers do not always have complete information about a product's or service's attributes; indirect measures may be their only basis for comparing brands. A product's durability, for example, can seldom be observed directly; it usually must be inferred from various tangible and intangible aspects of the product. In such circumstances, images, advertising, and brand names—inferences about quality rather than the reality itself—can be critical. For this reason, both Honda—which makes cars in Marysville, Ohio—and Sony—which builds color televisions in San Diego—have been reluctant to publicize that their products are "made in America."

Reputation is the primary stuff of perceived quality. Its power comes from an unstated analogy: that the quality of products today is similar to the quality of products yesterday, or the quality of goods in a new product line is similar to the quality of a company's established products. In the early 1980s, Maytag introduced a new line of dishwashers. Needless to say, salespeople immediately emphasized the product's reliability—not yet proven—because of the reputation of Maytag's clothes washers and dryers.

Competing on Quality

This completes the list of the eight dimensions of quality. The most traditional notions—conformance and reliability—remain important, but they are subsumed within a broader strategic framework. A company's first challenge is to use this framework to explore the opportunities it has to distinguish its products from another company's wares.

The quality of an automobile tire may reflect its tread-wear rate, handling, traction in dangerous driving conditions, rolling resistance (i.e., impact on gas mileage), noise levels, resistance to punctures, or appearance. High-quality furniture may be distinguished by its uniform finish, an absence of surface flaws, reinforced frames, comfort, or superior design. Even the quality of a less tangible product like computer software can be evaluated in multiple dimensions. These dimensions include reliability, ease of maintenance, match with users' needs, integrity (the extent to which unauthorized access can be controlled), and portability (the ease with which a program can be transferred from one hardware or software environment to another).

A company need not pursue all eight dimensions simultaneously. In fact, that is seldom possible unless it intends to charge unreasonably high prices. Technological limitations may impose a further constraint. In some cases, a product or service can be improved in one dimension of quality only if it becomes worse in another. Cray Research, a manufacturer of supercomputers, has faced particularly difficult choices of this sort. According to the company's chairman, if a supercomputer doesn't fail every month or so, it probably wasn't built for maximum speed; in pursuit of higher speed, Cray has deliberately sacrificed reliability.

There are other trade-offs. Consider the following:
• In entering U.S. markets, Japanese manufacturers often emphasize their products' reliability and conformance while downplaying options and features. The superior "fits and finishes" and low repair rates of Japanese cars are well known; less often recognized are their poor safety records and low resistance to corrosion.Tandem Computers has based its business on superior reliability. For computer users that find downtime intolerable, like telephone companies and utilities, Tandem has devised a fail-safe system: two processors working in parallel and linked by software that shifts responsibility between the two if an important component or subsystem fails. The result, in an industry already well-known for quality products, has been

spectacular corporate growth. In 1984, after less than 10 years in business, Tandem's annual sales topped $500 million.

• Not long ago, New York's Chemical Bank upgraded its services for collecting payments for corporations. Managers had first conducted a user survey indicating that what customers wanted most was rapid response to queries about account status. After it installed a computerized system to answer customers' calls, Chemical, which banking consumers had ranked fourth in quality in the industry, jumped to first.

• In the piano business, Steinway & Sons has long been the quality leader. Its instruments are known for their even voicing (the evenness of character and timbre in each of the 88 notes on the keyboard), the sweetness of their registers, the duration of their tone, their long lives, and even their fine cabinet work. Each piano is built by hand and is distinctive in sound and style. Despite these advantages, Steinway recently has been challenged by Yamaha, a Japanese manufacturer that has built a strong reputation for quality in a relatively short time. Yamaha has done so by emphasizing reliability and conformance, two quality dimensions that are low on Steinway's list.

These examples confirm that companies can pursue a selective quality niche. In fact, they may have no other choice, especially if competitors have established reputations for a certain kind of excellence. Few products rank high on all eight dimensions of quality. Those that do—Cross pens, Rolex watches, Rolls-Royce automobiles—require consumers to pay the cost of skilled workmanship.

Strategic Errors
A final word, not about strategic opportunities, but about the worst strategic mistakes. The first is direct confrontation with an industry's leader. As with Yamaha vs. Steinway, it is far preferable to nullify the leader's advantage in a particular niche while avoiding the risk of retaliation. Moreover, a common error is to introduce dimensions of quality that are unimportant to consumers. When deregulation unlocked the market for residential telephones, a number of manufacturers, including AT&T, assumed that customers equated quality with a wide range of expensive features. They were soon proven wrong. Fancy telephones sold poorly while durable, reliable, and easy-to-operate sets gained large market shares.

Shoddy market research often results in neglect of quality dimensions that *are* critical to consumers. Using outdated surveys, car companies

overlooked how important reliability and conformance were becoming in the 1970s; ironically, these companies failed consumers on the very dimensions that were key targets of traditional approaches to quality control.

It is often a mistake to stick with old quality measures when the external environment has changed. A major telecommunications company had always evaluated its quality by measuring timeliness—the amount of time it took to provide a dial tone, to connect a call, or to be connected to an operator. On these measures it performed well. More sophisticated market surveys, conducted in anticipation of the industry's deregulation, found that consumers were not really concerned about call connection time; consumers assumed that this would be more or less acceptable. They were more concerned with the clarity of transmission and the degree of static on the line. On these measures, the company found it was well behind its competitors.

In an industry like semiconductor manufacturing equipment, Japanese machines generally require less set-up time; they break down less often and have few problems meeting their specified performance levels. These are precisely the traits desired by most buyers. Still, U.S. equipment can *do* more. As one U.S. plant manager put it: "Our equipment is more advanced, but Japanese equipment is more developed."

Quality measures may be inadequate in less obvious ways. Some measures are too limited; they fail to capture aspects of quality that are important for competitive success. Singapore International Airlines, a carrier with a reputation for excellent service, saw its market share decline in the early 1980s. The company dismissed quality problems as the cause of its difficulties because data on service complaints showed steady improvement during the period. Only later, after SIA solicited consumer responses, did managers see the weakness of their former measures. Relative declines in service had indeed been responsible for the loss of market share. Complaint counts had failed to register problems because the proportion of passengers who wrote complaint letters was small—they were primarily Europeans and U.S. citizens rather than Asians, the largest percentage of SIA passengers. SIA also had failed to capture data about its competitors' service improvements.

The pervasiveness of these errors is difficult to determine. Anecdotal evidence suggests that many U.S. companies lack hard data and are thus more vulnerable than they need be. One survey found that 65% of executives thought that consumers could readily name—without help—a good quality brand in a big-ticket category like major home appliances. But when the question was actually posed to consumers, only 16% could name a brand for small appliances, and only 23% for large appliances.[6] Are U.S. executives that ill-informed about consumers' perceptions? The answer is not likely to be reassuring.

Managers have to stop thinking about quality merely as a narrow effort to gain control of the production process, and start thinking more rigorously about consumers' needs and preferences. Quality is not simply a problem to be solved; it is a competitive opportunity.

References

1. James F. Halpin, *Zero Defects* (New York: McGraw-Hill, 1966), p. 15.

2. This framework first appeared, in a preliminary form, in my article "What Does 'Product Quality' Really Mean?" *Sloan Management Review,* Fall 1984.

3. Roger B. Yepsen, Jr., ed., *The Durability Factor* (Emmaus, Penn: Rodale Press, 1982), p. 190.

4. TARP, *Consumer Complaint Handling in America: Final Report* (Springfield, Va.: National Technical Information Service, U.S. Department of Commerce, 1979).

5. P. Greg Bonner and Richard Nelson, "Product Attributes and Perceived Quality: Foods," in *Perceived Quality,* ed. Jacob Jacoby and Jerry C. Olson (Lexington, Mass.: Lexington Books, D.C. Heath, 1985), p. 71.

6. Consumer Network, Inc., *Brand Quality Perceptions* (Philadelphia: Consumer Network, August 1983), p. 17 and 50–51.

PART THREE

CHANGING AN ORGANIZATIONAL CULTURE

SECTION I
DIAGNOSIS

Changing an organizational culture is an enormous task that requires a systematic approach and a long term commitment. This part of the Sourcebook includes articles on the four major phases of a culture change process: diagnosis, development, delivery and determination.

The purpose of the diagnostic phase is to discover what norms, skills, and organizational support systems are needed to meet business goals.

This means talking to people—finding out their perceptions of where the organization is and where it is going. And that involves meeting with employees formally and informally at every level in the organization and gathering data through surveys. Diagnosis means finding out the expectations and concerns of top management so that it is possible to establish clear-cut, realistic goals. Also, focus groups are sometimes commissioned during this phase with a cross section of employees to find out "how things really" work in the organization so that barriers to long term change can be identified.

At the end of the Diagnostic Phase, a report is usually produced which summarizes all findings, identifies the causes of key problems and makes recommendations for improvement.

The Diagnosis Phase contains two articles. In the first article, "Assessing Cultural Change Needs," Michael Albert uses AT&T as an example of how a giant corporation altered its corporate culture.

In the second article, "A Tool for Tapping the Organizational Unconscious," Allen and Dyer present a powerful mechanism for analyzing corporate cultures.

Assessing Cultural Change Needs

By Michael Albert

In 1983, the birth of the new year brought with it, by Justice Department mandate, the creation of 23 independent Bell telephone companies. Out from under Ma Bell's umbrella, they were exposed to the inclemency of competition and consumer demand that forced them to become action-oriented and concerned with pursuing organizational excellence. New management concerns demanded the design and implementation of programs to initiate and sustain cultural change and development.

Because the training and organizational development staff will play a major role, they should be able to assess cultural change needs from a similar perspective. Presently, however, there is no widely accepted model that both groups can use to assess their organization's cultural change needs. Embracing a common model should result in more collaboration and synergy between the training and organizational development staff. This will provide cultural change and development programs that are more integrated and supportive of required individual and organizational change. After a preliminary overview of the model, I will discuss how it can be used to assess cultural change needs by describing a cultural needs analysis I prepared for a midwestern Bell telephone company.

The Dynamics of Corporate Culture

According to the model, culture results from the organization's pervading management style and the way the organization is run on a daily basis. These two factors, in turn, are directly affected by the roles and activities performed by all of the organization's managers. These describe ritualized patterns of behavior such as what is done to discuss problems, resolve conflicts, implement plans, report results, communicate and receive information, make decisions, manage change, reward performance, etc.

Because they are established at higher levels of management, such patterns directly affect culture, what lower level managers do and how workers are supervised. As we will see, during periods of cultural change, managerial roles and activities must be changed.

As the model illustrates, roles and activities should reinforce the key values and philosophy that are needed to support the organization's strategic direction. That allows the organization to adapt to environmental forces. Human resource specialists can assist management in determining two critical cultural change questions: what key values and philosophy should the organization embrace to support its strategy, and what managerial roles and activities are required to reinforce these key values and philosophy. An organization's key values represent those beliefs that have been determined essential to the organization's success. Key values include issues such as customer relations, innovation, quality, productivity improvement, growth, work ethic, community and managerial style.

The resulting corporate culture, in turn, affects the same elements that molded it. These include the way the business is run, the pervasive management style, the roles and activities that managers learn to perform, company values and philosophy, and its choice of strategic direction. In other words, corporate culture is both the result of and a contributor to numerous organizational dynamics. This is the primary reason why it is difficult to change culture in the short run.

In order to offer human resource personnel insight into how the strategic model can be used, it will help to consider the culture needs analysis prepared for a midwest Bell telephone company. This analysis was prepared by comprehensively reviewing contemporary business articles and industry reports focusing on the telecommunications industry. Human resource specialists using the model normally would gather data primarily through interviews, survey feedback, facilitated discussion, etc. This was not done in the following case study because it was the first contact with the organization. The primary objective of the analysis was to convey an understanding of the industry.

Using the Model: A Case Study

The Justice Department ruling formed the 23 Bell companies into independent businesses, organized into seven regional holding companies. Each regional company is legally and financially independent of AT&T. Prior to divestiture, the Bell companies operated in an environment characterized by little change. Low cost installation, maintenance and service were the key management issues. There was little concern or need to plan for and implement programs to respond to environmental change due to competition, customer needs or new technologies. The few strategic responses that were required in these areas were determined by AT&T and communicated to the operating companies as "things to do." Environmental analysis and strategy formulation was determined by AT&T, which functioned as a buffer from environmental

A Strategic Model for Assessing Cultural Change Needs

DRIVING FORCES IN ENVIRONMENT

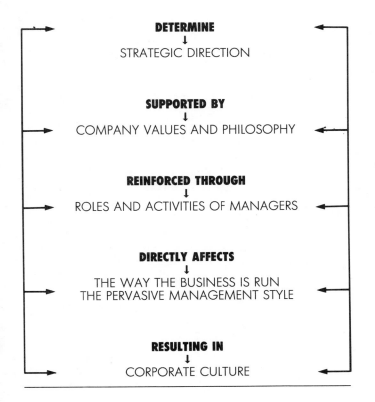

DETERMINE
↓
STRATEGIC DIRECTION

SUPPORTED BY
↓
COMPANY VALUES AND PHILOSOPHY

REINFORCED THROUGH
↓
ROLES AND ACTIVITIES OF MANAGERS

DIRECTLY AFFECTS
↓
THE WAY THE BUSINESS IS RUN
THE PERVASIVE MANAGEMENT STYLE

RESULTING IN
↓
CORPORATE CULTURE

change. Now, however, the regional and operating companies are responsible for environmental analysis and strategy formulation. This creates a difficult transition for an organization that was primarily operationally driven.

The environment that all Bell companies now face is primarily market-driven. Each operating company must respond to the competition, customer needs, technological developments, nonregulated opportunities and new financial constituencies. At the same time, they are still a regulated utility and must continue to provide low cost installation, maintenance and service. Whereas the low cost, operations-driven concern has molded their culture, they must now embrace new values and management practices in order to be successful in the rapidly changing, highly competitive telecommunications environment. Moreover, they must now determine and implement strategy.

Key values and philosophy should support an organization's strategic direction. Prior to divestiture, the values and philosophy of the Bell operating companies were implicitly defined. They were not formally assessed, written or communicated to employees. Nevertheless, they still had a significant impact on the day-to-day behavior of managers and employees. The midwestern Bell company is beginning just now to assess what values and management philosophy are required to support this new, market-driven strategic direction.

Managerial roles and activities directly affect the way a business is run and the organization's pervasive management style. It is important to emphasize that although these elements are segmented in the model, in practice they are inextricably intertwined. In other words, the day-to-day behavioral patterns and rituals of managers, are all part of the organization's management style and the way the business is run. It is important to emphasize that the way the Bell companies were managed prior to divestiture was appropriate to the environmental demands present then.

Prior to divestiture, environmental changes did not significantly affect the business of the local operating companies. Centralized control was appropriate for the company since it did not have to be concerned with new markets, technologies, customers, services, financial constituencies, etc. Its primary management concern was to provide low cost installation, maintenance and service.

Operations was the key factor to manage. Very little collaboration across departments or divisions was necessary. Information was primarily channeled from higher to lower levels. Functions with in the organization were highly segmented as each part of the organization did what was necessary to ensure that costs were kept to a minimum and day-to-day service was provided. Procedures and systems were developed to achieve these ends. Very little initiative, autonomy, or teamwork was necessary for the Bell companies to be successful.

After divestiture, however, the environment required a proactive rather than purely reactive response pattern. Management needed to learn how to respond to customer needs rapidly and to adopt a bias toward action and implementation. It also requires a problem-solving focus and substantially more collaboration and team work. Management must create an internal climate that provides more autonomy for individuals. Relevant departments and divisions need more integration, coordination, and horizontal and vertical communication. The Bell companies will not be successful if they remain highly segmented. In addition to developing these new capabilities, management must continue to provide low cost installation, maintenance and service to their customers.

A Valuable Tool

This strategic model, which training and organizational development specialists can use to assess cultural change needs, provides a foundation for the human resource staff useful in planning for and implementing cultural change programs. Human resource specialists can play a key role by facilitating the discussion of key values and management philosophy among management and staff. They can also use the model as an educational vehicle to provide an understanding of what culture is, how it develops, what the effects of culture are, etc. Perhaps the model's strongest characteristic is that senior management can relate to it because it emphasizes that corporate culture must be congruent with the organization's strategic direction. Equally important is developing programs that provide training to managers in the behavioral dimensions of the daily roles and activities that must be performed to reinforce key values and management philosophy.

A Tool for Tapping the Organizational Unconscious

By Robert F. Allen and Frank J. Dyer

The scientific conception of the individual unconscious has been with us since the time of Sigmund Freud and the beginnings of modern psychotherapy. It has helped us to understand the dynamics of individual behavior and, in some cases, to deal more effectively with its problems.

In dealing with group problems, it is quite possible—and useful—to envision another form of unconscious—an organizational unconscious that exerts a powerful influence on organizational behavior and has an immense impact on people's lives.

The organizational unconscious, as we theorize it, represents the patterns of social behaviors and normative expectations that become characteristics of organizational functioning without the members of the organization consciously choosing the behaviors in question. Thus, people in an organization frequently follow norms that have long since outlived their usefulness, as if these patterns of behavior were the only ones that could exist under the circumstances. For example, people in some organizations find it commonplace to be destructively critical of one another and not to get problems out in the open where they can be dealt with effectively, while at the same time assuming that such behavior is characteristic of human nature, rather than organizational choice. The behavior is so usual and so supported by the structures and way of life within the organization that the organizational members cannot consider other possibilities as real alternatives.[1]

A Powerful Mechanism

As is the case with much of the individual unconscious, there exist powerful mechanisms which prevent full awareness of the organizational unconscious' actual effects. Since it is painful to confront

genuinely emotionally charged problems, be they individual or collective, they are often left unexamined. The organization has a vested emotional interest in maintaining a relatively comfortable equilibrium by letting the sleeping dogs lie. It is precisely because of this, however, that negative (i.e. maladaptive) norms are able to exert such a powerful influence. The very fact that these norms operate at so dim a level of awareness ensures that they will seldom be directly addressed in typical problem-solving efforts directed at surface manifestations.

An excellent example of this problem is the course of events described in Fleishman's 1953 study of the effectiveness of human relations training for production supervisors.[2] Subjects were taken out of the organization for training in an entirely separate setting, where they seemed to acquire the target human relations skills. A follow-up evaluation of actual performance back on the job, however, revealed that after a brief period of time, the trainees reverted to their former human relations styles. From the point of view of the organizational unconscious model, the explanation for this finding is that the trainees were taught the target skills in a different cultural setting, but no attempt was made to prepare the home culture to sustain these newly acquired behaviors. When trainees returned to their familiar surroundings, they had no notion that there would be normative factors subliminally operating to undermine their new style of relating. Thus, a power which the trainees weren't even aware of exerted its subtle influence, eventually undoing the skills imparted in an alien setting.

Much the same type of thing occurs with individuals who constantly attempt new beginnings in order to change old patterns of behaving. The new beginnings are often dramatically successful at the outset—the individual stops drinking, or gives up gambling or treats others more benignly—but the unconscious factors that led to the original problem ultimately succeed in eroding the new gains. In such cases, it is not unusual for people to rationalize their backsliding in terms of some factor that is only marginally related to the real problem.[3]

Confront and Restructure

With these observations in mind, we now turn to the question of how people in organizations can uncover and deal with the real issues that they need to confront. Furthermore, how can they restructure the situation in such a way that effective action becomes possible? It is at this point that we part company from Freud and shift to a mode of action that is more akin to reality therapy, which deals with the here-and-now, with minimal emphasis on past causes.

The question of how the organizational unconscious developed its quirks is usually only academically relevant to their remediation. On the other hand, the identification of present dysfunctional patterns and direct confrontation of the buried attitudes and beliefs is as important in organizational work as it is in work with individuals. Also, too much emphasis on the past causes of these patterns too often results in unproductive blame placing or scape goating, practices which are the very antithesis of the model on which this discussion is based.

Fortunately, the process of identifying current problem patterns in organizations is far less laborious than might at first be assumed. It can often be a matter of simply asking the right questions of people who experience the negative effects of the dysfunctional norms. Experience has shown that under the right conditions, such as the confidentiality of a properly administered survey, individuals at various hierarchical levels of an organization will deliver hard-hitting yet truthful answers that shed a great deal of light on the dynamics behind the system's problems. Other uncovering techniques, such as focused group or individual interviews, may be used to supplement survey work if a more intensive procedure is desired.

As we said earlier, cultural factors are paramount in creating lasting changes. Any consciously chosen program for change must become absorbed into the everyday normative network of the organization if it is to survive as an element of that organization's culture. The demands of the program must be accepted and eventually taken for granted, so that they exert the same kind of subliminal influence as did the old norms that the program was intended to replace. In this way, those individuals who attempt to make a performance review procedure meaningful, or to adopt a more responsive supervisory style, or to set realistic and meaningful objectives, will not be regarded as outsiders or "rate busters" by their coworkers. Instead, their behavior will be accepted as normal and expected—thus giving them tremendous support in maintaining it.

Experience at our Human Resources Institute (HRI) has demonstrated that there are reliable ways of influencing cultures to ensure that new norms deliberately introduced into the system will "take" and maintain themselves over an extended period. In order to apply these influence strategies, it is first necessary to develop a precise picture of the existing normative patterns. By doing this, we generate sufficient information to target interventions toward specific areas of weakness, while avoiding wasted efforts in areas that are already strong. The work of HRI in identifying and restructuring the systems of norms that we have collectively termed "the organizational unconscious" has produced an action-oriented survey instrument, the Norms Diagnostic Index (NDI), that offers a detailed picture of this beneath-the-surface aspect of life in particular organizations. Most important, each segment of this picture is tied to a series of intervention strategies that can yield lasting results.

The Development of the NDI

The NDI was developed from an original pool of 86 survey items used by HRI over a period of more than 15 years' work with organizational cultures in diverse settings, ranging from migrant labor camps to large manufacturing and retail firms. Through a combination of factor analytic and pragmatic judgmental techniques, this pool was reduced to a final set of 38 statements dealing directly with organizational norms in 7 primary areas. To this was added an additional set of 13 items covering pay, communication, work itself and benefits, which fall in the area of traditional survey content. These items were included in the NDI's final form in order to provide in a single instrument both a comprehensive analysis of an organization's norms and a measure of popular job satisfaction dimensions. (See Figure 1.) The following discussion, however, deals with only the first 38 items.

Component Scales

Each of the seven primary scales of the NDI deals with specific areas which have been found to be significantly related to the success of cultural change programs. While they are, to some extent, inter-related with one another, both conceptually and statistically, they can also be viewed as separate focuses for organizational intervention.

1) Performance Facilitation: This factor of the NDI contains items measuring employees' perceptions of norms relating to job performance. In our work with change programs, we have found performance-facilitating norms to be extremely important. When these norms are positive within an organizational culture, people tend to agree with such statements as: "It is the norm in our organization to maintain the progress that is made," "...to care about and strive for excellent performance," "...to have a clear way of measuring results."

When such factors are low within the organizational culture, employees tend to disagree with these statements. According to the experience of HRI staff who have worked with this factor in field studies, effective performance of both individuals and work teams is directly related to the quality of norms in this area. This is in marked contrast to the typical findings of research studies using traditional job satisfaction instruments (such as Vroom's) where low relationships with performance are the rule.[4]

Specific cultural change interventions are available for organizations having difficulty in this area. Most often, these interventions seek to improve the performance evaluation and feedback process.

One of the most interesting findings of the NDI's factor analysis relates to the performance facilitation scale item, "to maintain the progress that is made." This item was found to be the most highly correlated with other items in the instrument. (In technical terms, it had the highest communality.) Thus, some aspect of what is measured by this item seems to underlie many norms in seemingly unrelated areas. This confirms one of the central principles of the normative systems approach to change described above: that maintenance of change depends on strengthening the entire network of related norms. The fact that the NDI's maintenance-of-progress item is so closely tied to the strength of norms in so many different areas would seem to provide convergent validity for that tenet of the normative systems approach.

2) Job Involvement: The next NDI factor consists of norms that reflect employees' emotional environment in their jobs and in the total organization. The items on this scale tap perceptions of those aspects of organizational climate involving goal directiveness, participation, pride, commitment

and support. Low agreement percentages on this factor would warrant interventions such as goal-setting programs, participative workshops, managerial training in modeling, and other strategies for sustaining subordinates' motivation. Such approaches have been found to produce substantial changes in response to items on this factor in HRI field studies. An excellent example of the success of a change approach, in which one of the primary goals was an increase in workers' emotional involvement in both job and community, is described in *The Quiet Revolution* by Harris and Allen (1978).[5] In this action research study, the culture of a Florida community of migrant workers was reshaped to provide more social and, ultimately, economic security for its members.

3) Training: This factor's component items focus on orientation of new employees and on meeting training needs. It has been the experience of HRI staff that employee orientation is one of the most underserved areas in the entire hiring process. It is frequently treated as a formality wherein information that would be picked up on the job eventually is simply given to the new employee in a concentrated dose. This attitude toward orientation of course creates a vacuum, which is promptly filled by other members of the work group, on whom the new person relies for knowledge of "what's what."

Unfortunately, the result of this informal process is often the very efficient transmission of negative norms. In a retail food business, for example, new checkstand employees were routinely apprised by their coworkers of the "accepted" practice of discounting fellow employees' purchases. This meant ringing up only a few items of rather large grocery orders. Of course, this wasn't really stealing, since it was perceived as a sort of perquisite enjoyed by employees of the store to supplement their base income. Any qualms expressed by unwilling newcomers were quickly squelched by group pressure. It was surprising how quickly and thoroughly new employees assimilated the attitude that this was an okay thing to do—a direct result of their "orientation."

4) Leader-Subordinate Interaction: The items of this factor measure respondents' perceptions of the extent to which leaders in the organization are concerned about their subordinates as people, take time to perform adequate follow-up, and are receptive to upward communication. Change and skill development programs involving modeling and listening effectively to other people have proved useful in instances where norms in

Figure 1
The Norms Diagnostic Index

Instructions: Norms are expected or usual ways of behaving in groups or organizations. This survey asks for your opinions concerning the norms that exist in your organization. You are to fill in the blank that best describes your agreement or disagreement with each of the statements in the survey. Some examples are given below. After completing the sample items, continue with the remaining survey items.

Example

The rating columns (left to right) are: Strongly Agree, Agree, Neutral, Disagree, Strongly Disagree, Don't Know

It's a norm around here:
A. for people to be rude to each other ( ) ( ) ( ) ( ) ( ) ( )
B. for people to be comfortably dressed ( ) ( ) ( ) ( ) ( ) ( )
C. for coffee breaks to be pleasant

It is a norm around here:
1. to maintain the progress that is made ( ) ( ) ( ) ( ) ( ) ( )
2. for people to regularly plan their work goals and review progress ( ) ( ) ( ) ( ) ( ) ( )
3. for new people to be properly oriented and trained to the job ( ) ( ) ( ) ( ) ( ) ( )
4. for leaders to take time to follow up on the jobs they've assigned to people ( ) ( ) ( ) ( ) ( ) ( )
5. for organizational policies and procedures to be helpful, well understood, and up-to-date ( ) ( ) ( ) ( ) ( ) ( )
6. for people to confront negative behavior or "norms" constructively ( ) ( ) ( ) ( ) ( ) ( )
7. for people to avoid blame placing and concentrate on looking for constructive solutions ( ) ( ) ( ) ( ) ( ) ( )
8. for people to feel satisfied with their pay ( ) ( ) ( ) ( ) ( ) ( )
9. for people to feel that their work is important ( ) ( ) ( ) ( ) ( ) ( )
10. for people to feel that the organization offers good job security ( ) ( ) ( ) ( ) ( ) ( )
11. for people to feel satisfied with the benefits programs offered by the organization ( ) ( ) ( ) ( ) ( ) ( )
12. for people to feel responsible for doing their own jobs right ( ) ( ) ( ) ( ) ( ) ( )
13. for people to have some input on decisions that affect their work ( ) ( ) ( ) ( ) ( ) ( )

14. for job orientation for new people to be more than just "sink or swim" ( ) ( ) ( ) ( ) ( ) ( )
15. for leaders to be equally concerned for people as well as results ( ) ( ) ( ) ( ) ( ) ( )
16. to review policies and procedures regularly and change them as needed ( ) ( ) ( ) ( ) ( ) ( )
17. for people to get feedback on how they're doing so they can develop as individuals ( ) ( ) ( ) ( ) ( ) ( )
18. for people to feel "turned on" and enthusiastic about what they're doing ( ) ( ) ( ) ( ) ( ) ( )
19. for selection and promotion practices to be fair ( ) ( ) ( ) ( ) ( ) ( )
20. for good performance to be rewarded through increased pay ( ) ( ) ( ) ( ) ( ) ( )
21. for people to get good feelings of accomplishment from their work ( ) ( ) ( ) ( ) ( ) ( )
22. not to have to rely on the "grapevine" as their best source of information about the organization ( ) ( ) ( ) ( ) ( ) ( )
23. to understand the organization's benefits programs ( ) ( ) ( ) ( ) ( ) ( )
24. for people to help each other with on-the-job or personal problems ( ) ( ) ( ) ( ) ( ) ( )
25. for people to follow through on programs that they begin ( ) ( ) ( ) ( ) ( ) ( )
26. for training needs to be adequately met ( ) ( ) ( ) ( ) ( ) ( )
27. for people to have an effective means of communication with peers and supervisors ( ) ( ) ( ) ( ) ( ) ( )
28. for people to share responsibility for things that go wrong in their work groups ( ) ( ) ( ) ( ) ( ) ( )
29. for a spirit of cooperation and teamwork to be felt throughout the organization ( ) ( ) ( ) ( ) ( ) ( )
30. for people to feel they are treated fairly in the area of pay ( ) ( ) ( ) ( ) ( ) ( )

Figure 1 (continued)

	Strongly Agree	Agree	Neutral	Disagree	Strongly Disagree	Don't Know
31. for people to like the kind of work they are doing	( )	( )	( )	( )	( )	( )
32. for people to work together effectively	( )	( )	( )	( )	( )	( )
33. for people to take pride in their own work and that of the organization	( )	( )	( )	( )	( )	( )
34. for work loads to be evenly distributed	( )	( )	( )	( )	( )	( )
35. to care about and strive for excellent performance	( )	( )	( )	( )	( )	( )
36. to feel really involved in the work of the organization	( )	( )	( )	( )	( )	( )
37. to have a clear way of measuring results	( )	( )	( )	( )	( )	( )
38. for leaders to help their work team members succeed	( )	( )	( )	( )	( )	( )
39. to point out errors constructively	( )	( )	( )	( )	( )	( )
40. for people working together to meet regularly on important issues	( )	( )	( )	( )	( )	( )
41. for improvement efforts to be based on facts	( )	( )	( )	( )	( )	( )
42. for people not to treat each other as just a "pair of hands"	( )	( )	( )	( )	( )	( )
43. to use time and resources effectively	( )	( )	( )	( )	( )	( )
44. for leaders to demonstrate their own commitment to what the organization is trying to accomplish	( )	( )	( )	( )	( )	( )
45. for leaders to make a strong effort to involve and motivate people	( )	( )	( )	( )	( )	( )

	Strongly Agree	Agree	Neutral	Disagree	Strongly Disagree	Don't Know
46. to give and receive feedback in helpful ways	( )	( )	( )	( )	( )	( )
47. for authority to be delegated appropriately	( )	( )	( )	( )	( )	( )
48. for people to share responsibility for what happens in the organization	( )	( )	( )	( )	( )	( )
49. for groups to define goals clearly before a task is begun	( )	( )	( )	( )	( )	( )
50. for people to get whatever training is needed to help them succeed in their work	( )	( )	( )	( )	( )	( )
51. for people to feel that the organization keeps them informed on matters that directly affect them	( )	( )	( )	( )	( )	( )

COMMENTS

Please use the space below for explanations of your answers to any of the survey questions or for other comments.

_____

_____

_____ _____ _____ _____

This concludes the survey. Please return this form according to instructions.
  Thank you for your participation.

this area were weak. Modeling, in particular, has been found to be related to many kinds of subordinate behavior. For example, a retail food chain was concerned over employee theft of fruit from open bins. It subsequently was learned in our study that it was the norm for managers to take a piece of fruit from the bin and eat it in full view of the employees.

5) Policies and Procedures: This factor relates to the efficiency of organizational policies and procedures and the extent to which they are effectively communicated to those who must implement them. In some organizations, this area is of the utmost importance to the successful resolution of performance problems. The impact of policies and procedures is clearly seen in instances where labor unions threaten, as their most disruptive job action, to follow them.

6) Confrontation: The last two scales of the NDI are perhaps of the greatest significance in terms of the organizational unconscious theory. The first of these scales, confrontation, consists of

NDI & The *Job Descriptive Index:* Correlations High and Low

A common practice, in developing psychometric measures such as general mental ability tests, is to calibrate new instruments against an accepted standard in the field. New IQ tests, for example, are frequently compared statistically with the *Sanford-Binet Intelligence Scale,* which is sometimes referred to as the "platinum-iridium bar of psychological measurement." The *Job Descriptive Index* (P.C. Smith, et al.) has come to occupy an analogous position in the field of employee attitude measurement.[6] This instrument, which measures individual satisfaction in the traditional content areas of pay, supervision, work on present job, people, and promotional opportunities, is generally regarded as the most thoroughly researched instrument of its kind. The JDI's normative sample included tens of thousands of workers in various areas of the United States, and it has been used in hundreds of employee attitude studies in major corporations since its standardization.

The authors performed a correlational study in which NDI factors were compared with JDI's content areas for a sample of 86 employees of a large manufacturing concern. This was a subsample of the original factor analysis sample of approximately 450 subjects. The sample employed in the correlation study included individuals in marketing, clerical and manufacturing job titles.

Correlations between the NDI's scales and the JDI's are generally low to moderate, with a few exceptions. This is to be expected on the basis of the two instruments' content, as reflected in the scales' labels. In general, then, it appears that individual satisfaction in the traditionally studied areas of pay, supervision, coworkers, promotional opportunity and work itself, is related in some degree to the various aspects of the organizational culture as measured by the NDI, even though the NDI is actually measuring something quite different. However, there were a few instances of surprisingly high overlap between certain NDI and JDI scales.

The NDI's Performance Facilitation factor, as would be expected from the description given above, shows only moderate correlations with the traditional areas of Work on Present Job, Supervision, and People on the JDI. While the pattern of correlations for the next factor, Job Involvement, resembles that of the Performance Facilitation scale, it is interesting to note the significant difference between the correlations of the two factors with JDI's Promotion factor, which asks respondents for their feelings about promotional opportunities within the organization. While Promotion has a negligible relationship with Performance Facilitation, it does have a moderately high correlation with Job Involvement, suggesting that measured satisfaction with advancement opportunities is more closely tied to the area of emotional involvement in work than to performance factors.

Among other interesting relationships is that of Leader-Subordinate Interaction to JDI's Supervision. As would be expected from the two scales' similar content, the highest correlation of Leader-Subordinate Interaction is to this corresponding JDI factor. On the other hand, Policies and Procedures, which has no overlap of content with any JDI scale, is seen to have essentially random relationships with all JDI factors.

Finally, the high correlations noted between NDI's Supportive Climate and JDI's Work and People factors are especially interesting. Supportive Climate is only a three-item factor and therefore would not be expected offhand to manifest such high correlations with JDI variables. The results are interpreted as reflecting the profound importance of the emotional component of daily working experience, especially in terms of feelings of belongingness, acceptance, and the assurance of being treated fairly when there is a question of responsibility for errors or failures.

---

three items relating to constructive responses to other people's behavior. This aspect of interpersonal interaction in organizations corresponds roughly to the process called "interpretation" in psychotherapy, where unconscious material is brought into the patient's field of awareness in such a way as to have a therapeutic effect. It is only through such confrontation that norms are deprived of the subtle but powerful influence that results from their operating at a dim level of awareness.

The first, and probably the most common way to handle confrontation is to simply bury the issue and avoid any direct confrontation at all. This usually results not only in a continuation of the problem, but also in pathological expression of the associated feelings, often in areas that have little to do with the original situation. The second strategy is to confront the problem bluntly, with little regard for the other person's ego. The popular image is that of the harried subordinate being called on the carpet by an authoritative boss. The third

approach is, of course, to create the kind of atmosphere where people speak freely to one another, but with regard for each other's feelings. Thus, everything gets out in the open, but without the need for defensiveness.

7) *Supportive Climate:* The last factor to be considered also consists of three items measuring emotionally supportive aspects of the organization's normative system. Avoidance of blame placing, excitement and enthusiasm, and an atmosphere of cooperation are what is meant here by emotional support. Strong norms in this area make the difference between employees who enjoy coming to work and those who feel emotionally drained at the end of the day from the effects of a hostile environment.

New Techniques, Old Cultures

Once the survey data have been gathered, it is possible to move directly to the subsequent steps in the change process. One of the major criticisms that is justifiably made of most survey programs is that the data often end up in file cabinets, rather than becoming the basis for successful change efforts. When this occurs, the survey tends to merely produce greater levels of frustration within the organization. One reason for this is that the survey data deal only with the symptoms of the organization's problems and not with the underlying culture, which is so much more influential.

Even the changes that are initiated as a result of some survey programs are such that they have little chance of sustaining themselves on an on-going basis. Thus, new MBO programs are often laid on top of an existing culture which calls for off-the-cuff or seat-of-the-pants management strategies. The older ways of doing things tend to win out in the process. This type of unsuccessful change effort can often be observed when zero-based budgeting programs are superimposed on cultures calling for more traditional types of budgeting procedures. When this occurs, people within the organization spend a great deal of time going through the motions of zero-based budgeting, but only after they have developed their budgets in the traditional way beforehand.

The use of the NDI is designed to cut through the surface symptoms so that management and employees are able to get at the underlying cultural issues in nondestructive ways. As they examine these cultural issues together, realistic programs for bringing about and sustaining change can be developed and implemented.

The Change Program

The total normative systems change program involves a four-step process, as shown in Figure 2. The initial phase— analysis and objective setting— is where the Norms Diagnostic Index is first used. Making use of the data obtained, the organization can then set appropriate objectives and develop a preliminary strategy for change.

This preliminary strategy is next introduced to the total organization in a series of workshops and meetings that constitute Phase II of the change process. As a part of these meetings, the NDI data are introduced at the various organizational levels, and opportunities are provided for each organizational group to contribute to the objectives and to the design of the change process.

Figure 2
The Normative Systems Change Process

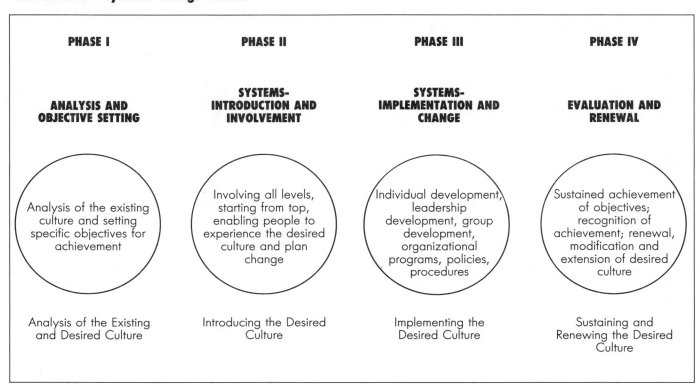

PHASE I	PHASE II	PHASE III	PHASE IV
ANALYSIS AND OBJECTIVE SETTING	**SYSTEMS-INTRODUCTION AND INVOLVEMENT**	**SYSTEMS-IMPLEMENTATION AND CHANGE**	**EVALUATION AND RENEWAL**
Analysis of the existing culture and setting specific objectives for achievement	Involving all levels, starting from top, enabling people to experience the desired culture and plan change	Individual development, leadership development, group development, organizational programs, policies, procedures	Sustained achievement of objectives; recognition of achievement; renewal, modification and extension of desired culture
Analysis of the Existing and Desired Culture	Introducing the Desired Culture	Implementing the Desired Culture	Sustaining and Renewing the Desired Culture

The third phase is the implementation of the change process, which is accomplished by focusing on individual, group, organizational and leadership factors as they affect the underlying culture.

The final phase is the evaluation and renewal of what has accrued. A second administering of the NDI helps to reveal to what extent the change program has been successful and to what extent additonal work is needed. The renewal element of the process is supported by additional NDI administrations and by renewal meetings where progress is observed and new goals are established.

Freedom for the Asking

The norms within the NDI factors constitute, as we have stated, a force that can be viewed as an organizational unconscious, roughly comparable to the individual unconscious of psychoanalysis. Just as projective and objective tests have been devised to generate profiles of the unconscious dynamics within individuals, so the NDI has been developed from 15 years' work with norms to provide profiles of the organizational unconscious. Specific strategies for change can be drawn from each NDI profile, based on interventions that have been proven effective in specific areas in numerous HRI field studies.

It is axiomatic that people are influenced in a very basic sense by the cultures of which they are a part. It is also true that people can, with directed effort, change their own cultures and deliberately choose the kinds of social influences they wish to exist as part of their interpersonal environments. This effort is a matter of uncovering and confronting that which already exists, setting goals relating to desired norms, and following proven methods for achieving a constructive readjustment of the normative system. The study of the organizational unconscious is not merely an exercise in information gathering; it is a means of helping people in today's organizations reach out to claim the freedom that is theirs for the asking.

References

1. Robert F. Allen and S. Silverzweig, "Changing the Corporate Culture." *Sloan Management Review,* Spring 1976.
2. L.A. Fleishman, "Leadership Climate, Human Relations Training and Supervisory Behavior," *Personnel Psychology,* 1953, pp. 205–222.
3. Robert F. Allen and S. Silverzweig, "Group Norms: Their Influence on Training Effectiveness," *Handbook of Training and Development,* Spring 1975.
4. V.H. Vroom, *Work and Motivation* (New York, John Wiley & Sons, 1964).
5. Sara Harris and Robert F. Allen, *The Quiet Revolution* (New York, Rawson Associates, 1978).
6. P.C. Smith, et al., *The Job Descriptive Index* (Bowling Green, Kentucky: Bowling Green State University, 1975).

SECTION II
DEVELOPMENT

In this phase, the emphasis is on developing the people and programs required for success. Effective and lasting change requires a broad base of leadership skills and support within the organization. Internal resources need to be trained as role models and exemplars for desired changes. It is also important during this phase to communicate the results of the organizational diagnosis and explain the effects of culture on organizational behavior, personal performance and business objectives. The key process objective is to involve people at all levels in the change effort. The specific outcome goals are internal productivity and profitability as well as customer productivity and profitability.

In the first article, "Thawing Out Your Management Culture," Albert and Silverman discuss predictable stages of culture change and suggest steps for preparing the organization for change. The second article, "Integrating Fiefdoms and Subcultures into Organizational Networks," discusses two of the major barriers to culture change—empire building and turfism. In this article, Mark Edwards suggests a system for transforming barriers into bridges.

Thawing Out Your Management Culture

By Michael Albert and Murray Silverman

The era of corporate cultural change is here, featured in a growing body of literature on America's most successful, and success-oriented, companies. These are the organizations that point the way for the rest. One principle they share is that values are the bedrock of any corporate culture and provide the essence of a company's philosophy for success.

The primary cultural value at IBM is customer service; at Pepsi it is being aggressive in winning; at Digital Equipment it is innovation; and at AT&T it is marketing. That everyone knows this demonstrates just how successful these companies have been in disseminating their particular values—to the members of the organization itself and to society at large. But in all that has been said and written on corporate cultural change there has been one major area of neglect: the failure to deal systematically with the process of translating cultural values at the organizational level into behavior at the individual level.

Just as general business objectives should be translated into more specific objectives to guide and direct a manager's performance, general management style philosophy statements should also be translated into specific managerial behaviors, activities and roles to guide and direct the way in which management gets work done through people. The benefits of human resource personnel taking this additional step beyond the generation of broad philosophy statements are: employees will share a common management philosophy and set of values; all managers will think and communicate with a common set of management activities and roles to guide their behavior; and a management effectiveness culture will develop that serves as a strong influence on future managerial behavior and performance. As a result, all of an organization's managerial resources will be working in an environment that has been shaped to achieve consistency.

Developing a Management Effectiveness Culture

The broad objective of a management effectiveness culture program is to develop a pervasive environment in which "work gets done through people." It is now widely agreed that in order to create effective long-term organizational change a three-step process is necessary: unfreezing; changing; and refreezing.[1] Basically, the unfreezing stage involves creating motivation to change; the changing state involves taking action that will change the individuals from their current level of behavior to a new level; the refreezing stage involves making the new level of behavior relatively secure against change. This three-step procedure is applicable regardless of the type of organizational change. Interestingly enough, many human resource personnel often talk about how some management development programs don't result in behavioral change back on the job. In most cases, the reason for this is that there was only an orientation to step two, changing, without also designing unfreezing and refreezing processes and programs.

In order to create long-term cultural change, processes and programs must be developed to change knowledge, attitudes, values and behaviors. Furthermore, the sequence of the change process must be appropriately integrated into the unfreezing-changing-refreezing procedures. A model of a process designed to create cultural change is illustrated in Figure 1.

The objective of the unfreezing stage is to provide all managers in an organization the opportunity to understand their values, attitudes and knowledge of management effectiveness and to understand how these differ from the organization's managerial expectations. Translating management philosophy statements into specific managerial roles and activities will provide every manager with a common set of specific behavioral expectations. As a result, a new awareness of "what is expected of me and what are the specific managerial behaviors, roles

Figure 1
Creating a Management Effectiveness Culture

and activities for me" develops for managers. Although commitment to and training in these behaviors, roles and activities occur at the changing and refreezing stages, the roots of the new management culture are planted and begin to spread through all managerial levels during the unfreezing stage.

Designing a Management Effectiveness Culture Program

Because the unfreezing stage focuses on management effectiveness, it is critical to reach agreement on what managers should be doing in their day-to-day behavior. The biggest breakthrough in this area has been developed by Henry Mintzberg.[2] Researching what managers actually do and how they spend their time, he found that *all managers, regardless of level or function, perform a combination of specific roles and activities.* Since these roles and activities are the actual things managers do when getting work done through people, it is critical for managers to understand that these roles and activities represent the organization's expectations for them when managing.

Mintzberg's management framework can provide all of an organization's management the opportunity to understand the various roles and activities that relate to management and organizational effectiveness. This is the seminal stage in developing a management effectiveness culture, when managers need to understand their current values, attitudes and knowledge about management effectiveness and how these differ from the organization's managerial expectations. To provide a use-

ful tool for these ends, we developed a management behavior questionnaire (MBQ).[3]

The MBQ contains 43 statements that describe various managerial roles and activities. Each activity is a value statement regarding specific behavior in which a manager should be involved, to some degree, in order for his or her department and organization to function effectively. The roles and activities specified in the MBQ can be modified slightly to adapt to the unique management culture that an organization or division desires to develop. As the context through which all organizational objectives are met, they also provide a framework to anticipate and react to opportunities and threats from outside the organization. To the extent that all managers in a company or division are involved in these activities and behaviors, and are performing them effectively, a new management culture will be developing. Selected items from the MBQ appear in Figure 2.

All managers participating in a management effectiveness culture program would complete the MBQ twice. During the first rating, managers indicate the relative importance they think their organization attaches to each activity in order for their department to be managed effectively. Participants rate each activity on a scale of 1 to 5 (5 = great importance, 1 = low importance). If they are uncertain, they indicate a question mark; this reveals to what extent managers are unclear of the roles and activities the organization considers important. During the second rating, managers indicate the relative importance they think should be attached to each activity, using the same rating scale.

The relative importance of these activities must first be determined for the various management

---

Figure 2
Managerial Roles and Activities
(selected items from The Management Behavior Questionnaire)

1. Receiving relevant information from an established network of contacts.
2. Providing opportunities for people in the department to discuss potential or real problems.
3. Playing a coaching role with subordinates.
4. Ensuring that subordinates keep their manager informed of the status of their projects.
5. Seeking input and reactions from people outside the department who may be affected by upcoming proposals and decisions.
6. Negotiating with managers from other departments or divisions on issues related to work flow, scheduling, informational requirements, etc.
7. Creating an atmosphere that allows subordinates to feel part of a team.
8. Taking action when a subordinate's performance does not meet standards.
9. Communicating guidelines to subordinates that serve as a frame of reference for their decisions.
10. Making sure that subordinates have specific goals in key performance areas.

Managerial Behavior Questionnaire: Selected items.

---

levels and positions throughout the company or division. This process occurs in a meeting with relevant staff and management personnel prior to the management effectiveness culture program. The result of this assessment is the first step in creating a new management culture. In essence, the MBQ provides all managers with an organizationally pervasive management effectiveness role model.

The discrepancy between the participants' scores and the formal assessment serves as a catalyst to change—a critical aspect of the unfreezing stage. Everyone gains a heightened sense of different perceptions and expectations, making them more receptive to the evolving culture of the organization. This heightened receptivity should hold through the further stages of change and refreezing.

The data base that is developed can provide human resource personnel with additional information. For example, because differences in ratings are found between higher and lower management levels, there is a lack of consistency in role expectations. It is critical for human resource personnel to develop a formal management culture that provides all managers with a pervasive management effectiveness role model—one that can be used for a variety of processes that are part of a culture program.

For example, participants at the workshop are asked to "Think of a situation in which a manager (either yourself, a manager you work for, or a manager you know of) was very effective in providing opportunities for people in the department to discuss potential or real problem areas. Make a list of the things this person did when performing this activity."[4] After completing this list, the participants discuss the many approaches to performing this activity.

Using this process for various MBQ activities serves to further unfreeze the participants. This happens because they see that there are many ways to achieve management results, some more and some less effective. The intent of this process is not to provide participants with formal training in actually performing these activities; that is something that the organization's human resource personnel should do at some later time. The intent is to increase their awareness of the issue of management effectiveness. Furthermore, since the managers are the one providing the examples, they see that each of them has similarities and differences with regard to managing. Peer group influence and a normative-reeducative approach to change result in a strong commitment to change.

Other processes used in the program ask: What do you do when performing this activity? List other occasions or situations when you might perform the activity. What might you do differently when performing this activity in the future?[5]

An in-basket exercise can also be part of the management effectiveness culture program. This would ask the participants to play the role of a manager who has numerous in-basket items to manage. After spending two hours managing these issues, there follows an analysis of their responses, why they chose to respond the way they did and a discussion of the relationship of their responses to management effectiveness.

Achieving Long-Term Cultural Change

In order for this new management effectiveness culture to take root and spread throughout the organization, attention must be directed to the changing and refreezing stages. Additional areas that may need redesign include:

- the orientation program for all new management personnel;
- the performance appraisal system;
- a systematic feedback process;
- the human resource planning system;
- the management development program;
- the compensation structure.

It is my view that this approach—viewing human resources as a priority—is substantially different from those approaches that are solely oriented to providing individuals with training and development in specific management skills. Both approaches are necessary and complement each other.

Unfortunately, many people do not view managing as an important activity. Although they manage, they perceive and identify themselves as engineering, marketing, financial, production or data processing people. People do not inherently believe managing is a less important activity. They have learned this attitude from their experiences in various organizations, from the way people behave and get rewarded. Productive organizational change and management effectiveness require an investment in time and human resources; they can't be done without focusing on managerial behavior.

References

1. Lewin, K. Group decision and social change. In *Readings in social psychology.* New York: Holt, Rinehart and Winston, 1958, 197–211.
2. Mintzberg, H. *The nature of managerial work.* New York: Harper & Row, 1973; and Mintzberg, H. The manager's job: Folklore and fact. *Harvard Business Review,* July–August 1975, 49–61.
3. Albert, M. & Silverman, M. *Managerial Behavior Questionnaire.* San Francisco: Albert, Silverman and Associates, 1981.
4. Albert, M. & Silverman, M. *Managerial activity role model analysis.* San Francisco: Albert, Silverman and Associates, 1981.
5. Albert, M. & Silverman, M. *Managerial activity action planning.* San Francisco: Albert, Silverman and Associates, 1981.

Integrating Fiefdoms and Subcultures Into Organizational Networks

By Mark R. Edwards

Abstract

Fiefdoms pose a critical problem that limits organizational effectiveness. The process of building work teams and group identify may create pockets of nationalism that interfere with effective across-group communication. Fiefdoms often build high walls to shield themselves from "outsiders," who may be internal to the organization. Measuring group behaviors and performances and rewarding group excellence communicates a change in cultural norms. No longer is empire building rewarded at the expense of productivity and service to internal and external customers. When evaluation and rewards are based on support given to internal customers, walls around groups are no longer useful to the groups, and barriers are replaced by bridges among work groups increasing organizational effectiveness and productivity.

Fiefdoms plague many organizations. A fiefdom exists when members of a department or work group operate as a subculture and cooperate very well internally but avoid people in other departments or divisions. Groups tend to create their own cultural norms and may eschew others. Naturally, by impairing communication and discouraging cooperation, fiefdoms can be extremely dysfunctional to organizational effectiveness. This article describes the fiefdom problem and provides an effective culture change solution that supports the norms of the total organization and makes managers more effective and organizations more productive.

Nature of the Fiefdom Problem

Boundaries occur naturally between functional areas within organizations. The fiefdom problem occurs when these boundaries become high walls

Reprinted by permission of the author.

designed to shelter those inside the group and keep outsiders away.

Unique terminology has evolved in different organizations to describe this phenomenon, including: turtles, ostriches, chimneys, peaks, turfs, thistles, mine fields, castles, armed camps, black holes, seminaries and "pop" (as opposed to "top") guns. These terms describe the effect of protecting insiders from outsiders. Often, these groups absorb considerable resources while contributing little to the organization.

Experience indicates that fiefdoms can occur in any functional area but are probably most common among specialized staff functions such as R&D, computer systems, management information systems, financial systems, and law. The fiefdom problem may evolve out of inflated self-perception of an individual or group regarding their importance to the organization. Ironically, even staff functions that exist to serve an organization may become so egocentric they believe the organization exists to serve them.

The fiefdom problem includes the following organizational dysfunctions:

1. *Reduces support.* Organizational members outside the group receive less support than they should. When fiefdoms occur, line and staff functions may not receive adequate support from the group.

2. *Poor communication.* Communication within an organization often breaks down when there are barriers designed to restrict passage. Often, external organizational members are frustrated when fiefdoms fail to receive or to act on important organizational information, such as information about participating in meetings or projects. Frustration increases when communication from the isolatist group is delayed substantially or fails to occur.

3. *Misdirected action.* The isolation associated with some groups leads to actions that conflict with organizational goals and objectives. Such misdirected action wastes critical organizational

resources that could be directed towards organizational priorities.

4. *Interference with development of individuals.* As organizational groups differentiate themselves from other parts of the organization, cross-training and internal assignments across organizational boundaries, critical for developing people, become more difficult. Fiefdoms may become much like competitor organizations which isolate themselves to the point where they receive and provide few development opportunities for insiders or outsiders.

5. *Competition rather than cooperation.* The nationalistic spirit within a fiefdom may cause a feeling of competition in place of a more constructive feeling of cooperation. Members of the fiefdom may feel more loyalty to the group than to the organization. Such feelings may translate into behaviors associated with protecting group identity at the expense of others, especially from "foreign requests," external to the group's membership.

Many other organizational dysfunctions may occur due to barriers erected to "protect" organizational turf, people, and resources such as time. Teambuilding offers an effective solution to the fiefdom problem.

The Teambuilding Solution

A primary reason for group isolation is egocentrism. Fortunately, egocentrism can also be an effective tool for teambuilding and for integrating isolated organizational groups into the organizational mainstream. Groups who feel superior naturally want extra rewards for being special. Teambuilding offers a mechanism for assessing the degree to which individual groups are indeed superior.

All organizational groups, independent of their barriers and isolationism, interact with organizations members external to the group, who may be called internal customers. These internal customers can provide high quality information about group effectiveness, internal service and productivity. Thus, much as organizations are evaluated in markets by their customers, organizational groups may be evaluated within the organization by their internal customers.

The key to this organizational intervention is to develop a *credible* set of internal customers who can provide accurate performance feedback to the organizational group. Such information, when used as a teambuilding tool, is hard to argue against. If, indeed, fiefdoms are extraordinary groups, internal customers will reflect such information in their evaluations of the fiefdoms. In addition, credible internal customers can identify both strengths and developmental needs for teambuilding and leadership enhancement.

Team Evaluation for Groups

Organizations can improve their effectiveness by adding information about group performance to existing evaluative information. A group-performance factor recognizes and rewards high-performance groups. Such information, when combined with traditional appraisal information, may be used to reward performers who might be rewarded inappropriately with individual appraisals:

1. Average or low performers in high performance groups;
2. Extraordinarily high contributors to high, medium or even low performance groups;
3. Innovative champions who support and develop others at the expense of personal gain and who help make their group a high performance group.

The team evaluation for group appraisal incorporates innovations not available in systems based on evaluation by a single supervisory evaluation. As a result, the group-performance factor:

—Clearly shows organizational members that team contribution and team performance will be rewarded;
—Builds the esprit-de-corps associated with team involvement and common objectives;
—Recognizes and rewards valuable team players;
—Identifies the most effective teams and team leaders (role models);
—Recognizes and rewards members of high-performance groups;
—Diagnoses organizational effectiveness issues and identifies training needs;
—Offers an opportunity for an entire new set of organizational rewards and a new system of recognition.

Implementing Group Evaluation

The steps involved in designing and using the Team Evaluation and Management System, or TEAMS, process are summarized in Figure 1.[1] Multiple-rater evaluation of groups has many similarities with multiple-rater evaluation of individuals, as illustrated in Table 1.

In the example that follows, Natural Nutrition, a fictitious international food corporation, used the TEAMS process to evaluate group performance. The first important activity is identification of meaningful work groups. National Nutrition segmented work groups into five levels or magnitudes.

1. **Functional Divisions** included groups such as marketing, engineering, systems and operations. Magnitude 1 groupings included the primary functional divisions that reported to a president or general manager.

2. **Sub-Divisions or Regions** included, for example, Western, Southeastern and European groups. Reporting responsibility for Magnitude 2 groups included vice president and director level management.

3. **Departmental Groups** included the departments that reported to each functional manager. For example, Magnitude 3 included marketing development, marketing research, international, institutional, promotion, and retail groups.

4. **Task Work Groups** included natural sub-groupings within departments. Magnitude 4 groups for marketing development included new product development, prototype testing, market evaluation, and consumer testing groups.

5. **Natural or Project Groups** included sub-groupings across departments or special projects. Magnitude 5 groups included, for example, quality improvement groups and temporary teams for productivity improvement.

Developing Team Performance Criteria

Participative development of group performance criteria can be an important organizational development activity. As organizational members examine factors associated with effective organizational performance, they begin to recognize the value of assessing group performance. The participative process of criteria development enables employees to shape the organization's future in terms of how they would like it to be.

At Natural Nutrition, criteria development yielded seven criteria, shown in Table 2, which is labeled according to the "7S Model" from Peters and Waterman's *In Search of Excellence*.[2] participants were first asked to submit criteria that represented effective group performance. After the approximately 120 criteria had been aggregated into 25, participants were asked to rate the importance of each performance criterion to group performance.

When results of a criteria development process of this type are subdivided by all relevant subsets, such as organizational level, protected group status, wage level and geographic region, they provide excellent information regarding the criteria different subsets within the organization perceive to be important for evaluating group performance. Further, a summary based on information from all

Table 1
Appraisals Adjusting for Group Performance
Steps to Implementation of Team Evaluation and Management System

Activity	Two-Factor TEAMS	Three-Factor TEAMS
Identify ratees	Performers are ratees	Work groups (divisions, departments, work groups) are ratees
Develop performance-related criteria effectiveness	For evaluating individual effectiveness	For evaluating and organizational and team effectiveness
Construct definitions and illustrative behaviors for performance criteria	Individual behaviors	Organizational and team effectiveness behaviors
Select raters	Selected by each associate*	Selected by each team
Appraise performance	Of each associate	Of work groups or teams
Provide Performance feedback	To associates	To work groups
Provide rater feedback about rating behaviors	To associate's evaluation team members	To work group evaluation team members
Use performance information for rewards distribution	For associate	For teamwork and team contribution

*"Associate" means participating employee.

Figure 1
TEAMS Performance Appraisal and Career Development

Step

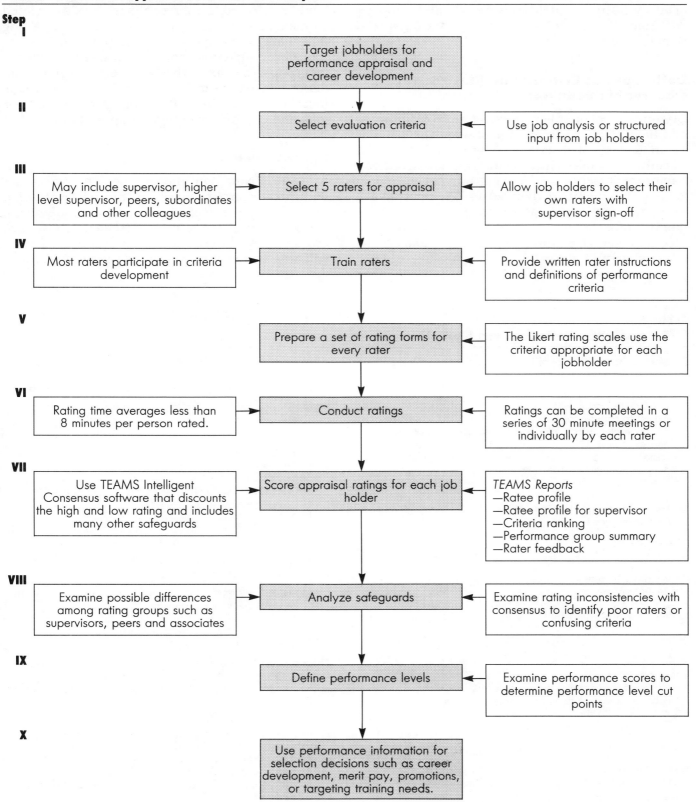

I — Target jobholders for performance appraisal and career development

II — Select evaluation criteria ← Use job analysis or structured input from job holders

III — May include supervisor, higher level supervisor, peers, subordinates and other colleagues → Select 5 raters for appraisal ← Allow job holders to select their own raters with supervisor sign-off

IV — Most raters participate in criteria development → Train raters ← Provide written rater instructions and definitions of performance criteria

V — Prepare a set of rating forms for every rater ← The Likert rating scales use the criteria appropriate for each jobholder

VI — Rating time averages less than 8 minutes per person rated. → Conduct ratings ← Ratings can be completed in a series of 30 minute meetings or individually by each rater

VII — Use TEAMS Intelligent Consensus software that discounts the high and low rating and includes many other safeguards → Score appraisal ratings for each job holder ← *TEAMS Reports*
—Ratee profile
—Ratee profile for supervisor
—Criteria ranking
—Performance group summary
—Rater feedback

VIII — Examine possible differences among rating groups such as supervisors, peers and associates → Analyze safeguards ← Examine rating inconsistencies with consensus to identify poor raters or confusing criteria

IX — Define performance levels ← Examine performance scores to determine performance level cut points

X — Use performance information for selection decisions such as career development, merit pay, promotions, or targeting training needs.

respondents can identify the most relevant criteria for appraising work groups. The criteria developed by Natural Nutrition were adopted into the "7S Model" to complement the desired organizational culture.

Definitions of Criteria and Illustrative, Observable Behaviors

Organizational members must agree on definitions and have similar perceptions of what the criteria mean in terms of observable job-related behaviors. Of course, the best source of information about behaviors representing effective group performance is the group members themselves. Therefore, Natural Nutrition asked each performance group to identify illustrative, observable behaviors associated with effective group performance. The criteria are shown in Table 2.

Although the seven dimensions of organizational effectiveness were common across all groups, behaviors selected to represent activities associated with effective group performance varied according to actual group behaviors. Development of illustrative, observable behaviors is a form of job analysis for groups; the illustrative behaviors for each group performance criterion represent the actions groups members take when effectively performing their jobs and creating effective group performance.

Rater Selection

At Natural Nutrition, the lead person or manager within each group chose an internal evaluation team, A, composed of three to six group members. These internal team members each chose two evaluators who were external to the group. The result was two evaluation teams for each group: A

Table 2
"7S Model" With Definitions and Illustrations

Structure: The framework of the organization, and the procedures used for reaching goals.

Framework and procedures:
  –Are simple and flexible.
  –Adjust to rapid changes.
  –Are characterized by informality, individual entrepreneurship, and evolution.
  –Foster personal and group achievement and innovation.
  –Support communication among members.
  –Are non-hierarchical.

Strategy: The skillful planning and directing of the organization that leads to success.

The organization:
  –Develops plan or mission statements that express a commitment.
  –Creates a setting for experimental action and career development.
  –Defines a clear direction, yet allows some flexibility.
  –Analyzes the competition and figures out how to do better.

Skills: The particular products or services that the organization makes or does best.

The organization:
  –Has customer service as its primary skill.
  –Is building skills it does not possess presently.
  –Assesses skills that have value to customers.
  –Tests limits and expands skills set.

Staff: The people supporting organization goals.

Staff Organization:
  –Is lean, with few administrators and many doers.
  –Is flat organization.

  –Is designed to promote ability to function in multiple departments.
  –Looks at the performance of people rather than personalities.

Style: Manner or method of running an organization for maximum performance

Leaders:
  –Interact and listen; they do not dictate.
  –Persuade instead of ordering.
  –Seek input from others.
  –Show willingness to share rewards and recognitions.
  –Empower subordinates.
  –Use teambuilding.
  –Move away from analytical, towards flexible.
  –Strive for more long-range enhancement, less short range.

Systems: An organization's orderly mechanism for implementing and using resources and ideas.

  –Ideas and information are moved around (not blocked).
  –Consensus decisions are used.
  –Innovation flourishes.
  –Systems encourage innovative ideas.
  –Positive reinforcement is encouraged and used.

Shared Values: Beliefs organization members project to themselves and their customers. The things done to give organization members pride and a feeling of belonging and dedication to the organization.

  –The customer comes first.
  –People are the most important asset.
  –Innovation is the lifeblood of the organization.
  –Stick to what is known about being the best.
  –A goal is to provide superior quality and service.
  –The importance of economic growth and profits must be recognized.

(internals) and B (externals). The Group Performance Factor was derived from ratings by evaluation team B composed of external raters. Evaluation team A provided an internal-to-the-group assessment, useful for self-diagnosis and teambuilding.

The Natural Nutrition TEAMS project allowed all five magnitudes of groups to be evaluated simultaneously. Participation by a large number of organizational members (about 30%) assured that most raters rated at least three groups.

Group Performance Feedback

TEAMS feedback includes a group performance profile (see Figure 2) that provides a summary of group performance. Isolated groups that are not meeting their organizational commitments get clear feedback about developmental needs.

The clustered bar chart format allows comparisons of ratings by group members with ratings by internal customers outside the group. Naturally, fiefdoms tend to be perceived more favorably by internal group members than by their internal customers. The profile has credibility because it represents the collective wisdom of the internal customers selected by group members. By clearly targeting areas of strength (support) and areas of developmental need, the profile makes it possible to focus teambuilding energy on areas where improvement is needed most.[3]

Discussion

The TEAMS process for profiling groups provides an excellent mechanism for teambuilding and for focusing attention on organizational integration.[4] Evaluation by internal customers can bring into the open issues related to internal organizational support, communication among groups, internal customer support and other factors that operate in the direction opposite to isolationism.

Even when no explicit rewards such as money are associated with the group profiling process, organizational leadership becomes highly motivated to improve their "picture" of organizational support. The process broadens the base of valuative information from a manager's boss to a wide variety of internal organizational members who have regular contact with each evaluative group.

Because management consists largely of activities directed towards accomplishing things through people, department leaders assume substantial responsibility for teambuilding activities designed to enhance the quality of service as rated by inter-

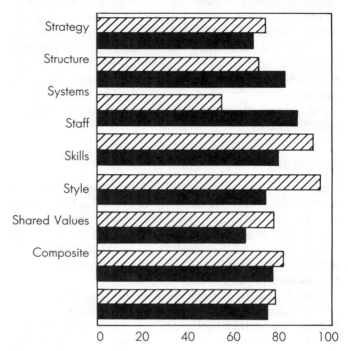

Figure 2
Team Evaluation and Management Systems Performance Evaluation for Financial Affairs

▨ Internal raters (within group)
■ External raters (outside group)

nal customers. Arguably, the esteem needs of managers provide stronger motivation than would extrinsic rewards such as money.

However, money still drives the reward system. Some organizations, such as Westinghouse and Red Lobster (a General Mills subsidiary), have begun to allocate merit budgets differentially based on group performance. More of the merit budget allocation goes to the high performing groups. Because behaviors tend to follow the organizational reward system, differential distribution of dollar rewards to high performing groups should substantially enhance the motivation of groups to cooperate and to serve internal customers.

Tapping Microcultural Norms

TEAMS group profiling can tap the cultural norms of various organizational groups. By asking participants to select evaluative criteria, an organization captures a picture of the relevant norms for various departments or work groups. The microcultural norms reflect the cultural style or behavioral norm emphasis of each manager whose leadership influences a group. The aggregation of information from different groups yields a higher-order norm profile for organizational functions of divisions.

Profiles of microcultural norms and aggregated cultural norms provide an excellent tool for identifying those who best support the desired organization norms. Credible identification offers an excellent teambuilding tool because it targets strengths and developmental opportunities. In addition, norm profiling meets employees' need to participate in decision making and management's need to have high quality information on leadership effectiveness.

Summary

Fiefdoms pose a critical problem that limits organizational effectiveness. The process of building work teams and group identity may create pockets of nationalism that interfere with inter-group communication. Fiefdoms can build high walls to shield themselves from "outsiders" who may be internal to the organization.

Ignoring subcultures creates the possibility that some units will not serve internal customers. Allowing virtual walls to separate organizational groups creates political infighting for turf and power—at the expense of organizational effectiveness. Such infighting disrupts internal support, intergroup communication, action toward the organization's goals, development of people and cooperative efforts.

The teambuildng solution described here holds promise to create culture change by evaluating group behaviors and performance. With independent sets of raters—specifically, one set of raters share group membership and a second set who share organization membership but are external to the evaluated group—a clear picture of group performance can be developed.

Feedback on group performance can include information on support of internal customers (outside the group) and factors such as organizational support, communication, action toward organizational goals, people development, and cooperation as well as other factors that impact group and organizational effectiveness. Such feedback identifies excellent targets for effective organizational development and teambuilding.

When organizations use measures of group performance in the reward system, a change in cultural norms is communicated. No longer is empire building rewarded at the expense of productivity and service to internal and external customers. When evaluation and rewards are based on internal customer support walls around groups are no longer useful to the groups, and barriers are replaced by bridges among work groups, increasing organizational effectiveness and productivity.

References

1. Edwards, M.R., and Verdini, W.A. "Engineering and Technical Management: Accurate Human Performance Measures = Productivity," *Journal of the Society of Research Administrators*, Fall, 1986, 18, 2, 23–37.
2. Peters, T.J., and Waterman, R.H. *In Search of Excellence: Lessons from America's Best Run Companies*, Harper & Row, New York, 1982, p. 10.
3. Edwards, M.R., and Sproull, J.R. "Making Performance Appraisals Perform: The Use of Team Evaluation," *Personnel*, March, 1985, 62, 3, 28–32.
4. Edwards, M.R., and Sproull, J.R. "Team Talent Assessment: Optimizing Assessee Visibility and Assessment Accuracy," *Human Resources Planning*, Fall, 1985, 8, 3, 157–171.

SECTION III
DELIVERY

The key thrust of this phase is to deliver the ideas and goal of the diagnosis and development phases through a multi-faceted intervention. Leadership provides the vision and commitment that drive the whole change effort. During this phase, the primary job of management is to help interpret, communicate and reinforce the organizational mission by supporting the belief that positive change is possible and helping people realize that they can do much more than they ever dreamed.

Delivery is a two-pronged approach emphasizing:

—Skills + Support. The training programs are designed to equip people with the skills they need to achieve their goals. At the same time, the organization and work teams provide a supportive environment for the acquisition and application of desired skills.

—Building Positive Norms. Leaders need to design systems to reward the norms that support desired culture. These reward systems should encourage such things as creative problem solving, quality improvement, responsiveness to customers and innovative teamwork.

The Delivery Section contains two samples of work done by one of the foremost pioneers in culture change, the late Robert Allen. Dr. Allen contributed significantly to the field of organizational development during his lifetime and these two selections provide an overview of some of his central ideas and principles. The first selection, "Changing Community and Organization Cultures," outlines a model for freeing people from cultural restrictions. The second article, authored by his son, Judd Allen, shows how the model evolved over the last decade and how three key themes emerged in importance.

Changing Community and Organizational Cultures

By Robert F. Allen and Stanley Silverzweig

Although cultural change has been considered the province of the anthropologist and academician, it is now beginning to interest the business, organizational and community leader. In offices, assembly lines, executive suites and city halls, people are discovering that they can make things happen—and make them stick—if they work in a cultural context!

This article describes some of the remarkable and lasting results stemming from this approach, as well as the system used to bring them about. The process used in the cases below, once learned for any one situation, can be applied to others, wherever there are problems to be solved or environments to be modified.

CASE I.
The Agricultural Operation of a Fortune 500 Company

Seven years ago one of America's largest employers of migrant workers embarked on a cultural-change program designed to significantly modify the norms of its agricultural operations and to increase worker productivity and income. Three years later it has accomplished its objectives.
- 200 per cent increase in worker production
- worker income tripled
- 75 per cent migrancy eliminated
- absenteeism reduced drastically
- turnover dropped to one-fourth former rate
- substandard company housing replaced by privately owned homes

Workers were no longer second-class citizens within the company. A new culture had been developed which was more in keeping with 20th century hopes and aspirations.

CASE II.
A Supermarket Company

Four years ago a supermarket chain set out to change those cultural influences which contributed to the 4 1/4 per cent "shrink" figure within the company—a measure of the loss of product through employee, customer and vendor theft, and through waste, damage and improper handling. "Shrink" amounted to more than $100,000 per year and more than equaled the company's profits at the time. Two years later:
- Shrink reduced by 70 per cent
- Company profits doubled

Through an extensive cultural effort, norms interfering with change were replaced by honesty, security and productivity norms. The supermarket is no longer a "school for crime."

CASE III.
Three Large American Communities

Two and a half years ago, three American communities (Tampa, Fla.; Macon, Ga.; Charlotte, N.C.) embarked upon what seemed to be an impossible task—changing the culture of their communities so that litter and littering behavior would be significantly reduced. After 16 months of effort, they reported some startling results. Litter in all three cities—reduced by over 60 per cent.

These communities had, in fact, changed their cultures and the results were being secured within standard budget allocations, almost entirely through the use of local resources.

CASE IV.
A Food Distribution Warehouse

Two years ago this company was seriously considering the closing of a new warehouse which had been plagued since its opening by problems of low productivity, low morale and wildcat strikes. A program to modify the cultural norms contributing to this sorry state resulted in:

- Productivity increased from 120 pieces selected per hour to 146.7 per hour
- Turnover was reduced drastically
- Absenteeism improved by 25 per cent
- Damage loss was reduced by 50 per cent

The company reported that negotiations with the union were no longer being conducted in a hostile and mutually belligerent atmosphere.

All four of these cases not only achieved results within a reasonable time period, but also maintained and extended the results after the initial project was completed. Thus, they were evidence, contrary to some of the beliefs about the immobility of cultures, that change is not only possible, but feasible and long-lasting within these organizational and community settings. The key to success in all four efforts was the focus that was placed, not on a temporary solution of the immediate problem, but on changing the culture that supported it.

The culture-centered approach utilized above was that of "Normative Systems," a cultural-change system designed by behavioral scientists of Scientific Resources Inc. and the HRI Human Resources Institute, Morristown, N.J. Developed and field-tested over a period of the past 15 years in a variety of settings ranging from prison to mental hospital to school to large corporation, the program seeks to free people from cultural restrictions that get in the way of achieving desired results. The cases above were selected from over 100 change programs that have been implemented.

The "Normative Systems" program is based on a relatively simple and straightforward concept that whenever people come together, over time they form a culture, and this culture has an immense impact on everything that happens thereafter. Whether the culture be that of assembly-line workers or an executive committee, its functioning will be tremendously affected by the culture that is created. Awareness of the power of the culture is a prerequisite to initiating a change process, for the culture influences the effective functioning of the group, and the functioning in turn determines whether or not meaningful results will be achieved.

But culture is not to be conceived of as a great, sprawling and elusive giant. Upon examination, it is found to consist of a network of norms—expected and supported behaviors that provide the basic building blocks within the organization or community. When norms are positive, a great deal can be accomplished; when they are negative, they can interfere with both individual and organizational

success. Norms of the assembly-line culture, for example, will influence factors like absenteeism, lateness, productivity; norms in the office will influence typing speed, errors in outgoing correspondence and the length of coffee breaks; norms in the executive suite will influence openness of communication, honesty and the ability to speak up when one disagrees with the boss.

Our theory holds that people can examine their norms, choose to strengthen good ones and eliminate negative ones. In this way, they can design and create the culture of which they are a part, rather than merely function on the basis of what already exists. It has been our experience that people can and will exercise intelligence and good judgment when they have an opportunity to do so.

To get results, a key factor is the participation of the group that will be affected by those results. This means that people at all levels in an organization or group will need to be part of the change effort, from the first look at negative and positive norms to the ongoing renewal meetings. We cannot expect a consistent success if changes are imposed from above, or if they are instituted without employees at all levels developing a sense of "ownership" in the program. They must have an opportunity to plan the effort, to get feedback on it, and to experience the new norms.

Win-Win Strategies

Results that are good for one person or group and not good for another will not be conducive to a good working environment and are not likely to be sustained. Traditionally, people are used to win-lose situations, where individuals or groups become scapegoats. Focusing on blame-placing severely impedes cultural change. Efforts to obtain results where all sides benefit are not as difficult as it might seem. Most people welcome a cessation to blame-placing and find it rewarding to put their energy into win-win situations.

If the focus is on activity that can be seen and measured rather than on changing people's personalities, there will be greater success in achieving objectives. Immediate results can be tremendously encouraging—a sign that we are not victims after all, but doers. By choosing to take small steps first, the usual attitude of "It's just human nature—you can't change things," can be quickly reversed. It is important that results are visible, recognized and publicized. They are the best feedback and the best impetus for working toward greater achievements.

No results are really worth the effort if they cannot be sustained. The external professional can play a crucial role in the analysis, training and early evaluation, but if the change process does not become internalized and a permanent part of the organizational function, accomplishments will dwindle away. The organizational leadership, and to some extent all members of a culture, must assume the change agent's role for results to be lasting. Crash programs with a pendulum return are all too familiar to us all. They can be avoided by strong and renewed commitment.

The proliferation of norms, good and bad, in any culture necessitates the use of a structure or model to bring some sense out of the chaos. To make it possible. to deal with critical change influences, we have developed a system for checking on key areas, for grouping norms into recognizable units, and for putting change efforts into a meaningful step-by-step sequence. Through a four-phase process (Figure 1), people are helped to examine their cultures, set objectives, experience new norms, install them and modify the culture to support them, and finally to sustain them with built-in renewal mechanisms.

Phase 1:
Analyzing the Existing Culture

The first step in getting results is to decide what results one wants. In the initial phase of this program, the culture is analyzed and objectives are set. With the guidance of professional consultants, employees at all levels do this for their own groups. The first question asked is, *"What are the norms at work in this situation?"* The second question is, *"Which norms do we want to change"*—i.e., *"What are our objectives?"* The cases in Figure 2 illustrate what can happen in this first phase of *Cultural Analysis and Objective Setting.*

It is apparent from these samples of typical specific objectives that "focusing on results" means setting detailed, specific and measurable goals, with some of them very short-range to provide immediate results and the impetus of hope, and some of them long-range to support sustained change.

Phase 2:
Experiencing the Desired Culture

The second phase is one of *Systems Introduction and Involvement.* "Peak-experience" workshops provide an opportunity for people to experience the new culture in a direct and immediate way. This is, in effect, an acting out of results before they are actually achieved—a sort of modeling of a hoped-for culture by the very persons who will be working toward it. By experiencing the new norms and seeing what the new culture can be like, people are given a chance to see that change is in fact possible. They see themselves and their group in a new light.

Special workshop designs during this phase help people become aware of cultural influences on their lives, and of how these can be changed if people care to do so. People see that there is a systematic process for bringing about change.

In the migrant labor camps, workshops brought together for the first time people of many different levels of the company. Senior officers shared feelings and aspirations with men and women who had lived all their lives as migrants. Black and white learned mutual respect.

In the supermarket, a cross section of managers, checkers, stockboys, supervisors and customers role-played each other's positions and found themselves stimulated to work together on the shrink problem. Instead of "our employees couldn't care less," there was developed a win-win atmosphere where all levels could forgo blame-placing and helplessness norms.

In the litter program, workshop participants, ranging from sanitation workers to Junior League matrons, attended by invitation of the mayor and

Figure 1
Normative Systems Model for Organizational Change

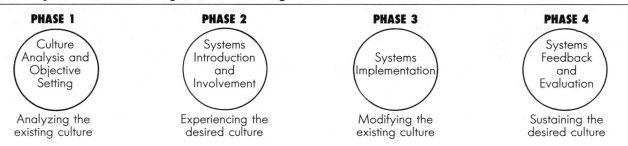

PHASE 1	PHASE 2	PHASE 3	PHASE 4
Culture Analysis and Objective Setting	Systems Introduction and Involvement	Systems Implementation	Systems Feedback and Evaluation
Analyzing the existing culture	Experiencing the desired culture	Modifying the existing culture	Sustaining the desired culture

Figure 2

Case	Some Norms To Change	Examples of Specific Objectives
The Agricultural Company	people don't identify with the company	absenteeism will be lowered to one day a week
	productivity and income are at low levels	productivity and income will both double in 18 months
	work force lives substandard or marginal existence	no employee will live in substandard housing
	pay is on piecemeal basis	licensed community health and social-service facilities will open in two years
	company is not sufficiently concerned about the migrants	

power structure. Initially there were two three-hour workshops which obtained a definite participant committee to take action on a permanent basis. People examined their own misconceptions about what litter was and what caused it, and about who was to blame (usually the ghetto resident who lived near litter sources bore the brunt of criticism). For local industry and government leadership, the focus was on "cleaning your own house." By the end of the initial workshops the sense of frustration over the long-standing problem was replaced by a determination to take positive steps. Later, a series of neighborhood workshops (including both formal and informal leadership) was held for each distinct subcommunity, leading to the later establishment of "zones of cleanliness."

In the food distribution warehouse there was a series of workshops designed to get workers and supervisors involved, to give them an understanding of the concept of culture and to help them identify influences that were affecting them. People were involved in planning strategies to move them in the direction in which they would like to go. They were urged to throw out the "experts" findings that didn't make sense and speak about their own ideas on improving management-labor relations, and worker-to-worker relations. Thus, in working on better norms they were actually experiencing them—a beginning step that eventually led to sustained good feelings.

Phase 3: Modifying the Existing Culture

Most cultural-change programs falter at the important phase of *Systems Implementation*. Too many companies' efforts unfortunately never get past developing a report on the problem, or a series of training sessions. What really changes cultures are strategies aimed at critical norm-influence areas. Normative Systems, through its work with many groups, has found eight persistent critical influence areas: Leadership Modeling Behavior, Work-Team Culture, Information and Communication Systems, Performance and Reward Systems, Organizational Policies and Procedures, Training and Orientation, First-Line Supervisory Performance and Results Orientation. All of these need to be checked out for positive and negative norms. However, the analysis of an organization usually points out the need for more improvement in some areas than others. The change effort of each group is tailored to its special needs. Our case logs illustrate different implementation focuses. In each, a sampling of some specific actions taken to modify the expected behavior is indicated.

Agricultural Company: In the area of *Leadership Modeling Behavior,* home-office corporate executives were in direct contact with migrant workers and attended every function of the program. They initially devoted 12 to 14 hours per day to the project and often worked full-time on weekends.

In the area of *Work-Team Culture,* worker involvement was maximized in planning and decision-making phases. Community boards responsible for budgets and programs were set up. Worker-management committees were established. Workers were involved with the architect-planner of the new community, and the project staff itself was drawn from the migrant employees.

In the area of *Organizational Policies and Procedures,* a multi-million dollar budget was provided by the company. The home office transferred a carefully selected corporate vice president to provide on-site support for the change program.

In the area of *Training and Orientation,* at the kickoff of the high-experience workshops the corporate executive announced that anyone who could not support the effort to upgrade migrant working and living conditions should resign immediately. Ongoing workshops in leadership and human relations were provided at all levels.

In the area of *Results Orientation,* when workers began to experience year-round work with fringe benefits, when new homes were built and commu-

181

nity centers opened, then the majority finally gave up their belief that the company was not serious in its efforts.

Supermarket Company: In the area of *Leadership Modeling Behavior,* executives no longer took fruit from the stores into their offices; "shrink" was openly discussed in meetings and manuals.

In the area of *Work-Team Culture,* shrink data was reviewed at regular meetings; action steps were taken to improve results.

In the area of *Information and Communication Systems* the accounting system was modified to provide department and store managers with specific shrink data.

In the area of *Performance and Reward Systems,* dollar rewards were paid for shrink control; a bonus system that evaluated shrink reduction was instituted.

Three American Communities: In the area of *Work-Team Culture,* after the "peak-experience" workshops, small community-action teams were established, comprised of formal and informal leaders of the community.

In the area of *Information and Communication Systems,* a way of measuring litter accurately was developed and quarterly measurements were conducted and fed back to the community.

In the area of *Performance and Reward Systems,* "Look What the People in Our City Have Done" was a positive reinforcement strategy publicized in the press and media. Blame-placing and scapegoating was avoided; from the beginning the media supported the efforts.

In the area of *Training and Orientation,* the high-involvement workshops cleared up misconceptions about litter. City council, municipal officers, community leaders and members, and sanitation workers attended.

In the area of *Results Orientation,* action and results were carefully tracked and publicized to counteract feelings that this might be just one more clean-up campaign. Improvements were made in sanitation collection and containerization. Specific legislation was introduced.

Food Distribution Warehouse: In the area of *Leadership Modeling Behavior,* tireless support and effective modeling of new positive norms was visible in the actions of the new director.

In the area of *Information and Communications Systems,* a series of new channels for communication was established—a comprehensive information system for all supervision, an open-door policy, regular task-force meetings, and Normative Systems meetings. Stewards and business agents of

the union attended the workshops.

In the area of *Organizational Policies and Procedures,* a decision was made to relieve several key personnel, including the corporate officer in charge of the warehouse and one superintendent. They were given less people-involved roles in the company and replaced by persons holding less of an authoritarian approach.

In the area of *First-Line Supervisory Performance,* to further facilitate leadership support of the new culture, extensive supervisory training was provided.

The implementation in all four cases proceeded simultaneously along three lines: first, a focus on leadership's role in each influence area; second, action-study task forces involving all levels of employees; third, regular meetings of all organizational work teams to improve their own on-the-job culture, accompanied by specific training of the work-team leader.

Phase 4:
Evaluating Results and Sustaining the Desired Culture

Evidence of results has proved to be one of the major factors in cultural change. Only hard data can convince people what they believed to be impossible is not only possible, but has actually already been accomplished. As the program is implemented and results are achieved, the focus shifts to sustaining the emerging positive culture. Just as regular evaluation is critical throughout the installation phase in order to clearly measure progress toward objectives, so ongoing evaluation is necessary to insure that results are sustained and to disclose the need for retooling and renewal of the change effort in one or more influence areas.

The purpose of the final step, *Systems Feedback and Evaluation,* is, therefore, to provide ongoing feedback on effectiveness and to establish renewal mechanisms. The emphasis is on development of an internal capacity to direct and sustain change and to continually re-evaluate.

Measurement of results is conducted along both normative and performance lines—that is, survey instruments measure modified perception of behavior in each influence area, and charts monitor performance objectives, including bottom-line results.

The fourth phase also provides an opportunity for extending the change program into other areas. Once expertise is gained while dealing with one problem, it can be used for others. The whole thrust of Normative Systems is from rigidity to flexibility—from stultification in a morass of negative norms to responsiveness and ability to take on new positive norms. Cultures which develop internal capability will be able to react meaningfully to new circumstances, new data and new phenomena.

Thus, the Agricultural Operation has not only accomplished a win-win financial picture for both migrant workers and the corporation, but company housing has been permanently replaced by a new community that governs itself. Health facilities and child-development centers were opened and workers began to experience year-round fringe benefits. The community services in health, child development, library, tutoring, etc., have become models for the entire state and have begun to attract outside, noncompany funding.

The Supermarket Company instituted regular meetings to review shrink data, and established a permanent bonus system. Every new employee was trained to understand shrink. Because these were established as ongoing activities, the new norms were continually reinforced and after four years, the low pilferage figure was maintained. Managers and supervisors now maintain the positive norm as part of the day-to-day functioning of each work team, and no outside professional expertise is needed. Periodically consultants are called in to review progress and activities, but they have found the new norms well-established.

In the litter program, follow-up accountability procedures are conducted by a permanent Clean City Committee, which monitor litter measurement and litter-reduction actions monthly, and provides public recognition for sustained "delittering." A task force from each workshop was formed to insure constant self-monitoring of the groups committed to sustained litter-reduction. In addition, enforced revision of the city ordinances provides ongoing confrontation of littering behavior.

Now that the industry and government groups have found they can "clean their own houses," and personnel on all levels have learned to deal with this particular problem, the people of the three cities have learned a technique which they can apply to problems of delinquency, drug addiction, etc.

The Food Distribution Warehouse sustained its new and positive atmosphere by periodic workshops involving all levels of the organization. The comprehensive information system that was established continues to give necessary feedback on results and further strengthens the positive steps. Union/management relations have been tremendously improved and the workers now joke about the "country-club" atmosphere in which they work. The union recently began to ask other companies to utilize the same type of program in their distribution centers.

The lessons learned from these experiences are clear: If the organization or community is treated as a culture, results can be obtained quickly and sustained at length. If critical norm areas are dealt with systematically, and if people are involved in planned programs, the support of the culture for new and positive norms is a crucial and powerful technique which any group can learn to use effectively. The systematic cultural-change process can bring about a great congruency between what people wish their group to accomplish and what actually happens.

A Sense of Community, a Shared Vision, and a Positive Culture: Key Enabling Factors in Successful Culture Change

By Judd Allen and Robert F. Allen

Abstract

In order to identify the features of the culture which enable program development, a retrospective study of culture change projects was conducted. Three core enabling factors were identified by those who had been responsible for past culture change projects. These factors—a sense of community, a positive culture, and a shared vision—have been found to make desired and sustained behavior change possible. The development of the core enabling factors as part of a culture change effort is discussed.

Most of the changes sought in communities and organizations will be of little value unless they can be sustained, and few changes will last unless the culture is modified to support desired goals. This desire for lasting change holds regardless of whether the goal is healthier lifestyles, reductions in littering, or increased caring for people with disabilities. Community and organizational change normally addresses needs which are ongoing. New cultural norms must be developed which enhance peoples' efforts to address the ongoing needs of their communities and organization.

Changing community and organizational cultures requires the continuing commitment of a significant number of organizational members.[1-4] Systematic culture change is more than periodic random offerings such as a needs assessment, a workshop, a packaged seminar, or a promotional flier. Culture change requires a comprehensive, systematized and continuing revision of cultural influence mechanisms such as rewards, social recognition, training, orientation, communication, and information systems. In order to bring about complex and sustained cultural change a supportive environment for change must be established. Three key enabling factors—a shared vision, a positive outlook and a sense of community—which have been found to account for much of the vitality generated through successful culture change efforts.

In the early 1980s, the Human Resources Institute (HRI), a behavioral science, research and consulting organization, received a grant to identify core cultural factors which enable organizations and communities to successfully approach change. This particular study focused on identifying: (a) factors that seemed to have been most important in blocking solutions to the problems prior to the introduction of the change project; and (b) factors that contributed most significantly to the solutions that were eventually achieved. In examination of the relationship between these factors, HRI expected to identify core cultural factors which would empower organizational members to initiate and adopt needed change.

Twenty culture change programs were identified for the study. Programs were selected for the sample if their development and outcome were well documented and if the staff who had worked on the project were available to participate in the current research effort. Although this was not a random sample or intended to be representative of the 616 programs originally considered for the study or of organizational and community settings in general, the analysis of this sample was expected to yield important information about enabling factors for culture change projects. The 20 programs in the subsample were those that most nearly corresponded to the criteria set for the selection of the subsample.

The staff members who had worked on the projects were asked to review the projects in order to identify key enabling and inhibiting factors. After initial lists were discussed, a series of meetings were held to consolidate the items that had been identified. In the course of these meetings, 19 factors were identified by two or more of the researchers as significantly contributing to or impeding successful project implementation. These are listed in Table 1.

Table 1
Initial Enabling Factors Identified

1. Leadership commitment
2. Involvement of people
3. Availability of financial resources
4. Availability of human resources
5. Win-win approaches
6. Support of the first line supervisors
7. Support of middle management
8. Viability of objectives
9. Agreement on objectives
10. Clarity of goals
11. Good communication
12. Belief in potential for success
13. Working on a team
14. Effective use of human resources programs
15. Results orientation
16. Measurement of effectiveness
17. Community support
18. Time commitment
19. Understanding of the influence of culture

From this list, three interrelated enabling factors were identified (see Figure 1) through discussion and consensual agreement. These three factors—a shared vision, a sense of community, and a positive culture—were seen as playing a significant role in determining the impact of 19 initially identified factors. In addition, it was felt that the relative presence or absence of these factors either before or during the implementation of a project would significantly affect the likelihood of the project's success or failure. Each of these factors is discussed in Figure 1.

A Shared Vision

When organization members have a shared vision, they know and are enthusiastic about what the organization is trying to accomplish and have a common view about the general mechanisms by which those goals can be achieved. A shared vision can be related to the organization as a whole or to a particular project within the organization. When no shared vision exists, people often end up working at cross purposes and there is little common agreement

Figure 1
Three Core Enabling Factors for Culture Change

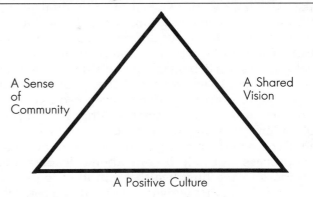

about what the organization or group is trying to achieve. It is as if there were insufficient liquid added to the flour in making bread. All the kneading in the world is not likely to help it to hold together, and additional flour is not likely to make a positive difference. Consequently, in order for people to work well together, they need to see themselves as working toward common goals. The need to develop clear project goals is particularly important during difficult periods in project development. Without it, difficulties that are encountered tend to become fatal obstacles to the project.

Such goals must be worthy of the commitment of significant amounts of time and energy. The term vision, rather than the more commonly used word, objective, was chosen because it suggests that these goals must be capable of inspiring participation. Furthermore, a vision is capable of bringing people with divergent views together in a commonly agreed upon and sustained effort. A vision implies something more than the mere number of dollars earned or the number of items produced or the number of health promotion courses taught, although it might include any or all of these. A vision is something that people can dream of and care deeply about as well as something that they can actually achieve.

Shared vision emerges when people have a chance to integrate their own personal goals and approaches with those of the organization, program, or project. This is particularly important in health promotion, because people have an opportunity to work toward their own health enhancement goals as part of the overall program design. People who are working toward the achievement of their own health objectives should be in a much better position to assist others, particularly if they are able to discuss their shortcoming, strengths, and difficultires with those they are trying to help.

The development of a shared vision is contingent upon working towards a group consensus which takes the hopes and wishes of individual group members into consideration. It has been our experience that talking out differences and concerns at the beginning of a project and reviewing shared decisions regularly helps to not only strengthen the vision but also to improve it. If group consensus is not worked towards, needed project resources and enthusiasm may not be forthcoming. Health promotion programs in particular stand to benefit from the process of developing a shared vision because this process can help organizational leaders and members to see how health promotion is not an add-on to their other activities, but rather a core feature of their work together.

If a shared vision is to be maintained and improved, a great deal of attention needs to be paid to its communication throughout the organization and particularly its communication to new organizational members. A simply and clearly stated vision consisting of not more than a few major statements is more easily communicated than lengthy lists of goals and objectives. A graphic image or an acronym can be useful to communicate the vision. The vision needs to be formulated in such a way that it can be communicated during the orientation of new members, in evaluating individual and organizational performance, in organizational planning meetings, and even during social occasions. As many organizational members as possible should be able to communicate the shared vision in a few short words and be able to tell how their decisions and actions, as well as the decisions and actions of the organization, fit with that vision.

It is the new and evolving vision of the organization which helps new norms to crystallize where old outmoded norms exist. The shared vision of the organization enables people to see that change is both desirable and necessary. The shared vision adds direction to the change. It helps people to believe that their energies will be well spent. The shared vision offers people an opportunity to develop common dreams and hope. It is the common acknowledgement to shared dreams which engenders a sense of community, and it is the element of hope which enables people to work in a positive culture.

A Positive Culture

A positive culture was found to be a critical second factor in promoting successful culture change projects. A positive culture is founded on the belief that goals can and will be accomplished when people work together and creatively toward their achievement. In a positive culture people look for opportunities rather than obstacles and for strengths rather than weaknesses in one another. Like a fisherman who thinks he is just about to catch a fish, a member of a positive culture is poised to take advantage of opportunity. Given such a positive outlook, multiple solutions are sought for every challenge. And, people think in terms of challenges and opportunities instead of problems or defeats. In a positive culture people look realistically at their assets and strengths as well as at their challenges and obstacles, recognizing that it is the former that will enable them to overcome the latter to move forward to new accomplishments.

A positive culture does not include unrealistic thinking, but rather a recognition that there are positives in most, if not all, people and situations, and they can be found through creative and persistent searching. And, it is these good things rather than the negatives in the situations that provide the basis for moving forward toward greater accomplishments.

Use of the term "culture" is intended to help people distinguish between the superficial "smiling face" posters, buttons and bumper stickers, and core values. Smiles are a feature of a positive culture, but they tend to be based upon the recognition of positive outcomes and opportunities rather than on a fixed facial posture. A positive culture is not a mask to cover problems and difficulties, but rather a way of thinking about problems and opportunities. It is not luck, but rather an attention to opportunities which improves results. And, having a positive culture does not mean that human suffering is ignored or that human values issues are taken lightly. In a positive culture joy is found in the process of working towards the solution of human problems.

Too often, the "nay saying" negative norms of our larger societal cultures sap energy and interfere with our achievements. To recognize the extent of this negativism, one needs only to look at the "bad news" that appears on television screens, in newspapers and in day-to-day interactions.

As one psychological study demonstrated, bad news makes people think of themselves and those around them as bad.[5] In this study, subjects who had just listened to a news broadcast reporting negative behavior were much more likely to predict negative human behavior in the experiments than those who had just listened to a news broadcast reporting positive behavior.

In a negative culture people tend to discount their resources and successes by looking for imperfections in the outcome. In a positive culture imperfections are seen as challenges for the future which can be better met as a result of current success. Instead of listing successes with failures on an additive score card, people operating from a positive culture would be more apt to list their successes and failures separately so that the successes could be fully appreciated.

In a similar fashion, a positive culture tends to promote win-win solutions to problems while challenging false dichotomies. Where it is customary to view health promotion as in opposition to curative treatment, for example, people operating from a positive culture are able to move towards integrated solutions by which both approaches to health are seen as vital. Thus, new approaches to analysis are sought in which conceptual grids replace linear dichotomies (as seen in the illustration in Figure 2 and Figure 3). Members of a positive culture tend to adopt a 9-9 position (see Figure 3) in which both factors are seen as contributing rather than competing with one another as illustrated in Figure 2. In this way, positive cultures avoid such common pitfalls as those associated with viewing the interests of management as different from those of employees or of viewing the concern for people as different from the concern for task.

Figure 2
A Dichotomous View of People and Task

Strong Concern for Task	A Moderate Concern for People and Task	Strong Concern for Task

In addition to fostering integrated thinking, cultures which succeed at becoming positive tend to utilize supportive performance review techniques. In positive cultures, the more typical fault-finding of the performance review process is augmented by an opportunity for individuals and groups to receive positive feedback on their accomplishments and to plan for future accomplishments based on solid initial successes. As part of this strength review process, associates sit down with their supervisors to answer four questions:

1. What are you particularly pleased with in your accomplishments during this past time period?
2. What would you like to do even better and how will you go about this?
3. What can I as your supervisor or other parts of the organization do to help?

Figure 3
A Grid View of People and Task*

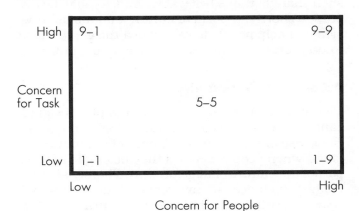

*Adapted from Robert R. Blake and Jan Srygley Mouton (1964). *Managerial Grid*. Houston, Texas: Gulf Publishing Company.

4. When shall we sit down again to review our program?

Such strength review questions can be extremely helpful in health promotion programs. In the process of identifying healthy activities in their behavioral repertoire, participants can move from the negative position of having to give up negative behavior to the more successful position of taking on enjoyable behavior. In addition, by enlisting the positive support of supervisors, family members and other members of the social network, those undertaking lifestyle changes can help to build a more supportive environment. These significant others will need to know how they can be of assistance.

Some organizations have difficulty working from strengths, and when this is true there is often a tendency for people to look for faults with one another and to engage in blame-placing and scapegoating rather than constructive problem-solving. Correcting this situation should be one of the first and primary tasks of a culture change agent. As organizational culture programs begin to succeed, more and more positive statements begin to appear. People begin to talk about what has already been accomplished as well as what remains to be done. They begin to point out strengths that exist in the organization and in their co-workers rather than focus solely on the weaknesses and limitations which so often command attention in more negative cultural settings.

The movement towards a positive culture makes it possible for organizational members to create the ingredients of success. A positive culture enables organizational members to create a worthwhile shared vision which is not bogged down in conditional statements or in solutions which rely on the failure of others. Furthermore, a positive culture makes such shared visions believable. And, as shall be discussed shortly, a positive culture and a shared vision can help people to establish a third ingredient to organizational success: a sense of community.

A Sense of Community

The third factor which was found to play a significant role in the success of culture change programs is a sense of community. A sense of community is found when people feel as if they belong to and are part of the culture change process. This sense of belonging includes an awareness that others will "care" and that, the individual, in turn, has a responsibility to care for the other members of the culture. Furthermore, a sense of community engenders meaning and connectedness. Inclusion in the community enables members of the culture to create a shared history and common destiny. It is a sense of community which fosters cooperative actions.

A sense of community is particularly essential when change is being planned. If there is a lack of a sense of community, each individual's resources and turf must be guarded and maintained exclusively for their own personal use. Information about strengths and weaknesses are kept secret so that people can feel protected from one another. The absence of community causes organizational members to look upon change with suspicion. Lower echelons in the organization equate change with manipulation. Leaders fear that their positions of power and privilege will be challenged by innovation. Participatory and democratic decision making is eschewed or used inappropriately when choices are really not available. The physical and creative energy of the organization is sapped by fear and scheming.

Too many groups and organizations endure low levels of community.[5-7] Organizational members tend only to know their co-workers in terms of their limited job roles.[8] Too many workers know little about their co-workers' families, their friends, their special interests, their hopes and dreams. The statement "give me a pair of hands" when asking for an additional employee reflects this attitude. Cut from a sense of community, too many organizational members have resigned themselves to "put in their time," to endure, to keep to themselves, and to hope that they survive a hostile environment. In order to cope, these people form protective groups or alliances. In extreme cases they may pay off others by looking the other way or sabotaging projects. These alliances are founded on a survival

mentality which fails to activate the collective potential of the organization.

People often look longingly at the times they felt community.[6-8] Such memories may stem back to time spent in a small town, or to when the organization was forming or to work in a particular department, or even to a time of their participation in a social movement or political cause. These memories can become a powerful force in individual and collective behaviors. There can be a reluctance to give up behaviors which are associated with the memory of community. As a result, some behaviors, such as overeating and the abuse of alcoholic beverages can be associated in peoples' minds with significant positive community-based experiences.

The creation of a sense of community adds immense power to the culture change effort. The new meaning and historical significance associated with creating a sense of community helps people to challenge older behaviors. By associating desired behavior with the creation of community, new chosen behaviors become emotionally reinforcing and more resilient to environmental pressures. Thus, a new sense of community frees organizational members to look more critically at behaviors which they had associated on a conscious or subconscious level with community. People are then in a better position, for example, to disassociate the smoking they learned in high school from the positive experience they had in building meaningful friendships. In a culture-based health promotion program, participants are better able to associate non-smoking with new positive bonds and meaningful experiences.

The trust and openness available in community is a necessary ingredient to collective innovation. Weaknesses and temporary setbacks need not be hidden and can be given the attention they deserve. And, given a sense of community, helping one another becomes a virtue allowing each individual to add to and to utilize available resources. These qualities of community make it possible, for example, to work on the often hidden problems of drug addiction and emotional distress. Perhaps most importantly, a sense of community helps all organizational members to recognize such issues as collective problems rather than strictly a concern of those directly experiencing the problem.

Although many program participants find their community building skills rusty, these same participants frequently give the most favorable ratings to those elements of the program which focus on community building opportunities.[9] Presentations and workshops which devote time to personal sharing and small group activities tend to be those which have a lasting impact on the group or organization.[9] It is not uncommon for organizational members who have worked together for years to learn about important, as yet unrealized, common interests in the course of simple sharing exercises. As sharing opportunities are scheduled into the daily workings of the organization, a sense of community evolves and the culture change programs moves forward.

In the same way that a sense of community contributes to the success of culture-based change efforts, the introduction of culture change programs serves a critical role in creating a sense of community in organizations. One organization that started a health promotion program for the purpose of reducing illness costs within the organization reported later that while the organization's financial goals had been more than achieved, the greatest benefit by far was the opportunities that the program provided for deepening the sense of community within the organization. Through the program, associates from various levels and departments in the company shared important health concerns with each other. In creating opportunities for associates to interact constructively, meaningfully, and playfully outside their normal work roles, a new appreciation of the organization and of individual associates was created. Furthermore, the recent involvement of associates' family members in the health promotion effort further strengthened the bonds which were emerging in the organization, and made it possible for the organization to be even more effective in accomplishing its goals.

A Matter of Degree

Few, if any, organizations or programs are ever completely successful in achieving these three enabling characteristics, and just as few are completely lacking in them. It is the degree to which they are present or absent that seems to make the difference in program or organizational success. Where a sense of community, a positive culture and a shared vision are relatively absent, they need to be increased, and where they are relatively present, they need to be celebrated, maintained and extended. Some suggestions for assessing the degree to which these factors exist in a given culture are presented in Table 2.

Programs and organizations which have many problems in implementing successful change tend to be lacking in these factors. Whereas, successful organizations tend to have these factors in greater abundance.

One example involves a group of migrant workers in central Florida and the company (The Coca Cola Company) that employs them.[1,10-12] At the beginning of this project, workers productivity, workers health, and company profits from operations were at an extremely low ebb. Accident rates were high, alcoholism was rampant, and absenteeism was commonplace. The operations of the division were also characterized by an almost complete absence of a shared vision, a positive culture, and a sense of community. People at different levels in the organization had little agreement as to what the organization was trying to accomplish and little

Table 2
Some Questions You Might Want to Ask About Your Program

A Shared Vision
Is it expected and accepted for people to support each other in efforts...
1. to discuss personal dreams and plans for their achievement?
2. to review the mission of the community when making plans?
3. to be fully aware of the mission of the community and how personal dreams relate to it?
4. to recognize the mission as an important aspect of community life?
5. to look for creative ways by which the mission of the community can be communicated and put into action?
6. to be able to tell about the mission of the community briefly and in their own words?
7. to regularly review the goals of the community and how these goals fit with the individual goals of various members?

A Sense of Community
Is it expected and accepted for people to support each other in efforts...
1. to get to know each others' personal history and dreams?
2. to develop a sense of belonging and appreciation?
3. to contribute in some regular way to the welfare of the community?
4. to love and be loved?
5. to respect the individual freedoms of community members?
6. to be involved in decisions affecting them?
7. to communicate openly?
8. to have many opportunities to have fun with one another?

A Positive Culture
Is it expected and accepted for people to support each other in efforts...
1. to take into consideration existing strengths when looking for solutions to problems?
2. not to discount strengths with weaknesses, but rather to overcome weaknesses through strengths?
3. to make more positive statements than negative statements?
4. to regularly review personal strengths and opportunities, and the strengths and opportunities of the organization?
5. to find ways to translate problems into opportunities for development?
6. to focus on hope rather than on despair?

shared commitment to the solution of the organization's problems. There was little in the way of a sense of community or relationship between people. Each person was on their own and each expected to succeed and fail—most of all fail—exclusively on their own merits or demerits. Cooperative effort was uncommon and high levels of distrust had developed between individuals and groups. High levels of negativism were evident. People tended to focus on the weaknesses in each other and in the organization, and they had low levels of hope and expectations and high levels of frustration and anger.

The culture change process was introduced, and over a period of months and years a shared vision, a sense of community, and a positive culture were developed. When these were achieved, the creativity and talents of the organization's members were unleashed in new ways so that the seemingly "unsolvable" problems of the past could be addressed. As a result, worker productivity, worker health, and company profits were increased, and accidents, alcoholism, and absenteeism were reduced. As one worker put it, "It used to be that we couldn't do anything to improve things, but now, by working together, we can really begin to address the problems that concern us."

A second example, drawn from the cases examined, involves a supermarket company that was having a great deal of difficulty in achieving its objectives, particularly as these related to customer service.[13] Its sales and profits were low, customers and potential customers were not pleased with performance, employee morale was problematic, and extremely high stress levels and dissatisfaction were being reported by everyone from the company president to the cashiers. The initial analysis of the organization showed that few people below the top management level could accurately describe the company purposes or philosophy, and that very few of the employees in day-to-day contact with the customers were even aware that the company was hoping to stress customer service in its marketing and operational programs.

It was also found that low levels of commitment existed at the employee level, and a general feeling of negativism permeated much of the organization's thinking. A great deal of time was spent in fault finding, blame placing, and in explaining why things could not work as opposed to finding ways to overcome whatever obstacles appeared. Relationship development was limited to narrowly defined role related activities, and very little in the way of a sense of community was apparent.

The culture change program, which was designed to confront these shortcomings, was successful in more than doubling the company's sales and profits, and in markedly improving both employee morale and customer satisfaction. The company was so successful in fact that it is regarded in independently conducted surveys as the most highly rated company in its trading area in customer loyalty and satisfaction. Employee surveys showed marked increases in employee understanding of and commitment to the organization's goals. Furthermore, dramatic improvements in quality of relationships were found.

Culture Change Systems and Enabling Factors

Enabling factors can be significantly enhanced by approaching change in a systematic manner. One such four-phase change approach, called Normative Systems, has shown its value in organizing change in such a way that people have opportunities to build a sense of community, a shared vision, and a positive culture (see Figure 4).[1-4]

In Phase I of Analysis and Objective Setting, members of the culture are asked to help identify the mission of the organization and how that mission might be enhanced by playing a more active role in choosing the culture. This process of identifying the common hopes of organizational members can further develop a shared vision. By focusing on identifying opportunities for win-win solutions to problems and by revealing existing strengths, the analysis can also aid in the development of a positive culture. Phase I efforts can lay the foundation for a sense of community by identifying mechanisms for people to learn more about each other and to care for one another.

Phase II, Systems Introduction, normally takes place during a participatory introductory workshop which is dedicated to helping all members of the organization to understand the impact of the existing culture, identify areas for change, and to develop an action plan by which change can be accomplished. By providing members of the culture with a common introduction to the change effort, Phase II can reinforce the key enabling factors. The introductory workshops offer opportunities for organizational members to tell about their personal history and interests, and in so doing help to create a sense of community. The introductory workshops also give participants a common knowledge base about how the culture is influencing the success of their efforts—making for a shared vision. The qualities of a shared vision and the positive culture are further augmented by workshop participant's efforts to devise individual and shared action plans for bringing about change.

The third phase of Systems Implementation tends to be carried out: (1) on an individual self-help basis; (2) with peer groups; (3) with leadership development; and (4) with the introduction of new organizational policies and procedures. By working on change at both an individual and a collective level, people can further develop a shared vision and a sense of community. The multi-level change strategy also enhances the opportunities for mutual success and a positive culture.

The fourth phase of ongoing Evaluation and Renewal provides an index of success, an opportunity to celebrate, and an opportunity to devise new plans for dealing with remaining problem areas. The celebration of success typically provides for further community building activity. By re-examining the goals of the project in light of current success, a renewed sense of a shared vision and positive culture tends to emerge.

Culture Change and Enabling Factors

A sense of community, a positive culture, and a shared vision have been shown to be important to the success of culture change efforts. When these factors become a part of the day-to-day workings of the organization, other goals, such as reduced levels of smoking or dietary changes, can more easily be achieved and integrated into the every day

life of the culture. Thus, the core enabling factors can be developed concurrently with other aspects of the culture change program and integrate with them as part of the ongoing implementation process. In Table 3 a number of suggested steps are outlined for the implementation of each of the three enabling factors.

In the process of developing a sense of community, a shared vision, and a positive culture, the organization will not only be in a better position to accomplish its immediate program goals, but will also be in a vastly improved position to undertake new change efforts. One community which had been involved in a culture-based litter reduction program spoke of their programs as "A place to begin." In building a new culture through their Clean Communities System, these community leaders recognized that they had created an environment which could support needed change.[14,15]

It is the view of the authors that everyone could benefit from monitoring surrounding levels of community, shared vision, and positive culture. Each of these factors can be strengthened, reaping dividends for individuals and for organizations. In changing levels of community, shared vision, and positive culture, people are in a vastly improved position to make differences in their health practices. When these factors are modified in organizations, new healthier cultures can take shape. And, perhaps most importantly, these enabling factors will help to insure that people will be in a position to choose healthier lifestyles.

Figure 4
The Normative Systems Culture Change Process

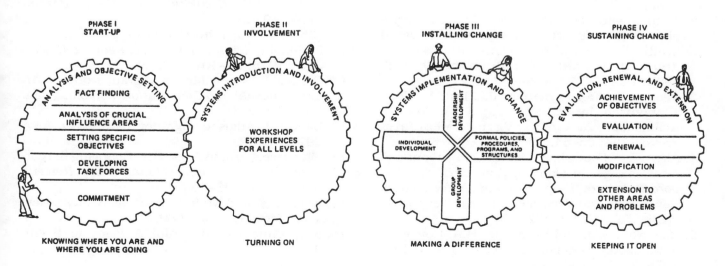

Table 3
Some Steps That Your Project Might Decide to Take

To Assure a Shared Vision
1. Include the development of a shared vision as one of the goals of the health promotion program.
2. Seek employee ideas for the development, installation, and improvement of the program so that the best ideas are developed and a sense of ownership is assured.
3. Tie in the objectives of your health promotion effort to the philosophy and the bottom line objectives of the organization.
4. Provide special briefing sessions for key groups, union leaders, shop stewards, top management, and first line supervisors to inform them and enlist their support.
5. Hold introductory workshops for all employees whether or not they plan to actively participate so that they can be supportive of the program.
6. Provide opportunities for all families to be introduced to and informed about the program so that they too can be supportive.
7. Regularly survey employees to determine their level of understanding and their suggestions for the improvement of the understanding and commitment.
8. Orient all new employees to the program as a regular part of the employee orientation process.
9. Involve participants in carrying the program to others in the organization.
10. Include the development of a shared vision as one of the goals of the introductory workshop.

To Assure the Development of a Positive Culture
1. Help people to understand the importance of positive cultures and the ways that they can go about creating them.
2. See to it that the program and the program leaders model the positive approaches that the program seeks to engender.
3. Regularly provide praise and positive feedback on the successes of participants and the program.

4. Make certain that mistakes are used as training opportunities rather than as occasions for blame placing and fault finding.
5. Recognize and point out ways in which negative cultures work to peoples' detriment and to the detriment of the wider society.
6. Use strength reviews and assessments as central features of the performance review and evaluation process.
7. Include the development of positive cultures as one of the goals of the health promotion program.
8. Include the development of positive cultures as one of the goals of the introductory workshop.

To Assure a Sense of Community
1. See that people understand the importance of a sense of community to the success of the program and achievement of individual health objectives.
2. See that all participants are introduced to the program in such a way that a sense of community with others is developed.
3. See that ways are found to include rather than to exclude people from participation and a sense of the participation (i.e., people who exercise at home can be included as program participants).
4. See that the program offers people the opportunity to be involved in helping and supporting others and in being helped and supported by others.
5. Regularly survey organizational members to determine the level of "community" that has been established and peoples' suggestions for increasing it.
6. Include the development of a sense of community as one of the objectives of the program and regularly measure the program effectiveness in achieving this objective.
7. Include the development of a sense of community as one of the goals of the introductory workshop.
8. Assure that people develop a sense of ownership about the program.

References

1. Allen, J. and Allen, R.F. Achieving health promotion objectives through culture change systems. *American Journal of Health Promotion,* 1986; 1:42–49.
2. Allen, J. and Allen, R.F. From short-term compliance to long-term freedom: Culture-based health promotion by health professionals. *American Journal of Health Promotion,* Fall, 1986; 1:39–47.
3. Allen, R.F. Transformations that last: A cultural approach. In *Transforming Work,* John D. Adams (ed.), Alexandria, Virginia: Miles River Press, 1984; 35–54.
4. Allen, R.F. Four phases for bringing about cultural change. In *Gaining Control of the Corporate Culture,* Ralph Kilmann, Mary Saxton, Roy Serpa and Associates (eds.), New York: Jossey-Bass, 1985; 332–350.
5. Holloway, S.M. and Hornstein, H.A. How good news makes us good. *Psychology Today,* Dec. 1976; 76–78, 106, 108.
6. Myerhoff, B. *Number Our Days.* New York: Simon and Schuster, 1978.
7. Nisbet, R. *The Quest for Community.* New York: Oxford University Press, 1953.
8. Slater, P. *The Pursuit of Loneliness: American Culture at the Breaking Point.* Boston: Beacon Press, 1976.
9. Gibbs, J. *The TORI Community*
10. Blank, J.P. Migrants no more. *Readers Digest,* July, 1975; 98–102.
11. Garner, P. A new life for migrant workers. *Atlanta Journal and Constitution Magazine,* Jan. 23, 1972; 8–14.
12. Larkin, T. Adios to migrancy. *Manpower,* Aug. 1974; 15–22.
13. Silverzweig, S. and Allen, R.F. Changing the corporate culture. *Sloan Management Review,* Spring 1976; 33–49.
14. Allen, R.F. and Kraft, C. *Beat the System.* New York: McGraw-Hill, 1980.
15. Keep American Beautiful A Place to Begin, 1979.

SECTION IV
DETERMINATION

In this phase the goals are to determine the results of the culture change efforts and recycle the process. Since change is a never ending process, this phase is both the end and the beginning of the 4D Process (Diagnosis, Development, Delivery and Determination). Leaders need to take a hard look at how far the organization has come and how far it still needs to go—and rekindle the desire to proceed. This phase provides the systematic follow-up that is crucial to lasting change. Leaders will need to create a consistency of purpose, adopt a philosophy congruent with the age we live in, and make change a well-orchestrated process instead of a series of isolated training events.

Since one of the most difficult challenges in culture change efforts is to maintain changes once they occur, the only article in this section focuses on a tested technology for sustaining culture change.

Sustaining Culture Change with Multiple-Rater Systems for Career Development and Performance Appraisal Systems

By Mark R. Edwards

Abstract

Supervisor-only evaluations contain fatal errors such as self-serving biases and other biases, severe inflation of ratings, non-comparability among ratings by different supervisors and problems with proof of accuracy, discrimination and validity. Peer evaluations overcome these problems but pose others, such as too great a loss of supervisory power. The compromise procedure, employee-supplemented evaluation, solves the culture shock problem associated with peer evaluation. Employees and management get many of the advantages associated with peer evaluation, such as high participation in the decisions that most affect them and an opportunity to identify strong, average and weak work associates. Supervisors find the process highly beneficial because the high quality information they receive from colleagues typically supports their own perceptions.

Possibly the most critical issues in the study of culture is sustaining cultural change. Much has been written about assessing, building and changing corporate cultures; yet relatively little is available on how to *sustain* culture change. This article presents a case for using fair and accurate multirater appraisal systems to credibly identify those who most support the desired cultures. By clearly identifying and rewarding those who support the new cultural norms, the rewards system drives organizational behaviors in a fashion that sustains the desired cultural change.

Accurate measures of job behavior provide the key to sustaining culture change. Traditional

mushy measures of performance, which result in all people receiving equal rewards or in rewards going to the wrong people, neither change behavior nor sustain behavioral change. In contrast, when an accurate measure is used, the rewards system reinforces behaviors consistent with the new cultural norms, and those new behaviors replace those consistent with norms of the past.

The multiple-rater process described here may be visualized as an assessment of the "micro culture" or the cultural norms (behaviors) exhibited by each organization member. With this process, assessment of the micro culture is based on information from the most reliable and valid source available, work associates. The participant's colleagues and the supervisor in the participant's immediate network provide an accurate and credible picture of work behaviors.

Multiple-rater evaluation requires some cultural change. The traditional, hierarchically dominated culture includes an extremely rigorous norm that supervisors alone should provide performance information. However, no method has been developed to overcome the problems with single-source evaluations, such as self-serving biases, other rater biases, and poor credibility to employees.

Motivating Employees: What Employees Really Want

A useful way to find out what motivates employees is to ask them. The American Productivity and Quality Center surveyed 383 employees, mostly top or middle managers, and asked them what they really wanted at work.

As shown in Table 1, employees want an organization culture typified by participative management where their opinions count. Employees want

Table 1
What Managers Want and What Exists

Factor	% Rating 4 or 5	% Saying Exists in Current Workplace	Difference Score
Challenging work	96.9	88.3	8.6
My opinion matters when decisions are made	96.0	68.5	27.5
Recognition for a job well done	90.9	54.5	36.4
Pay clearly tied to performance	88.7	49.6	39.1
Working for a company I can be proud of	87.2	79.1	8.1
Good, fair performance measures	85.0	38.7	46.3
Autonomy on the job	82.3	66.3	16.0
A competitive salary	80.9	81.3	−0.4
Clear performance goals	77.6	39.5	38.1
Opportunity to learn on the job	76.4	77.0	−0.6
Clear career opportunities	74.4	26.4	48.0
Harmonious relations with coworkers	70.7	75.1	−4.4
Job security	58.8	58.4	0.4
Generous benefit program	54.1	67.7	−13.6
Special incentives such as merchandise and travel	8.8	11.2	−2.4

Notes: 1. Responses were rated on a 5-point scale; 5 equals "very important."
2. Sample size: 383 top or middle managers.
3. Survey was conducted by American Productivity and Quality Center.

The survey shows the disparity between what employees highly value and what they actually receive in key areas. There were large discrepancies between what managers wanted and what they perceived to exist for several factors, including pay tied to performance, fair performance measures, and clear performance goals.

to be recognized for doing a good job. They want fair and accurate performance measures, pay clearly tied to performance, job autonomy, clear performance goals, and clear career opportunities.

For each of these desired cultural norms, there is a substantial gap between what employees want and what they perceive to be the current situation. A major obstacle to achieving participative management is the use of decision processes that do not allow participative input, but depend instead on hierarchically-driven, supervisor-only evaluation. How can an organization claim participative leadership when employees have little or no input to the decision process that most affects their career lives: performance measurement? Single-rater systems often fail to recognize good work, especially when supervision is poor. Supervisor-only evaluations contain many disincentives to fair and accurate performance measures, these disincentives make tying pay-to-performance difficult.

Multiple-rater appraisal systems offer participative management opportunities and substantial motivational benefits that make multiple-rater systems clearly superior to traditional, supervisor-only evaluation procedures. Compared with supervisor-only systems, multiple-rater systems offer improved motivation for supervisors and employees, due to social facilitation, improved accuracy and increased credibility. Possibly most importantly, multiple-rater evaluation shifts the supervisor's task from one of judging and defensive justification to filling a more constructive role as performance coach.

The Traditional Evaluation Model

Traditional systems of performance evaluation depend on hierarchically-based decisions by supervisors. The supervisor provides essentially 100% of the decision information associated with employee performance. Therefore, an employee's career life depends on the fairness and accuracy of supervisory evaluations. Culture change depends on each supervisor's ability to fairly evaluate and credibly communicate performance results.

Because nearly all American organizations use supervisor-only evaluations, most organizational cultures assume supervisors *should* provide the only information used in evaluating performance. Similarly, most organizational members have never seen an alternative model such as team evaluation and have no experiential base on which to evaluate a change.

When managers are presented with compelling empirical research demonstrating that obtaining input from work associates (rather than from

195

supervisors only) increases reliability and validity of information used in decisions about human resources, many managers respond only with skepticism. Such information may be counter-intuitive. It is certainly counter-cultural for many organizations.

Douglas McGregor, among many others, has warned that traditional appraisals of performance may do more harm than good.[1] Many managers prefer dental appointments to playing "God" in preparing appraisals. Supervisors often procrastinate or ignore appraisals entirely because they find the evaluation process time consuming and aversive. Supervisors realize that giving subordinates evaluations that are less than outstanding creates a situation where the supervisor must justify the evaluation, potentially demotivating a key subordinate. Consequently, supervisors have substantial self-serving bias to inflate performance ratings.[2]

Subordinates who receive a less-than-positive evaluation by a supervisor may attribute the low evaluation to the supervisor's poor judgment, lack of knowledge or bias. For some employees, the supervisor represents the least credible source of performance information. Therefore, judgmental information from the supervisor may have little, if any, positive motivational value. Such information lacks the credibility to create behavior change and is totally insufficient to sustain cultural change.

A supervisor may distort evaluations so much the results reflect the supervisor's bias more than they reflect employee performance.[3] A summary of the many disincentives (and the few incentives) to objective and accurate evaluations by supervisors is presented in Table 2.

Multiple-Rater, Team Evaluation

Multiple independent judgments are at the heart of our democratic political system, which was designed to ensure fairness to individuals. Multiple-rater decision systems can provide similar insurance to protect the career lives of employees within organizations. A summary of advantages and disadvantages of multiple-rater, colleague-supplemented evaluation is shown in Table 3.

Multiple-rater or team evaluation offers an effective way to obtain fair and accurate performance measurement. Team evaluation provides a compromise between hierarchically-driven supervisor-only evaluations and laterally-driven peer-evaluation systems. The team evaluation process yields a *colleague-supplemented evaluation*, in which evaluation bilateral associates provides high quality information to supervisors.

Table 2

Disincentives and Incentives to Objective Evaluation In Supervisor-Only Systems of Performance Measurement

	Disincentives or Self-Serving Biases
Confrontation:	A desire to avoid a difficult confrontation.
Documentation:	The difficulty of assembling definitive documentation.
Defensiveness:	A wish to avoid an awkward defensive reaction.
Reflective Attribution:	An apprehension that mediocre performance reflects negatively on the supervisor.
Action:	A desire to avoid subsequent performance monitoring or intervention.
History:	An acknowledgment that behaviors may have been "acceptable" for a long time.
In the Line of Duty:	A feeling that, because performance decrement is related to the job, the problem should be overlooked.
Personal Problem:	A belief that the organization should not become involved in personal problems.
Fear of False Accusation:	A fear of being mistaken about the seriousness of the problem.
Heartless Attribution:	A fear that others will view confrontation as unfeeling.
Demotivation:	A fear that confrontation will destroy vulnerable motivation.
Crystal Glass:	A fear that confrontation will shatter the weak performer's delicate self-image.
Coverage Holes:	A fear that a department's deficiencies in providing service to other internal and external customers will be brought to light.
Future Accountability:	A fear that subsequent mistakes by the weak performer will become the supervisor's responsibility.
Retention:	A fear that a poor merit rating means the supervisor will retain the problem employee.
Marshmallow Measurement System:	A wish to manipulate soft, mushy performance measures.
	Incentives
Integrity:	A feeling that supervisors "should do the right thing."
Knowledge:	An understanding that confrontation may save a career life.
High Dysfunction:	A recognition that the problem is harming the organization.
Exposure:	A fear that others may point out the supervisor's inaction.

Table 3
Advantages and Disadvantages of Colleague-Supplemented Multiple-Rater Evaluation

Advantages	Disadvantages
Is accurate, discriminating and valid	Is modest change from existing culture
Moderate biases	Poses modest threat to supervisor power
Moderates inflation of ratings	Poses modest threat to colleagues
Allows ratee and rater validation	
Permits comparisons across ratees and raters	
Is simple and time efficient	
Moderates politics and cronyism	
Supports participative culture	
Supports flat organizations	
Supports matrix management	
Shifts supervisor to coach's role	
Is highly credible to employees	
Provides substantial motivation	

Because traditional supervisor-only evaluations rely on a single judgment, they are severely deficient as measures of performance. Nearly every textbook on performance appraisal recommends the use of multiple raters.[4] Empirical research has provided compelling evidence that multiple-rater, team evaluation procedures are more reliable and valid for purposes of appraisal and promotion than supervisory judgments alone.[5] Additional research has shown that both employees and management prefer multiple-rater systems to single-rater procedures when they have an opportunity to experience a multiple-rater process.[6]

However, in 1988, less than 1 percent of American industry uses multiple-rater systems. The authors have helped develop over 100 multiple-rater systems in over 60 organizations, both public and private. Many of the firms conducted an internal assessment of the multiple-rater process and found support from more than two-thirds of the users. However, even among these organizations with positive user experience, fewer than half continue to use formalized multiple rater systems.

An Effective Multiple-Rater Model

One effective multiple-rater decision model, called Team Evaluation and Management System, TEAMS, provides an excellent example of fairness and accuracy in performance evaluation.[7] The TEAMS process consists of two components. The first component, the Team Evaluation, represents multiple raters who evaluate job-related behaviors of colleagues, as shown in Figure 1.[8] The second component, the Management System, represents the supervisor's evaluative judgment based on performance expectations or results. The TEAMS model uses input from multiple raters to improve the reliability of the most subjective part of performance evaluation, the behavioral judgments.

Which provides a better measure of performance, job behaviors or job results? The TEAMS answer is that a multiple-rater assessment of job behaviors combined with the supervisor's judgment of performance results provides the most reliable and predictively valid measure of performance.[9]

The use of multiple raters in the Team Evaluation component improves fairness by increasing the sample size for evaluation from one to five. Experience indicates that an evaluation team of four associates in addition to the supervisor usually provides highly reliable Team Evaluation results. The behavioral profile resulting from the Team Evaluation serves as input to the supervisor in the Management System, as shown in Figure 2.

Because the supervisor is the only automatic member of the evaluation team, the TEAMS model does not eliminate potential distortion by a supervisor who has personal bias. However, the TEAMS Intelligent Consensus software discounts the extreme high and low rater and thereby moderates the distorting effect a biased rater (whether biased positively or negatively) would otherwise have on the small samples of five ratings.

The Team Evaluation component usually leads to a highly reliable behavioral measure in which members of the evaluation team agree more than 90% of the time. In the unusual circumstance, when there is substantial disagreement among evaluation team members, a low Degree of Consensus of "C" score flags the Team Evaluation component as unreliable. The Degree of Consensus or "C" score indicates the reliability of each criterion evaluated, as shown in the profile (Figure 2). The "C" score is one minus the standard deviation, normalized to the rating scale used and also corrected for the portion of the scale used. More than 95% of the time, "C" scores are high (above 0.5), indicating

Figure 1
TEAMS Process

A Fair, Accurate, Simple, Trustworthy and FAST Decision Support Tool

1. Select Criteria

TEAMS

Ratee _____

Job Family: Merchandising

Communicates Effectively
Guiding and Motivating
Handling Crises and Stress
Creativity and Innovation
Interpersonal Skills
Teamwork/Teambuilding
Leadership
Organization Skills

To develop criteria, may use: job analysis, nominal group technique, survey or team evaluation rating. May differentially weight criteria.

2. Select Raters

TEAMS

Ratee _____ Title _____
Dept. _____ Location _____

Evaluation Team

1. _____
   Supervisor
2. _____
3. _____
4. _____
5. _____

_____

Supervisor's Signature

Select supervisor plus work associates.

3. Rate

TEAMS

Ratee _____
Rater _____

Communicates Effectively   1-10__
Guiding and Motivating   1-10__
Handling Crises and Stress 1-10__
Creativity and Innovation   1-10__
Interpersonal Skills   1-10__
Teamwork/Teambuilding   1-10__
Leadership   1-10__

Rate performers, positions, programs, projects, groups or strategies.

4. Score Score results using TEAMS® Intelligent Consensus™ software.

5. Profiles

Ratee Profile

TEAMS
Intelligent Consensus Report for Colleen Mahoney

Communicates Effectively
Guiding and Motivating
Handling Crises and Stress
Creativity and Innovation
Interpersonal Skills
Teamwork/Teambuilding
Leadership
Composite Score
1 2 3 4 5 6 7 8 9 10

Shows strengths and development needs.

Supervisor's Profile

TEAMS
Intelligent Consensus Report for Colleen Mahoney

Communicates Effectively
Guiding and Motivating
Handling Crises and Stress
Creativity and Innovation
Interpersonal Skills
Teamwork/Teambuilding
Leadership
Composite Score
1 2 3 4 5 6 7 8 9 10

S—Supervisor's actual rating

Shows supervisor's actual rating.

6. TE + MS Report

TE + MS Report
Colleen Murphy

TE
Communicating Effectively   9.2
Guiding and Motivating   7.1
Handling Crises and Stress   3.9
Creativity and Innovation   8.9
Interpersonal Skills   6.4
Teamwork/Teambuilding   9.8
Leadership   8.0
Composite Scores   TE = 6.8

MS
Completed TR3 program development (80%)
Solved 74 customer problems (85%)
Built network capability (40%)
                               MS = 7.9
TE + MS
TE = 6.8 MS = 7.9   Overall rating = 7.6

Shows combination of behaviors (TE) and results (MS) rating.

7. Other TEAMS Management Reports
Summary Report—Shows alphabetical history of all participants and scores.
Intelligent Consensus/Raw Score—Shows reliability between 3 and 5 raters
Safeguard Reports—Rater Feedback shows rater behavior and identifies rater problems.
Ranking Report—Ranks group by criteria and by composite score.
Speciality Report—May provide indicators of:
  • reliability and confidence intervals
  • cultural fairness
  • valid and invalid raters

**Figure 2
Profile**

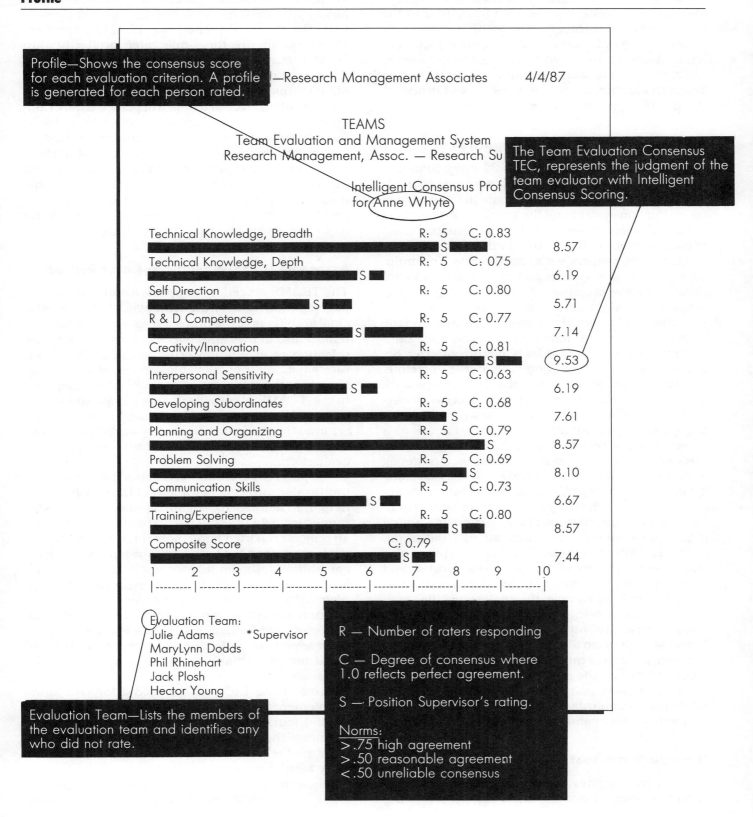

Profile—Shows the consensus score for each evaluation criterion. A profile is generated for each person rated.

—Research Management Associates   4/4/87

TEAMS
Team Evaluation and Management System
Research Management, Assoc. — Research Su

Intelligent Consensus Prof
for Anne Whyte

The Team Evaluation Consensus TEC, represents the judgment of the team evaluator with Intelligent Consensus Scoring.

Criterion	R	C	Score
Technical Knowledge, Breadth	5	0.83	8.57
Technical Knowledge, Depth	5	075	6.19
Self Direction	5	0.80	5.71
R & D Competence	5	0.77	7.14
Creativity/Innovation	5	0.81	9.53
Interpersonal Sensitivity	5	0.63	6.19
Developing Subordinates	5	0.68	7.61
Planning and Organizing	5	0.79	8.57
Problem Solving	5	0.69	8.10
Communication Skills	5	0.73	6.67
Training/Experience	5	0.80	8.57
Composite Score		0.79	7.44

1   2   3   4   5   6   7   8   9   10
|---------|---------|---------|---------|---------|---------|---------|---------|---------|

Evaluation Team:
Julie Adams   *Supervisor
MaryLynn Dodds
Phil Rhinehart
Jack Plosh
Hector Young

Evaluation Team—Lists the members of the evaluation team and identifies any who did not rate.

R — Number of raters responding

C — Degree of consensus where 1.0 reflects perfect agreement.

S — Position Supervisor's rating.

Norms:
> .75 high agreement
> .50 reasonable agreement
< .50 unreliable consensus

high agreement among the evaluation team. In the unusual case of disagreement among raters, the Management System provides a safeguard to the unreliable team evaluation consensus.

Experience indicates supervisors are reluctant to ignore a positive rating with high agreement among multiple credible work colleagues. Therefore, the Team Evaluation component enhances fairness of the performance measurement system.

Additional Procedural Safeguards

The TEAMS procedure includes 32 procedural and statistical safeguards to enhance procedure validity.[10] For example, employees participate in the design of the evaluation system and the selection of evaluation criteria. Employees select their own evaluation team of four evaluators, in addition to their supervisor—subject to their supervisor's concurrence. The multiple-rater decision system allows all raters who are chosen to serve on others' evaluation teams to participate as evaluators in the process.

Numerous statistical safeguards are built into the TEAMS Intelligent Consensus software. For example, rater feedback provides a picture of rater behavior for every participating evaluator.[11] Therefore, a rater who unfairly over or under evaluates a work associate not only loses a voice in the process by having the evaluative judgement discounted in the scoring system, but is identified by rater feedback as a person who displayed inappropriate rating behavior.

Rater feedback also identifies rater inconsistency with regard to individual criteria that may be causing confusion or high rater variation within the evaluation system. Such safeguards allow for better training and communication, and they permit fine tuning of the evaluation system to moderate such distortion.

The TEAMS Intelligent Consensus software also examines the pattern of ratings across all raters and ratees in order to identify systematic, unusual rating patterns. For example, the analysis can flag spurious or random ratings or ratings that are systematically unusually high or low. The Intelligent Consensus can also identify the ratings "footprint" or rating pattern of raters who attempt to collude in order to "game" the system.[12]

The net effect of the multiple procedural and statistical safeguards is to assure minimum distortion within the evaluation process.

The Two-Team Test

Possibly the toughest test for a performance measurement system occurs when the person being

evaluated is allowed to choose two separate evaluation teams. Assuming the person being evaluated has approximately equal visibility to members of both the A and B teams, the TEAMS procedure yields essentially the same ratee profile (within 10%) by team A and team B over 90% of the time.

An employee who can choose two different evaluation teams of work associates and can expect the same result from both teams will perceive the evaluation procedure to be reliable, accurate and fair. Even in the usual situation, where the evaluation criteria are subjective, the two-teams test demonstrates the objectivity of the multiple-rater decision process. Proven objectivity indicates a reliable measure, and when two separate evaluation teams provide essentially the same results, the measurement process is shown to be accurate.

Assessment of the Multiple-Rater Process

The TEAMS procedure supports a cultural norm of participation by allowing employees to be the principal architects of the human resource decision system. It also allows employees to participate in the selection of evaluation criteria and of their own raters (i.e., their own evaluation team) and to participate in the actual rating process. A key safeguard to the TEAMS process is the user evaluation component. Users, both employees and management, critique the procedure by survey and through staff meetings and special meetings for program evaluation.

The program evaluations reported here represent multi-rater projects with more than 6,400 participants across 16 organizations; project size ranged from 44 to 1,272 participants. In each of the 16 projects reported here, more than 40% of the participants responded to the critique survey. Each organization designed its own application using the flexible TEAMS model for colleague review as a *supplement* to supervisory performance and career development information. In nine cases, the information was used for career development only; in the other seven, the colleague review process provided *input* for performance evaluation and merit pay decisions.

Firms using the TEAMS model for colleague-supplemented evaluation included four regulated (utility), four public sector and eight industrial firms. Format of the process critique survey varied slightly across the organizations, but content was essentially similar as shown in Appendix 1.

The summary of results, shown in Figure 3, identifies strengths and weaknesses of colleague-supplemented evaluation. The bar graphs represent the percentages of people who agreed and disagreed with each statement. Each bar shows, for a given item, an unweighted mean percentage across all responding projects. The results show that 81% of the participants reported that colleague input *provides useful additional information.* Nearly the same percentage viewed the multiple rater process as an improvement to *fairness* and to the quality of *career development information.*

Another way to assess the issue of who should rate is to reverse the question by asking participants whether they prefer supervisor-only evaluation to colleague-supplemented evaluation. Responses indicated that most participants believed others besides the supervisor should be involved in the evaluation process.

More than 66% of the participants agreed with their performance profile. Over 80% recommended the use of multiple rater systems, but fewer, 72%, were satisfied with the process they had used. About 88% saw the rating form as simple and easy to use, and slightly fewer, 81%, felt the career profile was easy to interpret (see Figure 2). About 68%

Figure 3
TEAMS Program Assessment Composite Data Across 16 Projects Totalling 6400 Participants

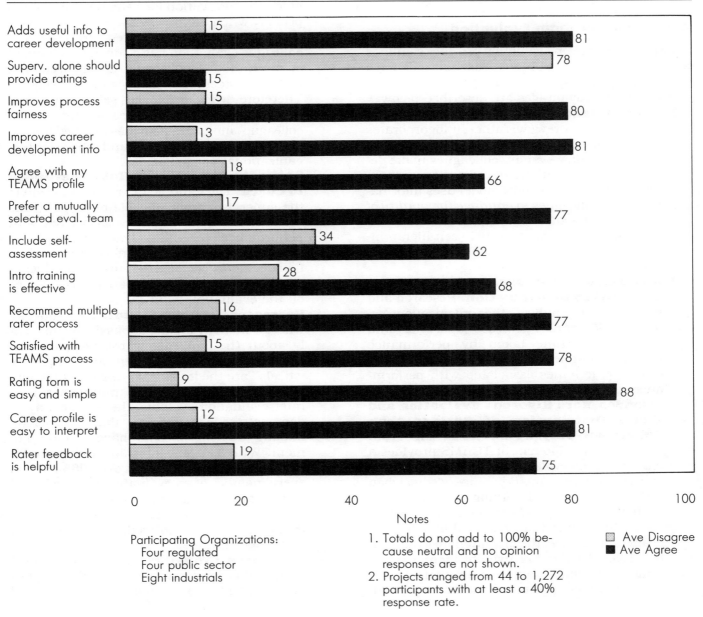

Notes

Participating Organizations:
Four regulated
Four public sector
Eight industrials

1. Totals do not add to 100% because neutral and no opinion responses are not shown.
2. Projects ranged from 44 to 1,272 participants with at least a 40% response rate.

Ave Disagree
Ave Agree

believed the supporting training was effective, and about 62% wished to include self-assessment in the multiple-rater process.

Additional survey information indicated that average rating time, per person rated, was approximately 7 minutes. Where tracked, higher rated performers answered survey questions no more positively than lower rater performers. Predictably, responses from projects targeted for career development were slightly more positive than responses from projects oriented to performance appraisal. Younger participants tended to be more positive, as a group than older participants. There were no differences in results based on organizational level or gender.

Advantages of Team Evaluation

Multiple-rater or team evaluation provides solutions to many of the problems associated with supervisor-only evaluations and peer evaluations. A few of these advantages are described below.

1. **Peer Evaluation.** The TEAMS model is not a model of peer review; rather, it incorporates a *colleague-supplemented evaluation* system. In a peer review system, colleagues make determinations about merit, promotion and other rewards. The TEAMS model uses information from colleagues to *enhance the quality of information available to supervisors.* TEAMS represents a compromise between hierarchically-based, supervisor-only evaluation and peer evaluation.

2. **Decreases Supervisor and Management Time Taken by Evaluation.** Research and field experience indicate that organizations using TEAMS actually decrease supervisory and management time taken by performance measurement, leaving more time for the constructive activities associated with performance management.

3. **Provides More Rigorous Evaluation and Wider Distribution of Ratings than Supervisor-Only Evaluation.** The Team Evaluation component of TEAMS provides a more rigorous evaluation than the traditional supervisor-only evaluation. Supervisors, when rating alone, have self-serving biases to *inflate* evaluation ratings. These self-serving biases are neither shared nor reflected in colleague evaluation. Hence, the discriminate validity of the Team Evaluation usually increases the range of the performance distribution by three to four times compared with traditional, supervisor-only evaluation. For example, if a five-point scale is used, supervisors rating alone rate nearly everyone into two performance groups (e.g., 3's and 4's). The Team Evaluation process typically distributes ratees across four groupings on a five-point scale, five groupings on a seven-point scale and six groupings on a nine- or ten-point scale.

Effects on Motivation

Experience shows users believe the strongest TEAMS features include the following points:

1. **Motivates Behavior Change (Social Facilitation).** Supervisory evaluations provide little motivation for behavior change, especially when the supervisor is not held in esteem by the subordinates. In contrast, colleague evaluation has a substantial impact on motivation. People have a strong need to be held in esteem by their work colleagues. Therefore, when employees select a personal evaluation team, the credible information from colleagues motivates activities directed toward performance improvement and the desired organizational norms.

2. **Shifts the Supervisor's Role from Judge to Coach.** The multiple-rater evaluation shifts the supervisor from the role of judge to the more constructive activities associated with performance coaching. The supervisor no longer must justify less-than-positive evaluation decisions, because the supervisor's evaluations are typically corroborated by colleagues on the evaluation team.

3. **Decreases the Noise Factor.** The "squeaky wheels" in many organizations complain loudly about the lack of rewards received. Experience indicates that often these "squeaky wheels" are the least deserving organizational members. However, with traditional single-rater evaluation systems, there is no way to demonstrate convincingly that the person making the noise does not have a valid argument. With TEAMS, interrater reliability for low performers is typically over 96%. When every member of an evaluation team selected by an employee agrees that the employee contributes relatively little to the organization, that employee has no credible argument for additional rewards.

4. **Moderates Cronyism.** Traditional single-rater evaluation systems tend to allow reward distribution based on political favoritism and

friendship. TEAMS moderates political and stereotyping behaviors and replaces them with performance-based assessments. For example, a supervisor will have difficulty ignoring information on highly rater subordinates even if those subordinates do not meet the supervisor's personal preference—the model the supervisor typically likes to reward. Similarly, supervisors are less likely to reward mediocrity when there is credible evidence to suggest a person is not making a substantial contribution to the organization.

5. **Provides Fairness and Accuracy.** The decision rules built into TEAMS represent state-of-the-art research on decision making. Most users believe TEAMS provides the fairest and most accurate method available for identifying those who truly deserve rewards such as merit pay, promotion, job assignments and opportunities for training and career development.

6. **Sustains Cultural Change.** When employees who support the desired cultural norms are accurately recognized and rewarded, a message is communicated that the new norms count. Tapping the "micro culture," the network around each person, yields highly credible feedback that sustains positive behaviors.

Some might argue that the motivational factors listed are theoretical. However, field experiences provide validation for these concepts.

Effects on Motivational Impacts—Theoretical or Real?

At Arizona State University, where team evaluation has been used in some academic units for four years, the motivational impacts have been substantial. When team evaluation was implemented, faculty who had not supervised a graduate student in over 7 years began soliciting graduate students in order to participate on graduate committees. Tenured professors who had not published for over a decade began to write articles when their accountability changed from the department chair only, to their colleagues. Similarly, faculty who had never submitted research grant proposals began participating in the grant writing process. Professors who had not served on university or department committees for years began volunteering for committee assignments.

Changes in a department of twenty-one faculty who began using team evaluation to provide input to the department chair's rating in 1985 illustrate a change in culture. Prior to 1985, performance evaluations had been conducted by the department chair alone. Table 4 presents evidence of productivity during the five years prior to the use of multiple-rater evaluation and during the three years after the department began using colleague-supplemented evaluation.

Interestingly, these improvements in academic productivity occurred during years when merit monies were either sparse or nil. Hence, *colleague-supplemented evaluation seems to have motivational value even when merit monies are not available.*

At Westinghouse, Steam Turbine Generator Division, a definite team building effect was associated with team evaluation. Prior to adopting team evaluation, the division used an objectives-based system of evaluation. The system credited performance, independent of the means for accomplishment. Therefore, some associates achieved substantial results, but at the expense of other associates and organizational effectiveness. Westinghouse developed multiple-rater appraisal to fit a change to a participative and collaborative culture. Mr. George Dann, Director of Human Resources for the power generator group at Westinghouse, reported a 28%

Table 4
Productivity of University Faculty Before and After Department Began Using Multiple-Rater, Colleague Supplemented Evaluation

Evidence of Productivity	Mean for 5 years (1981–1984)	Mean for 3 years (1985–1988)
Student Evaluations (of teaching effectiveness)	4.40	4.50
Refereed Publications	0.60	2.40
Reviewed Publications	0.71	2.34
Articles Written	1.40	3.40
Grants Received	0.40	2.10
Grants Proposed	0.85	2.05
Professional Presentations	3.40	6.20
Department Service	1.70	3.00
Colleague and University Service	0.30	1.30

Notes: 1. Multiple-rater, colleague-supplemented evaluation was used in 1985, 1986 and 1987.
2. Department size varied from 22 to 18 over these eight years.
3. First-year faculty and those on sabbatical leave were not included.

increase in productivity increase in the year following implementation of team evaluation. He attributed much of the increase to the team-building effect of multiple-rater evaluation.

At the Salt River Project, a large utility in the southwest, use of team evaluation improved internal and external customer service. When employees select internal customers to serve on their evaluation team, they gain substantial incentives for high performance that serve internal customers throughout the organization, as well as their boss. When employees respond effectively to the needs of internal customers, external customers also receive excellent service.

The Salt River Project experience illustrates another motivational value of team evaluation. This large utility uses matrix management for engineering, technical and other special project assignments. Employees were reluctant to participate in matrix structured assignments because participation often led to loss of contact with an employee's primary supervisor, who was responsible for performance evaluation, merit distribution and recommendations for promotion. When team evaluation was implemented to capture information from those involved in temporary work assignments associated with matrix management, the team evaluation process essentially served to "credit" employees for matrix management service from their work colleagues while they were matrixed. The process has substantially increased the number of employees electing to participate in matrix projects.

Summary

Multiple-rater or team evaluation provides a mechanism for driving culture change and sustaining the new organization norms. Traditional supervisory-driven evaluation systems lack incentives for fairness and accuracy and, in fact, impose severe disincentives to objectivity and accurate evaluation by supervisors.

Employees and managers want fairness and precision in the differential distribution of organizational rewards. Multirater systems allow for a high level of participative management and enhance the quality of information available for career development. Multiple-rater evaluation provides solutions to many problems associated with traditional supervisor-only review systems.

Supervisory benefits from team evaluation include improved performance information, improved visibility of subordinates' behaviors, and highly reliable feedback on the appraisal. The team evaluation process reduces supervisors' time requirement for performance measurement, releasing time for the more constructive activities associated with performance management. Team evaluation reduces supervisors' need to be defensive and to justify evaluations that aren't positive allowing supervisors to give objective, accurate feedback about performance.

Team evaluation enhances employee motivation substantially by improving the credibility of performance feedback. Many employees are motivated far more by the desire to be held in esteem by their work colleagues than by their supervisor alone. Rather than attributing a poor appraisal to the ignorance of their supervisor, employees typically view team evaluation feedback as highly credible and show substantial motivation to improve their evaluations by colleagues.

The experience-based recommendation here is for organizations to move from a hierarchically-based, supervisor-driven process of performance measurement to a participative, *colleague-supported process, in which information from colleagues provides additional input to enhance the quality of information available to supervisors for decisions about performance.* Such a procedure presents a less drastic culture change than a total shift from supervisor-only evaluation to peer evaluation.

Assessments by 16 organizations that critically evaluated their multirater systems indicate that about 3 out of 4 users preferred participative systems. Management and non-management employees perceived participative systems to be more fair, accurate and useful than traditional supervisor-only systems.

Not only do users prefer multirater systems, but such systems appear to increase motivation and actually change individual behaviors. Productivity of university faculty increased substantially when faculty members were evaluated by a combination of the department chair and their colleagues, rather than their department chair alone. Multirater systems developed by Westinghouse to improve a participative and collaborative culture did in fact improve productivity. Similarly, multirater systems reinforced internal and external customer service at a large southwestern utility.

These examples demonstrate the power of multirater systems for driving and sustaining culture change. The motivational power of multiple rater systems has been known for many years. However, only since the advent of supermicro computers and sophisticated software has the efficient use of multiple rater systems been possible.

Employees quickly recognize that the evaluation process is fair and that new behavioral norms are in place that reinforce the desired culture. When those who truly contribute to the new norms receive extra rewards, employees improve performance, leading to substantial increases in organizational productivity.

References

1. McGregor, D. "An Uneasy Look at Performance Appraisal," *Harvard Business Review,* May–June, 1978, 89–94.
2. Greenberg, J. "Explaining the Self-Serving Bias: Response Bias or Perceptual Bias," paper presented at the *Academy of Management 45th Annual Meeting,* San Diego, California, August 13, 1985.
3. Bedeian, A.G. "Rater Characteristics Affecting the Validity of Performance Appraisals," *Journal of Management,* Spring, 1976, 2, 1, 37–45.
4. Bernardin, H.J., and Klatt, L.A. "Managerial Appraisal Systems: Has Practice 'Caught-Up' with the State of the Art?" *Personnel Administrator,* 1985, 30, 79–86.
5. Harris, M.M., and Schaubroeck, J. "A Meta-Analysis of Self-Supervisor, Self-Peer, and Peer-Supervisor Ratings," *Personnel Psychology,* 1988, 41, 43–62.
6. McEvoy, G.M., and Buller, P.F. "User Acceptance of Peer Appraisals in an Industrial Setting," *Personnel Psychology,* 1987, 40, 785–797.
7. Edwards, M.R., and Verdini, W.A. "Engineering and Technical Management: Accurate Human Performance Measures = Productivity," *Journal of the Society of Research Administrators,* Fall, 1986, 18, 2, 23–37.
8. Edwards, M.R., and Sproull, J.R. "Making Performance Appraisals Perform: The Use of Team Evaluation," *Personnel,* March, 1985, 62, 3, 28–32.
9. Latham, G.P., and Wexley, K.N. "Increasing Productivity Through Performance Appraisal." Reading, MA: Addison-Wesley Publishing Company, 1981.
10. Sproull, J.R., and Edwards, M.R. "Safeguarding Your Employee Rating System," *Business,* April–May–June, 1985, 35, 2, 17–27.
11. Edwards, M.R., Borman, W., and Sproull, J.R. "Solving the Double Bind in Performance Appraisal: A Saga of Wolves, Sloths and Eagles," *Business Horizons,* May–June, 1985, 28, 3, 59–68.
12. Edwards, M.R. "An Expert System for Equitable Career Decisions," *Computers in Personnel,* 3, 1, Fall, 1988, 40–47.

Appendix 1
Performance and Career Development Systems Assessing the Current Rewards System and Considering Multiple Raters

SECTION I

This survey is designed to record your perceptions about the gainsharing and multiple rater evaluation system in your organization. The survey results will assist in designing improved performance and career development systems. For each item below, please circle the number from 1 to 7 which indicates your level of agreement/disagreement.

1	2	3	4	5	6	7	N
Strongly Disagree	Disagree	Somewhat Disagree	Neutral	Somewhat Agree	Agree	Strongly Agree	No opinion or Not applicable

Gainsharing:

1. All associates should receive equal rewards.   1 2 3 4 5 6 7 N
2. I believe I get accurate and useful feedback about my performance.   1 2 3 4 5 6 7 N
3. The current evaluation process provides helpful and constructive information to me.   1 2 3 4 5 6 7 N
4. I trust the current evaluation system to provide accurate information for fair gainsharing distribution.   1 2 3 4 5 6 7 N
5. I believe that high performers should receive more reward than poor performers, assuming fair and accurate performance assessment.   1 2 3 4 5 6 7 N
6. I believe it is possible to appraise performance accurately.   1 2 3 4 5 6 7 N
7. I prefer my supervisor to make career development decisions alone—wihout input from others.   1 2 3 4 5 6 7 N
8. I believe supervisory evaluation and career development coaching would benefit from multiple rater colleague input, assuming sufficient safeguards maximized information quality.   1 2 3 4 5 6 7 N
9. I am satisfied, overall, with the current evaluation and career development process.   1 2 3 4 5 6 7 N

TEAMS: What factors concern you most?

1. Designing the multiple rater evaluation system.   1 2 3 4 5 6 7 N
2. Developing appropriate evaluation criteria.   1 2 3 4 5 6 7 N
3. Selecting a fair set of evalutors (associates).   1 2 3 4 5 6 7 N
4. Some associates may be evaluated by an easier set of raters than others.   1 2 3 4 5 6 7 N
5. The time necessary for multiple rater evaluation.   1 2 3 4 5 6 7 N
6. Potential process acceptance by associates.   1 2 3 4 5 6 7 N
7. The system to provide accurate information for fair gainsharing distribution.   1 2 3 4 5 6 7 N
8. Difficulty to learn the process and to be trained as a rater.   1 2 3 4 5 6 7 N

SECTION II (Use the back of this page if necessary)

1. What concerns do you have about using the current evaluation system?

2. What recommendations do you have for improving the evaluation and career development process?

SECTION III—ABOUT YOU

1. How long has it been since your last performance review? _____ months

2. Have your performance reviews been helpful to you? _____

_____

3. Have you had support for career development? _____

_____

4. Sex: _____ M _____ F

5. Age: _____ 25 or under _____ 26–40 _____ 41–50 _____ 51–60 _____ 61 +

6. Department _____

PLEASE RETURN THIS SURVEY TO: Human Resources, ASAP.
Thank you for participation in this development survey!

PART FOUR

RESOURCE MATERIALS

This part of the Sourcebook contains overheads and exercises that can be used for presentations, seminars and course aimed at managing the change process.

The resources focus on a model for understanding the change process and for helping managers facilitate constructive change. For this Sourcebook, the target is cultural change which implies the need to establish the values of the "new" culture, to assess the existing culture and to develop and implement a plan to change the existing culture.

SECTION I
TRANSPARENCY MASTERS/
HANDOUTS

Culture Change

- **Identify the Desired Values**

- **Assess the Existing Culture**

- **Plan the Change Process**

- **Modify the Culture**

- **Evaluate the Results**

Sample Values

- **Valuing Differences**

- **Accountability at all Levels**

- **Think, Don't React**

- **Teamwork**

- **Customer Benefits**

Goals of Culture Change

- **Leadership Role Modeling**

- **Communication of Values**

- **Recognition and Rewards Aligned with Values**

- **Training Supports Value Shift**

- **Customer Benefits from Cultural Change**

Predictors of Employee Reaction

- **Unexpected vs. Expected**

- **Positive vs. Negative Perception**

- **Involvement in Process**

- **Amount and Timing of Changes**

Employee Signals of Stress

- **Unhealthy Behaviors**

- **More Illness**

- **Lower Energy**

- **Less work Done**

- **"Negative" Communications**

- **More Defensiveness**

- **People Leaving**

Causes of Employee Stress

- **Uncertainty**

- **Negative Changes**

- **Loss of Career Identity**

- **Lack of Direction**

- **Diminished Hope**

Organizational Signals of Stress

- **Decisions Pulled Up**

- **Constricted Communication**

- **Coordination Problems**

- **Crisis Climate**

- **Flip Flops**

- **Lots of Politics**

- **Turf Mentality**

Causes of Organizational Stress

- **Vision Not Clearly Defined**

- **Inadequate Planning**

- **Overcontrolling**

- **Go-It-Alone Mentality**

- **Fear of Failure**

- **Short-Term Thinking**

HEALTHY CHANGE PROCESS

Understanding	Accepting	Acting
• What happened	• Letting go of what can't be changed	• Setting goals
• What it means	• Planning for what can be changed	• Moving for-ward

TRANSITION CURVE

(For Events Perceived As Negative)

DENIAL/SHOCK

**COMMITMENT/
RESOLUTION**

SUFFERING/RESISTANCE

TRANSITION CURVE

| DENIAL/SHOCK |

COMMITMENT/
RESOLUTION

SUFFERING/RESISTANCE

Typical Behaviors During Denial/Shock

- **Acting as if nothing has changed**

- **Refusing to talk about changes**

- **Performing with no affect**

- **Talking as if changes will only affect others**

- **Making atypical errors**

- **Expressing confusion**

TRANSITION CURVE

DENIAL/SHOCK   **COMMITMENT/ RESOLUTION**

SUFFERING/RESISTANCE

Typical Behaviors During Resistance

- Absent more often

- Displays of anger

- Talking about why things won't work

- "Seeing" only the negative

- Communicating less

- Appearance goes downhill

- Performance drops

- Less contact with you

TRANSITION CURVE

DENIAL/SHOCK   **COMMITMENT/
                                    RESOLUTION**

                SUFFERING/RESISTANCE

Behaviors When Commitment Exists

- **Energy goes up**

- **"Can do" attitude shows**

- **Asking about how, not why**

- **More contact with you**

TYPICAL SHORT-TERM IMPACTS OF MAJOR ORGANIZATIONAL CHANGES

- Periods of uncertainty and ambiguity

- Questions of trust predominate

- People leave or are asked to leave

- Managers are expected to do more

- Reporting relationships change

- Stress levels increase

- Self-preservation becomes critical issue

- Career paths are modified

- Communication becomes constricted

- Rumors are rampant

- Loss of teamwork

- Productivity suffers

- Power struggles more visible

"TYPICAL" PROBLEMS FOR MANAGEMENT DURING MAJOR ORGANIZATIONAL CHANGES

- Not knowing what to expect from employees

- Giving "bad news" to good employees

- Putting aside their own career worries

- Dealing with stress

- Recognizing problems early

- Managing without sufficient information

- Building new teams

- Dealing with resistant employees

- Dealing with suffering employees

- Being proactive

TRANSITION CURVE

| DENIAL/SHOCK | COMMITMENT/ RESOLUTION |

SUFFERING/RESISTANCE

Typical Behaviors During Denial/Shock

- Acting as if nothing has changed

- Refusing to talk about changes

- Performing with no affect

- Talking as if changes will only affect others

- Making atypical errors

- Expressing confusion

TRANSITION CURVE

DENIAL/SHOCK

**COMMITMENT/
RESOLUTION**

| SUFFERING/RESISTANCE |

Typical Behaviors During Resistance

- Absent more often

- Displays of anger

- Talking about why things won't work

- "Seeing" only the negative

- Communicating less

- Appearance goes downhill

- Performance drops

- Less contact with you

TRANSITION CURVE

DENIAL/SHOCK

**COMMITMENT/
RESOLUTION**

SUFFERING/RESISTANCE

Behaviors When Commitment Exists

- Energy goes up

- "Can do" attitude shows

- Asking about how, not why

- More contact with you

GOALS FOR MANAGING CHANGE

Develop
Understanding
(Denial/Shock)

Facilitate Action
Commitment/
Resolution)

Encourage
Acceptance
(Suffering/Resistance)

HOW MANAGERS CAN HELP GROUPS AND INDIVIDUALS REACH UNDERSTANDING

OBJECTIVES: In this stage your objectives are to allow the employees to discuss what is happening, to listen to the employee's view of the change and demonstrate that you understand, and to communicate basic information about the change.

- Increase your contact with the group. Show your concern for your people, show confidence, and hope. Give them assurance of their worth. (Actions speak louder than words.)

- Meet with work group and individuals as needed to explain the vision for the future, what change is taking place, and why. More than one meeting will probably be necessary.

- Communicate what you know when you know it. Be honest; don't raise false hopes. Give people the facts so they can make their own decisions.

- Use active listening and empathy.

- Encourage people to come to you with rumors and not pass them around where they can increase anxiety. Respond to rumors by giving correct information or stating that there is nothing you know of to substantiate it.

- Don't be deceived or misled by people's initial calm and lack of emotion.

- Offer instructions and directions more slowly and carefully.

- Check for understanding; when people are in shock, they tend not to process data very well.

- Outline specific assignments, rather than leaving things vague and ambiguous.

- Assign definite timetables regarding when work is to be completed.

- Be patient. Take more time with people.

- Be nondefensive. Guard against fighting back.

- Check more closely for errors.

- Show better follow-up in general.

NOTE: You don't have to have all the answers. You can share your own loss, but always project confidence and hope for the future.

HOW MANAGERS CAN HELP GROUPS AND INDIVIDUALS ACCEPT THE CHANGE

OBJECTIVE: Your objective in this stage is to increase acceptance of the change through additional information, sharing your perspective, continuing to demonstrate that you understand the employee's point of view, and involving employees in decisions about the change.

- Hold a group meeting(s) to explain your perception of how the change will affect the group as a whole. You may want to use this meeting to overcome resistance by asking what concerns they have with the change. List all of the employee frustrations on a flip-chart, then have them identify which they have some control over. Your people need to accept what they can't change and make choices about what they can change.

- If the group is too negative, hold one to one meetings, encourage but don't force individuals to share how they feel the change will affect their families, their careers, their futures. Listen. Don't deny their view unless their view is based on misinformation--then correct the misinformation. Give your perspective if the employee seems ready for it.

- When possible, involve employees in planning or making decisions about how to implement the change.

- Provide rewards for those who help implement the change. The reward can take many forms: a letter, compliment in a meeting, or discretionary award.

- Continue hands-on management.

- Keep people involved.

- Re-recruit key incumbents—all of them that the company wants to keep.

- Don't hide bad news (but don't l,et it drive good news away).

- Maintain more of a managerial presence, or a higher profile in the work group.

- Spend more time with people one-on-one.

HOW MANAGERS CAN FACILITATE GROUP AND INDIVIDUAL ACTION

OBJECTIVES: Your objective is to get your employees constructively involved and reinforce their actions to implement change.

- Use group meetings to clarify goals, roles and responsibilities after the acceptance of change. Encourage questions and discussion to ensure that everyone understands not only their role, but everyone else's in the work group. Usually there is an opportunity at this point to involve employees in deciding how they will interrelate to accomplish the group's goals. Identify what responsibilities will require intergroup cooperation and assign those involved to figure out how they will process the work. At the end of this meeting, you may want to ask each individual to restate their understanding of their role and responsibilities.

- Provide the training and education employees need for their new roles and responsibilities.

- Provide rewards for changed behavior.

- Use group meetings to clarify new policies and procedures. Encourage questions and discussion.

- Involve employees in the planning and implementation of the steps of change.

- Expect setbacks.

- Respect the fact that some people grieve longer than others.

- Don't assume others are where you are emotionally.

- Continue to manage closely.

SECTION II
CORPORATE CULTURE AUDIT

INSTRUCTIONS FOR COMPLETING THE SURVEY

For each statement on the following pages, there are three things for you to do:

1. Indicate how often the state is true around here
2. Indicate how important the statement is to you personally and to the health of the organization
3. Indicate which way you see us heading on the statement (i.e., are we getting better or worse?).

EXAMPLE

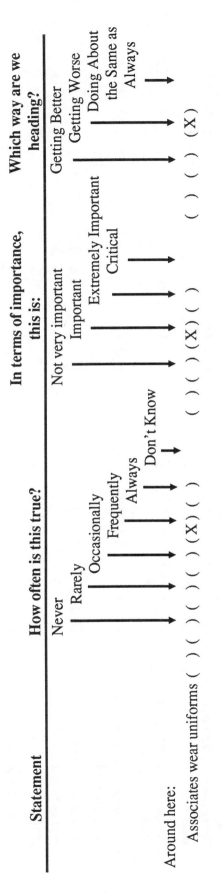

Statement

How often is this true?

Never
Rarely
Occasionally
Frequently
Always
Don't Know

In terms of importance, this is:

Not very important
Important
Extremely Important
Critical

Which way are we heading?

Getting Better
Getting Worse
Doing About the Same as Always

Around here:

Associates wear uniforms ( ) ( ) ( ) ( ) (X) ( )   ( ) ( ) (X) ( )   ( ) ( ) (X)

NOTE: You will find that this survey is divided into five major sections and several subsections. the major sections are: Commitment to People, Product, Communications, Mutuality, and Planning for the Future. Thank you for taking the time to complete this survey.

Statement

COMMITMENT TO PEOPLE

A. *Rewards and Recognition*
Around here:

Statement	How often is this true?						In terms of importance, this is:				Which way are we heading?		
	Never	Rarely	Occasionally	Frequently	Always	Don't Know	Not very important	Important	Extremely Important	Critical	Getting Better	Getting Worse	Doing About the Same as Always
1. Associates are well paid for their work.	( )	( )	( )	( )	( )	( )	( )	( )	( )	( )	( )	( )	( )
2. Associates are recognized for a job well done.	( )	( )	( )	( )	( )	( )	( )	( )	( )	( )	( )	( )	( )
3. Associates are recognized in a meaningful way.	( )	( )	( )	( )	( )	( )	( )	( )	( )	( )	( )	( )	( )
4. Associates are told about their mistakes in a constructive manner.	( )	( )	( )	( )	( )	( )	( )	( )	( )	( )	( )	( )	( )
5. Associates receive satisfactory benefits (e.g., health, vacation, sick).	( )	( )	( )	( )	( )	( )	( )	( )	( )	( )	( )	( )	( )
6. Associates are adequately protected when they retire.	( )	( )	( )	( )	( )	( )	( )	( )	( )	( )	( )	( )	( )
7. Associates have opportunities for advancement in technical areas.	( )	( )	( )	( )	( )	( )	( )	( )	( )	( )	( )	( )	( )
8. Associates have opportunities for advancement in management.	( )	( )	( )	( )	( )	( )	( )	( )	( )	( )	( )	( )	( )

Statement	How often is this true?						In terms of importance, this is:				Which way are we heading?		
	Never	Rarely	Occasionally	Frequently	Always	Don't Know	Not very important	Important	Extremely Important	Critical	Getting Better	Getting Worse	Doing About the Same as Always

COMMITMENT TO PEOPLE

A. Rewards and Recognition

Around here:

Statement													
9. Associates from the plant have the "first shot" at openings.	( )	( )	( )	( )	( )	( )	( )	( )	( )	( )	( )	( )	( )
10. Length of service is recognized in a meaningful way.	( )	( )	( )	( )	( )	( )	( )	( )	( )	( )	( )	( )	( )
11. Length of service is the deciding factor in advancement when skills and ability are equal.	( )	( )	( )	( )	( )	( )	( )	( )	( )	( )	( )	( )	( )
12. Performance evaluations of associates are helpful.	( )	( )	( )	( )	( )	( )	( )	( )	( )	( )	( )	( )	( )
13. Associates are evaluated fairly.	( )	( )	( )	( )	( )	( )	( )	( )	( )	( )	( )	( )	( )
14. Associates are treated with dignity.	( )	( )	( )	( )	( )	( )	( )	( )	( )	( )	( )	( )	( )

B. Training and Individual Development

Around here:

Statement													
1. Associates really do their job well.	( )	( )	( )	( )	( )	( )	( )	( )	( )	( )	( )	( )	( )
2. Associates have realistic opportunities to learn/improve their skills.	( )	( )	( )	( )	( )	( )	( )	( )	( )	( )	( )	( )	( )

Statement

COMMITMENT TO PEOPLE

B. Training and Individual Development

Around here:

Statement	How often is this true?						In terms of importance, this is:				Which way are we heading?		
	Never	Rarely	Occasionally	Frequently	Always	Don't Know	Not very important	Important	Extremely Important	Critical	Getting Better	Getting Worse	Doing About the Same as Always
3. Associates have opportunities to plan their future careers.	( )	( )	( )	( )	( )	( )	( )	( )	( )	( )	( )	( )	( )
4. Associates have opportunities to plan their retirement.	( )	( )	( )	( )	( )	( )	( )	( )	( )	( )	( )	( )	( )
5. Associates have opportunities to learn how to train other associates.	( )	( )	( )	( )	( )	( )	( )	( )	( )	( )	( )	( )	( )
6. Associates are told the real reasons they did not get a position they wanted.	( )	( )	( )	( )	( )	( )	( )	( )	( )	( )	( )	( )	( )
7. Associates get adequate orientation when they start a new job.	( )	( )	( )	( )	( )	( )	( )	( )	( )	( )	( )	( )	( )
8. Associates get the necessary training/help when they start a new job.	( )	( )	( )	( )	( )	( )	( )	( )	( )	( )	( )	( )	( )
9. Associates receive adequate help when they have problems that interfere with their ability to do their job.	( )	( )	( )	( )	( )	( )	( )	( )	( )	( )	( )	( )	( )

COMMITMENT TO PEOPLE

Statement	How often is this true?						In terms of importance, this is:				Which way are we heading?		
	Never	Rarely	Occasionally	Frequently	Always	Don't Know	Not very important	Important	Extremely Important	Critical	Getting Better	Getting Worse	Doing About the Same as Always

C. Involvement
Around here:

Statement													
1. Associates have opportunities to be involved in meetings.	( )	( )	( )	( )	( )	( )	( )	( )	( )	( )	( )	( )	( )
2. Associates have opportunities to be involved in problem solving activities.	( )	( )	( )	( )	( )	( )	( )	( )	( )	( )	( )	( )	( )
3. Associates have opportunities to be involved in planning for the future.	( )	( )	( )	( )	( )	( )	( )	( )	( )	( )	( )	( )	( )
4. Associates are involved in activities to prevent problems.	( )	( )	( )	( )	( )	( )	( )	( )	( )	( )	( )	( )	( )
5. Associates feel involved in how the plant operates.	( )	( )	( )	( )	( )	( )	( )	( )	( )	( )	( )	( )	( )

D. Freedom
Around here:

Statement													
1. Associates feel free to do what they think they should on their job.	( )	( )	( )	( )	( )	( )	( )	( )	( )	( )	( )	( )	( )
2. Associates feel free to say what they believe needs to be said.	( )	( )	( )	( )	( )	( )	( )	( )	( )	( )	( )	( )	( )

Statement	How often is this true?						In terms of importance, this is:				Which way are we heading?		
	Never	Rarely	Occasionally	Frequently	Always	Don't Know	Not very important	Important	Extremely Important	Critical	Getting Better	Getting Worse	Doing About the Same as Always
COMMITMENT TO PEOPLE													
D. Freedom													
Around here:													
3. Associates feel free to think about their job--make decisions and take action.	( )	( )	( )	( )	( )	( )	( )	( )	( )	( )	( )	( )	( )
4. Associates feel free to try out new ideas.	( )	( )	( )	( )	( )	( )	( )	( )	( )	( )	( )	( )	( )
5. Associates feel free to seek out new jobs and opportunities.	( )	( )	( )	( )	( )	( )	( )	( )	( )	( )	( )	( )	( )
E. Safety and Health													
Around here:													
1. Associates follow safety procedures.	( )	( )	( )	( )	( )	( )	( )	( )	( )	( )	( )	( )	( )
2. Associates report safety problems.	( )	( )	( )	( )	( )	( )	( )	( )	( )	( )	( )	( )	( )
3. The plant is kept as safe as it should be.	( )	( )	( )	( )	( )	( )	( )	( )	( )	( )	( )	( )	( )
4. Equipment is as safe as possible.	( )	( )	( )	( )	( )	( )	( )	( )	( )	( )	( )	( )	( )
5. Safety is monitored.	( )	( )	( )	( )	( )	( )	( )	( )	( )	( )	( )	( )	( )

Statement	How often is this true? Never / Rarely / Occasionally / Frequently / Always / Don't Know	In terms of importance, this is: Not very important / Important / Extremely Important / Critical	Which way are we heading? Getting Better / Getting Worse / Doing About the Same as Always
COMMITMENT TO PEOPLE			
E. Safety and Health **Around here:**			
6. Associates value good attendance.	( ) ( ) ( ) ( ) ( ) ( )	( ) ( ) ( ) ( )	( ) ( ) ( )
7. Associates are informed about how to prevent injury and illness.	( ) ( ) ( ) ( ) ( ) ( )	( ) ( ) ( ) ( )	( ) ( ) ( )
8. Associates are reluctant to abuse sick time.	( ) ( ) ( ) ( ) ( ) ( )	( ) ( ) ( ) ( )	( ) ( ) ( )
9. Associates are helped to improve their health.	( ) ( ) ( ) ( ) ( ) ( )	( ) ( ) ( ) ( )	( ) ( ) ( )
10. The plant is kept as clean as it should be.	( ) ( ) ( ) ( ) ( ) ( )	( ) ( ) ( ) ( )	( ) ( ) ( )
PRODUCT			
A. Quality **Around here:**			
1. Excellence is paramount.	( ) ( ) ( ) ( ) ( ) ( )	( ) ( ) ( ) ( )	( ) ( ) ( )
2. Excellent looking products are produced.	( ) ( ) ( ) ( ) ( ) ( )	( ) ( ) ( ) ( )	( ) ( ) ( )

Statement

Statement	How often is this true?						In terms of importance, this is:				Which way are we heading?		
	Never	Rarely	Occasionally	Frequently	Always	Don't Know	Not very important	Important	Extremely Important	Critical	Getting Better	Getting Worse	Doing About the Same as Always

PRODUCT

A. Quality

Around here:

Statement	Never	Rarely	Occasionally	Frequently	Always	Don't Know	Not very important	Important	Extremely Important	Critical	Getting Better	Getting Worse	Doing About the Same as Always
3. High quality materials are used.	( )	( )	( )	( )	( )	( )	( )	( )	( )	( )	( )	( )	( )
4. High quality packaging materials are used.	( )	( )	( )	( )	( )	( )	( )	( )	( )	( )	( )	( )	( )
5. High quality packaging is done.	( )	( )	( )	( )	( )	( )	( )	( )	( )	( )	( )	( )	( )
6. Associates are proud of the product.	( )	( )	( )	( )	( )	( )	( )	( )	( )	( )	( )	( )	( )
7. Associates understand what it takes to put out high quality products.	( )	( )	( )	( )	( )	( )	( )	( )	( )	( )	( )	( )	( )
8. Quality standards are well defined.	( )	( )	( )	( )	( )	( )	( )	( )	( )	( )	( )	( )	( )
9. Quality standards are enforced.	( )	( )	( )	( )	( )	( )	( )	( )	( )	( )	( )	( )	( )
10. Quality is adequately evaluated.	( )	( )	( )	( )	( )	( )	( )	( )	( )	( )	( )	( )	( )
11. Quality is more important than quantity in the plant.	( )	( )	( )	( )	( )	( )	( )	( )	( )	( )	( )	( )	( )

Statement

PRODUCT

B. Efficiency

Around here:

Statement	How often is this true?						In terms of importance, this is:				Which way are we heading?		
	Never	Rarely	Occasionally	Frequently	Always	Don't Know	Not very important	Important	Extremely Important	Critical	Getting Better	Getting Worse	Doing About the Same as Always
1. The plant is run efficiently.	( )	( )	( )	( )	( )	( )	( )	( )	( )	( )	( )	( )	( )
2. Associates think about ways to make their work more efficient.	( )	( )	( )	( )	( )	( )	( )	( )	( )	( )	( )	( )	( )
3. Associates are given the opportunity to use their talents to the fullest.	( )	( )	( )	( )	( )	( )	( )	( )	( )	( )	( )	( )	( )
4. Associates concentrate on reducing product waste.	( )	( )	( )	( )	( )	( )	( )	( )	( )	( )	( )	( )	( )
5. Emphasis is placed on reducing down time.	( )	( )	( )	( )	( )	( )	( )	( )	( )	( )	( )	( )	( )
6. Shift schedules maximize people efficiency.	( )	( )	( )	( )	( )	( )	( )	( )	( )	( )	( )	( )	( )
7. Equipment installation utilizes associate expertise.	( )	( )	( )	( )	( )	( )	( )	( )	( )	( )	( )	( )	( )
8. Equipment is adequately maintained.	( )	( )	( )	( )	( )	( )	( )	( )	( )	( )	( )	( )	( )

Statement	How often is this true?						In terms of importance, this is:				Which way are we heading?		
	Never	Rarely	Occasionally	Frequently	Always	Don't Know	Not very important	Important	Extremely Important	Critical	Getting Better	Getting Worse	Doing About the Same as Always
COMMUNICATION													
A. *Being Informed* Around here:													
1. Associates know what is going on.	( )	( )	( )	( )	( )	( )	( )	( )	( )	( )	( )	( )	( )
2. Information is provided when needed.	( )	( )	( )	( )	( )	( )	( )	( )	( )	( )	( )	( )	( )
3. Information is provided in an understandable way.	( )	( )	( )	( )	( )	( )	( )	( )	( )	( )	( )	( )	( )
4. Information is provided in a respectful way.	( )	( )	( )	( )	( )	( )	( )	( )	( )	( )	( )	( )	( )
5. Information comes directly from the appropriate source.	( )	( )	( )	( )	( )	( )	( )	( )	( )	( )	( )	( )	( )
6. Information is accurate, complete, and timely.	( )	( )	( )	( )	( )	( )	( )	( )	( )	( )	( )	( )	( )
7. Associates get answers to questions asked.	( )	( )	( )	( )	( )	( )	( )	( )	( )	( )	( )	( )	( )
8. Rules and policies are applied consistently.	( )	( )	( )	( )	( )	( )	( )	( )	( )	( )	( )	( )	( )
9. Associates know exactly what is expected of them.	( )	( )	( )	( )	( )	( )	( )	( )	( )	( )	( )	( )	( )
10. Associates understand the corporate vision and values.	( )	( )	( )	( )	( )	( )	( )	( )	( )	( )	( )	( )	( )

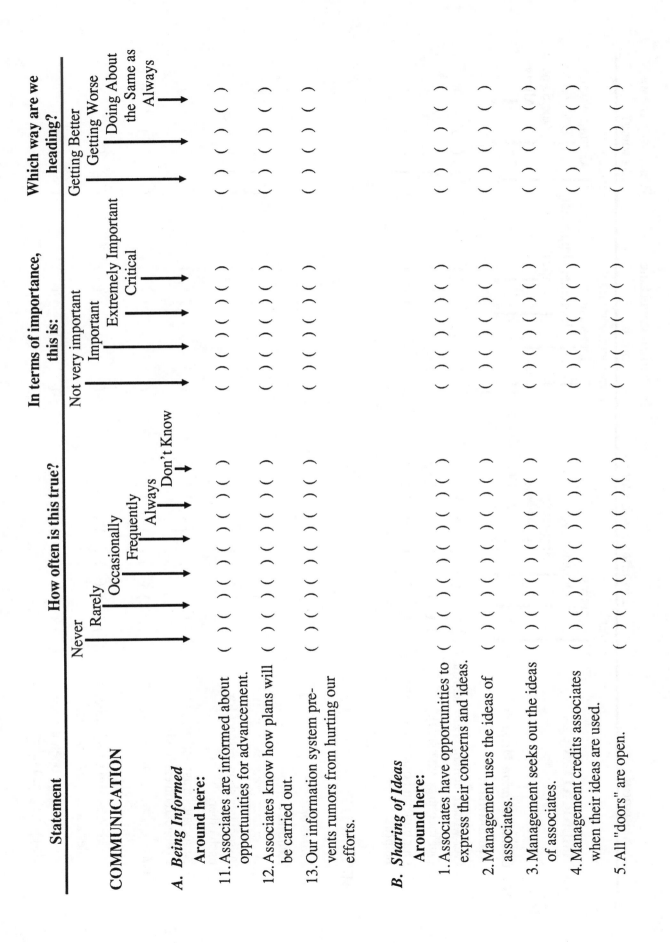

Statement

How often is this true?
Never · Rarely · Occasionally · Frequently · Always · Don't Know

In terms of importance, this is:
Not very important · Important · Extremely Important · Critical

Which way are we heading?
Getting Better · Getting Worse · Doing About the Same as Always

COMMUNICATION

A. Being Informed
Around here:

11. Associates are informed about opportunities for advancement.
( )( )( )( )( )( )   ( )( )( )( )   ( )( )( )

12. Associates know how plans will be carried out.
( )( )( )( )( )( )   ( )( )( )( )   ( )( )( )

13. Our information system prevents rumors from hurting our efforts.
( )( )( )( )( )( )   ( )( )( )( )   ( )( )( )

B. Sharing of Ideas
Around here:

1. Associates have opportunities to express their concerns and ideas.
( )( )( )( )( )( )   ( )( )( )( )   ( )( )( )

2. Management uses the ideas of associates.
( )( )( )( )( )( )   ( )( )( )( )   ( )( )( )

3. Management seeks out the ideas of associates.
( )( )( )( )( )( )   ( )( )( )( )   ( )( )( )

4. Management credits associates when their ideas are used.
( )( )( )( )( )( )   ( )( )( )( )   ( )( )( )

5. All "doors" are open.
( )( )( )( )( )( )   ( )( )( )( )   ( )( )( )

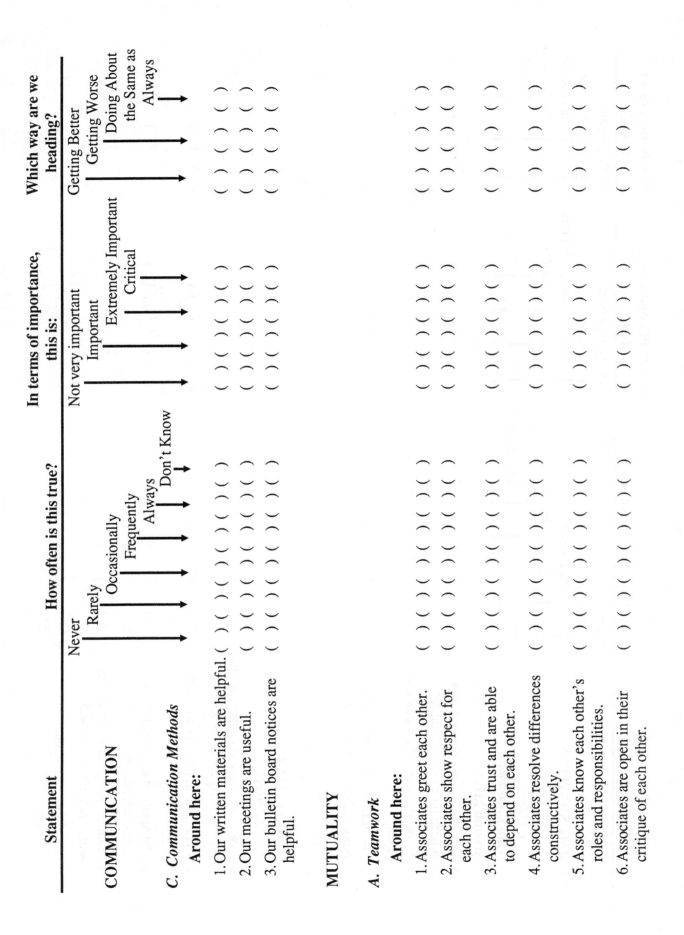

Statement	How often is this true?						In terms of importance, this is:				Which way are we heading?		
	Never	Rarely	Occasionally	Frequently	Always	Don't Know	Not very important	Important	Extremely Important	Critical	Getting Better	Getting Worse	Doing About the Same as Always
COMMUNICATION													
C. Communication Methods													
Around here:													
1. Our written materials are helpful.	( )	( )	( )	( )	( )	( )	( )	( )	( )	( )	( )	( )	( )
2. Our meetings are useful.	( )	( )	( )	( )	( )	( )	( )	( )	( )	( )	( )	( )	( )
3. Our bulletin board notices are helpful.	( )	( )	( )	( )	( )	( )	( )	( )	( )	( )	( )	( )	( )
MUTUALITY													
A. Teamwork													
Around here:													
1. Associates greet each other.	( )	( )	( )	( )	( )	( )	( )	( )	( )	( )	( )	( )	( )
2. Associates show respect for each other.	( )	( )	( )	( )	( )	( )	( )	( )	( )	( )	( )	( )	( )
3. Associates trust and are able to depend on each other.	( )	( )	( )	( )	( )	( )	( )	( )	( )	( )	( )	( )	( )
4. Associates resolve differences constructively.	( )	( )	( )	( )	( )	( )	( )	( )	( )	( )	( )	( )	( )
5. Associates know each other's roles and responsibilities.	( )	( )	( )	( )	( )	( )	( )	( )	( )	( )	( )	( )	( )
6. Associates are open in their critique of each other.	( )	( )	( )	( )	( )	( )	( )	( )	( )	( )	( )	( )	( )

Statement

MUTUALITY

A. Teamwork

Around here:

Statement	— How often is this true? (Never / Rarely / Occasionally / Frequently / Always / Don't Know)	In terms of importance, this is: (Not very important / Important / Extremely Important / Critical)	Which way are we heading? (Getting Better / Getting Worse / Doing About the Same as Always)
7. Associates seek ways to help each other develop.	( ) ( ) ( ) ( ) ( ) ( )	( ) ( ) ( ) ( )	( ) ( ) ( )
8. Associates put the group goals higher than any individual goals.	( ) ( ) ( ) ( ) ( ) ( )	( ) ( ) ( ) ( )	( ) ( ) ( )
9. Associates benefit when the plant does well.	( ) ( ) ( ) ( ) ( ) ( )	( ) ( ) ( ) ( )	( ) ( ) ( )
10. Associates do what is necessary to achieve the goal of the group.	( ) ( ) ( ) ( ) ( ) ( )	( ) ( ) ( ) ( )	( ) ( ) ( )
11. Associates feel they are part of the team.	( ) ( ) ( ) ( ) ( ) ( )	( ) ( ) ( ) ( )	( ) ( ) ( )

B. Assumption of Responsibility

Around here:

Statement	How often is this true?	In terms of importance, this is:	Which way are we heading?
1. Associates care about their work.	( ) ( ) ( ) ( ) ( ) ( )	( ) ( ) ( ) ( )	( ) ( ) ( )
2. Associates "pick up the over-load" when needed.	( ) ( ) ( ) ( ) ( ) ( )	( ) ( ) ( ) ( )	( ) ( ) ( )
3. Associates identify and report problems.	( ) ( ) ( ) ( ) ( ) ( )	( ) ( ) ( ) ( )	( ) ( ) ( )
4. Associates think about possible solutions to problems.	( ) ( ) ( ) ( ) ( ) ( )	( ) ( ) ( ) ( )	( ) ( ) ( )

Statement	How often is this true?						In terms of importance, this is:				Which way are we heading?		
	Never	Rarely	Occasionally	Frequently	Always	Don't Know	Not very important	Important	Extremely Important	Critical	Getting Better	Getting Worse	Doing About the Same as Always

MUTUALITY

B. Assumption of Responsibility
Around here:

Statement	Never	Rarely	Occasionally	Frequently	Always	Don't Know	Not very important	Important	Extremely Important	Critical	Getting Better	Getting Worse	Doing About the Same as Always
5. Associates care about the plant.	( )	( )	( )	( )	( )	( )	( )	( )	( )	( )	( )	( )	( )
6. Associates take initiative instead of "just dong their jobs" or "waiting to be told."	( )	( )	( )	( )	( )	( )	( )	( )	( )	( )	( )	( )	( )
7. Associates look for ways to be helpful even when there are no problems.	( )	( )	( )	( )	( )	( )	( )	( )	( )	( )	( )	( )	( )

STRATEGIES FOR THE FUTURE

A. Managing Change
Around here:

Statement	Never	Rarely	Occasionally	Frequently	Always	Don't Know	Not very important	Important	Extremely Important	Critical	Getting Better	Getting Worse	Doing About the Same as Always
1. Associates recognize that change is a part of growth.	( )	( )	( )	( )	( )	( )	( )	( )	( )	( )	( )	( )	( )
2. Associates are informed about why changes are taking place.	( )	( )	( )	( )	( )	( )	( )	( )	( )	( )	( )	( )	( )
3. Change is organized.	( )	( )	( )	( )	( )	( )	( )	( )	( )	( )	( )	( )	( )
4. Change happens at a realistic pace.	( )	( )	( )	( )	( )	( )	( )	( )	( )	( )	( )	( )	( )

Statement

How often is this true?
Never / Rarely / Occasionally / Frequently / Always / Don't Know

In terms of importance, this is:
Not very important / Important / Extremely Important Critical

Which way are we heading?
Getting Better / Getting Worse / Doing About the Same as Always

STRATEGIES FOR THE FUTURE

A. Managing Change
Around here:

Statement	How often is this true? (Never, Rarely, Occasionally, Frequently, Always, Don't Know)						In terms of importance (Not very important, Important, Extremely Important/Critical)			Which way are we heading? (Getting Better, Getting Worse, Doing About the Same as Always)		
5. All associates participate in making the change positive.	( )	( )	( )	( )	( )	( )	( )	( )	( )	( )	( )	( )
6. Change builds on present strengths and does not destroy what works well.	( )	( )	( )	( )	( )	( )	( )	( )	( )	( )	( )	( )
7. Alternatives are explored and discussed before being finalized.	( )	( )	( )	( )	( )	( )	( )	( )	( )	( )	( )	( )
8. The plant follows corporate values.	( )	( )	( )	( )	( )	( )	( )	( )	( )	( )	( )	( )
9. More information and "straight talk" are given during times of change.	( )	( )	( )	( )	( )	( )	( )	( )	( )	( )	( )	( )
10. changes have adequate follow-up and follow-through.	( )	( )	( )	( )	( )	( )	( )	( )	( )	( )	( )	( )

B. Leadership
Around here:

Statement	How often is this true? (Never, Rarely, Occasionally, Frequently, Always, Don't Know)						In terms of importance (Not very important, Important, Extremely Important/Critical)			Which way are we heading? (Getting Better, Getting Worse, Doing About the Same as Always)		
1. Associates assume leadership roles even when not given the authority.	( )	( )	( )	( )	( )	( )	( )	( )	( )	( )	( )	( )

Statement

How often is this true? — Never, Rarely, Occasionally, Frequently, Always, Don't Know

In terms of importance, this is: — Not very important, Important, Extremely Important, Critical

Which way are we heading? — Getting Better, Getting Worse, Doing About the Same as Always

STRATEGIES FOR THE FUTURE

B. Leadership

Around here:

Statement	How often is this true?	In terms of importance, this is:	Which way are we heading?
	Never / Rarely / Occasionally / Frequently / Always / Don't Know	Not very important / Important / Extremely Important / Critical	Getting Better / Getting Worse / Doing About the Same as Always
2. Associates want to be leaders.	( ) ( ) ( ) ( ) ( ) ( )	( ) ( ) ( ) ( )	( ) ( ) ( )
3. The leadership acts as they want associates to act.	( ) ( ) ( ) ( ) ( ) ( )	( ) ( ) ( ) ( )	( ) ( ) ( )
4. The leadership is "in touch" with associates at all levels.	( ) ( ) ( ) ( ) ( ) ( )	( ) ( ) ( ) ( )	( ) ( ) ( )
5. The leadership visits the floors.	( ) ( ) ( ) ( ) ( ) ( )	( ) ( ) ( ) ( )	( ) ( ) ( )
6. The leadership communicates effectively.	( ) ( ) ( ) ( ) ( ) ( )	( ) ( ) ( ) ( )	( ) ( ) ( )
7. The leadership is open to feedback and suggestions.	( ) ( ) ( ) ( ) ( ) ( )	( ) ( ) ( ) ( )	( ) ( ) ( )
8. The leadership can be trusted.	( ) ( ) ( ) ( ) ( ) ( )	( ) ( ) ( ) ( )	( ) ( ) ( )
9. The leadership cares about associates.	( ) ( ) ( ) ( ) ( ) ( )	( ) ( ) ( ) ( )	( ) ( ) ( )
10. The leadership is good.	( ) ( ) ( ) ( ) ( ) ( )	( ) ( ) ( ) ( )	( ) ( ) ( )

C. Planning for the Future

Around here:

Statement	How often is this true?	In terms of importance, this is:	Which way are we heading?
1. Associates think about the present and future needs of the plant.	( ) ( ) ( ) ( ) ( ) ( )	( ) ( ) ( ) ( )	( ) ( ) ( )

Statement	How often is this true?						In terms of importance, this is:				Which way are we heading?		
	Never	Rarely	Occasionally	Frequently	Always	Don't Know	Not very important	Important	Extremely Important	Critical	Getting Better	Getting Worse	Doing About the Same as Always
STRATEGIES FOR THE FUTURE													
C. Planning for the Future													
Around here:													
2. Plans include how to achieve the goals.	( )	( )	( )	( )	( )	( )	( )	( )	( )	( )	( )	( )	( )
3. Plans explain the "why" of the goal.	( )	( )	( )	( )	( )	( )	( )	( )	( )	( )	( )	( )	( )
4. Plans describe what is expected of associates.	( )	( )	( )	( )	( )	( )	( )	( )	( )	( )	( )	( )	( )
5. Associates are aware of future plans, the "big picture" for the company.	( )	( )	( )	( )	( )	( )	( )	( )	( )	( )	( )	( )	( )
6. Technology development is part of the future.	( )	( )	( )	( )	( )	( )	( )	( )	( )	( )	( )	( )	( )
7. Associate development is part of the future.	( )	( )	( )	( )	( )	( )	( )	( )	( )	( )	( )	( )	( )
8. Associates are encouraged to be creative.	( )	( )	( )	( )	( )	( )	( )	( )	( )	( )	( )	( )	( )

THESE QUESTIONNAIRES WILL ALL BE PROCESSED BY AN OUTSIDE CONSULT-
ING FIRM AND *YOUR CONFIDENTIALITY WILL BE STRICTLY PROTECTED*. HOW-
EVER, IF YOU FEEL THAT ANSWERING ANY ONE OF THE FOLLOWING QUESTIONS
WILL IDENTIFY YOU INDIVIDUALLY, THEN YOU CAN OMIT THAT QUESTION.

Please check the department you work in:

_____ Engineering   _____ Research and Development

_____ Maintenance   _____ Service and Finance

_____ Manufacturing   _____ Information Services

_____ Human Resources

Please indicate:

- If you are hourly _____ or salaried _____

- Your years of experience with the company. Less than 1_____   1-3 _____

   4-10 _____   11-20 _____   over 20 _____

- Your status: permanent _____   temporary_____

- Your shift: _____

- Your sex: _____

- Your age: 18-25_____   26-40 _____   41-50 _____   51-60 _____   61-70 _____